D1596560

Malinowski Among the Magi

International Library of Anthropology

Malinowski Among the Magi
'The Natives of Mailu'

Bronislaw Malinowski

Edited with
an Introduction by
Michael W. Young
Senior Fellow in the Department of Anthropology,
Research School of Pacific Studies,
The Australian National University

Routledge
London and New York

*In Memory of Bu'a of Mailu –
policeman, sorcerer, victim
(d. 1914)*

First published in 1988 by
Routledge
11 New Fetter Lane, London EC4P 4EE

Published in the USA by
Routledge, Chapman & Hall Inc.
29 West 35th Street, New York, NY 10001

Set in Times 10/12pt
by Witwell Ltd, Southport
and printed in Great Britain
by T. J. Press (Padstow) Ltd
Padstow, Cornwall

Library of Congress Cataloging in Publication Data

Malinowski, Bronislaw, 1884–1942.
    [Natives of Mailu]
    Malinowski among the Magi: The natives of Mailu/Bronislaw
    Malinowski; edited with an introduction by Michael W. Young.
        p. cm. — (International library of anthropology)
        Bibliography: p.
        Includes index.
        1. Mailu (Papua New Guinea people) 2. Malinowski, Bronislaw.
    1884–1942. I. Young, Michael W., 1937–   II. Title.
    III. Series.
    DU740.42.M35 1988
    995′.3 – dc 19   87-28769

British Library CIP Data also available

ISBN 0-415-00249-4

Contents

Editor's Acknowledgements

For permission to reproduce 'The Natives of Mailu', which first appeared in volume 39 of the *Transactions and Proceedings of the Royal Society of South Australia* (pages 494–706; Plates XXVI–XLIII), I am grateful to the Council of the Royal Society, and to the Honorary Secretary, Mr C. J. M. Glover, for his help in securing that permission. Mrs Helena Wayne (Malinowska) encouraged me to republish this early work of her father's, and I am grateful for her permission to quote from his correspondence, and for the photograph of the mission house on Mailu used on the cover. For permission to reproduce other manuscript sources I gratefully acknowledge the following: the British Library of Political and Economic Science, London; the Yale University Library, New Haven; the University Library, Cambridge; the Australian Archives, Canberra; and the Mitchell Library, Sydney.

I thank Mr Eric Saville and his daughter Margaret for their permission to quote from the letters of W.J.V. Saville.

Several people at the South Australia Museum have assisted me in various ways in my study of Malinowski's original typescript. Dr Peter Sutton, Head of the Division of Anthropology, and Mr Philip Jones, Curator of Aboriginal History, were especially helpful; my thanks are also due to Mr Graeme Pretty and Dr Eric Matthews. For their obliging correspondence concerning Malinowski's manuscript, I thank Mr Edward Booth and Professor Norman Tindale.

An early draft of the Introduction was read, with characteristic critical care, by Terence Hays, but along with my warmest thanks he is absolved of any responsibility for the final version. For sundry scholarly advice and inspiration, I thank Martha Macintyre, James Urry, Gilbert Lewis, Anthony Forge, John Morton, Jimmy Weiner, and (as always) Michael Jackson.

Malinowski Among the Magi
Editor's Introduction
Michael W. Young

I Mailu in Malinowski's Myth

In September 1914, when the world's attention was focused on momentous events in Europe, Bronislaw Malinowski – a thirty-year-old expatriate Pole and citizen of the Austro-Hungarian Empire – arrived in Australian Papua on the first of three anthropological expeditions. Although it was an inauspicious time to begin fieldwork, the single publication that resulted has some retrospective significance as the apprentice work of the consummate ethnographer who was to revolutionize social anthropology. Malinowski's Mailu expedition was greatly overshadowed by his longer expeditions to the Trobriand Islands between 1915 and 1918. It was the Trobrianders who received the limelight when he duly returned to Europe, became a powerful academic impresario (self-proclaimed 'godfather and standard-bearer' of functionalism), and, in a series of polemical treatises and influential monographs, displayed the ethnographic riches he had won. Thus was the charter myth of the British fieldwork tradition created, with an exile and prisoner-of-war as its culture hero.

The present decade has seen many attempts to evaluate this myth and place it in historical perspective.[1] The more serious purpose has been to debate it, not debunk it, and to this end many of Malinowski's writings – including his published field diaries – have been examined minutely. The task is unfinished, and since each generation of scholars must rewrite the history of its discipline and reassess the worth of ancestral figures, the task is interminable. Much attention has rightly been given to the circumstances and achievements of Malinowski's Trobriand work, particularly to that first expression of his mature genius, *Argonauts of the Western Pacific*. This remains the most celebrated of his monographs and the most artful demonstration of his 'ethnographer's magic'. Critical demystification begins typically with his methodological Introduction (1922: 1–25). Here he had announced his credo: a mix of detailed prescription, personal experience, and mastery of the vernacular – all made possible by the essential 'condition of the performer', which entailed dwelling 'right among the natives', closely observing them and participating in their activities.

From this complacent later standpoint, the first expedition that Malinowski undertook, to the Mailu or Magi-speaking people of the southern coast of eastern Papua, was something of a failure. He was to speak of it condescendingly as a 'trial run',[2] and his field *Diary* gives blow-by-blow testimony to the manner in which the experience blooded him. Yet it was during the Mailu trip that Malinowski could learn from his mistakes, gain confidence as an ethnographer, and formulate the working strategies he was to deploy in the Trobriands. Mailu was important to him as his first military campaign is to any ambitious commander. Just as important, however, was the strategic decision to publish in Australia the report of his first field campaign. This enabled him to secure the funds and the government support which saw him through his first expedition to the Trobriands. In the sensitive political circumstances of 1915, his modest monograph on the Mailu was thus instrumental in advancing his career. To that extent, certainly, the discipline of social anthropology can be grateful it was written.

Malinowski's report on the Mailu appeared in the annals of an Australian scientific society, under the cautious title of *The Natives of Mailu: Preliminary Results of the Robert Mond Research Work in British New Guinea*. It was 'read' (formally presented) on 14 October 1915, by Sir Edward Stirling of the Royal Society of South Australia, and published in December 1915 in volume 39 of that body's *Transactions and Proceedings*. Despite its length (212 pages of text and 17 pages of plates), Malinowski's 'article' was not even the longest offering of that thick volume of some 900 pages. It is sandwiched between an article on exotic fishes of the genus Aracana, and scientific notes on an expedition to the outback regions of South Australia.

While not, strictly speaking, inaccessible, *The Natives of Mailu* has been less readily available than any other of Malinowski's English works, and partly by reason of its unlikely location it has remained a wallflower, if not exactly a Cinderella. It received no publicity and was assured of a limited circulation: a printing of about three hundred, of which one hundred were received by members of the Society and perhaps a further hundred were procured by libraries throughout the world.[3] The *Transactions and Proceedings* is unlikely ever to have sat on the shelf of a bookshop, and only the most dedicated scholars of Malinowski or Melanesia would have sought to obtain it directly from the Royal Society in Adelaide. If not quite inaccessible, then, it was certainly invisible.[4]

Despite the obvious failings of *Mailu* when measured against his later work, it represents a considerable amount of industrious recording in a very short time. Malinowski's energetic intellect and keen powers of observation asserted themselves despite the lethargy, the sickness, and the 'poor circumstances' of which he complained in his *Diary*. The *Natives of Mailu* is deservedly less famous than any of his half dozen Trobriand monographs. We cannot claim it to be a neglected masterpiece, a forgotten classic. It is an apprentice work, conventionally structured, hastily written, and between the flashes of brilliance, clumsy in style. One could say it was an early product of his talent, not of his genius. For all that its re-publication is warranted, I believe, not only by the revival of interest in Malinowski during recent years, but equally by its intrinsic worth as the earliest study of an important cultural group in Papua New Guinea.

II Anthropologists and Administrators in the Antipodes

Why did Malinowski, a budding social scientist, publish his report in such an unlikely serial – one devoted almost exclusively to the natural sciences? The answer will emerge in a later section, but first I shall adduce some biographical details necessary to understand the circumstances of Malinowski's sojourn in the antipodes, particularly those of his fieldwork among the Mailu.

As is well known, Malinowski went to London in 1910 to study anthropology under Edward Westermark and C. G. Seligman at the London School of Economics. He had earned a doctorate in philosophy at his *alma mater*, the Jagellonian University in Cracow, then spent a year studying under Karl Bücher and Wilhelm Wundt in Leipzig. After completing *The Family among the Australian Aborigines* (a work which together with *The Natives of Mailu* earned him a DSc in 1916), he was eager to do fieldwork.

Seligman had tried, and failed, to get him funds to work in the

Sudan; but through his own influence in the University of London he succeeded in obtaining for Malinowski a Robert Mond Travelling Studentship and, commencing 1 January 1915, election to a Constance Hutchinson Studentship. The former was worth £250 a year for five years, the latter 100 guineas a year for two years. One of the stipulations of the Hutchinson scholarship was that its holder should present a thesis to the University within three years or forfeit the last two quarterly instalments. There was a further condition: 'When the thesis is completed it is to be understood that the School series will have the first option of its publication'.[5] As it transpired, Malinowski completed his 'thesis' within six months of being offered the scholarship, but his circumstances were unusual to say the least.

British New Guinea (renamed Papua after Australia took over its administration in 1906) was an obvious country in which to do fieldwork. The very term 'field work' had been introduced into anthropology by one who worked there – Alfred Cort Haddon of Cambridge, who had begun his academic career as a natural scientist, and was largely responsible for generating a sense of urgency in the study of vanishing primitive cultures (see Haddon 1901, Quiggin 1942, Urry 1982). Arguably the most influential British anthropologist of the first two decades of the century, Haddon had begun survey work on the south coast as early as 1898–9 while leading the Cambridge University expedition to Torres Strait, and he planned to return for a further six months in 1914. Seligman had been a member of the Torres Strait expedition and had revisited British New Guinea for a longer period in 1904–5 to conduct the extensive survey that resulted in his monumental book, *The Melanesians of British New Guinea* (1910). W. H. R. Rivers, greatly admired by Malinowski and probably the most brilliant British anthropologist of his time, had also been a member of Haddon's Torres Strait team, though in August 1914 he was bound for a different part of Melanesia. In the immediate pre-war years, Diamond Jenness (a student of R. R. Marett's at Oxford) had worked on Goodenough Island in the D'Entrecasteaux group; Gunnar Landtman and R. W. Williamson (students of Haddon) had worked, respectively, on Kiwai Island in the Fly delta and among the Mafulu people of the interior. No other possession of the British Empire, then, had given such a head start to professional anthropology.

In the company of many of his colleagues from England,

Malinowski sailed to Australia in June 1914 to attend meetings of the British Association for the Advancement of Science, which was held like a travelling fair in one state capital after another. He went as Marett's secretary (who was Recorder to Section H) and at the expense of the Australian Government. News of the outbreak of war in Europe reached the itinerant scientists in Adelaide. Malinowski's status immediately became one of 'enemy alien' (or as he put it more dramatically, 'Austrian Subject, member of the Landsturm, or second reserve'). But well-armed with references from the University of London, and with Haddon's personal introduction to a top government official, Atlee Hunt, Malinowski was allowed to proceed to Papua as he had originally planned.

A. Atlee Hunt C.M.G. was Secretary of the Department of External Affairs of the Commonwealth Government of Australia. In view of all he did for Malinowski during the following six years he deserves recognition for what, indirectly, amounted to a considerable service to anthropology. The official file on Malinowski, covering the whole period he was in Australia and Papua (1914–1920), is a couple of inches thick, and most of the paperwork it contains was initiated by Hunt. He wrote innumerable letters of introduction for Malinowski, pressed his Minister for substantial grants when difficulties arose over the transfer of Malinowski's funds from England, arranged free travel passes for him whenever he could, defended him against rumours of his untrustworthiness and pro-German sympathies, protected him from a suspicious and hostile Sir Hubert Murray (Lt-Governor of Papua), smoothed over difficulties with military commandants, and generally eased some of the irksome restrictions which hindered his movements. Hunt even arranged for Malinowski to purchase photographic supplies at discount, to have his prints done at little or no expense, and to borrow from the Government a camera (3A Graflex fitted with a Zeiss Kodak Anastigmat F.6.5 lens) and a tent – the famous tent which was to become a symbol of the ethnographer's intimate style of fieldwork.[6]

Atlee Hunt did all these things not merely to oblige Haddon and Baldwin Spencer, another of Malinowski's eminent patrons, but because he held an enlightened belief in the practical value of anthropological research, and an unshakable faith in Malinowski's capacity to carry it out. No other public figure demonstrated such support for Malinowski. If Lt-Governor Murray had had his way, Malinowski would not have been permitted to return to Papua in

1915, except on condition that he was employed by the Papuan government. It annoyed Murray that the grant (£250 over a two-year period) Hunt secured for Malinowski was drawn against his own administration's budget; if Murray was paying for Malinowski's research he wanted some say in where he went and what he did. It was Hunt's intercession with his Minister that kept Murray at bay and ensured the continuation of Malinowski's fieldwork. While Malinowski was suitably grateful to Hunt for his patronage, he could not have known the extent to which he was being protected by him – all too often from the consequences of his own gaffes.[7]

III Fieldwork in Mailu: 'Covering the Ground'

Malinowski's plan to go to Mailu was not entirely his own. Seligman apparently urged him to investigate this area, one he had been obliged to neglect during his survey of British New Guinea in 1904–5. It was of particular ethnological interest to Seligman as a zone of transition between the two ethnic groups he had identified as the eastern and western branches of the Papuo-Melanesian stock.[8] Although there were a great many other peoples to be found in the Territory who had not yet been investigated, many of them temptingly exotic, Malinowski appears to have been content on this first expedition to follow Seligman's advice. It called for no great intrepidity or complex logistical plans, for Mailu had been in regular contact with Europeans since about 1885, had hosted a resident missionary since 1896, and was comparatively well-served by coastal steamers. Roughly midway between Port Moresby and Samarai, then the administrative and the commercial capitals of Papua respectively, Mailu probably saw as much sea traffic in 1914 as it does at the present day.

Although he eagerly anticipated his arrival in Papua as beginning a 'new epoch' in his life, Malinowski was worried about his status as an alien, his shortage of funds, and whether his health was equal to the ennervation of the tropics. He spent the first month in and around Port Moresby, visiting officials, learning Police Motu, and doing some ethnographic work on Motu and Koita peoples with considerable help from an experienced, even 'professional' informant.

In his first letter to Seligman, dated 20 September 1914, Malinowski wrote:

> Here I am at last in the Promised Land – and so far I find it in all respects better and promising more success than I had ever anticipated...
>
> I am so far entirely conforming with your orders and waiting for the first opportunity for going East to Mailu, where I propose to settle for my first period of work ... [He says he is learning Motu and working with Ahuia Oval] who after being started by you and tapped by Barton and others has become a passionate Anthropologist (by the way he ought to be made honorary Member of the RAI). At any rate I am learning much in the way of technicalities of inquiry and I am facing quite hopefully the future – even in the case I would not be able to find an interpreter half as good as Ahuia...
>
> I find investigation and description of technical details (technology) more difficult than anything else. When this reaches you, you will probably know how matters stand with my further monetary supplies. I am now much more eager to be able to extend my visit here than I was ever before. Of course, I have not yet really tried my forces and worked on my own; here I am still guided by you and undergoing a kind of practical training in your school. But I have a concrete idea of what the difficulties will look like and I have lost my original diffidence (SP 20.9.1914).

After hiring a young Motuan, Igua, to serve as his cook and factotum, Malinowski departed for Mailu, arriving on 16 October. He was immediately welcomed by the local missionary, William Saville of the London Missionary Society, whom Seligman had met ten years previously. Saville courteously offered Malinowski food and board, conducted tours of local villages and an introduction to Mailu culture. Malinowski, however, soon found himself in disagreement with the missionary. Early the next month he visited the mainland and met the local planter Alfred Greenaway, an English Quaker of 'working-class background' whom he found to be a more congenial source of information than Saville (Malinowski 1967: 31, 39).

On 3 November, Malinowski wrote a long letter to Seligman

detailing his progress. It is worth quoting at some length as it shows
that he had already grasped the essentials of Mailu culture. This
letter also reveals the extent to which he had expected to depend
upon the local missionary (as his anthropological mentors had no
doubt encouraged him to do) as well as upon bilingual informants.

> I am here for over three weeks already and I have gathered
> a nice store of information, though by no means as much as
> I could have done under less unfavourable circumstances. The
> missionary is really very busy; after 3 months absence he
> came back for 8 weeks and is soon starting on a few months
> leave. So that he is of very little help to me. No one else
> speaks two words of English. If not for the miserable shade
> [?] of Motuan I have got I would have to close shop, for my
> Motu boy is far too stupid to be used as an unchecked
> interpreter. But I picked up a certain amount of Motu before
> and I am rapidly perfectioning it [sic]. Thus, slowly but at a
> definite rate I am working out the material. There is however
> [?] a great scarcity of men just at present, as many have been
> making sago for the great feast, which in fact is not going to
> be very great this year. The war scare has upset even pig-
> trading in New Guinea and the Mailu (of Mailu Island) who
> depend on their *boraa* (pig)-supply from Aroma, have not
> gone there this year...I have, so far, seen only this village
> (Mailu on the island) and Unevi village on the coast,
> opposite Mailu. From what Saville says, they seem to be
> nearly identical in their social and cultural features. They do
> not seem to go far inland, some 10–20 miles inland there are
> villages speaking a different language.

Malinowski then proceeded to summarize his observations
concerning housebuilding, clans, *dubu* (men's house), gardens, and
trading. His comments on trade are interesting for he later
reproduced them, with amplification but no major amendment, in
his monograph.

> On Mailu Island gardens played a very little role and the
> community is not self-supporting. They trade for food with
> some of the adjoining coastline villages and for pigs with
> AROMA. They had a sago supply on the mainland, which
> they had an exclusive right to exploit and did it on
> communal principles. Their trading line extended from

Bonabona east to Aroma west and was somewhat complex –
I have got many details; thus f[or] e[xample], raw shells were
bought in Aroma, made in Mailu and sold again as TOEAS
[i.e. armshells] in Aroma. I could not...[?]...so for the
overland trading line, though I am sure it must have existed,
for various reasons.

He goes on to mention family life, kin terms, 'superstitions' of *vada*
sorcery and ghosts, taboos and taboo signs, the absence of totemism,
etc., indicating their similarity or otherwise to Koita practices as
Seligman had documented them in his book. Malinowski concluded
his survey with some notes on feasting, and these too deserve to be
cited:

Public feast system is developed as among the Koita and as
much important in public life. Main features: dances and
distribution of food (MADUNA), the collection of food for
MADUNA governs the whole tribal life during the latter part
of the S.E. trade and beginning of monsoon. Vegetable food
supplied by clan giving MARU feast...Pigs supplied by other
clans. The brunt of pig-giving falls to the men, who married
girls from the clan giving [the] feast. Marriage usually settled
when girl small, though no infant marriage used. A system of
feasts and payments (details in Notebooks). Payments in pigs
continued after marriage at MADUNA occasions. These
returned at reciprocal MADUNA, but never with equal
balance. (I have made some pig-statistics for a couple of
MADUNAS and figures show, that the pigs given by a man to his
people-in- law always outnumber the returned pigs.) I have got
some notes on the disposal of the dead ... on the division of the
seasons and on some technical points (pot-making, house-
building, canoes). But I feel I have not got yet into the
'heart of the people'...
    The weather is fair so far and I had no serious breakdown
yet, though I have days of collapse, when I cannot
work...(SP 3.11.1914).

Scrutiny of the relevant pages of his *Diary* (1967: 26–34) suggests that
Malinowski could have put in no more than 14 days' work in Mailu
by the time he wrote this letter. He had already collected and
synthesized a good deal of information, yet was beginning to

reproach himself for not having seen into the 'heart of the people'. A few days later, Professor Haddon and his daughter visited Mailu during their tour of the southern coast; Haddon was investigating canoes, Kathleen collecting string-figures. Malinowski did not enjoy their visit (what novice would welcome the world's foremost authority on Melanesian ethnography in his village three weeks after starting work?), but he showed Haddon his notebooks and won some praise. Later Haddon was to write to Seligman that his protégé will 'make an excellent fieldworker'.[9]

On 24 November, after several days of sickness, depressed spirits, and a therapeutic immersion in Rudyard Kipling's *Kim*, Malinowski wrote again to Seligman. But the 'nervous disorganization, sentimentalism, agitation' he noted in his *Diary* (1967: 42) are scarcely evident in this reassuring letter:

> Just a few words, as there seems to be soon an opportunity
> for sending out mail. I am going on not at a tremendous
> pace, but steadfastly. Haddon was here for a couple of days
> and you will have seen him, before this reaches you. I think
> I have now got a fairly complete all round picture of the
> Mailu – but it is a rough sketch in black and white so far
> and the touches of colour are much more difficult to get. I
> am trying to *see* as many things done, as I can. I hope I
> shall be able to see a couple of feasts in the end of
> December or beginning January – the great annual feast. In
> the meantime I am going East – there is the mission launch
> going to Samarai – and I shall, on the way back, stop in
> one or two places, especially at the very point where the
> Mailu and the Suau touch. This will be only rough sounding,
> but it will be very helpful in discovering the touches of
> Eastern culture here. I have had no serious breakdown of
> health so far, though for a week or so I felt seedy and my
> work was very slow. My weakest points are photographs and
> phonographic records. I have taken very few photos so far –
> but I have ambitious schemes of recording much of their
> dances, children's plays [sic] and economic activities (fishing,
> making gardens etc.) and technology. But whenever skill
> comes into play I am not much good (SP 24.11.1914).[10]

As arranged, on 26 November, having spent five weeks in Mailu, Malinowski accompanied Saville on a trip to the east, visiting

Charles Abel's mission on Kwatou Island, and then Samarai, where he interviewed prisoners at the gaol. Between the 8 and 19 December he investigated some Suau coastal villages and visited the Riches', another L.M.S. missionary family. On returning to Mailu, alone this time, he spent the following five weeks doing his most intensive work (with a few days' break for Christmas at Greenaway's plantation). On 24 January he boarded the Lt-Governor's ship (to be greeted by Murray 'with a distinct blunt, cold reserve'), relieved and happy finally to depart Mailu ('a sense of freedom – as if I were starting a vacation' [1967: 74]). He immediately wrote a cheerful letter to Seligman from Port Moresby:

> Last night I arrived here from Mailu. My fortunes there, after the Rev. W. J. V. Saville B.B. (you know what those initials mean in NG), were very varied. In fact the missionary has done his best to interfere with my work...[with his?]...subterranean ways, and after he left I got on with the natives infinitely better than before. I got in fact a fairly good amount of information about Mailu. I am sticking to my previous plan to go South for 60 days and work out everything clean and neat before I proceed. I shall send you samples from Australia. I hope I have got some fairly good plates – though I didn't develop the last 2 dozen. I neglected only scandalously the purely anthropological side (measuring) of the business, but I may be excused that as on the one hand I really did work whenever I got the opportunity and on the other, I think I am much better fitted for the other work and I consider it more important – I shall send you a good deal of technicalities – in fact a short abstract of all I have got, when I go over my stuff (SP 25.1.1915).

After spending a week in Moresby, Malinowski sailed a little way down the coast to work with Ahuia among the Sinaugolo. They returned to Moresby after a productive stay of nine days in Rigo. A week later Malinowski boarded a ship which took him back to Samarai, and from there he made a week's excursion to Woodlark Island, which proved to be another fruitful trip. Then he sailed for Australia via Samarai and Moresby again, reaching Cairns on 1 March 1915.

IV   Fieldwork in Mailu: Lessons of Experience

The recital of dates I have given above serves to establish that Malinowski was engaged, on this first expedition, in 'survey' rather than 'intensive' work – a methodological distinction which Haddon and Rivers had begun to make in recent years (see Urry 1972; 1984; Stocking 1983). As Stocking (ibid: 108) has noted in another connection, Malinowski's time reckoning was 'somewhat unreliable'. His claim to have been 'living quite alone with the natives' for 'the best part of December, January and February', can be seen to be a generous exaggeration. If the *Diary* presents an accurate record of his movements, then of the 73 days he spent among the Mailu proper, only 37 days were spent without some social intercourse with Europeans. ('I don't feel too cut off', he remarked in his *Diary* on 19 December after His Excellency and his entourage had stopped by and given him supper and 'free friendly conversation' aboard the Government boat, and before he listed all the 'well-disposed' and 'hospitable' white families he had met in recent days [1967: 58–9].)

He mentions the time he spent 'living quite alone with the natives' not in order to boast, however, but to establish a methodological point which had the force of a personal discovery. The importance of his Mailu research for him seemed to lie in such lessons. He had begun to articulate a couple of them even before he began work in Mailu, while he was conducting his 'ethnological explorations' in Port Moresby. 'They suffer from two basic defects', he noted, '(1) I have rather little to do with the savages on the spot, do not observe them enough and (2) I do not speak their language' (1967: 13). Following his Mailu trip he was to write: 'I found that work done under such circumstances [i.e. living alone with the natives] is incomparably more intensive than work done from white men's settlements, or even in any white man's company; the nearer one lives to a village and the more one actually sees of the natives the better' (p. 109).

If this prescription represented an ideal he did not live up to in Mailu, he certainly tried to achieve it in the Trobriands the following year. Meanwhile, a foretaste of life in the heart of the village was granted when he visited the Suau coast while a *Soi* feast was in progress. He was suffering a light fever and was 'greatly irritated' by the conditions: 'the stench, smoke, noise of people, dogs, and pigs'. The three or four nights he spent in the village exhausted him ('I awoke feeling as if just taken down from the cross'), and he later rebuked himself for his limited powers of endurance: 'On the whole, these few days which might have been extremely fruitful... were greatly spoiled by my lack of strength' (1967: 53–5). As Stocking gently puts it, 'total immersion was not easy for him' (1983: 97).

Another important lesson Malinowski had learned in Mailu, one he raised to a fieldwork principle which he never tired of stressing, was the imperative need to speak the vernacular. Although his Mailu notebooks are sprinkled with Mailu terms, he made no systematic attempt to learn the language (leaving the field entirely to Saville, who had already published a grammar in 1912). But Malinowski was proud to inform his readers how quickly he had managed to learn Motu (though it was actually the simplified trade version), and he claimed to have found it 'a completely satisfactory instrument of investigation'. It also enabled him to eavesdrop: 'Over and over again I was led onto the track of some extremely important item in native sociology or folklore by listening to the conversation of my boy Igua with his Mailu friends' (pp. 109).

Other fieldwork lessons he learned in Mailu are more imponderable, though they include what Stocking has called 'a more intimate ethnographic style'. This was in part enjoined by the proximity he had sought ('living right among the natives'), but it also ensued from the simple fact of being present in the village as things were happening, of becoming caught up in an event and then turning it to ethnographic advantage. There is the example he gives of drawing out reticent informants by feigning concern about ghosts and asking their advice; he elicited in this way information which previously had been 'withheld' from him (p. 273; also Stocking 1983: 96). Pontifically, he generalized the lesson: 'My experience is that direct questioning of the natives about a custom or belief never discloses their attitude of mind as thoroughly as the discussion of facts connected with the direct observation of a custom, or with a concrete occurrence in which both parties are materially concerned' (p. 275). The recording of 'concrete instances' or 'actual cases' became another keystone of his method and laid the groundwork for both 'the statistical documentation by concrete evidence' and the 'imponderabilia of actual life and of typical behaviour' (1922: 20). 'Concrete illustrations' of the kind he later used to help bring Trobrianders to life make a more modest appearance in *Mailu*, most effectively as devices to explicate inheritance (p. 258–60) and mourning practices (pp. 312–14). But he mentioned them frequently, obviously mindful of Rivers' first rule of method from *Notes and Queries*: 'the abstract should be approached through the concrete' (NQ 1912: 115).

The most intensive period of his work began, as I have noted, when he returned to Mailu on 19 December after his trip to the Suau coast. Saville had remained in Samarai, shortly to go on furlough, so Malinowski moved into 'a disused mission house, not far from the present Mission Station' (p. 272). But he was unsure of how to begin: '... I really do not know, or rather I do not see clearly, what I am to do. Period of suspense. I came to a deserted place with the feeling that soon I'll have to finish but in the meantime I must begin a new existence' (1967: 49). (In the event, he spent the day usefully enough by catching up on his diary of the previous week.) He was still living outside the village and observing its activities at set times each day rather than continuously. As before, he made a morning and a late afternoon visit to the village in search of informants and scenes to photograph. Occasionally he strolled to the village in the evening if there was any dancing to watch. The names of Mailu informants recur in the *Diary* and the monograph: Papari, Kavaka, Dagaea, Velavi, Dimdim, Puana, Omaga, Pikana. Malinowski paid them tobacco for enduring lengthy, openended interviews. His highest praise for an informant (as in all his subsequent monographs) was 'intelligent', which he occasionally qualified with 'very', 'extremely' or 'exceptionally'. But there were many occasions of frustrated communication, which he was peevishly inclined to blame on the stupidity of his interlocutors.

Two days before he was to leave Mailu, he wrote in his *Diary*: 'I am *"covering the ground"* of my territory more and more concretely. Without doubt, if I could stay here for several more months – or years – I would get to know these people far better. But for a superficial short stay I have done as much as can be done. I am quite satisfied with what I have done under the poor circumstances' (1967: 76). Why the circumstances were 'poor' during his last month in Mailu he does not explain. Discounting the bouts of sickness and depression, his material circumstances appear to have been tolerably good. He refers to no shortage of supplies, no impediments to collecting information (save for a period of nine or ten days when the men were absent on a trading trip), and he was within easy reach of a white planter's haven at Mogubu (where he spent Christmas). Notwithstanding his brave claim that Motu was a 'completely satisfactory' medium of communication, one must infer that 'the poor circumstances' were due to his inability to communicate as well as he would have liked with his subjects.

We must not forget the emotional circumstances. The forays into the village were sometimes made in the teeth of an inner resistance. An index of his misery is the frequency with which he succumbed to the escapist lure of 'trashy novels'. On 6 January a crisis of sorts developed, when the wind changed and 'absolutely everybody left Mailu' to sail to Domara on a trading voyage. (Some women presumably remained behind, but Malinowski was unable to speak to them [p.173].) He had tried to accompany the men but refused to pay the £2 demanded by the expedition leaders, so they sailed without him. Malinowski was 'infuriated'. It was a unique fieldwork opportunity missed, and a few days later he was to regret not having paid the sum – exorbitant though it was.[11] For solace he turned to a Dumas novel and read without respite for six days – 'as though I were reading myself to death' (1967: 62–9).

Under the 'poor circumstances' that prevailed in Mailu, even throughout the period of his most intensive fieldwork there, it is astonishing that Malinowski managed to amass as much information as he did. And when he came to reflect upon his achievement (modest though it was to seem compared to later ones), there is a mood of self-congratulaton in the retrospective *Diary*. One also hears a great sigh of relief:

> At moments I was very exalted; I have been in N.G., I have
> accomplished a good deal. I have prospects of far better
> work – fairly certain plans. And *so* – it's not as hopeless as I
> thought when I arrived here. Moreover I don't feel a bit
> worse than when I came. I am a better sailor and I walk
> much better – the distances no longer terrify me. – Gazing at
> the sea I have a strong feeling of happiness. True, it's not all
> over yet; but in the light of old fears and uncertainties I
> have decidedly won a victory (1967: 97).

V An Adelaide Autumn: The Politics of Publication

Aboard the *Marasina*, nearing Cairns in northern Queensland, Malinowski admonished as well as congratulated himself:

The most important thing now is not to waste my stay in Australia but to use it carefully in the most productive way. I must write an article about Mailu – maybe a few others in addition, but Mailu first and foremost. I must check the museums insofar as possible. So there won't be time for nonsense! I must give a detailed account to Mr Atlee Hunt and try to impress him (1967: 93).

During this interlude of less than three months Malinowski somehow managed to do almost all of these things – and evidently also found time for some 'nonsense': he fell in love.

The providential suggestion to publish his first report in Australia appears to have been made well before Malinowski had finished it. Most closely involved were his two most influential academic patrons, Sir Baldwin Spencer and Sir Edward Stirling. Spencer was Director of the National Museum of Victoria in Melbourne and a seasoned fieldworker in his own right. Like his friend Haddon, he was a zoologist turned anthropologist, and Malinowski had become thoroughly familiar with his ethnography while writing *The Family among the Australian Aborigines*. Stirling was Professor of Physiology at the University of Adelaide and Curator of Ethnology at the South Australian Museum. He too had done field research (some of it with Spencer) into the physical anthropology and material culture of Aborigines in Central Australia. Although he built up the largest museum collection of Aboriginal artifacts in the world, he published very little of his ethnography.[12] When Malinowski returned to Australia following his Mailu expedition he stayed as a guest in Stirling's Adelaide home (having narrowly escaped imprisonment for failing to report to the military authorities in Melbourne), and it was there that he wrote up his Mailu research.

Malinowski must have written his report at a furious pace. He appears to have begun it while still aboard the *Marasina* (1967: 97–8), but he is unlikely to have written much until after he had arrived in Adelaide on 18 or 19 March. Yet he had substantially completed it by the end of April, when he was back in Melbourne reporting in person to Atlee Hunt. On 7 May he was in Sydney ordering supplies and arranging his finances, and two weeks later in Brisbane, waiting for the boat that would take him back to Papua. He penned the Preface to his 'memoir' on 9 June in Samarai, *en route* to Kiriwina.

The speed with which he dashed off *The Natives of Mailu* is all the more remarkable in view of the fact that he was sick with malaria for some of the time he was in Australia; he was also obliged to write official letters to Hunt and others, and spend time reassuring the local authorities that he was not a security threat. Not only did he write a full-length monograph, prepare 34 photographs and sketch 50-odd figures during those six or seven weeks, but he found time to captivate Stirling's daughter Nina, to whom he became unofficially engaged (Wayne 1984: 194). The sole half-page entry in his *Diary* for the first year he spent in the Trobriands – dated 1 August 1915 – focuses precisely upon this event: 'If in the end I marry N., March and April 1915 will be the most important months in my emotional life' (1967: 99).

As his Adelaide host, Edward Stirling must have exercised a persuasive influence on Malinowski during this brief period of intensive writing. Stirling had been elected F.R.S. in 1893 (South Australia's first), and in all probability it was he who urged Malinowski to offer his report to the Royal Society of South Australia. He even undertook to edit it for publication, though this proved to be no light task. By 4 May Malinowski had finally decided to place it with the Royal Society, and on that day he wrote to Seligman from Melbourne, with a mixture of apology and defiance, seeking his supervisor's approval. One section of this lengthy letter is worth quoting in full, since it shows how finely balanced Malinowski saw his immediate and long-term obligations to be, and how accurately he had perceived the political advantages of publishing in Australia:

> I came down here [i.e. Australia], among other reasons, also
> to write my results into a final or semi-final form, and thus
> to check my methods of fieldwork thoroughly. As I was
> mainly working among the Mailu, I went straight to a
> monograph of these b.bs. I wrote it as if I were going to
> print it, and when I got the stuff typed, I be-thought myself
> that it looked quite printable. But it will be about 120–150
> pages octavo and there would be not the remotest chance of
> it seeing the light under the grey skies of England, in the
> present troubled times. I thought the easiest [thing] to get it
> through somewhere here. The Royal Society of S.A.
> (Adelaide) opened its arms to receive the new born Papuan
> infant (excuse bad taste) – on one word they said they will

print the stuff at *once* as a separate memoir, with plates etc.
a *discrétion*. I got it through Stirling, who has been as kind
to me here – nearly as you have been over there. He read
my M.S. and corrected the English and the stile [sic] in its
logical aspect and took great interest in the stuff. He was
very good to me in general – I was very seedy in Adelaide,
he took me up to his house in the hills and I stayed there
for over a month, most awfully kindly treated by the whole
family. Another man in Adelaide did the typing for me in his
office, free of charge. When I came here to Melbourne, I
produced some of my stuff to Baldwin Spencer, who seemed
to have thought it quite worth printing – he even suggested
that I ought to send it over to England in order to get a
better *résonance*. He backed me up energetically at the
External Affairs and undertook to read the proofs and see
the book through. So he has been also extremely kind – and
I gather that Spencer is not a soft person – I think he would
be fairly critical with fieldwork. So I feel encouraged and I
hope that my next [?] will be much better, Insh' Allah! But I
want to tell you emphatically that all the real kindness I
have received here, has not blunted for a moment my
genuine gratitude for you and that I consider my stuff as
always being under your supervision. I have made all
arrangements for the thing being printed here, and I consider
that under the present circumstances, the conditions I have
obtained are perfectly advantageous: 1) I'll have my stuff
ready printed, say in September, October next – and you and
I will be able to say and show that something has been done
– and I may be at a very bad pinch, because the external
affairs have cut me down to £150 from £200. So that I'll
have £250 for the year, which will not allow me to do inland
work, on which I am very keen. 2) I'll have my work printed
in Australia, and as I am pumping money from this soil, it is
only fair (and what is more, it's wise for the future) to let
my sweat manure the same soil. 3) I would have not been
able to discuss with you matters and give you the same hints
and data as to technicalities, as I was able to do Stirling and
Spencer who will kindly see my thing through. But in spite
of all that, I have not finally decided, whether I shall have
my things printed here, because the final decision rests with

you. I wrote to Stirling that if he receives a cable from you: 'Stop Malinowski Printing' (the cable money I would return to you with all my other debts – if you trust that I shall not die etc.) – my stuff is not to be printed. At the same time I shall forward to you a set of T.S. of the stuff as soon as it is ready. If you, however, for any reason should not agree, I shall not feel in the slightest offended, or hurt, or touchy, though I may swear at you a little bit. If Stirling does not get the cable before end of June, I'll tell him to let things go. Title: 'The Natives of Mailu, British New Guinea: Preliminary Account of the Robert Mond Ethnological Investigations in Papua'. I think I better put R.M. in the subtitle. He gave the coins awfully nicely – and I'll write to him from Papua, though I of course, don't expect him to shower any more money on me.
... As a matter of fact my stuff about the Mailu was the poorest I got. Sinaugholo, bits of Koiari, scraps of Woodlark, much better quality though small quantity. I expect I shall be able to get some really good stuff if I don't get seedy or something else.
... Another point: The School, which stipulated first option on publication of my results, has no claim on this lot, as I did it without their assistance (SP 4.5.1915).

*

Malinowski appears to have been banking on Seligman's amenable nature as well as on the fact that it took several months to exchange correspondence with England. When he wrote this letter, Malinowski had already committed himself to publishing with the Royal Society, and had Seligman withheld his approval it would have been embarrassingly difficult to withdraw the T.S. Indeed, a great deal more was at stake than Malinowski himself guessed, and from one point of view his *Mailu* monograph was a political document. A week before writing the above letter to Seligman, Malinowski had submitted to Atlee Hunt a brief but formal report on his Mailu research. He carefully pitched his account for government approval:

In the investigation of the natives I have paid special attention to the economic and sociological aspects of native

life, as well as to their beliefs and general psychological
features. I did not neglect the sociological problems, arising
from the transitory stage of the native society and I studied
the extremely interesting (both theoretically and practically)
process of adaptation to their new conditions. I was unable
to pay serious attention to physical anthropology and to
broad racial problems as well as to speculations about origin
(AA 28.4.1915).

Here Malinowski was not merely distancing himself from the
ethnological concerns of Haddon and Seligman, but positively
stating his interest in social change and the 'sociological problems' of
direct concern to the colonial administration. In subsequent
paragraphs he outlined his future plans for research (see Young 1984:
12) and justified his request for funds. He referred to his
'monograph' on the Mailu: 'Parts of it are ready for print and have
been favourably commended by such authorities as Professor
Stirling, F.R.S. of Adelaide, and Professor Spencer, F.R.S. of
Melbourne . . .' (ibid).

Acting with an alacrity uncharacteristic of modern bureaucracies,
Hunt sent the report to his Minister. Hunt's accompanying
memorandum makes it clear that the local availability of
Malinowski's writings was a substantial argument in favour of
granting him government money for research. It is also a loud (and
quite early) hint of the potential value of an applied social
anthropology for colonial administrations. The implication of this
memorandum, moreover, is that if Malinowski had been more
engaged in the kind of 'technical' ethnological investigations that
Seligman had wanted him to carry out, and less committed to
developing his own 'sociological' interests, then Hunt's advocacy
would have been that much less forceful. Again, without Hunt's
active support, Malinowski would have been most unlikely to have
been given any money at all:

I have spent some little time with Dr Malinowski and have
been greatly interested in the very practical work on which
he has been engaged. It will be noted from his letter that the
class of investigation which he has been conducting is one
likely to be of much use to the Government in our dealings
with the natives. He has not concerned himself with the more
technical branches of the science such as are involved in the

measurement of bodies, etc., but deals with the mental attitudes and peculiar customs of the people.

I have glanced over the monograph to which Dr Malinowski makes reference. It will be found of great interest by all connected with the Government of the Territory. It is to be published in Australia by the Royal Society of Adelaide.

Dr Malinowski is especially desirous of pursuing his enquiries already commenced into the native ownership of land ignorance in regard to which has frequently caused considerable trouble. His request for £200 to cover all expenses, transport, carriers, assistance, provisions, etc., appears extremely moderate.

I have consulted Professor Spencer who has made himself conversant with Dr Malinowski's work and he speaks in the highest terms of him and regards him as one well worthy of getting assistance. In this view I understand he is confirmed by Professor Stirling of Adelaide.

As all the results of his investigations are made available for this Government I recommend that a grant of £200 for the current year be made (AA 28.5.1915).

By 1 May the Minister had given his approval, and on 4 May (the same day that Malinowski wrote to Seligman) Hunt wrote to Malinowski, informing him that he would get his £200:

I am to add that in approving this grant the Minister understands that your investigations will include careful examination of the system of native ownership of lands and will generally deal with aspects of all native life any records of which will be of practical advantage to officers carrying on the government of the country and, further, that all papers prepared by you will be made available for the Government of the Territory and will be published in Australia or Papua (AA 4.5.1915).

When he placed his arguments before Seligman, Malinowski was doubtless unaware that Hunt had made publication in Australia a condition of his government's further support. But writing from Sydney on 7 May, Malinowski warmly thanked Hunt and dutifully acknowledged the conditions under which he was being financed:

In accordance with the instructions given me in your letter, I
shall pay special attention to the sociological, legal and
economic problems of native life, which might be useful for
practical purposes of administration and legislation, and I
shall make a report on the results I obtained. As far as the
purely theoretical results of my work are concerned I shall
consider it my duty in the future to offer them to Australian
Scientific Journals etc. for publication, as I have done with
my first M.S. There might be technical difficulties with the
publication of a large volume in this country, however, unless
financial subsidy were forthcoming (AA 7.5.1915).

In case his *Mailu* monograph set an awkward precedent,
Malinowski shrewdly left himself a loophole. And indeed, he was
later to excuse any attempt to publish in Australia his book on the
Kula by grossly exaggerating its proposed length and likely expense.
With the sole exception of an article he was invited to contribute to
the *Australian Encyclopaedia* (1926a), he published nothing more in
Australia – least of all in Papua.[13]

*

Fortunately, Seligman was agreeable to Malinowski's plan and
replied favourably: though Malinowski appears not to have received
his letter until September, by which time he had been in the
Trobriands for three months. 'I am delighted you are getting your
Mailu stuff printed in Australia', Seligman wrote, and he expressed
his appreciation at the 'friendliness and delicacy' Malinowski had
showed in allowing him the final veto. 'I shall write to Stirling, thank
him for all he is doing, and tell him how grateful I am to hear that he
has been able to arrange for you to publish at once. Probably I'll
suggest smoothing out your sub-title a little...' Seligman told
Malinowski he had written to Reeves, Director of the L.S.E.,
informing him of the publishing arrangements and pointing out
'what a good omen it was for the work you would do on behalf of the
School' (SP 16.6.1915). Only three days before, Malinowski had
written yet again to Seligman : 'I have spent two weeks of my time –
or rather lost them in a way – in Samarai. I was finishing my Mailu
M.S. Yesterday I posted the finished thing for Adelaide, where, if it
has your sanction, it will be, Insh' Allah, printed' (SP 13.6.1915).

Malinowski had good reason for feeling pleased about the outcome of publishing in Australia. It gratified his local academic patrons and promised to advance his cause. It was instrumental in securing him the financial wherewithal for almost a year (as if he had actually sold *The Natives of Mailu* to the government for the price of £200). It might even have mollified Hubert Murray in Papua if only he had been sent a personal copy. Not least, perhaps, it was also an honourable way of paying a debt forced on Malinowski by the circumstances of the war.

To demonstrate the political importance of his *Mailu* monograph we must follow the story one stage further. Volume 39 of the *Transactions and Proceedings* duly appeared in December 1915. Malinowski returned to Australia from his second expedition (his first Trobriand trip) during late March 1916. In August, Lt-Governor Murray wrote to Hunt suggesting that the Papuan Government 'be supplied with say a dozen copies of all books or pamphlets which may have been published in connection with that gentleman's work in the territory'. The government secretary of Papua, H. W. Champion, had been sent a copy 'as an act of personal courtesy', but Murray had not (AA 10.8.1916).

Baldwin Spencer wrote to Hunt on Malinowski's behalf, explaining that although the author had received 25 copies of the 'pamphlet' he had distributed them 'to various Scientists and Scientific Bodies', and therefore could not comply with the request for more than one copy; besides, the Mailu work had been done before Malinowski received any funds from the Australian government (AA 14.9.1916). (As we have seen, Malinowski had used the same argument to Seligman, in reverse, to justify his printing in Australia rather than in England.) Hunt conveyed this information to Murray and thereby defended Malinowski, adding that his Department too had received only one copy (which he duly forwarded to Murray). But Murray was not to be put off, and his reply was corrosive:

> I have the honour to suggest that as this Government paid Dr Malinowski's salary more than one copy of his book should be supplied to us. I do not think that this gentleman has ever realized that it was the Papuan Govt. that was paying him, and I feel certain that if this is pointed out to him he will readily admit that he owes us some return (AA 30.10.1916).

The record does not state whether Malinowski complied with this request. The following year, one copy of his *Baloma* article was sent to Murray by Hunt with the explanation (given by Malinowski) that 'a number' of them had been 'lost at sea' (AA 29.8.1917). By the time he came to write his acknowledgements to *Argonauts*, Murray's name had been dropped from the list of his benefactors; but then, so too had Baldwin Spencer's and Edward Stirling's, notwithstanding the sincerely warm thanks he had given them in his Preface to *The Natives of Mailu*. Patently, of all his eminent Australian patrons only Atlee Hunt remained high in Malinowski's esteem.[14]

VI *Notes and Queries* and the Writing of *Mailu*

Now that we understand something of the personal and political circumstances under which Malinowski wrote his monograph, we can return to the work itself and examine it as an ethnographic text. *The Natives of Mailu* is essentially a survey report of the kind that Haddon or Seligman would have been pleased to author. It treats of many of the visible and some of the less visible aspects of Mailu culture. It has none of the textual richness of his best Trobriand ethnography, however, and there is an awkward juxtaposition of discrete areas of enquiry: a consequence of following too slavishly the format of *Notes and Queries*. The monograph has no institutional focus, no functional plan, no unitary topical theme, and it does not narrate a story as, in the most exemplary case, *Argonauts of the Western Pacific* was designed to do. Such literary and theoretically informed devices of presentation were to appear later in Malinowski's corpus, beginning with his extended essay on *Baloma*.

Comparison with *Argonauts* is invidious but inescapable. Historically speaking, if *Argonauts* is a window on the future (post-1922), *Mailu* is a window on the past (pre-1915). As is well known, it was through *Argonauts* that Malinowski began to publicize his 'revolution': radical changes to the practice of ethnography in the field and, no less important, to the writing of ethnography in the study. *Argonauts* was written for – made readable for – a far wider audience than were the spare, technical reports such as Haddon and Seligman approved. Though many of their generation came to mistrust Malinowski for 'popularizing', the fact could not be ignored that *Argonauts* inaugurated a highly influential mode of ethnographic authority. As James Boon nautically pictures it, 'the Malinowskian monograph was launched as the flagship *Argonauts* on Frazer's literary vogue' (1982: 13).

Such self-proclaimed, heroic authority is merely latent in *The Natives of Mailu*, with which its relatively unknown author took few chances. It had, after all, to be acceptable to the anthropological establishment in Australia and England, as both a useful factual report and a respectable academic thesis.

A large proportion of the text is technical description; this, along with the diagrams and photographs, carried its own authority. But Malinowski was on shakier grounds when he reported custom, conduct and belief. Then he frequently cites his indigenous or European sources, sometimes by name and sometimes by reference to an anonymous 'intelligent native'. This is one of his means of establishing credibility, but it also has to do with persuading himself of the accuracy of his facts. He tends to cite local authorities (whites with so many years' experience of the district or 'exceptionally intelligent' natives) when he senses the possibility of dispute about his findings. When the information is uncontentious he need cite no one (the reader is not told, for example, that many of the observations on toilet and cleanliness at pp. 151–2 were recorded from Alfred Greenaway). But let us note too how tentative and diffident Malinowski is on many matters, how willing to admit that his information is incomplete. The author who confesses his ignorance in this way is all the more trustworthy about what he does claim to know. Malinowski is also scrupulous in telling the reader what events he has or has not witnessed (see p. 110 for his statement of this point of method, and Chapter V for several examples).

*

The influence of the 4th edition of *Notes and Queries on Anthropology* (NQ 1912) on the textual construction of *Mailu* is pervasive and easy to demonstrate (Urry 1972: 52; Langham 1981: 173; Stocking 1983: 96). Malinowski carried a copy of this handbook with him on all three of his expeditions. He mentions it in the Introduction to *Mailu* (p. 110), and occasionally alludes to it in his *Diary*; 'Reading Rivers' (1967: 64ff) almost certainly refers to the important central section, 'A General Account of Method', contributed by Rivers. Malinowski's personal copy survives,[15] and there are some interesting marginalia in his hand, a few of which I refer to below.

The 'fairly systematic division' of chapters ('Geography, Sociology, Economics, Magico-religious matters, etc.') that he adopted (p. 110), bears close comparison with the topical organization of *Notes and Queries*. Chapter II of *Mailu* (Social Divisions) takes its main cues from the section on Social Organization written by Rivers (NQ 1912: 143–9). Chapter III (Tribal Life) is a more composite chapter; thus, section 1. (Daily Life) begins with 'divisions of daytime' (cf. ibid: 140), but the remainder of the section (on sleep, toilet, dress, cleanliness, food preparation, cooking, narcotics etc.) closely follows the categories of the Technology chapter of *Notes and Queries*. Section 5 of this chapter, on 'legal institutions', is only notionally based on the *Notes and Queries* section titled 'Government: Politics'. The proof of this connection is the pencilled 'III.5' that Malinowski had written at the head of this section in his personal copy (NQ 1912: 172). He was obviously dissatisfied with these unhelpful pages, and there is a revealing comment in the top margin of the following page on Morals (ibid: 175): 'Neither here, nor foregoing paragraph, do they give hints for study of *sanctions*, of binding force; of underlying ideas' (see also 1926b: 4, where he published a restated version of this criticism). In Chapter IV, Economics, Malinowski put together several headings from the Technology and Sociology parts of *Notes and Queries* (i.e., notably on hunting and fishing; on canoes and sailing; on land and labour; on industry and trade; on property and inheritance – the last by Rivers). In his personal copy Malinowski had bracketed (and marked with 'Ec.') the relevant items on the contents page, items distributed between Technology and Sociology. Chapter V is another composite one, but it reveals throughout the influence of Marett's methodological strictures on 'The Study of Magico-Religious Facts' (NQ 1912: 251–62). Malinowski explicitly acknowledged this influence (p. 110). Section 2 deals with the *Maduna* festival as ceremony, though it fits uneasily in this chapter and would have been better placed in the previous one. Neither feast nor festival appears in the *Notes and Queries* index; nor does the text suggest any category into which they might be placed. (Malinowski's treatment of this important topic warrants further comment, see section XII of this Introduction.) The final section, on death, burial and mourning, takes its cue from the pages on 'Death and Funeral' (NQ 1912: 137–40). Finally, Chapter VI, Art and Knowledge, which Malinowski seems to admit is his weakest chapter, was guided by Part IV of the handbook.

Quite evidently, then, Malinowski relied heavily on *Notes and Queries* for the categories which structured his text. While he used it intelligently, regrouping various sections to suit his own purposes, the skeleton of the report is plainly visible beneath the flesh of description. The frame was also procrustean: some sections are too abruptly begun, others too suddenly terminated. Had Malinowski not been so constrained by his 'adopted' model he would surely have written a more interesting report. It is precisely at those junctures where he departs from the tight structure that his ethnography is most lively and characteristically Malinowskian in its rhetorical combination of vivid observation, elicited native comment, reflexive anecdote, and theoretical aside. The sections on 'legal institutions' and 'the feast', for example, are unconstrained by *Notes and Queries* guidelines for the simple reason that there were none, and these pages are arguably the most original in the report. He presented the material in a thoughtful and challenging way, and it matters little that his theories of law have been dismissed or that his interpretation of the *Maduna* feast now seems unbalanced in its over-emphasis on the ceremonial aspects.

There was, of course, one important practical consequence of using *Notes and Queries* the way Malinowski did. It saved him much time. If, as I have argued, it was diplomatically important for him to write a report as quickly as possible (and to publish it in Australia), then the guide played a modest role in getting Malinowski to the Trobriands. However we may deplore the haste with which he wrote *Mailu*, a haste which left him so little time to cogitate on his data and none whatever to polish his prose, the task was immensely facilitated by *Notes and Queries*. Notwithstanding his disclaimer on p. 110, the structure he derived from *Notes and Queries* was riddled with, indeed founded upon, 'preconceived ideas'. He was thereby spared a great deal of the time and effort otherwise needed to think about that other kind of ethnographic experience – 'writing up'.

VII   Field Notebooks and the Writing of *Mailu*

Three of Malinowski's Mailu notebooks survive (of an original four or five). They were written in English in a fairly legible hand, with proper names and Mailu terms printed in block capitals. It is instructive to examine them for further clues as to how he composed his monograph. In particular, they illustrate how his writing in the field (notebook entry) and his writing in the study (monograph) were often remarkably congruent. This fact does not invalidate Malinowski's later statement that 'the distance is often enormous between the brute material of information... and the final authoritative presentation of the results' (1922: 3–4). But it does show that, in his Mailu ethnography at least, the distance could also be very small.

The sample passages that I reproduce below were selected for their legibility and internal coherence; I have also chosen entries that are (or can be) dated and attributed to particular informants, so that they can be 'triangulated' with respect to the *Diary* as well as the monograph. Besides conveying something of the flavour of Malinowski's fieldwork inscriptions they indicate the way his personal style leaked into the finished monograph; the way, that is, the mediated text of the report reproduces the more immediate ethnographic expressions of his notebooks. Of course, of the three kinds of document, the *Diary* (written in Polish) is the most personal and multivocal, and however experimental its literary tropes it must be privileged as the most authentic expression of Malinowski's fieldwork experience. At the other extreme, as an intentionally public document, the monograph is the most guarded and impersonal. Somewhere in between are the field notebooks, though their authorial voice is much closer to the modal one of the monograph.

The following entry is undated and the informant unspecified, but from internal evidence of adjacent entries it could only have been written on 10 or 11 November when, according to his *Diary*, Malinowski worked with Alf Greenaway, the planter, and Puana, a Mailu man. Haddon was also in the village at the time (1967: 36).

> *O–O* [i.e. *o'o*] is a custom analogous to Amok running. The spirit makes them bad. Shooting stars called in Mailu KARAVENI enter the man or woman and make them *o–o*. There need not be any cause; no angry [sic], no sorry [sic]. They simply get seized by this spirit. In olden days they used to kill a man or a woman, destroy property, chop up a canoe; throw spears at a house. Sometimes they run away to the camp [i.e. gardens] and run about and then fall down exhausted and go to sleep. Next day all right. A LAURUOLO woman, Vaila by name, used to have such fits

> regularly; she used to dress up with weeds on her head and round her waist; she used to take a spear or drum and perform some of the customary dances. Taoplie[?] used to tie up such *o–o* boys. (This is a kind of hysteria and not an Amok. Amok is not known) (MPY 194: 240–1).

Although Malinowski does not identify them as such, *karaveni* are what he was to call 'witches' in the Trobriands. Checking this entry against pp 276–7 of the monograph, we see that Malinowski expanded it slightly (possibly from another source) and smoothed the English. This is a positive instance of notebook/text congruence, and would have made for rapid writing up. There are many such examples.

More intriguing are examples of self-censorship, in which notebook entries have been suppressed or radically re-written to meet prevailing conventions. The following passages, which come close on the heels of the one above, do not occur as such in the text. In view of their mildly salacious tone it is not hard to guess why, though Malinowski was less prudish than his British contemporaries. The alternately coy and spicy section on 'Sexual Life before Marriage' (pp. 174–9) was probably about as far as he dared go without risking Royal Society censure. Since standards of decorum were likely to have been adjudicated by his editor and prospective father-in-law, Sir Edward Stirling, the irony was a delicious one for Malinowski:

> Coitus is performed in the usual position, girl underneath, man on top. Kissing was not known before. They do not kiss during copulation. A case is related by Mr. G. of a father holding his daughter in order to be humped by a man to whom she was married and whom she did not like (194: 242).

> During the *Maduna* general licence prevails. It is usually during the dances. The two agree & sneak away. Sometimes 12 boys hump one girl. It takes place outside the village in the garden (194: 243).

In his report Malinowski mentions only kissing (p. 175) and gives no details of the licence during *Maduna*, merely stating that he did not see 'any sign of quickening sexual life' at the two *Soi* feasts he witnessed (p. 306).

The notes taken from Greenaway are characterized by a rather more lucid style and greater generality. In the notes taken directly from villagers there is a more liberal sprinkling of Motu and Magi terms. Contrast the following entries in the notebook. The first identifies Greenaway as the informant, the second Dimdim (or Owani) of Loupom. Dimdim was lightskinned if not a half-caste – the nickname means 'whiteman' – and he was the 'modern Orestes' who had killed his mother, possibly as 'a case of *o'o'* possessions (pp. 195, 277, 1967: 39). Spent at Greenaway's plantation, 12 November was one of Malinowski's better days ('exceptionally active'), and thanks to the obvious availability of both Greenaway and Dimdim, he 'accomplished a great deal, wrote and collected information efficiently' (1967: 36–7). His output was about twenty pages of handwritten notes that day:

> *Cleanliness. Greenaway.* 12.XI. An old coconut is scraped (shell). Then fold the scraped stuff in their hand put a drop of water over it then squeeze it all over their heads and rub it well. That kills the lice. Then they rub the remainder over the body. The man would hold the stuff over the back and another boy would rub the fluid. They like to bathe sometimes, not for cleanliness – for coolness. No washing in the morning. No soap. After eating: They rinse their hands and rinse their mouths with salt or sweet water. They use the wood dishes (ABOMA) as water receptacles, if there is no sea or creek near at hand. Every time after food this custom is observed (194: 270).

Compare this with pp. 151 of the monograph. As in the text, the notes which follow the above passage deal with mourning dress, perfume, hairstyle, depilation, ear and nose perforation, genital deformation etc.

> 13.XI. *evening. Dimdim:* Marriage. D. represents it a little bit queerly. Every year one pig to be given for wife. This called AVEISA & VOEVOE. Part of this pig returns to giver, his wife cooks it. If pig not given, wife he cries [sic]. Dimdim married to UDAMA OF BOILADUBU, Mailu. He gives a pig to BANIA . . . If neither Boiladubu nor Maradubu have got feasts D. does not give any pigs. Girls of a given clan usually marry at the time of their clan's Maduna so that the

pigs are given to their people. No pigs are given to anyone at a time when there is no Maduna (194: 280).

A sketch of Dimdim's wife's genealogy appears in the middle of this entry, together with a list of men (and their clan affiliation) to whom Dimdim had given pigs at previous *Govi Maduna*. The men listed are all affines (WiBr or WiFZS) and these pages' contain some of the data on which Malinowski bases his discussion at pp. 181–3. This entry is followed by notes on the *tselo* dance which he saw at. Kurere, so the interview with Dimdim was undoubtedly the one of which Malinowski wrote in his *Diary*: 'became extremely impatient – I closed the notebook' (1967: 37).

A more reflective example, for which no informant is mentioned, can be dated to 16 or 17 January 1915, and it is of additional interest as belonging to the period when Malinowski was 'completely alone' in Mailu. He expanded this entry at pp. 172–3 of his text. Possibly deferring to the squeamishness of his imagined audience, he suppressed the details about delousing. (There are further observations about 'lousing' elsewhere in the notebooks, but they were not published either.)

Public Life. Women and men keep strictly apart from each other in public. When a house front is occupied by women no men will as a rule sit there, even if the front of the verandah be crowded as in the performance of a dance. Again during such public occasions men and women form separate groups. Women sit in a ring, men sit apart. When recently the village was quite deserted on account of everybody having gone to Domara, the few remnants were sitting in strictly separate groups. In their economic activities in village and outside men and women are separate. Even when fishing on the reef. When I join a group of women my male informants leave me. There is a great sense of decency in speaking in front of women. Thus my informants told me that certain details about the men's form of dress were not told me in the village, because of the presence of ladies. I was also warned not to use the word for the arrangements of the male genitals in the old fashion of dressing, when in the presence of ladies. Indecent speech is never used... Lousing and eating the lice and giving the breast to babies is not considered a matter to be queasy[?] about. Whenever sitting down the ladies are careful about the arrangement of their ramies (194: 506–8).

Insofar as *Mailu* was composed as a compendium of ethnographic 'facts' reproduced directly from the author's notebooks, then the writing was easy. He was able to transcribe whole pages with minimal re-drafting, though as we have seen, some thoughtful conflation (and occasional censorship) was also necessary. The consequence was a lightened intellectual task and hence a shorter time necessary for its execution. On some topics, however, he had to work harder. The facts had also to yield to interpretation – if only to find some way of writing them down. Malinowski was obliged to give thought to law, taboo, land tenure, the big feast, and other topics, and handle them within some discursive and theoretical frame. They were manifestly social facts of a different order from those practical, technological or otherwise self-evident customs that were at the time deemed to be unproblematical: personal decoration, canoe construction, dancing, gardening, and the like. Accordingly, Malinowski's sections on the complex institutional structures are the longest and most theoretically informed. How he wrote them is impossible to deduce from the notebook entries, and it is not surprising to find that material on these subjects is scattered piecemeal throughout the several notebooks, indicating that he returned to their investigation again and again as opportunity offered.

VIII   The Writing of *Mailu*: Rhetorics and Style

A number of incisive analyses of Malinowski's literary style have recently been made by American scholars (notably Payne 1981; Stocking 1983; Clifford 1983, 1986). All have focused on *Argonauts* as the exemplary ethnographic text, the 'euhemerist myth' (in Stocking's phrase) which divinized 'the European Jason who brings back the Golden Fleece of ethnographic knowledge' (1983: 109). While it would be futile to seek any such validating charters and ambitious literary endeavours in *The Natives of Mailu*, it is possible to detect some of the stylistic features and rhetorical conceits that characterized Malinowski's later work.

Malinowski's rich ethnographic experience of the Trobriands

saturates the text of *Argonauts*. He exploited it as a powerful narrative device, such that the Trobrianders' *Kula* voyage becomes an extended metaphor of the anthropologist's meandering voyage of discovery. By contrast, his more impoverished ethnographic experience of Mailu barely seeps into the over-structured text of his report. Within the constraints of the format he had adopted, and the no less pressing constraint of the limited time he had for reflection, there was scope only for anecdote and apt illustration. These enliven the pages, however, and allow his literary talent momentary expression in a flash of colour.

Malinowski dramatized some of his field experiences as ethnographic data, showing how his own interaction could generate valuable information. Such anecdotes can often be read as 'fables of rapport' (in Clifford's phrase), devices for confirming the ethnographer's authority by saying 'I was there', though they were primarily intended to embellish an ethnographic point (see pp. 269, 300, 306 for some instances). An elaborate example occurs at pp. 280, where Malinowski 'took part in negotiations' between Igua (his Motuan cook) and a Mailu man, Pikana, who was willing to 'sell' to Igua a special stone as part of his dugong magic. Malinowski played devil's advocate and persuaded Igua not to buy it, the clinching argument being that Pikana 'would be very likely to fake a spell and give him a false stone, and thus avoid the danger of having his magic spoilt, while at the same time he got money'. Igua withdrew from the negotiations and thereby saved his hard-earned wages; but the modern reader is left to ponder the ethics of this 'experimental' intervention.

All such anecdotes say as much about the nature of Malinowski's role as a dominant party in the taken-for-granted colonial situation as they do about the 'traditional' native society. It was not a slip of the pen that caused him, on one occasion, to refer to Igua as his 'Motuan valet' (p. 304), and he was obviously at one with other Europeans in feeling that 'Having a crowd of boys to serve you is very pleasant' (1967: 40). Yet his relationship with Igua was more complicated than the exploitative role of master might suggest. What is one to make of the following entry in his *Diary*? 'Igua massaged me and told stories in *delightful* Motu, about murders of white men, as well as his fears about what he would do if I died in that way!' (1967: 73; original italics).

In *Argonauts*, Europeans appear as 'the stock of strawmen', both to 'set the natives off' and to act as a foil to the Ethnographer as hero (Payne 1981: 421). In *Mailu*, the device is more subdued, and where such characters appear at all it is usually as named personages with some dignity still clinging to them. A notable exception, mentioned in the footnote to p. 282, is the anonymous representative of a 'class of white men only too eager "to put down the native superstitions"'. Malinowski used such men to explain his principled decision not to divulge the vernacular text of a Mailu incantation. (A remarkably modern scruple, to protect one's informants thus.)

In *Mailu*, the personal anecdote is virtually the only means by which Malinowski depicted the European colonial culture, the otherwise unarticulated background to his ethnography.[16] Some of the sentiments conveyed by these stories are uncomfortably racialist to modern sensibilities (like the notorious epithet 'nigger' so many commentators on the *Diary* have struggled to explain and excuse). Malinowski states, without irony, how Mr Greenaway 'actually forced the natives to tell me truthful details by shaming them in my presence for their pretended ignorance, thus allowing me a share of the unlimited confidence he enjoys among them' (p. 311). Again, we might wonder at the ethics of his oft-reported bribery and cajolery with sticks of tobacco (the local currency of colonial Papua) to challenge men's observance of a taboo or adherence to a principle (pp. 185, 300), or to test their fear of darkness (p. 269). The methodological justification for this form of 'experimentation' (1954 [1916]: 246–7) surely does not apply in the following instance: 'I came back in the dark and once again frightened a little boy whom I call Monkey; he utters strange sounds when frightened; I persuaded him to come a stretch of the way with me, bribing him with tobacco, then I would suddenly disappear in the bushes, and he would begin to squeal' (1967: 63). This is more a case of wanton teasing.

In connection with the colonial (and wartime) circumstances of Malinowski's Mailu ethnography, it is hardly coincidental that the theoretical disquisitions he offered broadly converge on the subjects of most pressing concern to local Europeans. This is so notwithstanding his presumed audience of disinterested academics and natural scientists. Thus, his discussion of sanctions and 'law', his paragraphs on the problem of understanding land tenure and native attitudes to 'work', and his meta-theoretical observations on the 'communism' of property relations, were all contentious topics in the colonial situation of 1914. Law and order, property ownership (especially land), and labour (including servants), were a tangle of linked issues which perennially warmed after-dinner conversation on the planters' and mission house verandahs. And they likely sparked the most heated arguments, generated the most ideological obfuscations and fuelled the most blatant racial bigotry. As Atlee Hunt indicated in the memorandum I cited earlier, the colonial administration could never have too much information about such matters: here was anthropological knowledge essential for stable government and the maintenance of peace, for the dispensation of justice and the framing of legislation, and – perhaps most important of all – for optimal exploitation ('development') of the colony's economic resources. What Malinowski thought about such things in 1914–15 is not explicit in *Mailu* and has to be read between the lines of the *Diary*. The following year, however, he was to declare himself on the subject of 'native labour' when he gave evidence to an Australian Parliamentary Commission on trade in the South Pacific.[17]

*

In several places in *Mailu* Malinowski exercises the persona that he will use to great effect in his later works. One, as we have seen, is the probing Ethnographer extracting reasonable explanations from more or less 'intelligent' informants; another is the urbane gentleman-scholar who moves with such ease between the native village and the salons of Europe. A splendid example occurs at p. 184, where Malinowski tries to make intelligible Mailu affinal taboos by referring to some of the absurd conventions of polite bourgeois society. The text at this point is appropriately littered with French *mots*, as if 'our own rules of *savoir faire*' illuminated Mailu mores, and the coercive power of convention can be amusingly illustrated by 'the rigidly observed custom' of wearing the correct dress for the occasion, whether flannels and necktie, or dinner jacket with black tie. The device of reducing 'us' to the ethnographically distanced 'other' is rhetorically effective and became one of Malinowski's favourite gambits.

Another, more complex, figure joins a personal observation or brief anecdote to the cumulative rhetoric of an ethnographic point cast as argument, an argument which finally teeters on the edge of polemic. A telling example appears at p. 269. I treat this paragraph in some detail as an illustration of how Malinowski's ethnographic rhetoric might be seen to work. The proof that he was pleased with this early demonstration – the form of the argument rather than its content – is that he repeated it in his very next essay.

The first sentence of the paragraph is pure Frazer in style; it 'emphatically' states that the Mailu 'hold in great fear the terrors lurking in the shadows of night'. The second sentence, while giving an extra twist to the Frazerian hyperbole, offers a spuriously quantitative image: 'Nothing would induce a man to venture out alone at night, even for a few hundred yards from the village.' The third sentence brings the ethnographer's observation to bear, a reminder of his witness. The fourth sentence can now furnish the extreme case: even 'one of the oldest and wisest men in the village', his best informant Papari, 'was quite as unprepared for such risks as any of the boys and young men'. The fifth sentence tells of the author's contrived 'experiment' with tobacco and thereby offers further quantitative data: even ten sticks would not induce any of the young men to walk 'about a quarter of a mile'. The manner of their refusal ('smilingly declined') carries conviction. The sixth and seventh sentences tell of further manifestations of their fear (of the darkness of their houses and of leaving them at night 'to satisfy a necessity of nature'), fears which give rise to two customs: keeping a fire burning all night and taking a companion when one went outside. Mr Greenaway's witness is invoked for the second, lest the prudish reader's credulity be strained. The next brief paragraph consists of two generalizations. The first states that, in the author's belief, all Western Papuo-Melanesians 'share this intense dread of darkness'. The second commences with what might be called Malinowski's Aunt Sally trick: 'it is interesting to note that the general fear of the night is not an essential characteristic of this stage of culture or even of this type of human society...' He then goes on to announce his discovery that Woodlark Island men are unafraid of walking about alone at night. The Aunt Sally of 'the general fear of the night...' is actually a weaker version (substituted by editor Stirling) of the original typescript's 'the universal fear of darkness...'.[8]

The rhetoric of this passage obviously pleased its author for he wrote a strikingly similar one, in his *Baloma* article, concerning the Trobrianders' absence of fear of darkness:

In general, there is a remarkable absence of superstitious fear of darkness, and no reluctance to go about alone at night. I have sent out boys, of certainly not more than ten years of age, a good distance alone at night, to fetch some object left on purpose, and I found that they were remarkably fearless, and for a small bit of tobacco quite ready to go. Men and youths will walk alone at night from one village to another, often a couple of miles, without the chance of meeting anyone. In fact, as such excursions are usually carried out in connection with some love adventure, often illicit, the man would avoid meeting anybody by stepping aside into the bush. I well remember having met on the road in the dusk solitary women, though only old ones. The road from Omarakana... to the beach passes through the *raiboag*, a well-wooded coral ridge, where the path winds through boulders and rocks, over crevasses and near caves, at night a very uncanny type of surrounding; but the natives often go there and back at night, quite alone; of course, individuals differ, some being more afraid than others, but in general there is very little of the universally reported native's dread of darkness among the Kiriwinians (1954: 152; a footnote refers to the Mailu, who are 'conspicuously afraid of darkness').

Comparison of the two passages shows striking parallels; indeed, they are rhetorically homologous, though the argument of one is the inverse of the other. The opening statement of the second passage (not Frazerian on this occasion) calls attention to a 'remarkable absence' of fear. This lack is then made the subject of a number of observations, including the author's personal witness, and a similar experiment with tobacco. A 'small bit' will induce Trobriand juveniles to do what Mailu young men would not do for the 'large reward of ten sticks'; 'a couple of miles' is a measure of Trobriand courage, as against the 'quarter of a mile' measure of Mailu timidity. Malinowski found solitary old women wandering about at night, whereas in Mailu his old informant Papari was as fearful as the young men. The Aunt Sally of the last sentence, we may note, is actually closer to the original formulation of the *Mailu* typescript: 'the universally reported native's dread of darkness'. Once again, not a single authority is cited for this view, though towards the end of

Baloma Malinowski rehearses the argument to make a methodological point concerning his tobacco experiments, 'as the first approach to exactness, to treat elements of belief expressed by behaviour as types' (1954: 247).

The questions remain, not only why Malinowski found these ethnographic arguments worth making at all, but why he thought they deserved the deployment of his most powerful rhetoric? If he wished simply to overturn a conventional generalization or contest the received wisdom, why not cite authorities for them? The reader is inclined to suspect that the subject, and hence the experience, of fear of the dark held some personal fascination for him (one is reminded, for instance, of the bleak Conradian moods of the *Diary* and his pointed allusions to *Heart of Darkness* [see Stocking 1974, Clifford 1986]). It is curious, too, that he thought it worth mentioning in yet another place: the final paragraph of his article on the Papuo-Melanesians for the *Australian Encyclopaedia* (1926a). But whatever the source of his fascination, given the rhetorical effort he made in the passages I have discussed here, they overdraw and exaggerate the case to little ultimate effect. The rhetoric is inordinate to its end, and the effect of succeeding paragraphs is to countermand some of the claims made in the opening statements.

In short, in both contexts these passages presage an anticlimax. In the Mailu case the explanation of the fear of darkness is less convincing than the depiction of that fear: '...it seems absolutely beyond doubt that the Mailu...are exclusively afraid of evil magicians, as constituting the one and only dreadful danger threatening them out of the darkness of the night' (p. 270). In the Trobriand case, the 'remarkable absence' of fear of darkness is in the very next paragraph considerably qualified, for 'there is an enormous increase of superstitious fear' following a death, when female witches, *mulukuausi*, are believed to be abroad. Then the Trobrianders, it seems, are very much afraid of the dark, perhaps even as much as the Mailu, though '...there was never the slightest doubt that the only beings to be dreaded were the *mulukuausi*' (1954: 154). So Malinowski judges the fear, in both cases, to have an intelligible if not fully rational cause. But the reader is entitled to wonder why he did not hint at this in his opening statements: something to the effect that 'The Mailu/Kiriwinians are/are not normally afraid of the dark...' Too much hinges on his refusal to specify the 'normative' condition. Something of the categorical difference that his rhetoric sought to establish lingers, however. The Mailu are afraid of the darkness *all the time* owing to their belief in male sorcerers, whose threat is persistent and unrelenting; the Trobrianders are afraid of the darkness *some of the time* owing to their belief in female witches, whose threat is occasional and contingent. The Aunt Sally begins to seem even more foolish in the light of these qualifications.

*

While on his last stint of fieldwork in Kiriwina, Malinowski wrote prophetically to Haddon: '... my next article or book ought to be as much ahead of the "Baloma" article as that is of the "Mailu"' (HC 7. 25.6.1918). His *Baloma* essay is indeed structurally and stylistically transitional between *Mailu* and *Argonauts*, and any reader of the three works must be struck by the growing maturity of style over the six-year period in which he wrote them. His written English became as adroit as his native Polish – though it was never to approach the literary power and grace of that of his compatriot hero Conrad, nor did it fulfil the poetic promise of his *Diary*.

In a recent essay on Conrad and Malinowski, James Clifford (1986) has compared their early attempts to shape, integrate, and even 'rescue' themselves through the act of writing 'cultural fictions' in a language other than their mother tongue. In a process which Clifford calls 'ethnographic self-fashioning', a crucial (though unrecoverable) period in Malinowski's biography is the 'writing cure' he undertook in the Canary Islands during 1920–21. As Clifford suggests, Malinowski had by this time accepted 'three major commitments: (1) to writing, (2) to marriage, (3) to a limited audience, language, and culture' (ibid: 159). One might also conjecture that among the circumstances present in 1920 that were absent in 1915 – such as more time to reflect and, despite his persistent health problems, greater peace of mind – the close companionship of his bride Elsie Masson was the supreme factor.

There is documentary support for the likelihood that his wife played a more prominent role in Malinowski's literary productions than has generally been supposed. Raymond Firth testifies to her 'fine sense of style' and 'good critical mind', and recalls how she 'spent much time reading and discussing his work' and how 'he relied very greatly upon her judgement' (1981: 107). Elsie Masson had published a book of her own in 1915, an account of a year spent in the 'untamed' Northern Territory of Australia. Historical, descriptive and anecdotal, it is – if for different reasons than *The Natives of Mailu* – another window on the past. Stylistically lively, it offers a fair share of the faintly purple prose beloved of travel writers of any era. Her precise turn of phrase is demonstrated in this excerpt from a chapter on 'The Servant Question':

> Cook is stout, beetle-browed, and deep-voiced, always jovial and imperturbable in any circumstances, and an excellent chef. Through the kitchen window his black head can be seen bending over his saucepans, or his burly form, in white singlet, wide black trousers, and blue cummerbund, moving from oven to dresser with incredible swiftness. At the same time he pours out a flood of Chinese. Then his voice, which in speaking English is only a deep guttural, rolls up and down in a sonorous torrent of words, pausing every now and then for a deep-toned note on a long vowel till it sounds like the tuning up of violins and 'cellos in an orchestra. His conversation is generally addressed to Chin Sing, the laundryman, who brings the washing to and fro from his little house in Chinatown. Chin Sing is lean, brown, and withered, like an old pea-nut. He looks as if he might at any moment slip through a crack in the verandah ... (1915: 43).

Here are more engaging ethnographic portraits than the stock characters who populate Malinowski's Trobriand monographs, but the passage would not seem too out of place in them. There is the same minute observation, the same active voice and 'syntax of agency' (Payne 1981: 428), the same immediacy of a richly visual world, and the same piling up of adjectives. The cheery, slightly patronizing tone ('servants are amusing') is, of course, an inadvertent echo of the writer's class position in the multi-ethnic society of colonial Australia.

Malinowski's youngest daughter, Helena, has recently confided that her father was 'impressed' by Elsie's book, 'and soon after they met [he] asked her to help him with his work: and so they started to collaborate in the few hours she could snatch from her hospital training' (Wayne 1984: 194). He did not acknowledge her help with *Baloma*, though this was written during the months of their budding courtship. 'Bronio and Elsie's friendship was at first only a working relationship, a "stern acquaintance" as he called it, as she helped him with his Trobriand field notes...' (ibid: 195). It was during the first year of their marriage, spent in Melbourne, and the following year spent in the Canaries that *Argonauts* was written. In Tenerife, 'the happiest time of their life together... Elsie acted as aide and critic, not least with his style. She also continued with her own writing, short stories of a Conradesque nature' (ibid: 196). Malinowski did not refer to his wife's help in *Argonauts*, however, and his acknowledgement had to await the publication of *The Sexual Life of Savages*. Then he wrote: 'My greatest debt in this book, as in most I have written, is to my wife. Her counsel and practical co-operation have made the writing of *Argonauts of the Western Pacific* and of this an agreeable task instead of a drudgery. If there is any value and interest in these books for me personally, it comes from her share in the common work' (1932 [1929]: xlix–l). Later still he dedicated *Coral Gardens* to her, 'because I believe it is the best I have produced or am ever likely to produce. Her critical advice in this, as in other aspects of my research, have been the most valuable and effective inspiration to me' (1935: xxii). This work, alas, was the one that she gave least to, for during its writing she was dying of multiple sclerosis and did not live to see it in print (Wayne 1984: 198).

I do not think one can go much further than to say that Elsie Malinowska subtly influenced her husband's style by direct comment and criticism, particularly during the early years of their marriage when she acted as his amanuensis and he was still fashioning his idiosyncratic 'English' voice. That he was an accomplished writer in Polish there seems little doubt; even in translation some passages of the *Diary* have a highly wrought poetic effect. More so than when writing in English, Malinowski was capable of creating stunningly sensuous images, as anyone can testify who has seen a frangipani ('a tree with an elegant silhouette, its green bouquet with blossoms carved in alabaster, smiling with golden pollen'), or smelled a tropical rainforest ('sultry, and saturated with a specific smell which penetrates and drenches you like music') (1967: 85). But Elsie Masson Malinowska, although similarly gifted, could scarcely have written his Trobriand works for him or influenced his style to the extent of choosing his tropes. Even so, Clifford's suggestion that Malinowski fashioned a writing Self by his own lonely striving does not take into account this wifely assistance. It would never do to suggest that Joseph Conrad's spouse had played such an intimate role in his literary productions!

*

The remarkable thing about *The Natives of Mailu* is not that it is so thin compared to the plenitude of his Trobriand works, but that if it manages to be as richly detailed as it is. While it falls far short of later standards of ethnography (standards which Malinowski himself was largely responsible for setting), we must remember that it was based on less than four months' fieldwork. Judged in the light of his close contemporaries' monographs on Papuan peoples – those of Williamson (1912), Jenness (1920) and Landtman (1927) – each of which were based on at least a year of fieldwork, *Mailu* loses little in the comparison. I have found only one review of it. Sidney Ray, the linguist who joined Haddon's Torres Strait team, reviewed it for *Nature* a full two years after it appeared. More in the style of a synoptic notice, Ray's evaluation is blandly approving: 'a fine piece of work, and an extremely valuable and interesting contribution to the ethnography of New Guinea'; *Mailu* was 'a credit' to the Royal Society that published it (Ray 1917).

But how did Malinowski come to view *The Natives of Mailu*? Accurately, perhaps, in view of the physical context in which it appeared, he variously referred to it as a 'memoir', 'paper', 'article', 'pamphlet', 'essay' or 'booklet'. Such labels literally belittled it, but he disparaged it more directly when referring it to others. To Seligman he had written from the Trobriands on 30 July 1915: 'I don't know yet whether you allowed my Mailu monograph to be published in Adelaide. I don't know either what you think of it. (I know that I do not think very much of it, now in the light of my new work – but I am afraid it is impossible to do *final* work.)... If that stuff could be accepted by my stern examiner as [a] thesis I could take my time with the subsequent publications, which I would prefer' (SP 30.7.1915). A few months later he wrote to Rivers about his Trobriand work, referring to *Mailu* in a postscript: 'As it is my first attempt, it is of course very weak, and if ever it comes into your hands, please don't condemn me on its account' (HC 12055, 15.10.1915). Clearly, Malinowski had no intention of sending Rivers a copy. He wrote also to Haddon the same day: '... my work in Mailu was a time of trial and learning of method and I made of course lots of blunders and wasted half my time. The only thing I can urge as a plea on my behalf is that I am making a little progress and that this year's work ought to be somewhat better than the Mailu stuff' (HC 7, 15.10.1915). And two years later, when he met Saville on the beach at Samarai, they talked about his 'booklet' on Mailu: 'I deprecated it, he praised it, not too sincerely' (1967: 133). Thus was Malinowski prepared to be quite candid about the shortcomings of his monograph and the quality of the fieldwork on which it was based (see also 1927: 89n; 1935: 457n). His main dissatisfaction, however, springs from his discovery that only prolonged and intensive fieldwork can generate the kind of ethnographic text that will rank, with Frazer's, as both a scientific treatise and a literary masterpiece.

IX   The Missionary's Mailu

If Malinowski had been the only ethnographer to describe the Mailu his work would be virtually inaccessible, if not to criticism, then to correction. But he was not. Discounting works on the language, three major studies of the Mailu have been published since Malinowski's report: a semi-popular ethnography by Saville (1926), a monograph on social structure and modernization by Abbi (1975 [1964]), and a study of prehistoric local trade by Irwin (1986 [1977]). Each of these works sheds interesting light on Malinowski's ethnography by way of enlarging and modifying our understanding of the Mailu. In the sections that follow I deal with each work in turn, though in the case of Saville something more needs to be said about his personal relationship with Malinowski.

William James Viritahitemauvai Saville was born in Surrey in 1873, the son of a missionary. He had first been a draper's assistant (not 'a petty greengrocer', as Malinowski's invective styled him [1967: 136]), but he was ordained in 1900 and sailed for British New Guinea the same year. He was not even the first white missionary to dwell on Mailu Island, where a site had been purchased by the London Missionary Society as early as 1894. But Saville outstayed all his local colleagues and by the time he finally departed Mailu he had spent almost thirty-five years among Magi people – fourteen of them before Malinowski's arrival. Saville seems never to have doubted his vocation; though at times the recalcitrance of the Mailu made him despair (he quickly realized that they were more interested in his tobacco than in his message). In quarterly letters to his younger brother, a schoolteacher who remained in England and sent him regular bundles of newspapers, Saville told of his frustrations among the 'proud, ungrateful, selfish' Mailu; though he was equally inclined to be scandalized by test cricket scores, the Roman Catholic church, Australian manners and English trade unionism.

The correspondence spanned three decades, and there is a notable mellowing of Saville's tone with respect to the Mailu over this period. One of his earlier letters gives cause to wonder why he became a missionary at all, so great was his manifest distaste for the people among whom he was living. He listed ten 'laws in dealing with Mailu-speaking natives'. Based on the presumption of their innate inferiority, these rules reveal Saville's preoccupation with the preservation of white dignity and his profound fear of caste pollution:

1. Never play the fool with a native.
2. Never speak to a native for the sake of speaking.
3. [?] swear at a native when he is alone.
4. Never call a native, send some one for him or go inadvertently to him.
5. Never *touch* a native, unless to shake hands or thrash him.
6. Always let a native see you mean what you say.
7. Never let a native see you believe his word right away, he never speaks the truth.
8. Rarely argue with a native and then only when he is alone.
9. Warn once, afterwards proceed to action.
10. Don't try to be funny, a native can never see a joke.

He possesses one joke and that is beastly talk (SML 8.10.1902).

Having recently read Livingstone's *Missionary Travels in South Africa*, Saville lamented: 'Poor New Guinea, it is awfully low in the scale of mankind'. He defined the Mailu for his brother by what he perceived them to lack, enumerating the 'graces' which the Mailu had 'no word for': no respect, no gratitude, no sense of honour, no love, no obedience, no charity, no sacrifice nor gift; they took no pains, did nothing gently or with care (ibid, also SML 23.8.1904). It is in mitigation, then, to add that Saville rarely had a good word for any race, creed or nation not his own. 'Australia I love, the Australian I have no time for' (SML 8.2.1915). He thought the French (and other

'Continentals') 'godless, selfish and full of greed' (SML 8.10.1902); while the 'so-called labouring classes' of England were 'spoiled at home' – this at a time when so many of them were being trained as cannon-fodder! (SML 29.9.1915). If Malinowski found him parochial and petty-minded one can begin to guess why, though it is perhaps as well that Saville had nothing to say about Malinowski in his letters home.

It is only fair to observe that Saville mellowed as he aged. He spent many of his later years writing English school readers, commissioned by the government and used throughout the country. Although he forever complained of overwork and bemoaned his lack of time, he grew more forgiving and tolerant towards his unruly flock. By the time he came to write his book he had developed an affectionate respect for the Mailu; later still it grew into a kind of paternal love. But even after thirty-odd years among the Mailu their material existence, no less than their spiritual lives, continued to baffle him. (He began one of his chapters: 'He is a clever man who can understand the Mailu man on his material side; but I do not know how to describe the individual who can describe his spiritual side' [1926: 283].) 'I still can't make out how these people live', he wrote to his brother during a severe drought. 'Even though there is only one meal a day, where does it come from to fill the 600 stomachs in this village?' (SML 26.3.1931). A remarkable admission, surely, for one who had a modest reputation as a missionary-anthropologist. If there was any intellectual (or spiritual) problem that preoccupied him, however, it was the religious mainspring of Mailu life. He returned to it repeatedly in his letters and in his book (1926: 293–6), and it was the subject of his only other anthropological publication, revealingly titled 'Are the Papuans Naturally Religious?' (1930–1). The resounding 'yes' of his answer, one suspects, was dictated by his commitment to his vocation and the particular field in which he had exercised it.

*

While the 'field' construed by a missionary is very different from the 'field' as defined by an anthropologist, their radically divergent professional interests were only beginning to emerge in 1914. Since Haddon's Torres Strait expedition in 1898 a kind of 'partnership' (actively fostered by Haddon himself) was presumed to exist, and anthropologists routinely consulted missionaries as expert informants. Treating mission stations as havens of civilization, anthropologists sometimes even lived within them (as Diamond Jenness, in 1911–12, had stayed with his sister and her missionary husband while studying the Bwaidogans of Goodenough Island). Initially Malinowski was no exception, and he appears to have been comfortably installed in Saville's splendid mission house with its walnut study and varnished hardwood fittings, its spacious verandahs commanding sweeping views of the sea and the mainland mountains, its gardens, orange groves, tree-shaded croquet lawn and cricket field. Also on that mission station, discreetly out of sight, was the teachers' house and a boarding school for 50 children. In that year, too, the village school had the names of a further 123 children on its register. English was taught, 'but we cannot get the children to speak it to us' (Saville 1914–15: 64). Malinowski records none of these interesting facts, or the extent to which his Mailu fieldwork was conducted by courtesy of the mission.

Yet one of the most significant changes Malinowski was to introduce in fieldwork practice was the renunciation of this facile reliance on local field missionaries. It is notable how often (and with what vehement 'hatred') he refers to missionaries in his Mailu *Diary* of 1914–15, compared to the infrequency with which they rate a mention in the Trobriand *Diary* of 1917–18. The process of professional disengagement began, so far as Malinowski was concerned, during his uneasy personal relationship with Saville. From the generally unflattering remarks in his *Diary*, we may surmise that Saville was among those Malinowski had in mind when he wrote the following:

> The habit of treating with a self-satisfied frivolity what is
> really serious to the ethnographer; the cheap rating of what
> to him is a scientific treasure, that is to say, the native's
> cultural and mental peculiarities and independence – these
> features, so well known in the inferior amateur's writing, I
> found in the tone of the majority of white residents (1922: 6).

The first phrase is a re-statement of Malinowski's reason for disliking Saville so soon – just three days – after he met him: 'Very much disillusioned regarding his friendliness and disinterestedness and, from that time on, *this*, combined with S's casual attitude to my work, has made him loathsome to me' (1967: 27).

Malinowski's long-term relationship with Saville was something of a symbiotic one. Despite his disappointment with him ('I had done no work as yet, waiting for the help S. promised me' [1967: 26]), Malinowski 'prepared a plan of campaign' with Saville, and accompanied him on visits to other villages and districts. His 'underhanded dealing' notwithstanding, the missionary (and sometimes his wife) were among Malinowski's most accessible informants (see 1967: 30–31, 41, 45; the early Mailu notebooks frequently mention 'Mr S.'). But Saville cast a long shadow on Mailu ('a caricature of a petty sovereign') and Malinowski had to learn to live with it. Ironically, their positions were reversed when Saville came to London and spent a summer studying under Malinowski; thereafter the deference was all on Saville's side, though it was never publicly expressed. Several times in his report Malinowski graciously acknowledged his debt to Saville, and he did so again in the congratulatory Foreword to Saville's own book. But Saville, apparently, did not reciprocate this acknowledgement, nor make even a single reference to *The Natives of Mailu*.

*

In 1920, the London publishers Seeley, Service invited Saville to write a book about his experiences in Papua. He told his brother that he thought he would 'have a try at it', and had begun 'to collect information and make notes'. What he had in mind 'would hardly suit the general public', he said, as he wished 'to do it on more scientific, that is anthropological or ethnological lines... What I should like most of all to deal with is native belief. But that is awfully scanty, and hazy too' (SML 3.10.1920). It took him almost five years to complete the book. 'I cannot say that I am flushed with pride over it', he wrote to his brother after posting the typescript. He feared it was 'so terribly amateurish & so filled with petty detail', but he had written it 'as an attempt at a permanent record of these people' (SML 11.7.1925). *In Unknown New Guinea* was published in 1926 and remaindered after five years, though nowadays it fetches a modest price in antiquarian bookshops. While Saville was not responsible for the descriptive subtitle of his book (nor even the title, so he claimed), it is worth quoting for its eighteenth-century flavour.

A record of twenty-five years of personal observation & experience amongst the interesting people of an almost

unknown part of this vast island & a description of their
manners & customs, occupations in peace & methods of
warfare, their secret rites & public ceremonies.

In the real world of the twentieth century, however, the missionary
had 'followed a comprehensive course of lectures on primitive
sociology and economics' delivered by Malinowski at the London
School of Economics in the summer of 1922.[19] This is some
indication of how seriously Saville approached his task. It is not clear
at what stage he asked Malinowski to write an introduction to the
book, but characteristically, Malinowski readily agreed and made the
most of the opportunity. His Foreword manages to be both sincerely
complimentary and faintly patronizing. It raps the author gently on
the knuckles for terminological imprecision, but praises him for 'the
rare union of rich detail with firm outline . . . the full flavour of native
life . . . combined with a good grasp of the underlying scheme of
native organization' (1926c: 9). He declared the book 'an excellent
anthropological contribution', superior to most writings of amateurs
for the very reason that Saville had sought 'to fashion himself into an
anthropologist'. As elsewhere, Malinowski used his Foreword as a
platform, an opportunity to preach the new professionalism of
fieldwork-based anthropology (though not yet, we might note, the
self-conscious creed of functionalism):

> The difficulty of direct research among savages lies in the
> rare combination of two elements indispensible to good field-
> work: intimate personal acquaintance with the people and a
> good knowledge of the principles of the science of man.
> Unfortunately the two are seldom united in the same
> person . . . (ibid: 7).

The Reverend Saville was one of the exceptions. The book's
authority, so Malinowski in effect declares, derives as much from
Saville's brief training as an anthropologist as from his long
experience as a field missionary, a 'man on the spot'.

W. E. Armstrong – a Cambridge student of Haddon who in
1920–21 had been Assistant Government Anthropologist in Papua
and knew Saville personally – reviewed the book for *Man*. He
pronounced it 'most readable and . . . a contribution to Papuan
ethnology of great value'. So it remains today. But Armstrong was
also impressed by its 'scientific' trappings, as ' . . . an ethnological

account presented with that eye to system and sociological significance which is usually found only in the writings of professional ethnologists' (1927: 59). Surprised and even embarrassed by the seriousness with which his book was received, Saville protested that he had no pretensions to being even an amateur anthropologist.

The influence of Malinowski's teaching and the direct example of Malinowski's text are indeed apparent in Saville's adoption of several analytical categories, and in his occasional use of identical phrasing. The plan or narrative sequence of *In Unknown New Guinea* emulates that of *The Natives of Mailu*, though Saville uses short chapters instead of the 'section' format favoured by Malinowski. The only chapters in Saville for which there are no corresponding sections in Malinowski deal with initiation (XI) and the inland Dimuga people (XXXII). To read Saville, then, is to re-visit the Mailu of Malinowski, though accompanied by a more lively and discursive guide. The extraordinarily detailed correspondences of the two monographs does not mean that Saville was a plagiarist (any more than Malinowski had been one in publishing the information given him by Saville). Clearly, however, they learned a great deal from one another in their differently defined, yet geographically identical fields of work.

As one might expect, Saville's book is more reliable than Malinowski's on matters of language, and it is richer in quotidian detail. His photographs are also better. The facts about the Mailu that Saville offers his readers were based upon his personal observations, but he does not need to present his observer's credentials so often as Malinowski had done: Saville's authority as an ethnographer was of lesser consequence for him to establish. Befitting a more popular account, his book was written with a lighter tone and in a more accessible style: that faintly jocular approach adopted by missionaries who have won their colours in the field; an easy confidence that comes of having God and your fireside-travelling reader on your side. The Natives are not mocked, for they are admired despite their imperfections. But look how funny they can be, how curious their ways, yet how recognizably human beneath the dark masks of savagery! And look, too, how the missionary, in his patient, well-meaning way, makes human errors of judgement and is gently humbled, only to be rewarded with a better understanding of God's mercy . . . Saville has just a touch of this homespun missionary style.

It is beyond my task to augment Malinowski's account by adducing Saville's or even to document all the topics which Saville covers more thoroughly, and I will assume that readers interested in pursuing some point of Mailu ethnography will consult both sources without favour. But let us return to Malinowski's Foreword, for this sheds as much light on Malinowski the proselytizing anthropologist as it does on Saville the diffident ethnographer. Malinowski honestly admits that Saville gives a more '"full-blooded" account of kinship relations' than he had done. He allowed that in the areas of ritual and belief, and of defunct practices such as warfare and head-hunting, 'the superiority of the long-term resident becomes obvious' – thanks to his intimate knowledge of the vernacular. 'I had not even discovered the existence of initiation,' Malinowski ruefully confesses. But he is pleased to note that 'most of the information on kinship' in his own monograph 'is confirmed by the subsequent research' of Saville; and he is not too modest to forbear mention of those technical topics concerning which his own discussion is superior to Saville's: 'land tenure, the regulation of public life, and the nature of property and inheritance' (1926c: 10). Malinowski does not, however, draw attention to various factual and terminological discrepancies in their respective accounts. For example, his own and Saville's section entitled 'Division of the Day' are wildly at variance. Malinowski is shaky indeed on time reckoning, as even cursory comparison of their accounts will show. Both agree that the sun's position marks the Mailu time of day, but few of their terms are in agreement. One can only bow to Saville's linguistic mastery in this and like matters.[20]

It was hardly Malinowski's job, in introducing the work of another, to point out details of his own defective ethnography. Yet he clearly felt obliged to make some comparisons, even those unfavourable to himself, because Saville had not only failed to engage with Malinowski's text but had unaccountably neglected to refer to it at all. It was left for Malinowski coyly to alert the reader:

> ...I may perhaps be allowed to mention that certain aspects
> of the sociology, economics and belief of these Papua-
> Melanesians [sic] have been already described in a
> monograph on *The Natives of Mailu*... When soon after its
> publication I was able, on the beach of Samarai, to present a
> copy to Mr Saville, I expressed my hopes that he would

freely use my essay, incorporate into his own book what he
found correct, pull the rest to pieces and remake it into a
more perfect vision. Mr Saville however, with great restraint
and generosity, abstained from publishing anew of those
passages and documents which he evidently found correct and
to which there was nothing to be added (1926c: 9–10).

Any reader of Saville must pause to wonder at this 'great restraint
and generosity', for it smacks of a deliberate suppression of
Malinowski's name. But there is a plausible, if unexpected,
explanation. Three of Saville's letters to Malinowski survive, written
from Mailu Island during 1926 (MPY 557).

The first, dated 7 April, thanks Malinowski for writing a
Foreword, though Saville had not yet received a copy of his book nor
seen any proofs. Malinowski had obviously praised it in a letter to
Saville (not extant, but acknowledged as 13 January 1926), and
Saville modestly replies: '. . . it is very encouraging to think that one
so "high up" as yourself can appreciate anything in the book . . . The
whole thing of course is amateurish and I hope I have not given any
other idea of the work. I do not pose as an anthropologist.' Then, in
reply to Malinowski's comment to the effect that he should have
made explicit reference to *The Natives of Mailu*, Saville sounds a note
of alarm: 'Does this mean that you have not seen the preface I wrote?
Or that they omitted to include my preface? Or do you mean I should
have made explicit reference in the text to your memoir?' Saville
decides that the most excusable of these possibilities is the last, and
proceeds to explain:

As a matter of fact except in classification and method I
referred very little to your memoir while writing the book.
Indeed I purposely put it from me. Yours therein is a strong
style and I wanted the style of the book to be as much my
own as possible.

Malinowski had told him it was most gratifying that their findings
had accorded so well. Saville turns the compliment and tells
Malinowski he can congratulate himself, for '. . . you go so much to
the root of things in comparatively so short a time with the people,
especially [considering] that you did not understand the language.
My 25 year residence and a fairly accurate knowledge of the language

should certainly have placed me in a better position for getting at the facts'. Malinowski would have concurred that getting quickly 'to the root of things' was what professionalism in anthropology was all about – with or without a knowledge of the vernacular (cf. Clifford 1983: 121–2).

Saville's second letter, dated 3 May 1926, confirms the worst. Having just received a copy of his book he is mortified to find the preface missing. The publishers had also chosen an 'unimaginative title' (he had favoured 'The Fish Hawk Folk', as Mailu people referred to themselves), and they had deliberately omitted a chapter on language, an appendix on kinship terms, many photographs and line drawings... But worst of all, 'the wretched book goes before the public without those acknowledgements and I am humbled to death'. Saville is profoundly, almost abjectly apologetic:

> The mere fact that you could have written so kind (too kind) and so generous (too generous) a foreword as that you have written, in face of the fact (as it appeared to you and unknown to me) that they had not published my preface makes me think very highly of you, and puts me in a deep debt of gratitude to you... In my preface I wrote to the effect that if in anyway I had acquired any scientific manner of arrangement of fieldwork details I owed it all to you, your personal contact, your Researches [i.e. *Natives of Mailu*], and having attended your course at London University. I think my words were 'above all I am indebted etc....' Will you accept my personal apologies for a catastrophic lack of imagination on the part of the publishers?

The third letter, dated 4 October 1926, released another round of apologies. In the circumstances, it seems, Malinowski's Foreword was nothing short of magnanimous: 'Reading between the lines of your letters it seems as if you must have been terribly upset at no mention having been made of your monograph on these Mailu people, and I can quite understand it'. What he cannot understand, Saville says, is how he was nevertheless able to write such a 'generous' Foreword:

> Too generous, I think. For what reviews of the book I have seen, give me credit for what I personally cannot take to

myself as true that I am an even amateur anthropologist...
You know I am no student, I never have been and I am afraid I
never will be.

Saville then admits that 'in the said preface' (of which he had kept no
copy): 'I in no way discussed nor did it ever occur to me to discuss
your Monograph...', and further admits that while 'collecting'
information and 'writing up the material' he 'hardly referred' to
Malinowski's monograph. 'Method, yes, I did gather from you not
only from the monograph which I may as well confess never once
having read consecutively right through, but also from your lectures
in London'.

Between the lines he seems to be protesting, not simply against the
role of anthropologist, amateur or not, that Malinowski has cast him
in, but against the scholarly obligations that Malinowski appears to
have wished upon him. This leads Saville to disparage his own work:

> Nor was this book intended as a scientific treatise to prove
> that any thing that may have been previously written about
> these people was either right or wrong... If there is any
> scientific method in the book I owe a very great deal of that
> through being, shall I say, one of your scholars, but as
> regards matter in the book, that I have learned from a long
> residence among the people themselves.

He confesses, finally, that he had not read *Argonauts*, and as a final
rejection of the role of anthropologist, he dismisses Malinowski's
suggestion that he should write something for the *Journal of the
Royal Anthropological Institute*: '...I do not quite understand on
what lines or subjects I should write.'

Thus ends the correspondence, and it is possible that the two men
never wrote to one another again. How sincere were Saville's
protestations? We cannot be sure, though it is curious that he said
nothing about the publisher's sins of omission when writing to his
brother who had, ironically, written to Seeley, Service on his own
behalf, 'appreciative... of the way in which [the book] has been
turned out' (SML 10.3.1926). Saville spent a further nine years in his
Mailu field before retiring to England. He died in 1948 at the age of
seventy-five.

X   Mailu Re-visited

Forty-five years after Malinowski worked in Mailu, an Indian postgraduate student embarked on a re-study. Bahari Verma (later Abbi) of the Research School of Pacific Studies in The Australian National University was interested in social change, specifically in the transformations that traditional local groups made to cope with modernization.[21] He investigated in detail (in a different manner and under different circumstances) what Malinowski had merely used as bait in his report to Atlee Hunt: 'the process of adaptation of the natives to their new conditions' (see above). Abbi's study, however, is an historically informed analysis of modern associations – cash crop cooperatives, the local government council, church organization and village clubs – as they developed in Mailu after the Second World War. His findings were presented as a doctoral thesis (Verma 1964) and published a decade later – though regretably, he did not bring the book up to date (Abbi 1975). Abbi's work nonetheless provides useful correctives to the descriptive and analytical deficiencies of Malinowski's account of traditional Mailu social structure. I mention here only those topics Malinowski had dealt with: village confederacies, the village community, the clan and subclan, and the household.

Malinowski described 'village confederacies' as groups which 'maintained friendly relations between themselves' and 'constituted the most extensive tribal or political units of the Mailu' (p. 121). He saw the Mailu 'tribe' as divided into a number of such units, each with its established boundaries. Yet his list of confederacies differs slightly from Saville's (1926: 23), a simple discrepancy which indicates that 'confederacy' might be too firm a label for an impermanent set of alliances. 'In traditional Mailu society', writes Abbi, 'neighbours were usually connected by kinship and marriage, political friendship, common feast-group affiliation, or exploitation of common natural resources, such as a reef, sago swamp, or hunting ground. Often they were connected by ties of common origin and common clanship as well' (1975: 51–2). The picture that emerges from Abbi's account of village 'confederacies' is of 'shifting alliances of varying duration between individual villages', and of friendship and enmity resulting from 'several sets of cross-cutting bonds' (ibid: 51). This view is more consistent with the comparative evidence for such political groupings in Melanesia.

Abbi states that 'people preferred to marry in their own village if they could' (ibid: 54) but does not otherwise discuss Mailu marriage strategies, so the relationship of marriage to the formation and maintenance of village 'confederacies' remains unclear. The kinship terminology suggests that cross cousin marriages was permissible if not preferential, but such marriages, if they occurred, went unremarked by all three ethnographers of the Mailu. Abbi gives some figures for intervillage marriage pertaining to the period of his fieldwork. Mailu Island, for instance, had 105 existing marriages, of which 95 were between Mailu Islanders. Only 12 women were from other Magi villages or beyond (ibid: 55).

With regard to village social structure, Abbi challenges Malinowski (and Saville, who followed him closely) on a number of important points and he offers different terms for some of the units described by Malinowski. Where the latter wrote of the village on Mailu Island as being 'divided into clans and subclans', Abbi identifies wards, clan sectors (i.e. segments) and lineages (ibid: Chapter 3).

The village, according to Abbi, is 'the largest stable local group whose members were linked to each other by marital and kinship ties' (ibid: 18). Malinowski observed that the clans of Mailu Island were larger and more internally differentiated than the clans of other villages, though he does not appear to have asked himself why this was so. He stated categorically that subclans were always 'subdivisions' of clans, but does not say how he imagined such subdivisions might have occurred. Abbi argues persuasively that what Malinowski regarded as atypically large clans on Mailu Island actually represented another level of social organization, local groups Abbi refers to as wards (though in his 1964 thesis he had called them phratries). Thus the four 'clans' Malinowski lists at p. 130, are actually residential aggregations of several clans. The sub-clans (in Malinowski's terminology) of Mailu Island are structurally coordinate with the clans of other Mailu villages. Hence, it was not the mainland villages that were anomalous in having small clans and no subclans, as Malinowski thought, but Mailu Island which was anomalous in having clans grouped into named wards: local groups which look and to some extent behave like 'superclans'. Abbi's characterization of the ward makes better sense of Malinowski's statement that 'at feasts the individuality of the subclans was not entirely merged in that of the clan' (p. 132). This can be rephrased in

Abbi's terms: at feasts the identity of the local clan sector was not subsumed by that of the ward. Indeed, why should it be, if feasts are primarily occasions for exchanges between kin and affines and not between local groups as such?

Abbi redefines Malinowski's subclans as 'clan sectors', since many Mailu clans are dispersed and segments of them are to be found in several villages. 'Thus while in any single village a *dubu* was one of several subdivisions, in the inter-village context it was a descent group cutting across village boundaries and creating wider ties' (Abbi 1975: 19). In anthropological parlance, then, the local 'clan sector' (Malinowski's subclan) is a named, exogamous, agnatically recruited group (albeit subject to non-agnatic accretions), with corporate ownership of property (land, canoes, pig and fish nets, with their associated magic), and which acknowledges the leadership of one man, nominally the senior male member of the senior descent line within the group. The clan sector's members occupied, on average, 3.3 houses. As a refinement of Malinowski's assertion concerning property rights being vested in the clan, Abbi notes: 'A person had rights in land and other property by virtue of his membership of the clan sector, not of the clan as a whole' (ibid: 19).

The lineage represents another level of social organization which Abbi identifies in Mailu, but which Malinowski neglected or subsumed under household and subclan. Abbi defines it as comprising at least three generations of agnates, usually but not always dwelling together in a single large household. In marrying women are (in Murray Groves' term) 'contingent members' of their husbands' lineages (ibid: 34; Groves 1963: 20). But some men too are contingent members, having been adopted as children, or having been invited to join other, non-agnatic, kin. Malinowski depicted the normative patrivirilocal composition of the household ('the greater family'), but Abbi found a great deal of 'deviation' from this ideal, so much so that Malinowski's model of the Mailu household now seems overly simple. He said nothing about adoption, though it apparently was and still is quite common. Agnatic descent ideology notwithstanding, a child belonged to his mother's brothers until its father validated his claim by the gift of a pig or two (ibid: 32–3). A childless man, moreover, might adopt a sister's child by waiving this payment from his brother-in-law and keeping the child as his own. In short, as elsewhere in Melanesia, descent group structure in Mailu was flexible just as household composition was fluid.

The large and heterogeneous Mailu households were obviously quite complex, though Malinowski is cursory on the structure of authority and division of labour within them. Abbi found, for example, that each adult woman of a household took turns to prepare the main daily meal. 'The day she cooked she was the mistress (*gubina*) and, as such, had the privilege of distributing food to the household, as well as to certain kin and affines in other households' (ibid: 28). *Veveni*, the day-to-day exchange of food between households, was clearly very important (Malinowski 159; Saville 1926: 49–50), and although it was principally between close agnates, consanguines and affines, others too exchanged cooked food under this rubric. According to Saville (ibid: 50), *veveni* also passed between *isigoina* (*wizhus*), who appear to have been exchange partners. Despite the internal segmentation of a household based on its several nuclear families, it was apparently treated as a unit for purposes of village feasting (Abbi 1975: 31).

These criticisms of Malinowski, articulated or implied, are perhaps unfair or unjust. It is anachronistic to judge his Mailu study by the standards of fieldwork he was to establish with his Trobriand work; it is likewise unfair to compare the work of the apprentice Malinowski with that of another novice ethnographer nearly half a century later. Again, it would be unjust to take Malinowski to task (or Seligman for that matter) for having failed to research the history of early European contacts with this coast. Many such sources and reports were less readily available then than they are today, and perhaps equally pertinent, it was the 'ethnological' question of origins that exercised them more profoundly than the relatively recent 'first contacts'. (One must recall, however, that Malinowski was in process of breaking from this tradition, and it is with a defiant note that he told Atlee Hunt he had not investigated 'physical anthropology or questions of origin'. In any event, a prehistorical perspective on Mailu was either unavailable or irrelevant to him.)

Abbi's study took the historical changes of Magi people as part of his data when trying to understand their social structure in 1960–2. His base line was the second half of the nineteenth century, particularly after 1884 when the area became part of the Protectorate of British New Guinea (1975: 63–4). But there had been a tragic early contact between Mailu and Europeans nearly three centuries earlier, so long ago that its effects had been absorbed virtually without trace. Neither Malinowski nor Abbi knew of the event.

XI Mailu Prehistory

Chance brought Mailu Islanders a traumatic introduction to European civilization and a violent foretaste of a proselytizing Christianity. Indeed, theirs was the dubious distinction of being one of the very first New Guinea communities to be contacted by Europeans. The date was 24 August 1606, when Luis Torres and Diego de Prado anchored at Mailu, which they named St Bartholomew Island after the day in the Church calendar. (They were seeking a route to Manila from Espiritu Santo where they had left – or rather lost – Quiros; in previous weeks they had casually killed and plundered at the eastern extremity of the mainland.)[22]

Don Diego de Prado y Tovar (to grace him with his full aristocratic title) described the encounter in his *Relación* (Stevens 1930: 151–5). It is a distressing tale of massacre and abduction, perpetrated with little apparent provocation. When the Spaniards landed they found the men of the island ('more than a hundred Indians') waiting in ambush. After trying to parley, the commanders lost patience with the natives' hostile demeanour ('brandishing their arms... which was a sign of battle'). They knelt to pray and then opened fire. The Spaniards seized the islanders' position and drove them towards the village ('shooting them as they fled'), where the survivors embarked on twenty-six canoes and sailed for the mainland. Some were shot on the open sea, from a distance, 'and this caused them greater fright and terror'. The village, Prado mentions in passing, 'had about three hundred houses very well enclosed by planks and big canes'. The soldiers then stormed a clifftop 'fortress' and slaughtered some of the defenders. Prado continues: '... the living and the wounded came down, they would be about three hundred, three parts were women and I was sorry to see so many dead children they were carrying in their arms. I selected fourteen boys and girls of from six to ten years and sent them on board; the rest I let go free and they ran up a hill like goats.' Having taken 'possession of all the country in the name of his Majesty the King our Lord', the explorers sailed on to discover the strait named after Torres. The fourteen kidnapped children were later baptized in Manila, where they presumably remained until the end of their lives, and Mailu people resumed their historical anonymity for another two hundred and eighty years. But it is clear from Prado's account (even if all his figures are halved) that Mailu had been a populous and prosperous community as early as 1606: as indeed, Saville and Malinowski had found it in the early twentieth century.[23]

*

In 1973, a prehistorian from The Australian National University made a thorough study of Mailu Island and neighbouring mainland settlement sites. Geoffrey Irwin's findings explain why Mailu Island was so prominent at the time of European contact, and why it had a rather more complex social organization than other Magi communities. This materially reconstructed and scientifically calibrated past is a far cry from Malinowski's vaguely pastoral notion of 'olden days'.

Archaeological evidence reveals that the Magi area was settled by pottery-using people some 2,000 years ago. They lived in functionally unspecialized settlements along the coast and offshore islands, and subsisted by gardening and fishing. There is no evidence of any major intrusive immigration throughout that period, and Mailu Island itself shows continuous occupation, by what appears to be the same culture, for the past 6–800 years. When Malinowski arrived on the scene, and demonstrably for at least three decades before that, the community on Mailu Island was larger, more economically specialized, and more influential than any of its Magi neighbours. In Saville's apt phrase it was 'the hub of their universe' (1926: 29). While it appears to have been self-sufficient in tree fruits and fish it was unable to support itself in garden produce, and ultimately it was reliant upon the sale of pots to obtain vegetable food. The island was the centre and point of articulation of local and long distance trading systems, both inland and coastal.

The engine of Mailu's commercial success was a double monopoly: pottery manufacture and seagoing transport. The pot-making of its women provided, as Saville put it, 'the daily bread and the maintenance of the community' (ibid: 153). (Armshell manufacture, although not a monopoly, came 'a very close second, for it is closely associated with marriage...and therefore with the maintenance of the community as a social organization' [ibid].) Because Mailu Islanders alone had a fleet of seagoing canoes they dominated local trade as middlemen and 'merchant venturers' (Seligman's romantic term for the people of Tubetube Island, a similar entrepôt in the southern Massim). Thus, at the end of prehistory, Mailu Island was a 'central place': central, that is, with respect to the regional network of communications along more than a hundred miles of coastline and inland as far as the main range.

But it had not always been so. Irwin found evidence of the earlier existence of a number of other potting settlements on the mainland. For many centuries, it seems, Mailu Island was no more favoured than any other Magi village. The record then reveals that, over the past few hundred years, Mailu developed a specialized pottery industry to the point where it became (in another coinage of Saville) the 'metropolis of Magi man' (1926:19). The varied pottery styles of the earlier periods became transformed into a finer but stylistically uniform trade ware. This transition, Irwin argues, must surely reflect increasing production for export and the acquisition of a monopoly by Mailu Islanders. Several advantages accrue to the producers of thinner pots: a more economical use of clay, faster drying time, and reduced chance of damage during firing. From the consumers' point of view, finer pots are preferable for their faster boiling time and a more economical use of fuel, though they break more easily. Irwin suggests that there was 'something akin to inbuilt obsolescence' in Mailu pot manufacture, though this is not to say the potters refined their technology with a view to increasing their sales (1978: 409; 1985: 241).

Spatial analysis of prehistoric Magi settlements also yielded evidene of Mailu Island's emergence as an entrepôt. Irwin used connectivity analysis (a method for quantifying the relative centrality of interacting settlement sites), to show that Saville's metaphor of 'the hub of the Mailu universe' was spatially as well as socially apt. Mailu Island's 'economic specialization coincided with a distinct locational advantage over other sites'; in spatial terms, its monopoly was 'situated at the precise point from which a large area could be supplied with pots most efficiently from a single source'. Mailu, indeed, became more 'central' with the passage of time (1978: 410; 1985: 241).

The rise of Mailu seems to have been associated with an increase of population in the region. This is not to claim that population growth as such was the cause of Mailu's pre-eminence, though once Mailu's local dominance was achieved, an expanding market would have reinforced its influence. Nothing succeeds like success, and with its own growth in manpower the community would have been able to maintain its trading hegemony by force of arms. The archaeological record shows that after a period of population expansion, the mainland communities retreated from the exposed littoral and began to occupy defensive hilltops. This put them at a further disadvantage to Mailu with respect to their own trading prospects; it also meant that they had to relinquish whatever share of the coastal trading market they once possessed. They would have had no further use for large canoes. Given its excellent natural defences, its growing size, its command of canoe transport, and its monopoly of distribution of essential imported goods such as obsidian, it is perhaps only to be expected that Mailu Island maintained its local dominance by raiding as well as trading. Evidence from the maritime *Kula* trading network to the east now suggests that there was, in the nineteenth century, a complex interplay between warfare, trade, and ceremonial exchange (Macintyre 1983; Young 1983).

Radical shifts of settlement from the coastal fringe to defensive ridges inland clearly indicate that the threat of warfare had increased. This is not to insist that Mailu Island and its colonies were the only aggressors in the area; other 'confederacies' also were likely to have fought one another. Malinowski and Saville state that Mailu men needed human heads for initiation ceremonies, but it is not known when this particular cultural 'demand' came into existence. It is reasonable to suppose, however, that rather than committing themselves to warfare, Mailu men would have found it more worthwhile to expend their 'leisure' on producing armshells for export and maintaining their fleet of canoes. Notwithstanding the occasional demand for human heads, it would scarcely have been to Mailu men's advantage to harass their pottery customers, the very people who supplied them with subsistence food. Supported by the potting industry of their womenfolk and released from some of the drudgery of garden work, Mailu men could turn their energies to the annual cycle of long distance trade. By this activity, Mailu achieved the breakthrough to a higher cultural standard of living. With this went a qualitative change of social complexity, itself a likely response to a burgeoning population. Internal segmentation, such as the emergence of phratries, moieties and so forth, is characteristic of Melanesian communities of larger than optimum size (see Forge 1972). This dynamic of a changing political economy would seem to offer the most satisfactory explanation for the anomalous local group organization described by Malinowski and Abbi.

*

Although it was changing in scale and organizational complexity, there is little or no evidence that Mailu Island was also becoming more stratified. Given the egalitarian ideology common to the whole genus of Melanesian society, it would indeed be surprising if Mailu had developed true chiefs or a class of 'nobles'. As elsewhere, the political economy of production, distribution and exchange militated against the emergence of rank. Thus, the annual cycle of long distance maritime trade seemed designed to bring a 'trade surplus' of full-grown pigs into Mailu. Pigs represent a form of wealth that can be invested in social relationships, notably affinal ones. The large pigs obtained from Aroma were distributed at the great *Govi Maduna* festival when marriage and mortuary debts were repaid. Malinowski correctly identified the *Maduna* as 'a central feature in the social and mental life of the natives' and of 'paramount social importance' (p. 288). As in other Melanesian trading systems, overseas expeditions were ultimately motivated by the quest for local influence and prestige; they served to fund the internal exchange economies of the traders' own communities. 'Profits' in the form of pigs were not invested in capital enterprise but consumed forthwith. Thus was a ceiling, commensurate with the egalitarian ethic, maintained on economic expansion.

*

By Malinowski's time, the Mailu had long since renounced warfare and headhunting, and boys' initiation ceremonies were greatly attenuated (p. 189; Saville 1926: 109). The *dubu* or men's club houses had almost disappeared. There were further familiar consequences of pacification: safe travel was conducive to the expansion of trade, as was the increased leisure permitted by the use of steel tools. 'More men went on sailing and trading trips, covered greater distances, and spent longer time on voyages' (Abbi 1975: 77). So more canoes were built. Saville mentions one trading voyage that reached the furthermost point in Papua: Rossel Island, over 350 miles distant (1926: 152). Mailu men began working for Europeans as early as 1891, and by Malinowski's day many would have travelled throughout coastal Papua trying a variety of jobs. Understandably, they were most in demand as skilled boat crews.

Abbi confirms that the traditional pattern of production, exchange, and consumption persisted: 'Though the people increased their economic production and to some extent their capital, their main purpose was not to accumulate savings for further production but to collect pigs, tobacco, and vegetable foods for large-scale feasts' (1975: 77). In 1927 Saville told a government officer that the previous year Mailu men had spent 'nearly £2000 in money and trade' in Aroma for the purchase of pigs: 'the whole lot being eaten in one feast' (Abbi 1975: 77n). Predictably, too, the elaboration of feasting, reported from so many parts of Melanesia in the wake of colonial contact, brought to Mailu intensified competition for prestige and hence a modified, more 'democratic' system of leadership (cf. Young 1971: 254–8; 1985). Traditional headmen began to lose the assets which represented the material basis of their authority (club-houses, war magic, large war and sailing canoes, big fishing and hunting nets, etc.) at the same time that positions of leadership were appointed by the government and lesser men were able to procure new forms of wealth by working for Europeans (Abbi 1975: 78).

XII The *Govi Maduna*

One of the most interesting sections of *The Natives of Mailu* is that devoted to the 'big annual feast', and Malinowski's treatment deserves some comment. He was in no doubt about the central importance of the *Govi Maduna* festival to the Mailu, and he exhausted his stock of superlatives to get this point across (p. 288). Reflecting its importance, his field notebooks dwell repeatedly on aspects of the feast, and it obviously engaged his aesthetic and intellectual interests as an irresistible confection of dramatic ingredients: magic, dance, personal adornment, and the spectacular display of food wealth.

Malinowski was correct in declaring that the annual feast in eastern Papua was everywhere essentially similar (p. 288n). At the time he wrote, Seligman (1910) and Newton (1914) had already described the *Walaga* of Bartle Bay, and a few years later W. E. Armstrong (1920–21) was to give a brief account of the *Soi* feast of Suau and the *Toleha* feast of Tawala in Milne Bay. The mango sapling played a symbolic role in all of them and remains something of an ethnographic mystery, but the organizational features of the feasts are clear.

The festivals are transitively linked in local series or cycles. Each feast is joined to the preceding and succeeding one, not only by means of the delayed exchange of pigs, but also by the ceremonial transmission of part of the previous feast's mango sapling to the next feast's sponsor or 'master'. Each feast is also a commemoration, the final mortuary ceremony for one or more dead persons of the sponsor's lineage. (Advisedly 'also', because this feature is not especially emphasized and may not even be evident to observers; the memorial aspect may even be subsumed under 'ideological rational'.) The ceremonies of seclusion and fasting by the masters, with the object of increasing their 'heat' (*gigibori* in Suau) or magical power to attract pigs, are virtually identical throughout the region. Similar observances are entailed during the erection of special structures, notably guest houses and dance platforms. The quest for pigs, for which journeys are undertaken by land or sea, is another standard feature of the festival. The main contributors of pigs (other than the sponsors) are invariably sons- or brothers-in-law, affines of the hosts, who are indebted to them for the women they have received in marriage. This applies equally, it seems, to the matrilineal peoples of Suau, Milne Bay and Bartle Bay, and to the patrilineal Mailu. Other common features are a sequence of minor preliminary feasts, colourful 'entertainments' of dancing and singing to drums, a degree of sexual licence, and an excitable mood of incipient violence preparatory to, and even during, the culminating food distribution. It seems that a measure of hostility between hosts and guests was enjoined, the blustering and threats being conventional expressions of traditional enmity.

The most salient aspect of Malinowski's description of the *Maduna* is his insistent search for 'ceremonial' elements. Although it appropriately belonged to the chapter on Economics, he dealt with it under the rubric of 'magico-religious activities and beliefs'. Yet his descriptions of the events and preparations leading up to the *Maduna*, of the dances, of the other minor feasts to which it is linked, and of the final distribution, are decidedly thin on beliefs. Malinowski had inherited this preconception of feasting and ceremonial exchange, and as I mentioned above, *Notes and Queries* provided no guide: neither 'feast' nor 'festival' occur in the index, and they receive no more than passing mention in the text.

The candour of Malinowski's treatment shows he was uneasy with this perspective, but he was not yet ready to question it directly. He was subsequently to make a significant contribution to the study of 'primitive economics' by disentangling it from the study of 'religion', and then reintegrating the two in a new, functional relationship. Indeed, he had begun to do so as early as 1912 in his *Festschrift* article for Westermarck on 'The Economic Aspect of the Intichiuma Ceremonies', in which he argued that totemism provided economic incentive and promoted cooperative activity.[24] In *Argonauts*, he presented the *Kula* as an economic institution as well as a ceremonial enterprise, and by that time he had more or less broken completely with the flat-earth view that 'savages' were in thrall to superstition, 'bound in the chains of immemorial tradition' (1926b: 10, citing Sidney Hartland). *Baloma*, Malinowski's only extended essay on Trobriand religion, was an implicit attack on this view by way of a sensitive exploration of dogma, socially constructed but individually variegated. In *Crime and Custom* he edged an economizing sociological principle, reciprocity, to centre stage to rout the masques of Custom and Ceremony once and for all. In *Mailu*, however, he was not quite ready to admit that the *Govi Maduna*, as a religious festival, was something of an Emperor without clothes.

On what evidence did Malinowski claim it to be a magico-religious ceremony? In introducing it he enumerated the things with which it was closely associated as 'the mainstay of the native's social organization': display, marriage and sexual life, trading, agriculture, clan organization – in short, the entire system of cultural and social reproduction. In the middle of this Tylorian miscellany, there are 'certain forms' of taboo, which are 'exclusively practised in connection with the feast' (p. 288). This is the only magico-religious element he discusses in detail, though he had already dealt at length with taboo in a previous chapter. The dances too had magico-religious significance.[25] But in circular fashion Malinowski seems to have identified the 'sacredness' of particular dances by the degree of taboo they involved. Moreover, despite the 'feeling of real fear and awe' associated with some dances (p. 305), he noted that even 'the principal ceremonial dance may ... degenerate into a mere pleasure dance' (p. 303). The economic aspects of the *Govi*, on the other hand, loomed very large indeed, and the lavish display of pigs and vegetable food obliged him to admit that 'as far as the interest of the native goes, undoubtedly the most important part of the feast' is the final distribution – which is the literal meaning of *maduna* (p. 304).

Wherever Malinowski looked he found secular attitudes and pragmatic explanations; his informants could not or would not confirm his expectations (pp. 301–2). The taboos, *udini*, were revealed to have a practical intention, for the whole purpose of fasting, seclusion, and incantation was to enhance the supply of pigs (p. 301). Again, '...all the ceremonial and magical activities connected with the feast are directed towards the increase of food at the *Maduna*' (p. 305). Whatever the equivocations of his informants, and his own preconceived reasons for according it magico-religious significance, he was unable honestly to deduce that any religious or supernatural agency was involved. Ostensibly, the *Govi* neither celebrated any deity nor communicated with any spirits, even ancestral ones. Saville, by contrast, did so deduce. But while maintaining that the *Govi* festival was in essence the communication of its chief sponsor with his dead ancestor, even the missionary had to confess that by the end of the feast: 'Religious feeling has vanished. Economics has got what it wanted from religion, and now religious feeling can take a rest' (1926: 264). This could have been written by Malinowski, though more in triumph than regret.

Towards the end of his own account Malinowski was wondering aloud what might constitute the 'religious' in the *Govi Maduna*. 'The main magico-religious elements are contained...in the preliminary feasts, preparations, and taboos. There is obviously less *belief* embodied in the practices of the feast itself' (p. 301–2). In a disarming footnote he justifies these observations as 'only statements of fact', cautiously adding: 'How far the feast is to be regarded as a mere social revelry, as a magical ceremony, or else as a religious ceremony, is a theoretical question, which it is not necessary to discuss in this place' (ibid). To whom did he address this note? Evidently mentors (Marett? Crawley?) who might otherwise have chided him for failing to discover the magico-religious motivations of the Mailu.

Malinowski missed or neglected several important features of the pig festival in this region. One of them, ironically, might have alleviated some of his concern about its equivocally 'religious' status. Armstrong wrote of the *Soi*:

> The feast is the expression of a Cult, which is almost a
> religion, and the elaborate and lengthy story of its origin is
> the most important legend of the people. The central figure,

> Taufo, taught the Suau people, and also Mailu, the method
> of distributing pigs peculiar to the *Soi*-area and the elaborate
> ceremonies... [during the]... period of fasting prior to the *Soi*
> (1920–21: 42).

Malinowski does not mention this culture hero, Taufo or Tauhau,
though Saville does briefly (1926: 165–6). The Mailu version given to
Saville calls him Tau or Samadulele, and has him sailing from the
West with his mother, introducing pigs, sago, coconuts and betel nut
along the coast.[26] Born of a pig mother in some versions, the hero is
also known in Mailu as the founder of the annual trading expeditions
to Aroma. Notwithstanding its likely role as a 'charter myth' for
Govi, Saville does not claim the same constitutive importance for the
hero's legend as Armstrong does for the *Soi*.

It is a pity that Malinowski did not give more details of the
distributions in the festivals he witnessed, particularly the different
categories of gifts and their recipients. He underestimated the politics
of feasting, too, and his comment on the role of the sponsor having
'no scope for much initiative' because the 'details of the feast are
strictly regulated by custom', betrayed an ignorance of the
interminable negotiations that sponsors and their helpers become
involved in while staging their festivals (p. 309). We cannot justly
complain, however, that Malinowski failed to note the efflorescence
of feasting as a post-contact phenomenon. Apart from his lack of
quantitative data and comparative evidence, the 1915 *Maduna* (which
he did not wait to see) was expected to be smaller than usual. Even
during a much longer stay, it is unlikely that he would have
suspected, let alone have been able to demonstrate, any inflationary
tendency in competitive feasting.

XIII The Text and its Editing

A bound copy of the original typescript of *The Natives of Mailu* is
held in the library of the South Australian Museum, Adelaide. It is a
surprisingly complex, not to say puzzling document. It consists of
about 400 quarto, doublespaced typed pages, most of them heavily
corrected by one or two, and often three, different hands. Neither the
pages of the typescript nor the pages of its constituent chapters are
numbered consecutively; the pages are numbered according to each

section alone. This is ample proof that Malinowski had the sections typed up in batches, or in chapters at best, and likewise delivered them piecemeal to Edward Stirling for reading.[27] Three of the sections are bound out of order (that is, the sequence in which they appeared in the printing), but this is more likely to have been a simple error of collation than an alternative sequence intended by Malinowski. Second and third carbon copies are represented, as well as some top copy pages, probably from a retyped version. All show varying degrees of editorial rewriting. Only parts of this typescript were marked up for the printer, however, so there must have been other copies in use. In short, the 'original' typescript is heterogeneous and composite, a mixture of at least two copies of at least two drafts.

The most important problem of the typescript concerns the three editorial hands. One is easy to identify as Malinowski's, though his is not the most prominent. The heaviest and most drastic editing was done by Edward Stirling, and Malinowski acknowledged none other (p. 104). But there is another hand evident in the interventions on some pages, and this belonged to Arthur M. Lea, assistant editor of the *Transactions and Proceedings*. (Lea was an entomologist with a remarkable passion for classifying beetles; by the time of his death in 1932 he had named and described 5,432 species, more than anyone else before or since.)[28] In 1918, Norman B. Tindale joined the South Australian Museum as Lea's assistant. It was he who inherited Malinowski's typescript and, sometime in the 'thirties, had it bound in a scarlet cover with gold lettering on the spine – just like the thesis it was meant to be! Professor Tindale still believes that 'much of the revising of Malinowski's Polish English fell to Lea', but 'not being aware of local happenings', Malinowski was unable to acknowledge him as he had Stirling.[29] The evidence of the typescript suggests otherwise, however, and although I have not scrutinized every page to determine whose editorial pen predominates, there can be little doubt that Stirling's changes – including additions and deletions – are far more numerous than those made by Lea.[30]

The present editing of *The Natives of Mailu* does not seek to overwrite the general good sense of the previous editing and its printing. As I have indicated, the 'original' typescript is so heavily compromised that an archaeology of the text designed to uncover a pristine 'Malinowskian' stratum would be an impossibly tedious as well as quite spurious exercise. Except in the case of a few pages we are dealing with multiple editorship not authorship. I have followed a simple principle: where it seemed that Malinowski was poorly served by his previous editors, or where the ambiguity of his phrasing led them to misread him, I have offered an optional reading by citing his original words in the endnotes. In some cases, I believe, Malinowski's phrasing was clearer and stylistically preferable; and in a few cases a different meaning can be recovered.

Concerning more technical aspects, I have preserved the original printing so far as is consistent with modern conventions of orthography. Typographical errors have been corrected, some redundant cross-referencing deleted, genealogies redrawn, neglected references supplied, and additional notes (signalled by square brackets) appended where they seemed necessary or deserving. On expert advice, Malinowski's Mailu orthography is retained, though all students of the language since Saville have used a simpler one. The original printing persisted in italicizing (and unwarrantedly capitalizing) all 'native' words, proper nouns of place and person as well as vernacular terms. This was an unusual convention for the ethnographies of the day, but perfectly proper for the natural scientist majority who contributed to the *Transactions*. At any rate, it was another editorial practice which overrode Malinowski's preference, and where his typescript had names in Roman type a red editorial pen converted them to italics. I have countermanded this order.

The plates, negatives, or prints of *The Natives of Mailu* were not bound in with the typescript, and I have been unable to locate them, in either the South Australian Museum or any of the Malinowski archives. Presumably they are lost. The plates in this edition have been copied from those in the *Transactions* with, unfortunately, some loss of quality.

Notes

1   The list is by no means exhaustive, but of items published in the
    last few years, see especially: Ardener (1985); Boon (1982); Clifford
    (1983, 1986b); Firth (1981); Gross (1986); Kuper (1983); Langham
    (1981); Payne (1981); Stocking (1983, 1986); Symmons-
    Symonolewicz (1982); Thornton (1985); Urry (1984); Wayne (1984);
    Young (1979, 1984, in press). There is also a rapidly growing
    body of studies of Malinowski by a generation of young Polish
    scholars principally concerned with the early intellectual influences
    of his youth; see, for example, Paluch (1981) and Kubica (1986),
    also the comments of Ellen (1985) and Gellner (1985) on this
    posthumous repatriation of Malinowski.

2   In a letter to Haddon (HC 25.5.1916). But the context of this
    condescension towards a 'trial run' is important, for he had
    recently spent eight months in a single Trobriand village. The
    letter continues: '... this proved to me, how even a poor observer,
    like myself, can get a certain amount of reliable information, if he
    puts himself into the proper conditions for observation' (ibid). The
    'condition of the performer/observer' was one of Malinowski's
    most important Mailu lessons. This letter shows he had also learnt
    the British virtue of diplomatic understatement.

3   I am grateful to Mr John Glover, present Honorary Secretary of
    the Royal Society of South Australia, for these estimates.
    Malinowski himself received twenty-five copies, one of which –
    disappointingly unannotated – is preserved in the Yale archive of
    his papers.

4   In one instance it was actually disguised. Writing to him from an
    Omaha reservation in 1930, Margaret Mead told Malinowski that
    the Columbia University Library had his Mailu book 'bound in a
    cover which says La Divina Comedia' (MPL 9.8.1930).

5   Reeves to Malinowski (MPY 617: 18.12.1914). These grants were
    not ungenerous. Had he been guaranteed the full £350 a year (if
    only for two years), Malinowski would have been quite
    comfortably off. By comparison, Resident Magistrates in Papua
    (Mr Armit of Abau, for example) received £250 per annum, and
    the Lt-Governor's Private Secretary £300. Malinowski's problem, of
    course, lay in the fact that neither of the grants could be
    guaranteed in wartime; hence his need to press the Australian
    Government for additional or alternative support.

6   Malinowski's tent (see plates I and II in 1922: 16; though first
    mentioned at 1954 [1916]: 254) has a secure place in his myth and
    has attracted some thoughtful comment (Wax 1972; Young 1979:
    13; Stocking 1983: 97 and plate at p. 101; Clifford 1983: 123;
    1986: 1–2). Accordingly, it is interesting to note its negotiated
    identity as a valued object and not simply as a symbol. It appears
    that the tent Malinowski used in the Trobriands was loaned to
    him by the local Assistant Resident Magistrate and doctor, R. L.

Bellamy, in July 1915. 'This tent suffered considerably from the wear, incidental to prolonged use, and on leaving the islands [i.e., in March 1916] I offered to Mr J. Campbell, ARM, to return its value to the Government, should this be expected of me. As my own tent, which was anyway too small, has been lost, I would be very much indebted to the Papuan Government, if I were allowed to use the old tent again' (Letter, Malinowski to Hunt, AA 29.10.16). Hunt arranged this promptly, but the ultimate fate of the tent is unknown. Should we seek any significance in the curious fact that Malinowski's own tent was unserviceable, and that the 'fragile canvas artifact of civilized Europe' (Stocking, ibid) which sheltered and consoled him throughout his Trobriand fieldwork actually belonged to the Papuan Government, and hence to the Australian taxpayer?

7 This assessment of Hunt's patronage is based on the material in the Australian Archives (AA). For Malinowski's relations with officialdom generally and further details of his financial circumstances, see Laracy (1975). Mulvaney and Calaby (1985: 267, 323–5) also deal briefly with Hunt's (and Baldwin Spencer's) dealings with Malinowski, though these authors view Malinowski in an unsympathetic light.

8 See Malinowski (1915: 497–8, i.e., pp. 105–6 below; hereinafter references to *Mailu* will follow the pagination of the present edition); also Stocking (1983: 95). Young (1984) reviews the wider ethnographic options open to Malinowski on his arrival in Papua.

9 As repeated by Seligman in a letter to Malinowski (SP 14.2.1915).

10 Malinowski expressed his concern about the war in Europe in all his letters to Seligman. In this one, for instance, he wrote: 'The last war news seems to be a trifle better... but I am very distressed about my mother and it is awful that the war is going on right within Polish territory'. In a postscript to this letter he tells Seligman he has already decided to go 'South' (i.e., Australia) for February-March or March-April.

11 Ironically, Malinowski bungled a similar attempt to sail with a Trobriand fleet later in the year when the Omarakana chief refused to let him accompany a *Kula* expedition to Kitava (1922:479).

12 Last (1986) gives biographical notes on Stirling; his only major work on Aborigines was published as volume 4 of the Horn expedition report (1896). Concerning Spencer, see Mulvaney and Calaby (1985); Stocking (1983: 78–80); Urry (1984: 39–40). In a review of Spencer and Gillen's *Across Australia,* Malinowski had claimed that 'since the publication of their first volume, half of the total production in anthropological theory has been based upon their work, and nine-tenths affected or modified by it' (1913). Stocking suggests that in Baldwin Spencer's work 'Malinowski no doubt also recognized an ethnographic style that was closer to his own than Haddon's...' (ibid: 79). *The Natives of Mailu,* however,

did not reflect so much as ignore Spencer's ethnographic innovations.

13   There is no evidence that Malinowski ever wrote a report for the Australian or Papuan Governments on land tenure (or anything else for that matter). In *Coral Gardens*, his massive treatise on Trobriand horticulture, he admitted that he had 'failed' in Mailu 'to find out all that really matters about land tenure', but that this awareness led him to develop 'a strategy of frontal attack on the subject' in Kiriwina (1935: 326). Atlee Hunt died the year *Coral Gardens* was published.

14   Edward Stirling had died in 1919, but his stiffly polite, final letter to Malinowski was dated 2 April 1916. It informed him that 'there must be no further personal association' with his daughter, though he permitted them to correspond 'not too frequently' (MPY 590). Mulvaney and Calaby (1985: 322-6, 332-3) detail the full extent of Spencer's support for Malinowski, despite what seems to have been a marked personal antipathy. They argue that Malinowski's almost paranoid suspicion of Spencer (as testified to in the *Diary* and letters to Seligman) was quite unwarranted, there being no evidence that Spencer did anything whatever to undermine Malinowski's academic reputation. On the contrary, Spencer supported him throughout by urging Hunt to continue funding him, and later by recommending his work to his own publisher, George Macmillan. Wayne (1984: 195) agrees that Spencer caused no harm to Malinowski, but disagrees that Spencer was altogether blameless of seeding Malinowski's suspicions.

15   In the possession of Richard Randolph of Santa Cruz, University of California; I possess a photocopy.

16   For an historian's analysis of colonial attitudes in Papua during the period 1906-1914, see Nelson (1969); a summary is given in Young (1984: 3-5).

17   See Malinowski (1918). Although more sympathetic to the plight of Papuan labourers than the majority of submissions, his views could hardly be called humanitarian, and he delivered himself of some startlingly unanthropological judgements. For instance: 'The native Papuan cannot really see even seven or eight days ahead, though he may be very intelligent in many matters; he has no mental grasp of a further perspective'. The context of this remark was the villagers' reluctance to plant coconuts for copra, but as a generalization about native mentality it was made in total disregard of all that he already knew about the *Kula*, not to mention Trobriand gardening and Mailu feasting. Insofar as he concluded that, 'Broadly speaking, I think it would be best to leave them [i.e. the "natives"] to their own conditions', his views were probably regarded as unhelpful to, if not subversive of, the whole colonial enterprise.

18   For more on Malinowski's Aunt Sallys and strawmen, see Fortes (1957: 157); Young (1979: 6); and Strathern (1981: 666-8).

19 Malinowski (1926c: 8) gives the year as 1921, but Saville's letters clearly indicate that the course he attended was in the summer term of 1922 (see also Firth 1957: 4).

20 Haddon followed Saville rather than Malinowski when he reproduced Mailu canoe terminology. Without directly comparing them, Haddon conventionally praised both ethnographies: Malinowski's was 'an admirable detailed study of the Mailu', Saville's 'an extremely good description of the people and their culture' (1937: 231).

21 Raymond Firth foreshadowed this project in 1951 during a brief visit to two Mailu communities (Boru and Domara); he published some observations on changing settlement patterns, social structure, and modernizing economic activities (Firth 1952).

22 The identification of Mailu (or Toulon) Island with the Spaniards' St Bartholomew has been convincingly made by a number of historians, including Irwin, and only Parsonson (1967) disputes it. Irwin even found fragments of an oral tradition about the abduction of children by early white visitors (1985: 9).

23 Saville was sent a copy of Stevens' book in 1931, shortly after its publication (Prado's long-lost *Relación* had been recovered in 1929). In a letter to his brother Saville wrote: 'It is wonderful to think that in 1606 old Torres and Prado anchored their old tub just opposite where our house now stands – they had a fracas with the natives here. Shooting several and taking some women and girls ("for the use of the sailors") and incidentally a man or two. This they did with smug R.C. hypocrisy. But what great men some of these ancient mariners [were]' (SML 3.2.1931). Prado said nothing about the abduction of women from Mailu, and Saville probably conflated a later event at the 'Islas de los Perros' (supposedly one of the smaller islands in Torres Strait): 'We selected three of the youngest women and put them on board for the service of the crew of the ship' (Stevens 1930: 159). Errors aside, these are surprisingly unsympathetic and partisan comments for a missionary to make.

24 Malinowski (1912); see Firth's comments (1957b: 212). See also Malinowski's version of this bit of intellectual history in *Coral Gardens*, concerning the functional connection between magico-religious belief and economic activity, a relationship which impressed him 'strongly' on his first field expedition, and which '...needless to say, is perhaps the dominant motive [sic] throughout this book' (1935: 457). A large claim indeed.

25 Murray Groves wrote of the Motu, '...the dances of an *iduhu* [subclan] were psalms to its ancestors' (1954:80). Much earlier, Marett had written in a throwaway remark '...savages do not think out their form of cult...but rather live it out, or, one might almost say, dance it out' (NQ 1912: 258).

26 In the Suau and Milne Bay region Tauhau is claimed to have introduced many more cultural features besides these; see Kaniku (1975) for an epic version of Tauhau's myth.

27   Stirling wrote to Malinowski in Melbourne, just before the latter's
      departure for Papua on his second expedition: 'I shall be glad to
      look over the rest of your MS but it has not yet reached me. I
      also note what you say concerning Seligman's approval and will
      act accordingly' (MPY 590: 14.5.1915). This is confirmation that
      Malinowski did give Seligman the veto over his publishing in
      Australia. (Stirling's letter is a reply to Malinowski's of 4 May,
      which does not survive.)
28   The same issue of the *Transactions* contains a lengthy 'article' by
      Lea; at 238 pages it is even longer than Malinowski's. I am
      grateful to Dr Eric Matthews for information about Arthur Lea.
29   Professor N.B. Tindale, personal communication, 18.3.86.
30   I am grateful to Mr Edward Booth, Stirling's grandson, for
      identifying Stirling's handwriting on sample pages of the typescript
      (personal communication, 19.2.86).

Editor's Addendum

Several months after this book went to the publisher, Ms Margaret
Saville, the missionary's granddaughter, sent me a letter she found
while sorting family papers. Dated 4 August 1926, it was Malinowski's
reply to Saville's two letters mentioned above (7 April and 3 May
1926), and was written while Malinowski was travelling in North
America. This letter, excerpted below with the kind permission of Ms
Saville, is important for the additional light it sheds on Malinowski's
relationship to the missionary and the mystery of the missing Preface
to his book.

My Dear Saville,

I was delighted to get your two kind letters from Mailu & to
see that you like my Preface – in spite of all!
    The fact is that I not only did not receive or see your
Preface, but I was positively told by both Seeley Service &
your L.M.S. friend that there was *no* Preface! As a matter of
fact I got first my Secretary (a pupil of mine, a New
Zealander named Raymond W. Firth) to ring up S.S. & the
L.M.S. & when he gave me the message, I was so surprised
that [I] rang them up myself. I take it from your 2nd letter
that the L.M.S. man is innocent, but S.S. played a nasty tric
[sic] on both of us!

I shall speak now plainly – since I find with delight that you are as correct as possible in the matter – but I hinted already in my previous letter an acknowledgement on your part & a reference to my previous publication was the natural thing. As you see, I tried to solve the difficulty writing as if I had been instructed by you to make the references. You will no doubt appreciate the diplomatic feat involved!

But what a damned shame that I did not see the Pref. you wrote! It would have given such pleasure – not of vanity, but of this personal [?] which two people who worked & at times squabbled & at last came out friends – to see it. And again I am so angry that I could not simply pour out my blessings. I resented your not putting [in] a kinship table – after all our talks – & now I see [you] *did* it!

Now as to the remedy: we are not going to get on the wrong side of S.S. & Co. – I warned you against them several times, you'll remember! Mulching a MSS. is a dirty tric [sic]. However, it is done not only by Missionary Societies or their publishers! The Rev. E.C. Fox of the Solomons sent his MSS. to the famous Rivers, who died & the MSS got into the hands of Prof. Elliot Smith, F.R.S. & Mr W.C. Perry – and Fox wrote to me that $\frac{1}{3}$ of the MSS has been cut out! and that *without* acknowledgement of the fact!! Here you have a number of men of science cutting and altering the MSS of a Missionary who is too far to control them – and all in order to bolster their silly theories.

To return to our position. It is a thousand pities that your kinship tables & other more 'dry' data got cut out. I am also specially sorry that it has not been said that you collected your data independently of my monograph. The substantial coincidence of fact would be a very valuable & unique proof of our having been correct.

What would you think of writing up an article (some 6–15 thousand words) for the Journal of the R. Anthrop. Institute, giving your K[inship] table & working out some of the more abstract problems? You might collect your evidence again without looking at my pamphlet & then control my data, correct my errors, point out where I was on the right trac [sic] etc. I might then add a *P.S.* showing that for once a

Miss[ionary] & an Anthrop[ologist] can work parallel,
correcting and completing each other & not quarrelling about
any difference....

Yours ever,

B. Malinowski

THE NATIVES OF MAILU: PRELIMINARY RESULTS OF THE ROBERT MOND RESEARCH WORK IN BRITISH NEW GUINEA

By B. MALINOWSKI, Ph.D., Cracow,
Robert Mond Travelling Student in the University of London

Plate 1.

Plate 2.

Plate 3.

Plate 4.

Plate 5.

Plate 6.

Plate 7.

Plate 8.

Plate 9.

Plate 10.

Plate 11.

Plate 12.

Plate 13.

Plate 14.

Plate 15.

Plate 16.

Plate 17.

Plate 18.

Plate 19.

Plate 20.

Plate 22.

Plate 21.

Plate 23.

Plate 24.

Plate 25.

Plate 26.

Plate 27.

Plate 28.

Plate 29.

Plate 30.

Plate 31.

Plate 32.

Plate 33.

Plate 34.

collectively forming a ~~rig~~
~~Cylindrical~~ *bodes* ~~surface~~ hanging ~~under~~ *beneath* the ear conch.

Here fig 12.

Sometimes these tortoise shell rings are   alter-

nat~~ing~~ *ed* with perforated discs of *the* red ground shell,   well

known as "native money of the Pacific."   These

are placed with their plane perpendicular to that of the tortoise-shell disc,

so that they present   their broad surface to the

eyes. Rather ~~rare~~ *uncommon*   is a (white) fairly large shell-
                                                                external border
disc, with a   serrated ~~outward contour~~,

Here fig 13.

placed in the lobe.

Here fig 14.

All of these ornaments, the tortoise shell rings (Gebóre), the shell-
                                        of local manufacture.
discs (Agéva), and the white, serrated disc (Kúre) are ~~made in Vailu.~~

The teeth are artificially blackened ~~and have~~ *additions* sometimes *to* a jet black
        (To effect this)
colour. They mix the decayed root of the Badila tree with green leaves of
    other   *apply to*
some kind of tree. This mixture they ~~fix over~~ the teeth with a piece of
            allowing it to remain
~~bast~~ ~~bark~~ ~~and keep~~ overnight. The process is repeated from time to time.

All the women tatoo the face and the body in a pattern identical with

that of the Massim and undoubtedly borrowed from them. The tatoo is done
                                                                    lawyer
by pricking the skin with a thorn of the sago palm or of the ~~larger~~ cane and

CONTENTS

CHAPTER III

TRIBAL LIFE

CHAPTER IV

ECONOMICS

CHAPTER V

MAGICO-RELIGIOUS ACTIVITIES AND BELIEFS

CHAPTER VI

ART AND KNOWLEDGE

PLATES

Map (facing page 117) showing Mailu, or Toulon, Island and adjacent coast of Papua.

1. Village of Mailu seen from the north-west.
2. Village of Mailu seen from the east.
3. Scene on Mailu beach showing a double canoe (*oró'u*) which has been temporarily converted into a house-boat.
4. A section of the village of Bórebo seen from the sea.
5. The village street in Mailu looking westwards. The houses seen here belong to the clans Maradúbu and Moráu. Some of them are decorated with rows of sago bundles which, in view of the approaching feast, hang under the thatch eaves.
6. Western end of Bórebo village, showing the *dúbu* standing in its characteristic position in the middle of the street.
7. Front view of a house in Mailu, showing the typical manner in which the natives occupy verandahs, or lower floor of the house.
8. Side view of a native house. In front a row of girls in their gala petticoats.
9. Group of men in gala dress and decorated for the *bára* dance.
10. Woman in mourning petticoat.
11. A man squeezing coconut shavings for making coconut cream (*górogóro*). He has moved into the middle of the street for the convenience of the photographer.
12. Boiling of sago for a small feast. Men are stirring the contents of the pots with long wooden spoons. A temporary shade, removed for the purposes of photography, has been constructed. Only on festive occasions are men concerned with cooking.
13. Group of girls in festive dress. They are wearing glass beads.

14. Two women in gala petticoats, and one in mourning petticoat. They show the method of carrying babies.
15. Flotilla of Mailu toy canoes. The boy owners stand each behind his boat.
16. The toy canoes floating on the small bay in front of Mailu village. The boys have been grouped together for photographic purposes; usually they are scattered all over the shallow water.
17. Mailu double canoe (*oró'u*) beached.
18. Side view of beached *oró'u*.
19. An *oró'u* with hoisted sail.
20. Scooping out the large logs which are to form the dug-outs of an *oró'u*. To the right an end-on view of a dug-out; to the left a side view. Over the latter a shade has been erected. This plate shows the 'backs' of Mailu village.
21. Hoisting of the crab-claw sail.
22. An *oró'u* ready to sail.
23. Native dressed, and provided with the magical requisites, for the performance of arm-shell magic.
24. Arm-shell magic.
25. Wrapping a bunch of bananas in leaves to protect it from flying foxes. (Photograph taken on the Laróge River, Koíta district.)
26. Nets as set for wallaby hunting. The scene is after the hunt; the men have picked up their spears which, during the hunt, lie on the ground near at hand. (Photograph taken in the Koíta district.)
27. Pot making in Mailu.
28. Final stage in the making of arm-shells; polishing of the shell.
29. Group of natives dressed for the *bára* dance and holding boars' tusk ornaments in their teeth.
30. A figure of the *bára* dance.
31. A *bára* dance; ready for the quick step which is danced to the sound of the drums without singing. The houses in the background are decorated with 'sausages' of sago, and bunches of bananas are seen hanging from posts erected along the street.
32. Dancing the quick step of the *bára*.
33. A Pantomime figure of the *bára*.

34. Women decorated for the *damoréa* dance. (Photograph taken in a Southern Massim village.)

PREFACE

The ethnological information presented in this memoir was collected during a stay of six months in Papua, from the beginning of September, 1914, till the end of February, 1915. The expedition was suggested by my friend and teacher, Prof. C. G. Seligman, and its organization and scientific direction has also been in his hands. I owe him a further debt of gratitude in that he has made himself responsible for the financing of the expedition, the funds for which were to a great extent supplied by Mr. Robert Mond, F.R.S.E., the well-known scientist and benefactor of science. In every way I am under the greatest obligation to Prof. Seligman, and I hope my work will prove not altogether unworthy of the great trouble and kind care he has taken to make it possible.

I would not have been able to conduct my investigations with any hope of success without the kind and very effective assistance given me by the Federal Department of External Affairs, and by the Papuan Government. Both Mr. Atlee Hunt, C.M.G., Secretary to the Commonwealth Department of External Affairs in Melbourne, and His Excellency Judge J. H. P. Murray, Lieutenant-Governor of British New Guinea, have taken a friendly interest in my work and have given me the best opportunities for carrying it out. To both these gentlemen my sincere thanks are due.

For much help in my investigations I have to thank the Hon. H. W. Champion, Secretary to the Papuan Government, and Dr. W.M. Strong, of Port Moresby.

I also owe much to the kindness of the Resident Magistrates of the Divisions which I visited – Mr. L. P. B. Armit, of Abáu; Mr. C. B. Higginson, of Samarai; and Mr. A. H. Symons, of Woodlark Island.

In actual field work I have been greatly helped by the Rev. W. J. V. Saville, of the London Missionary Society, missionary in Mailu, and by Mr. Alfred Greenaway, a resident of long standing in that district. I had also the good fortune to meet Dr. A. C. Haddon, F.R.S., in the field during his short visit to Mailu.

Prof. E. C. Stirling, C.M.G., F.R.S., of Adelaide, has read and corrected my manuscript and given me his invaluable advice on many points. He has also undertaken to edit this memoir. I owe him personally and scientifically more than mere words of acknowledgement can express.

Prof. W. Baldwin Spencer, C.M.G., F.R.S., of Melbourne, whose investigations have marked an epoch in ethnology, gave me the benefit of his unique experience in field work. The personal interest he has been good enough to show in the work of a beginner has been the greatest encouragement I could have received.

My thanks are due to Dr. R. Pulleine, of Adelaide; to Mr. C. Hedley, F.L.S., of the Australian Museum; and to Mr. W. Howchin, F.G.S., Lecturer on Geology in the University of Adelaide, for much help given me in connection with the publication of this memoir.

The drawings in the text have been executed by Miss P. F. Clarke, partly from actual specimens and partly from rough sketches made in the field.

Some parts of the manuscript might have been amplified by adding comparative notes and by incorporating such information as has been obtained among the kindred and neighbouring tribes, the Southern Massim to the east and the Sinaughólo and Motu to the west. I hope, however, that I shall be able to collect some more material, especially among the Southern Massim of Suá'u and Bónabóna, and I am eager to resume field work as soon as possible.

B. M.

Samarai, Papua, June 9, 1915.

INTRODUCTION

Seligman's classification of the Papuo-Melanesians; the Mailu problem

In his well-known treatise on the 'Melanesians of British New Guinea', Prof. Seligman has laid the foundations of Papuo-Melanesian ethnology. He classifies the natives of the territory in the following manner, taking into account physical, linguistic, and cultural data. Calling all the inhabitants of the 'Great Island' Papuasians, he says: – 'The term "Papuan" ... will be limited to the geographically more western Papuasians, a congeries of frizzly haired and often mop-headed peoples, whose skin-colour is some shade of brownish black. The eastern Papuasians – that is, the generally smaller, lighter coloured, frizzly haired races of the eastern peninsula of New Guinea and its archipelagos – now require a name, and since the true Melanesian element is dominant in them, they may be called Papuo-Melanesians.'[1]

These latter (the Papuo-Melanesians) present again two entirely different types, both from the anthropological (physical) and ethnological (cultural) points of view. In this pamphlet I shall adopt Prof. Seligman's classification and terminology and, with him, 'shall call the two great divisions of the Papuo-Melanesians the Massim (Eastern Papuo-Melanesians) and the Western Papuo-Melanesians respectively'.[2]

In his book, Prof. Seligman has given the results of his researches among five different tribes, or groups of tribes. These may be considered representative of the different cultural types found in the Papuo-Melanesian area. The Roro-speaking people and the Mekeo are typical of the most westerly of the Western Papuo-Melanesians. Their culture shows signs of some modification, due to the influence

---

[1] C.G. Seligman: *The Melanesians of British New Guinea*. Cambridge, 1910, pp. 1 and 2.
[2] *Loc. cit.*

of pure Papuan tribes in their neighbourhood. The Koíta, described in the first part of Prof. Seligman's work, represent a perfect type of the pure Western Papuo-Melanesian culture, as it exists amongst the bulk of tribes inhabiting the (administrative) Central Division of the Territory. The two last parts of the treatise deal with the two subdivisions of the Massim, the Northern Massim, who inhabit the Trobriand Islands and Woodlark Island, and the Southern Massim, who live in the extreme eastern end of the mainland and on the islands which run south-eastwards from it – the D'Entrecasteaux Group, the Louisiades, and the minor groups lying around and between. Thus we owe to Prof. Seligman a complete picture of the ethnographical area covered by the term Papuo-Melanesian.

Prof. Seligman says, however, in the introduction to his book: – 'Very little is known concerning the population of the country between Aróma and Mullins Harbour in the neighbourhood of which the territory of the Massim begins, in fact, this is one of the least-known portions of British New Guinea.'[3] It is with this area that the present study is concerned.

'A people who may be called the Mailu inhabit the country around Port Glasgow and Milport Harbour...'[4] The name Mailu, by which Prof. Seligman calls these natives, has also been adopted in this paper. Mailu is the name of the most important village of the tribe, which is situated on a small island (called Toulon, or Mailu Island), some four to five miles off the mainland, opposite Amazon Bay. The Mailu islanders have played quite a special and prominent part in the trade of the southern coast, and they also possessed certain industries (pottery, canoe-building, etc.) unknown, or hardly known, to the other natives of the district. Physically, they are undoubtedly much more robust and healthier than the average mainland native. They seem also to enjoy a certain amount of aristocratic prestige among the neighbouring villagers. Thus the term Mailu, applied to the natives of the whole district, is a fair use of the *pars pro toto* figure. I have also reason to believe that the whole district was known by that name to the other tribes on the southern coast, even before the white man's advent. The natives of the district sometimes call themselves by the generic name Mági, which term I have occasionally used when I wished to imply that a statement referred to the whole district.

[3]*Op. cit.*, pp. 22 and 23.
[4]*Ibid.*, p. 24.

The natives of Mailu, or Toulon Island, and the Mailu-speaking inhabitants of the mainland

The natives of Mailu Island differ in several points from their fellow-tribesmen, though in broad outline their culture and their social institutions seem to be identical. The bulk of my work was done in a Mailu village on Toulon (or Mailu) Island. Since I made only a few short visits to three points on the mainland, I was unable to do more than to ascertain broadly whether certain statements were true of the whole district, or applicable exclusively to Mailu Island. On the other hand, many of my Mailu informants had spent much time on the mainland, and, knowing the differences and similarities, were able to enlighten me in this respect on many points, and I have always been as careful as I could to state the geographical range of my statements. Generally speaking, where there is no special reservation, a statement, though obtained in Mailu village, has been considered by me to hold good for the whole district.

Ethnic position of the Mailu; their relation to the Motu-speaking tribes; use of the Motuan language

The Mailu are the most eastern of the Western Papuo-Melanesians; in fact, their immediate neighbours on the east belong to the southern Massim stock. The social constitution of the Mailu and the essential features of their culture are of the same type as those of the Koíta, described by Seligman in the first section of his treatise as representative of the Western Papuo-Melanesians.

This masterly outline of a Western Papuo-Melanesian culture and sociology I always kept before me as a model.[5]

---

[5]In fact, being obliged to wait in Port Moresby for over three weeks for a boat to Mailu, I had the good fortune to work with Prof. Seligman's own informant Ahúia Ova, a man of great natural intelligence, who, moreover, had been trained by Prof. Seligman and Capt. Barton as an accomplished native ethnologist. Since Seligman and Barton have left the territory Ahúia has been conducting investigations on his own account for the last ten years. I have been able to obtain a certain amount of information through my conversations with Ahúia and during two native hunting expeditions at which I was present. Thus I had, on the one hand my own raw materials, and on the other similar materials skilfully shaped into a final form by Dr. Seligman. By comparing the two sets of information I was able to learn in the way of method a great deal more in those few weeks than I could have done in many months had I been obliged to depend entirely upon my own efforts unaided by Dr. Seligman's previous experience.[1]

The cultural resemblance of the Mailu to the Koíta and allied tribes is the reason why I am giving in the text frequent footnotes referring the reader both to Prof. Seligman's description of the Koíta and to some data I was able to collect among the Motu and Sinaughólo tribes, who live in close contact with the former but differ from them in some respects. I had specially good opportunities among the Sinaughólo, as I went there (at the end of my stay in Papua) in company with my friend Ahúia, by whom I was introduced to a number of well-informed, intelligent, and outspoken natives. The Sinaughólo customs and folklore closely resemble those of the Mailu, and in many cases comparison is very useful.

Besides the Mailu names of things, customs, etc., I am also giving as many Motuan terms as possible. This is partly because the Motu is a universal language among the natives in British New Guinea, or, at least, it is beginning to become such. If it were adopted (as was partially done by Dr. Seligman, who has given the Motu equivalents of all Koíta terms) as an ethnological standard language for all the Papuasian tribes it would greatly facilitate matters, since it would bring into prominence identities and correspondences between the customs, ideas, and material culture of various tribes. I have been able to give the Motuan terms the more easily as I used that language in my conversations with the natives, especially towards the end of my work. I had been advised to acquire as much as possible of Motu, and I studied the grammar and vocabulary of the late Mr. Lawes before arriving in Papua.

During my first weeks in Port Moresby I made the most strenuous efforts to get a conversational smattering of the language. I took with me to Mailu a Motuan cook-boy, Igua Pipi, whom I used to employ as interpreter when talking with the natives. He translated my English into Motuan, and then the natives' statements back again from Motuan to English. I was sufficiently advanced in Motuan by that time to be able to check the conversation, and this was indeed essential, as my interpreter often misunderstood my questions. Gradually I began to ask questions in Motu myself, and relegated Igua from the position of an interpreter to that of a personified pocket dictionary, which was brought into requisition whenever a word was lacking or if the natives refused to penetrate the somewhat barbarous Motuan I was using. It must be added that it is much easier to speak and understand Motu when conversing with a non-Motuan, since he speaks it more slowly, less elaborately, and uses a much narrower range of words. In fact, a kind of 'Pidgin-Motu' is now in process of formation. This 'Pidgin-Motu' is, however, a form of the pure Motuan which, though simplified, is by no means distorted.[2] It is infinitely better adapted to the natives' forms of thinking, and infinitely more expressive for him and for the investigator, than that dreadful mixture called 'Pidgin-English'. Moreover, in Mailu absolutely no one spoke the latter, whereas practically all men under forty, and some of the elderly men, spoke Motu, some of them even excellently. Towards the end of my time in Mailu I was quite able to talk freely with my informants, discuss matters, raise objections, and, in short, use Motu as a completely satisfactory instrument of investigation. When I returned to Port Moresby, and then went with Ahúia to the Sinaughólo country for a fortnight, I was able not only to talk with the natives in Motu, but to follow their discussions in that language, though they speak it in the pure, unsimplified form. I am afraid I must explicitly boast of my facility for acquiring a conversational command of foreign languages, since I understand that the time in which I learned to speak the Motu would have been normally too short a period for acquiring a foreign, and especially a native, tongue. I wish also to state that the ability to speak Motu and to follow a conversation was of no small advantage in my work. Over and over again I was led on to the track of some extremely important item in native sociology or folklore by listening to the conversation of my boy Igua with his Mailu friends, who used to come from the village to see him.

Remarks on the conditions of work and on the methods of presenting the material

I may also mention that during the best part of December, January, and February I was living quite alone with the natives, except for short periods of about two or three days, when I travelled on board a steam launch, or stayed at Port Moresby. I found that work done under such circumstances is incomparably more intensive than work done from white men's settlements, or even in any white man's company; the nearer one lives to a village and the more one sees actually of the natives the better. In fact, as I work out my notes, I see that only such information is quite satisfactory as has been obtained by witnessing an occurrence or seeing a thing, and subsequently (or previously) discussing it with the natives. In the course of this memoir I am always careful to state explicitly what I have not seen, and what therefore is described merely from information gathered by questioning natives. I also try to convey to the reader, as clearly as possible, under what circumstances and with what degree of accuracy every item of information has been collected. The somewhat personal data just given have the object of allowing the reader to visualize and to judge the methods of field work used in collecting this material.

The division into chapters and sections which I have adopted needs also a word or so of explanation. By adopting a fairly systematic division – Geography, Sociology, Economics, Magico-religious matters, etc. – I have, of course, deviated from a purely topical presentation of facts. I shall undoubtedly be taken to task for having thus 'put some theory into the facts', and, in the first place, for having swerved from the native forms of thinking and abandoned the native classification.

A thorough reply to such an objection would require a long philosophical digression, for which there is no room here. I wish, however, to emphasize the fact that I have always tried to leave all preconceived ideas on one side when working among the natives, and to classify and register facts according to their essentials as I saw them then and there. In discussing facts, which may be called religious or magical, according to the student's point of view and definition, I have followed Dr. Marett's excellent advice and hints, given in the 'Notes and Queries', and, in accordance therewith, I have called them throughout by the impartial term Magico-religious. I have tried to preserve the same attitude in all the various subjects investigated.

Again, I have always endeavoured to preserve as far as possible the natives' own way of looking at things, and whenever I was able to obtain a native classification of facts – as, for instance, that implied in the term *góra* (chap. iii., sec. 5) – I was careful to record it and to state it as exactly as possible.

In the spelling of native names I have adopted the system recommended by the 'Notes and Queries,' which practically consists in the use of the consonants with their English sounds and the vowels with their Italian values. I found this system entirely sufficient with Mailu. The only sign I found necessary to introduce refers to the distinction between the diphthongal sounding of two vowels and their separate sounding. Wherever the vowels are simply juxtaposed they are to be sounded diphthongally. Wherever the two vowels retain their separate values I have indicated this by putting an apostrophe between them, but it is important to note that the apostrophe so placed does not imply any pause or any specific sound, similar to the Arabic *ain*. Thus in the word *bó'i* the apostrophe between *o* and *i* means that the vowels have to be pronounced as in the Italian *poi*, and not as in the English *boy*. I have also put an accent upon nearly every word, except those in which I failed to record it through haste in taking the notes. On some compound words I have put a double accent. As a matter of fact, the natives join the component parts and pronounce them like one word, though they place the accent on each component more or less as is done in the German compound words.

It must be remembered that the sounds *r* and *l* ought to be replaced by an intermediate sound, as the natives do not distinguish between them. It is certainly a fact that the natives, nowadays, sound very distinct *r*'s and *l*'s when pronouncing words slowly and clearly for the European to take them down. There is not the slightest doubt, however, that this is a phonetic corruption, under European influence. Originally the natives had one 'intermediate' sound, and there was no distinction between *r* and *l*. This is the reason why they, at the present time, always mix the two sounds. The same native will, on the same day, say both *Mailu* and then *Mairu*; or mix freely *Kurére* and *Kuléle*, if you press him for clear *r*'s and *l*'s.

The same holds good in Mailu with reference to the sounds *t* and *s*; these are always mixed, a Mailu native saying quite as often Tamarai as Samarai, for instance. There is, or rather was originally, no distinction between *t* and *s* among the Mailu, the 'intermediate' sound *ts* (Polish and Slavonic *c* – the sound in *car* = *tsar*). In contact with Europeans, and under the necessity of adapting their words to our spelling, the natives have learned to split the sound *ts* into *t* and *s*, the result being that the two latter sounds are interchangeable, as they cannot really decide which to use. I have used the spelling *ts* throughout. Whenever the Mailu natives talk to each other they always use the original sound *ts*; never *t* or *s*.[3]

CHAPTER I

GEOGRAPHY

The country of the Mailu; rainfall; rivers; flora and fauna; reefs; quarries

The Mailu inhabit the seaboard from Cape Rodney in the west to the middle of Orangerie Bay in the east. Near Cape Rodney there is a belt of flat alluvial soil, extending far inland, and eastwards as far as Cloudy Bay. Near the latter the hills, which in this part of the continent run in a series of longitudinal parallel ranges, rising one beyond the other and culminating in the Main Range, approach the sea, though they do not rise to any great vertical height.

Cloudy Bay is closed on the east by Dedéle Point; then comes Baxter Bay terminated by Table Point, so named after the flat table-topped hills which rise a couple of miles beyond the level foreshore of the Cape. From Table (or Batumata) Point to Cape Mogúbo (Greenaway Point) an alluvial flat again stretches for some distance inland. From the sea the ranges, rising in succession one above the other, here and there broken by deep gorges, and with the dim, bluish profile of the main range in the background, present a fine scene. Towards Mogúbo Point the hills approach the shore again, and beyond the small Amazon Bay a range of little hills rises straight from the sea, forming a series of extremely picturesque bays, surrounded by heavily timbered, and luxuriously green, slopes, with here and there a fringe of coconut palms running along the shore in the neighbourhood of the villages.

After that the hills recede again to a certain extent and the vast expanse of Orangerie Bay opens, running in a slightly curved line as far as the entrance to Mullins Harbour. Only the western shores of Orangerie Bay are inhabited by the Mailu. Almost exactly through its centre, at a village called Gadaísiu, runs the boundary line between the Mailu and the Southern Massim.

The Mailu country is situated beyond the so-called dry-belt. It has a fairly heavy rainfall, especially during the north-western season, but there are good rains even at other times.[4] It is clothed with tropical vegetation, and the hills are always green. The contrast with the parched brown slopes near Port Moresby, when one goes eastwards in the dry season, is very striking. The small island of Mailu and the two flat coral islands of Laruóro and Loupóm are exceptions to this luxuriance, as they do not get the same rainfall, in consequence of their distance from the hills. The steep slopes of the Mailu hills are covered with *lalang* grass, and, in the dry season, are parched yellow. There are no big rivers in the district which are navigable for any appreciable distance even for small craft. The alluvial flats of Amazon Bay, Table Bay, Cloudy Bay, and those near Cape Rodney are drained by a series of streams, some of which may be navigated by light-draught vessels, though for a few miles only. There are also swamps throughout the district, on which sago grows freely.

The high tropical jungle yields a rich supply of all the kinds of timber used by the natives, as well as of many sorts of fibre, bast, cane, and of other raw materials for native industries. The fertile and well-watered soil encourages the growth of all the native garden plants, such as taro, bananas, sugar cane, yams, and *taitu*, as well as the introduced sweet potato, pawpaw, and sago. It must be noted that the dry tracts of the New Guinea coast are deprived of some of these vegetables (especially taro), as well as sago.

The Mailu district has, of course, the same supply of animals as the other parts of the continent – *viz.*, wild pigs, small kangaroos (wallaby), cuscus, bandicoots, etc., as well as an enormous variety of birds, with magnificent plumage, and edible for the natives.

The shore, and especially the reef, affords splendid opportunities for fishing and for the collection of shell fish. The shells constitute an important raw material for implements and decorations.

The barrier reef runs along some parts of the coast, though it is absent on others. It extends from Cape Rodney in the west to the middle of Table Bay. Then there are again patches of reef off Mogúbo Point. In Amazon Bay there are ring-barriers of coral encircling the islands.

There were no stone quarries affording really good material in the district, and the majority of stone implements was imported. The only place whence stone was taken for making sago-pounders and other implements was in the island of Abá'u in Amazon Bay. There was, however, good pottery clay on Mailu Island.

The villages

The Mailu or Mági inhabit the coast of this country, some of their villages lying directly on the beach, others, built before the advent of white man's influence, on the hills, which rise straight from the sea between Amazon and Orangerie Bays. Again, on some parts of the coast, natives speaking a different language, and probably belonging to a different stock, came quite close to the coast, though there were no non-Mailu villages on the beach. It will be best to enumerate the Mailu villages and characterize them briefly, as well as to say a few words about their neighbours on either side and inland.[6]

Beginning from the east, Gadaísiu is the first place inhabited by the Mailu. As a matter of fact, it is a mixed village, about half the houses being built in the Massim manner and inhabited by the Massim (Bónabóna subdivision) and the rest showing the Mailu style and tenanted by Mailu-speaking natives. Succeeding Gadaísiu, westwards, comes a group of Mailu villages – Gogotsíba, Oibáda, Orí, Nabá – some built on the shore, some a few miles inland. These villages have some specific customs, by which they differ from the other Mailu. Beyond these, all of which lie on the shores of Orangerie Bay, come the places situated on the hills between Orangerie and Amazon Bays. All the latter were built on the hilltops for purposes of defence. Under the influence of the new conditions of existence and of the complete personal security which these assured, these villages moved to the shore. On the hills overlooking the first bay (Port Glasgow) stood the villages of Banóro, Géagéa, and Gíma, the last-mentioned being the only one that has not migrated, while Banóro and Géagéa now stand on the shores of Port Glasgow. In the next bay (Millport Harbour) are the villages of Tsaviríbo and Pedîri, which removed to the shore relatively recently. In the next bay – a broad and shallow one – the villages of Bórebo, Dágobo, and Unévi are situated; further west comes Dérebai itself, occupying the whole shore of a small bay. The Tselái, Wowuóro and Kurére villages lie in Amazon Bay. The first two came down from the hills, and the last-mentioned is a fairly recent Mailu colony, which came over in the

---

[6]I am indebted to Mr. Saville for much of the information on this subject.

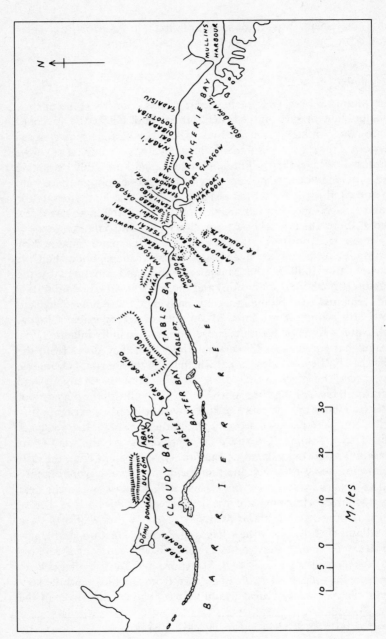

Map. 1 Map showing Mailu, or Toulon, Island and adjacent coast of Papua.

first years after the establishment of the white man's rule and security in the district.

In Amazon Bay, or, rather, opposite it, lie, as said above, the two flat coral islands (Laruóro and Loupóm) and the rocky island of Mailu (Toulon Island). Each of them harbours a village. Mailu is, as has been stated, the most important and largest village in the district. Besides Kurére, it has sent out the colony of Oraído or Bóru. It was the leading trading centre on the whole southern coast from Hulá'a to Suá'u, and it was also the village most dreaded by the mainland communities, with the majority of which it was constantly at war.

Going westward from Mogúbo Point (the western end of Amazon Bay) we come upon the village community of Magóri, who now live on the plain up the Baírebo River, some five miles from the beach. This community, which came down from the hills only a couple of years ago, forms a non-Mailu speaking village. There is another non-Mailu village, Deba, now on the seashore, which recently came from the hinterland.

Beyond these we meet with the villages of Daláva, Magaúbo, and Bóru or Oraído. The first-named is a colony from one of the Amazon Bay island villages, Laruóro. Oraído is a Mailu colony, and Magaúbo seems also to be one, dating from an earlier period. All these villages are said to speak exactly the same dialect as the Mailu proper. In Cloudy Bay there are a few villages, not far from the shore, which speak non-Mailu languages, but I was not able to ascertain their names. Between Cloudy Bay and Abá'u there are the villages of Duróm, Domára, and Dómu, all of which speak Mailu, and it is said, even the same dialectic variety as the Mailu villages.[5] These latter are also in very frequent communication with those villages of the extreme west, where they used to, and still, call on their westward expeditions (see chap. iv., sec. 4). I have not, however, been in this part of the district. Beyond these settlements begins the next ethnographic district, that of the Aróma natives.

The neighbours of the Mailu

As the Mailu – and especially the Mailu islanders – came under the influence of their neighbours, it seems advisable to say a few words about these, though I cannot give much information about the intercourse which takes place, or did take place in the past, between the mainland Mági and the tribes of the hinterland. There were a few things traded, such as some kinds of feather ornaments, bamboo, etc., which the inland tribes could easily obtain in exchange for the shell ornaments that were only accessible to people on, or near, the seashore; one or two Mailu dances also were said to come from the inland tribes. But on the whole the mutual influence does not seem to have been of great importance. I am not able to say anything about how far the sociology and material culture of the inland peoples resemble or differ from the Mailu.[6]

The western neighbours of the Mailu, the Aróma people, possess a similar type of village, the same style of houses, and the same system of clans with paternal descent. They are, as far as I am able to judge, very much akin to the Mailu, and they were apparently always on friendly terms with the Mailu villagers, who yearly visited Aróma on trading expeditions, importing shell ornaments and exporting pigs. The cultural influence could not have been very great, owing to the great similarity of the two peoples. The Aróma were the link uniting the Mailu with other Western Papuo-Melanesians and, in that way, their contact with, and influence upon, the Mailu was important. The Mailu use the drums of the Hood Bay type, and they have adopted a dance – the *bará* – originally coming from Kerepúnu in Hood Bay.

With their eastern neighbours, the Southern Massim, the Mailu were also in constant intercourse, and the influence of their culture upon the Mailu is more conspicuous, if only because of the fundamental difference between the two – the Mailu being Western Papuo-Melanesians, with definite communities, patrilineal clans, patrilocal marriage; and the Massim having their own different forms of social institutions and material culture, as well as many different beliefs and ideas. The influence of the Massim on the Mailu was both on the side of material culture and artistic production, but I could not trace any influence upon the social institutions of the tribe. Thus the tattoo of the Mailu women is identical with that found among the Southern Massim. Again, their technique and ornamentation in pottery is the same as that of their eastern neighbours. Some of their beliefs are parallel to those of the Massim, and they also dance a considerable number of dances originating from the east end. These similarities will be pointed out subsequently, when describing the different customs and institutions.

In order to make clear subsequent allusions to the various tribes, I shall give a brief outline of the anthropogeography of the Massim tribes of the Southern Coast.

The Western boundary runs, as we know, through the village of Gadaísiu, just at the centre of Orangerie Bay. The eastern half of the bay, the island of Bónabóna, at the entrance to Mullins Harbour, and the southern shores of that harbour are inhabited by people who are said to speak the same dialect. They are known by the generic names of Dahúni or Bónabóna. From the entrance of Mullins Harbour to Farm Bay live a people almost identical with the former, but said to speak a slightly different dialect. Their collective name seems to be Dau'úi. They have the same type of irregularly built village as the other Massim. Scattered over a large area, amid coconut palms and gardens, they are composed of what Dr. Seligman calls 'hamlets' – *i.e.,* small groups of houses; a number, sometimes twenty or more, of such hamlets compose a large village.[7]

These natives also build the same kind of house as the other Southern Massim, and the resemblance extends to the internal arrangements, household implements, decorations, etc.

The line of demarcation running through the western end of Farm Bay is, however, important, since it is the boundary of cannibalism on the south-eastern coast of New Guinea. The first village in Farm Bay, Saváia, was the first Southern Massim village in which anthropophagy was practised. I have inquired carefully into this matter on both sides of the dividing line, and a thorough agreement between a great number of independent informants leaves no doubt as to this anthropogeographical boundary. The natives of Farm Bay, of Suá'u Island, and of the mainland coast as far as the Bay of Modéva, speak the same dialect, and they can be called the Suá'u, by which name they would also be best known to other natives. The last Suá'u village to the east in Modéva Bay is called Núria.

The next groups of Southern Massim, also speaking a slightly different dialect, are the Rogéa and Sáriba peoples, inhabiting the two islands of that name and the extreme end of the southern coast. Their first village on the coast is called Guavíli. Another group is formed by the Milne Bay people, generically called Tavára, which is the native name of the bay. With these we arrive at the Southern Massim area, comprised in Prof. Seligman's description, to which the reader is referred.

---

[7] Comp. Seligman, *op. cit.*, chap. xxxiv., for a detailed description of the Southern Massim village system.

CHAPTER II

SOCIAL DIVISIONS

1 THE TRIBE

General remarks

The tribe, village community, clan, and household, or family, are the most important social divisions among the majority of native peoples, and consequently they must be described in connection with Mailu sociology. Among the natives of that district the village community, the clan, and the family are all extremely important units, and it would be impossible to give an account of the customs of the Mailu, or of their social life, without having drawn a clear outline of these social groupings. The 'tribe', on the other hand, is a term which could scarcely be used when dealing with the social institutions of one district. The Mailu people, as a whole, possess a distinct cultural unity, but they by no means form one great social group bound by ties of solidarity; thus the term 'tribe' may be applied to them to express the fact that they form one class in the ethnological sense, but not that they are a unit in the same sense. The formation of smaller groups within the 'tribe' – confederacies of several villages – is, and was in olden days, of a much greater social importance than the cultural uniformity of the whole district.

In this chapter I shall only give an outline of the social organization of the village community, clan, and household, and of the relations between the villages and village confederacies within the tribe. In order to understand thoroughly a form of social grouping it is necessary to see it in its active, functional aspect; to see how it acts as a unit in social life; what are the internal relations of its members, and what are its external relations with other groups. Such data will be supplied throughout all the chapters of this memoir in the detailed description of the different customs and institutions when the sociological aspect of the various customs, ceremonies, and beliefs are considered. But to be able to use the terms 'tribe', 'clan', 'village community', etc., it is necessary to give a preliminary definition of these terms.

The Mailu tribe and the relations between the different villages

As stated, the Mailu people as a whole have no social solidarity. Nevertheless, their linguistic unity, their local contiguity, and the identity of their material culture and social institutions make it necessary to treat them as a unit in this description. In the relations of village to village, however, the ethnographical unity does not find its sociological parallel. There were several groups of villages, which we may design by the name of 'village confederacies'. The villages of such confederacies maintained friendly relations between themselves, and were, broadly speaking, on terms of enmity with the others. Some of these confederacies were also on permanently good terms with villages outside the Mailu district. Thus the social and political unity of the Mailu tribe was divided not only by internal dissensions, but also by the adhesion of certain portions of the tribe to external centres.

In the foregoing chapter the various Mailu villages have been enumerated. I shall now briefly state how those villages are grouped into small confederacies, which constituted the most extensive tribal or political units of the Mailu.

The most important of such groups was the Mailu village itself, with its recent colonies: Oraído and Kurére. This group was undoubtedly the most powerful politically, the Mailu being the most populous village of the district, and possessing the greatest number of war canoes. It is also the most important economically, inasmuch as it is the seafaring and trading community of the whole district, and even of the whole south-eastern coast. The group was also in possession of certain industries (pottery and canoe-building) which were unknown to the other villages.

The scattered Mailu villages to the west of Amazon Bay – Daláva, Magaúbo, Duróm, Domára, and Dómu – formed, as far as my information goes, another group. These are, on the whole, practically identical with the Mailu group in all cultural respects, though they hardly did any trading to speak of, did not build the big canoes, and knew not pottery in olden days, except perhaps the Domára. Nowadays things have changed considerably, all the natives adopting industries and activities from which, by pure inertia of custom and possibly by other factors, they had been excluded in the past. The western villages were on friendly terms with the Mailu group.

The two villages on the coral islands in Amazon Bay, Loupóm and Laruóro, form a group apart. They were both living under identical conditions, and they were similar in their economic activities and sociological features. They were keen fishermen, but in olden days they did not do much sailing, nor had they any big canoes. They were on good terms with each other, but they were not permanently friendly with the Mailu. This was especially the case with the village of Laruóro, which was nearer to Mailu, and used to make war with the latter. Thus tradition says that some time ago the Laruóro attacked the Mailu successfully, killing some, and forcing others to take flight on the boats. The Mailu retaliated so thoroughly that they drove the whole village away, after killing many. The fugitives sailed as far as Gadaísiu, the frontier village of the Southern Massim. There part of them remained, forming the Mailu half of the settlement, and part returned to their island village.[7]

The villages of Wowuóro, Tsélai, and Dérebai, all of which are now on the coast, form another group. In olden days they were perched on the tops of hills round Amazon Bay. They were on permanent friendly relations with each other and with the village of Mailu.

The next group was formed of several villages, situated on the hills, towering above the three picturesque bays – Mayri Bay, Millport Harbour, and Port Glasgow. There was a long gap between Dérebai Hill, the place where the most eastern village of the foregoing group was situated, and Dágobo Hill, where the first village of this group lay in the olden days. The group consists of Dágobo, Unévi, Bórebo, Pedíri, Tsaviríbo, Géagéa, Banóro, and Gíma. All these villages were mutually friendly, though I was told that there was a closer bond of union between the first five and the last three respectively. All these villages used to be at war with the Mailu and with the Amazon Bay confederacy. They were linked with each other by several co-operative functions, as, for instance, by the common arrangements with regard to the annual feasts, which they gave in turn, and again by certain agricultural arrangements with regard to sago swamps.

The next group of villages comprised the communities living on the western shores of Orangerie Bay – Oibáda, Nabái, Ore, and Gogotsíba. They had certain cultural characteristics in common

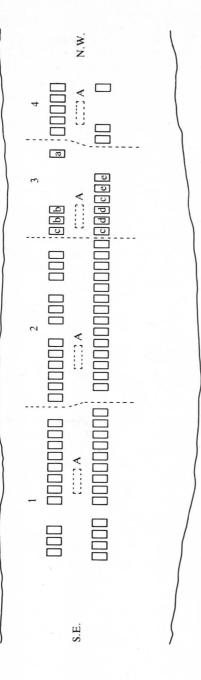

Coconut and banana plantations.

S.E.

N.W.

High-water mark.

Plan of Mailu village showing the division into clans[8]

1. Bodéabo.　2. Urumóga.　3. Máradúbu.　4. Moráu.

A, A, A, indicate the position of the *dúbus* (club-houses) of each clan. This is a reconstruction, as the *dúbus* no longer exist in Mailu village. Subdivisions of the Máradúbu clan: – a, Aritsadúbu; b, Barádúbu; c, Máradúbu; d, Dibodúbu; e, Mótsodúbu. The separation of one of the Máradúbu houses (a) from the others of the block is quite exceptional.

(burial customs, sorcery; see below), and they seemed to have been on terms of political friendship with each other, whereas they were dreaded, disliked, and fought by the other Mailu, though the latter villagers seem to have been on better terms with them than with their own immediate neighbours, the Bórebo, Pedíri, Géagéa, etc.

These groups, or confederacies, were, as said, political units on account of their mutually friendly relations and common foes. They were also to a certain, though limited, extent social units on account of the trace of co-operation between them.

As there was a close resemblance between villages of each group in their culture and customs, and possibly also in the dialectical variety of their speech,[8] those groups form ethnological subclasses. My studies have been, however, made nearly exclusively among one group, consisting of the villages of Mailu and Kurére, which in fact are identical, so that I am not able to do justice to the differences among the various groups, though I noted them in the few cases where, from being prominent, they were brought under my notice by my informants.

2   THE VILLAGE COMMUNITY

Type of Mailu village; its surroundings; village buildings

Perhaps the most important social division among the Mailu is that into village communities. These are the real political, economic, and sociological units of the Mailu tribe. The Mailu villages are of the Western Papuo-Melanesian type, consisting of one compact group of houses, as opposed to the scattered villages of the Southern Massim.[9] They are extremely regularly built, more so than the villages of the Sinaughólo, which can be considered representative of the Western

---

[8]As I have no knowledge of the Mailu language, I am unable to speak with any authority about linguistic matters, and I am here only repeating what I was told by Mr. Greenaway and by my native informants, none of whom was reliable on this point. I missed the opportunity of discussing the subject with Mr. Saville, who knows the language well and who has studied the problem scientifically (cf., his 'Grammar of the Mailu Language' in the *Journal of the Royal Anthropological Institute* Vol. 42, 1912).

[9]Prof. Seligman draws attention to this feature as one of the cultural differences between the Southern Massim and the Western Papuo-Melanesians; comp. *op. cit.* Introduction *passim*.

Papuo-Melanesians of the Central District. They were all built on land, the houses standing on piles.

All the villages with one exception – Gíma – are now built on the shore, and they all represent the same type (see p. 123 for plan of Mailu village). They consist of two parallel rows of houses, forming a street some 10 to 15 metres broad, and, usually, they are quite close to the beach. Thus in Mailu there is a belt of some 30 metres between the high-water mark and the houses. The same holds good with reference to Bórebo, Loupóm, Tsélai, Banóro, Géagéa, etc. (comp. pls. 1, 2, 3, 4). Some villages, however, like Kurére, are about 100 metres distant from high-water mark.

The fronts of the houses are always turned towards the street, so that the fronts of the two rows face each other, while their backs are turned to the sea and to the gardens (see pls. 3, 4 and 5, 6). There is again a space of 10 to 20 metres between the village and the gardens (see pl. 20).

I am unable to say for certain whether the same type of street, formed by two parallel rows of houses, was also typical of the mainland villages at the time when they were still on the tops of the hills, though I was told by the natives that this was the case, and that Gíma, the only remaining hill village, which I have not seen, is also built in the same manner.

The villages of the mainland east of Amazon Bay have all recently moved, and there are no extensive coconut groves near their present sites except near Bórebo, Banóro, and Géagéa, which were in olden days situated quite close to the shore and had their coconuts on the beach (see pl. 4). The villages on the islands and the older Mailu settlements in the west lie among coconut plantations. In Mailu village the palm trees overlook the houses on all sides (see pls. 1, 2, 3, 4, 5, 6). The street and the spaces on the beach and garden side are quite bare, all grass and weeds having been trampled down (see pls. 5, 6, 31). The beach is lumbered with canoes, the large *oró'u* forming in Mailu a fine decoration for the sea front (see pls. 3, 4, 18). On this side of the village the nets are spread for drying and the canoes to be overhauled are beached above high-water mark. All preparations for sailing and fishing take place also on this side.

The women occupy themselves either on the beach or on the garden side of the house, making pottery or doing household work. It may be said that as a rule the street is kept clear of human encumbrances, being reserved by étiquette for thoroughfare.

Dancing takes place in the street, as well as the ceremonial preparation of food (see pls. 11, 12, 29, 30, 31, 32, 33, 34).

Small children, dogs, and pigs are, of course, exempt from every rule in Papua, and they very often adorn the main street.

A village consisted in olden days of two kinds of buildings – the family houses and the men's club houses, or *dúbu*. Nowadays the latter class has almost completely died out in the Mailu district, though it still flourishes among their eastern neighbours, the Southern Massim. The houses and *dúbu* were differentiated by their position in the village. The former stand transversally, ranged in two rows, each house with its long axis perpendicular to the line of the street. The *dúbu* stood in the middle of the street, with their longitudinal axes coinciding with the median line of the street.[10]

The style of building of the houses and of the *dúbu* was positively stated to have been also different, though this information refers to the village of Mailu only.[11]

The difference in structure between the ordinary houses in Mailu village and a *dúbu* was that the latter was built in the Southern Massim style. That means that the ridge line of its roof was markedly concave, instead of forming a straight line sloping slightly downwards from front to rear. Again, the arrangement of piles which form the foundation structure is different in the case of the Mailu and in that of the Southern Massim. The Mailu house is described below, but I am not able to give a description of the Southern Massim style of building. The excellent picture of a Southern Massim house, given by Prof. Seligman (*op. cit.*, pl. liii.), will, however, be sufficient to show the difference referred to.

The tree houses, or tree platforms, described later (chap. iii., sec. 6) formed also another class of village buildings. These were only possible on the mainland, because there only existed trees high and strong enough for their support.

As temporary erections may be mentioned the ceremonial platforms made during the feast for the killing and distribution of pigs and for the *góvi* dance; the small huts and shelters usually erected near the houses, on the beach, where people go to sleep

---

[10]Comp. the plan of the Mailu village on page 123.

[11]The only *dúbu*, which is built in the characteristic position in the middle of the street, is that in Bórebo, figured on pl. 6. This *dúbu* is built exactly in the same style as all the other houses, and I was told in Bórebo that in the olden days the *dúbu* and houses were all built alike.

during the stifling hot nights at the end of the dry season; and similar structures in the gardens and on distant points of the sea beach, which were used when gardening or fishing (such a shelter may be seen on pl. 4).

Sometimes the large canoes are used as houses. The platform is covered with a roofing of nipa palm mats, and the shelter thus obtained is used as a dwelling-room. It is always so used whenever people go on distant and protracted visits (see pl. 3).

The sanitary arrangements near the villages are well regulated by custom, and carefully observed by both sexes. In the villages on the shore both sea and land are used for these purposes. In daytime, when people are not afraid to go a few hundred yards from the village, people utilize some thick patch of bush near the village, where a certain portion is always reserved for the women and another for the men. In Mailu those places are so sheltered by rocks and bushes that they are invisible either from the village or from any of the main approaches to it. Similar arrangements were said to exist in all villages. At night, when anybody would be too frightened to venture any distance from the houses, the sea is chosen.

The village community as social unit

As said at the beginning of this chapter, the village community is a most important social unit in the tribal life of the Mailu. As a matter of fact, the village community is a body of people living perpetually, and normally, in very close contact, to the exclusion of all others – at least under ordinary conditions, feasts, trading visits, etc., being the exceptions. They see each other constantly, they co-operate in many ways, they are all on permanently friendly, and fairly intimate, terms, though the bonds between clansmen and kinsmen and those of personal friendship were very prominent within the village, and were by no means merged in the broader and looser ties of village solidarity.

Strangers are not often to be seen in the villages, even at present, and in olden days they must have been quite exceptional.

The difference between such a closely-linked village community, bound by permanent local proximity and by constant contact, and a community, even such as that of the Southern Massim who live in scattered hamlets, is undoubtedly very prominent, and although I had but a short time in which to study the Southern Massim, the effect of this difference was apparent.

Thus the village community is the local unit of the Mailu. It is also the real political unit. Both in aggressive and defensive warfare fellow-villagers would, of course, always fight on the same side, and in raids the whole male population would very likely take part as a single unit, though the war canoes were separately allotted to the various clans and subclans. Again, in the economic sense, the village community was the joint owner of land as far as certain rights were concerned; it was also the joint owner of fishing rights, and, though the hunting rights were subdivided among the clans, it was the village, as a whole, that possessed the final economic benefit of those rights, as far as actual consumption of the goods is concerned. In the legal arrangements and institutions the village very often functioned as one body, as one 'legal person' (cf. the *tóna góra* arrangements, or the *nebúru* in the case of an influential man, chap. iii., sec. 5). Again, it was so in the giving of the feast, though the individuality of the clan then came strongly to the fore, especially in Mailu. The village as a body also played an important part.

Thus the village was the real πόλις of the Mailu man, and its limits formed the social horizon within which he moved.

3 THE *DÚBU* (CLAN AND SUBCLAN)

Description of clan, subclan, and their relation; the clubhouse

The village community is not an entirely homogenous social body. It is divided into clans and subclans. These subdivisions possess a distinctly local character; the houses of a clan always form one block in the village, and usually there is a certain distance between the different blocks. The houses of a clan lie on both sides of the street, so that at one end of the village there is one clan, then after one has passed its houses one enters the next, and so on. In other words, the village consists of a series of local subdivisions ranged in a row.[12] The native name for a clan is *aúra*, or *dúbu*. The first name is as a rule used with reference to the rather large clans of Mailu village, where the term *dúbu* is usually applied to the small subclans. On the mainland, where the clans are smaller than in Mailu, the term *dúbu* is universally applied to clan, subclan, and clubhouse, which last is the

---

[12]Cf. plan of Mailu village on p. 123.

original meaning of the word. Originally the word *aúra* means side, spot, direction – it has the same meaning as the Motuan word *káha*.

Each clan is, or more correctly was, connected with a house, or clubhouse of the men (*dúbu*), which stood in the middle of the street, between the houses of the clan. The style of this building has been outlined in the preceding section. No women or children were allowed to enter the *dúbu*, nor was it safe for a stranger to go there without an invitation. The young unmarried men, after 'initiation', used to sleep there, as also the widowed old men, and at times the married men made similar use of the *dúbu*.[13]

Thus the clan was a local unit with the *dúbu* as a symbol, so to say, of its individuality and independence, and it is not merely a figure of speech to say that the village was not a texture of *dúbu* (clans and subclans), but a juxtaposition of these. The clans were really fairly independent, and the forces of social cohesion in a village community which bound the different clans together were much weaker than those holding together the members of a clan. Thus, whenever there were emigration, colonization, or gregarious shifting of people it was either a clan (or clans), or else a subclan (or subclans) that moved. Thus, for instance, in the two migrations which took place from Mailu, it was the clan of Oraído that moved to settle in Table Bay. Again, when the village of Kurére was founded in Mailu, several subclans of Maradúbu and Moráu moved there, no men of Bodéabo or Urumóga joining them.

The clans of the Mailu are exogamous; they are also patrilocal and with paternal descent. In other words, the wife always comes from outside the clan; she joins her husband, moves to his home, and the children belong always to the same clan as their father.

There is, however, no tradition of a common male ancestor of the clan, and as genealogies are seldom remembered beyond the third generation back, it is, of course, impossible to ascertain how far the clansmen are really related by blood.

The number of clans varies, and so does their size. Historical events, such as a raid in which one particular clan suffered exceptionally, or such as the exodus to Kurére, for example, in which two clans furnished the majority of emigrants, easily account for the varying sizes of the clans and for their unequal number.

---

[13] All the details referring to the various uses and functions of the *dúbu* will be described below in their respective places.

There are four *aúra* in Mailu village, each having had its *dúbu*-house in the olden days.

The following names of clans and clubhouses, going from west to east, are enumerated:–

Clan name	*Dúbu* name
Moráu	Agiu'óro
Maradúbu	Omou'óro
Urumóga	Dariavára
Bodéabo	Goise'óro

To be added to these is the emigrated clan Oraído. The only clan name which seems to have a meaning is Bodéabo, *bodéa* being the name of the south-east trade wind and of the easterly direction in general. Curiously enough all the *dúbu* names have a geographical derivation, thus Agiu'óro is originally the name of a hill on Mailu Island; Omou'óro is the table-shaped hill at the back of Table Point; Dariavára is a rock near Oníbu Point; and again Goise'óro is a rock on the island of Mailu.

There are five clans in the village of Dérebai – Oraído, Boíladúbu, Góbu, Warátsa, and Abá'u. I failed to record the *dúbu* names.

In Bórebo village there are six clans – Tírihi, Abá'u, Wó'u, Warúbo, Atsána, Gadóbo. In this village there is one *dúbu* house still standing in the middle of the street, while the *dúbu* of all the other clans stand in line with the ordinary houses (see pl. 3).

There are four clans in the village of Banóro: Arúme, Oraído, Danó'a, and Bará'u; and two in Géagéa: Arítsa and Góbu.

In Loupóm there were two clans:–

Clan name	*Dúbu*-house name
Góbu	Lapilaóro
Boimará'i	Moguraóro

Here, again, the *dúbu* houses are named after some hills, *oro* (in Mailu) meaning hill.

There seems to be always a headman in each clan, or, more correctly speaking, perhaps, a man of greatest importance, whose opinion commands a certain amount of respect, and who would act as the authority and representative on all occasions in which the whole clan was concerned. The position of such a clan headman was, however, far from being clear and well defined, and I think that in reality there was no clan headman as such, but that he was only either the most important and influential among the headmen of the subclans, or else the headman of the most important and influential subclan.

Each clan is subdivided into subclans, which are also local – that is, the houses of each subclan form a separate group within the clan's block. The subclan is also to a certain degree an independent social unit. As mentioned before, they are the units of cohesion in all cases when a village community splits up. Again, each subclan has its headman, whose position, functions, and authority within the subclan is very well defined; much better, indeed, than is the case with the headman of the clan.

It is obvious that the subclan is also patrilocal and patrilineal. But though I have recorded a considerable number of genealogies, I was unable to ascertain the actual relationship, by blood, of the members of any of the subclans of Mailu village.

These were the clans and subclans of Mailu village:–

Clan	Subclan	Clan	Subclan
Moráu	Bumadúbu Maraoraído	Urumóga	Bánagadúbu Boíladúbu Díadúbu Gónidúbu Gáradúbu Bára'idúbu
Maradúbu	Maradúbu Díbodúbu Bará'udúbu Mótsodúbu Aritsadúbu	Bodéabo	Bodéadúbu Aritsadúbu Wáratsadúbu Bánidúbu

I believe there were no subdivisions of the small clans in the mainland villages.

In order to make clear the relation between the clans and subclans, it must be first remarked that the latter are always subdivisions of the former. The main difference between a clan and a subclan was, first, that a clan had an independent *dúbu*, whereas a subclan always had to share it with other subclans. Again, a clan would act as an independent unit in giving the big annual feast, *Madúna*; hence also it was called *Madúna dúbu*, in distinction to the other meanings of the word *dúbu* (i.e., subclan and clubhouse).

Sociological character of clan and subclan

As in the case of all other social groups, it is only the study of their respective functions which makes clear the relation between the clan and the subclan. Those functions will be described in detail further on, and I shall now only briefly enumerate them, so as to give the sociological contour of the two groups in question.

The social structure of the clan and subclan must be borne in mind: the subclan consists of a few houses, one of which is the 'chief's house', and the house of the *dúbu* headman.[9] The clan consists of a few subclans, of which again one is the most important, and its headman occupies the somewhat ill-defined position of the clan headman.

The subclan is, or was in the past, the joint owner of the large seafaring canoes, the headman being the owner *en titre*. Again, the large *gaúma* nets are owned jointly by the subclan.

The clan is, as often mentioned, the joint owner of the *dúbu* and the real giver of the annual *Madúna* feast. The master of the clan was also master of the *dúbu*. The feast was given by a clan as a whole, but the various headmen of the subclans acted in turn as masters of the *Madúna*. Thus at feasts the individuality of the subclans was not entirely merged in that of the clan.

In the mainland villages the clan was the most important social group in connection with land tenure, and the clan, as a whole, was the owner of the war canoes (*bobóre*). The unity of the clan was expressed in its being an exogamous group.

4 THE HOUSEHOLD AND THE FAMILY – KINSHIP

Household and family

The household and family are two very important units in the sociology of the Mailu. The distinction between the family and the household corresponds to that between family and what in comparative sociology is sometimes called 'greater family'. The term 'family' usually denotes merely a married couple and their children, such as are not independent. By 'greater family' is meant the group consisting of a married couple, all their children and grandchildren. The house, among the Mailu, is usually tenanted by as many generations as there are alive in the male line, and if there are several married, grown-up brothers they usually occupy the same house. Thus the 'household' – the group consisting of the occupants of a house – corresponds broadly to the 'greater family'.

I have made a genealogical census of the Mailu village, drawing genealogies of the inmates of each house. The results may be summed up as follows:– Every house is habited by people related by blood on the agnatic side and by women married to members of the family. The children always live with their parents. Nowadays they continue to live in the paternal house, the girls till marriage, the boys indefinitely. In olden days the boys moved to the *dúbu*, or clubhouse, after puberty, and remained there until their marriage. After marriage the man, in former times, lived in the same house with his parents, his wife joining him. This is also the present state of things. If there are several sons in the family, two or three would live in the paternal house, the others building a new home.

Thus, as stated above, three generations, comprising several families, may form a Mailu household. In a few cases only a house is occupied by a single family – a married couple and their children. Usually two or three, sometimes as many as four or five, families live in one house.

The ownership, or 'mastership', of a house is hereditary in the male line, the eldest male of the household being always regarded as its 'master' (*gubína*). Of course, this title does not confer any special economic privileges upon a man; in spite of which, however, the natives attach to it a certain importance, and are never in doubt as to who is the master of a house.

As the house is the scene of family life, this is the proper place to give its description.

Houses and house-building

The Mailu houses are built on piles on dry land. They comprise two compartments – an upper room, formed by the upper floor and by the oval-shaped thatch, and the lower verandah, roofed by the upper floor and open on all four sides (comp. figs. 2 and 3; also pl. 4, and pl. 8). The upper room is practically closed all round, there being no windows or doors, access being gained by a small opening in the floor, where one climbs up by a ladder (the opening and ladder have not been shown in the diagrams, figs. 2 and 3). The lower verandah is

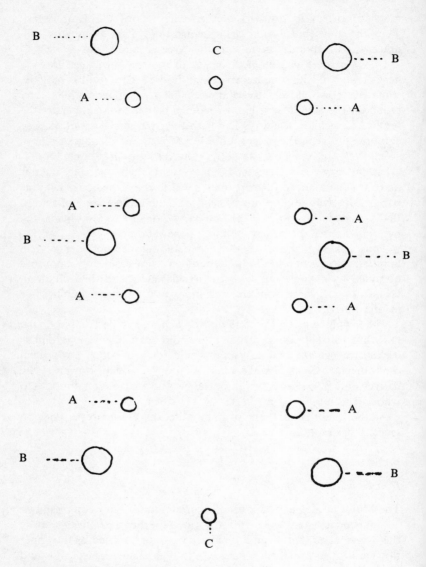

Fig. 1 Ground plan of house piles

A. Piles of the lower floor, or verandah (*dóu dogóta*).
B. Piles of the upper floor (main piles; *dogóta*).
C. Piles, supporting the roof.

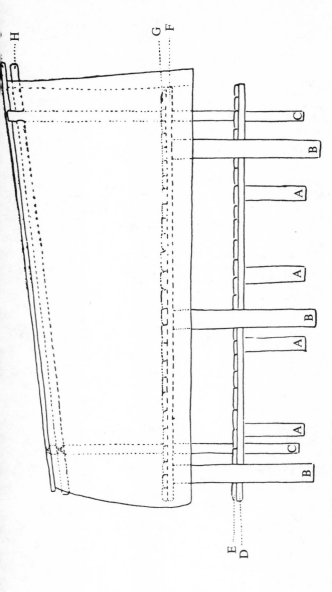

Fig. 2 Lateral elevation of the house

A. Piles of the lower floor or verandah (*dóu dogóta*).
B. Piles of the upper floor (main piles; *dogóta*).
C. Piles supporting the roof (*góragóra*).
D. Longitudinal poles, on which the lower floor rests (*dóu búisi*).
E. Lower floor (*dóu*).

F. Poles on which the upper floor rests (*otu*).
G. Upper floor.
H. Lower ridge-pole (*dagira*).
I. Upper ridge-pole (*oúre*).

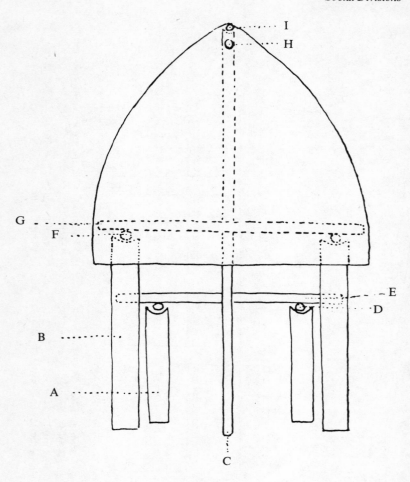

Fig. 3 Front elevation of house

A. Piles of lower floor, or verandah (*dóu dogóta*).
B. Piles of the upper floor (main piles; *dogóta*).
C. Piles, supporting the roof (*góragóra*).
D. Longitudinal poles, on which the lower floor rests (*dóu bútsi*).
E. Lower floor (*dóu*).
F. Poles, on which the upper floor rests (*otu*).
G. Upper floor.
H. Lower ridge-pole (*dagíra*).
I. Upper ridge-pole (*o'úre*).

overhung by the thatch, forming fairly long perpendicular eaves; it may also be sheltered on any side by portable screens, made of pandanus mats (*elaki*), plaited coconut leaves (*tsináu*), and reed mats (*eba*), the latter being the kind used for sails. (The verandah in the house on pl. 7 is partially screened with mats.)

Both the verandah and the upper room are used as general living places. The household members sleep, have their meals, cook the food, and do their work either in the lower or upper compartment – according to the weather. Of course, when engaged in work the people prefer to sit on the verandah because the upper compartment is dark; whereas they sleep usually in the upper room. But there is no sharp division of functions between the two parts of the Mailu house, both serving broadly the same purposes, according to circumstances.

From the point of view of construction, the house consists of three practically independent parts, each possessing its own foundations and each being scarcely connected in structure with the two others. The lower floor, or verandah, rests on eight to ten thick fairly short piles (about 1.5m. high); the upper floor rests on the six main piles of the building; the roof is supported by two wooden pillars, slenderer than the main piles and much higher (comp. figs. 1, 2, and 3). The order of construction is as follows:– First, the six main piles are sunk; then, before the upper floor, which rests on these six main piles, is laid, the lower platform or verandah is made, its size and position being determined by that of the six main piles (hence the reason for its subsequent construction). The men can now stand on the lower platform or verandah and carry out the construction of the upper floor. When this is finished the builders have a scaffolding ready for the making of the roof. Thus they are able to construct the whole house, which is a fairly high erection, without the necessity for making a special scaffolding of any description.

The preparatory work of supplying the material for construction (the posts, poles, and boards) was undoubtedly the most difficult part of the task, especially in olden days, when everything had to be done with stone implements. There is also a great difference between the material employed nowadays in the construction of the houses, and that used previously, the better tools now available enabling the native to obtain timber much superior to that which was previously used.

The six main piles had to be cut in the bush and brought to the village, as well as the two higher ones which support the roof, and the eight to ten short piles for the verandah. The preparation of the boards was still more laborious in olden days. A tree had to be cut down; a deep and fairly narrow longitudinal groove was then scooped out. After that the log was turned upside down so that the groove was now underneath, and another longitudinal groove, opposite the first one, was scooped out. Then, with the aid of three pairs of poles wedged into one of the clefts, the log is levered asunder. The tree trunk has now been split in halves, and the resulting two, fairly thick, logs were subsequently planed by thin broad adzes – the type most approaching the fine ceremonial blades.

A   B   C

Fig. 4 Showing the mode of preparing boards

A. The trunk in section; a deep longitudinal groove has been scooped out on one side.
B. A second groove has been cut on the opposite side.
C. The trunk split in two halves with three pairs of poles, wedged into one of the grooves. The two halves are subsequently planed with an adze.

Besides the piles and the boards a number of, more or less, thick poles is necessary in the construction of the house, and a sufficiency of sago leaves is collected to be used for making the thatch.

The piles and boards of the recently-made houses are made of the fairly hard *bedíla* tree. In olden days the much softer timber of the *dubúna* tree was used for boards, and the piles were made either of *móda* tree wood in the better houses or of coconut palm trunks in the inferior ones. The thinner poles and stakes are, and were, made of red mangrove. The preparatory work was by no means easy. On Mailu Island, where the natives had to fetch everything from the mainland, the preparations might (according to my native informants' estimate) take as much as two to three moons' time. Of course, this implies the native rate of working, which is not very fast.

After the material had been collected the natives proceed to the construction of the house. As mentioned, the first thing done is the

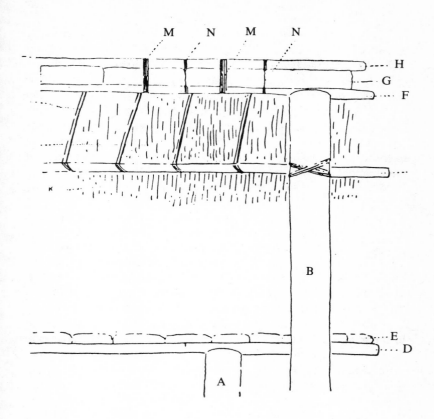

Fig. 5 View of a house in vertical section from within, showing construction of lower and upper floor

A. *Dóu dogóta* (verandah piles).
B. *Dogóta* (piles of upper floor).
D. *Dóu bútsi* (horizontal supports of the verandah planks).
E. Planks of the verandah or lower floor.
F. Poles on which the upper floor rests (*otu*).
G. Planks (*wawá'u*) of the upper floor, lashed to the *otu* and *abába*.
H. *Abába*, longitudinal pole, parallel to the *otu*.
M. and N show the mode of lashing the planks to the *otu*; at M holes have been drilled in the planks for the purpose of the lashing. N indicates an interstice between the planks, which has been used for passing the cane.

implantation of the six main piles (they are called *dogóta*) in deep
holes, about the depth of a man's height.[14]

The work of sinking the piles is done by many men, who help the
owner.[15] It is thus done quickly, the work being finished in about a
day. After that the lower platform, or verandah (*dóu*) is erected. The
eight or ten short piles (*dóu dogóta*) are sunk, but only to about half
the depth of the *dogóta*. On the slightly concave tops of the *dóu
dogóta* rest two long poles (*dóu bútsi*), running the whole length of the
house, and on those the boards (*dóu wawá'u*) are laid. Neither are the
dóu bútsi attached to the piles, nor are the boards secured in any way
to the *bútsi*. They simply rest one on top of the other. The boards of
the verandah are moreover much inferior to those of the upper floor.

Standing on this lower platform, the builders construct the upper
floor. This is done, of course, much more carefully, any insecurity or
unsteadiness in this part of the house being considerably more
dangerous a matter than in the case of the verandah.

The construction of the upper platform is, in principle, quite
identical with that of the lower one, the difference being that the
single joints are fastened together and not merely superimposed.
There are also two longitudinal poles resting on the concave tops of
the six main poles. And on these the boards are transversely placed
and firmly lashed. The two longitudinal poles (*otu*) are not fastened
to the main piles, but rest securely in the carefully cut concavities in
the top of the latter. The boards (*wawá'u*) are laid in close
juxtaposition and with their ends well trimmed, so that the upper
floor presents a regular rectangle, bounded on each side by regular
straight lines. The fastening of the boards to the *otu* is made by
means of another longitudinal pole (*abába*), thinner than the *otu*, laid
on top of the boards, parallel to the *otu*. Holes are drilled in the
boards and through them, as well as through the spaces between any
two boards, the *otu* and *abába* are lashed to each other with split
lawyer cane (fig. 5).

Thus the lower and upper platforms are ready. The native
architects proceed now to the construction of the roofing (see fig. 6).

---

[14] The Motu, in constructing their pile dwellings in the sea, sink piles by pointing them
at the lower end and driving them into the mud of the seabottom by a rotatory
motion. Two ropes are lashed to the top of the pile, so that the four ends radiate at
right angles in four directions. By pulling on these four ends the rotatory motion is
imparted.

[15] Comp. chap. iv., sec. 5.

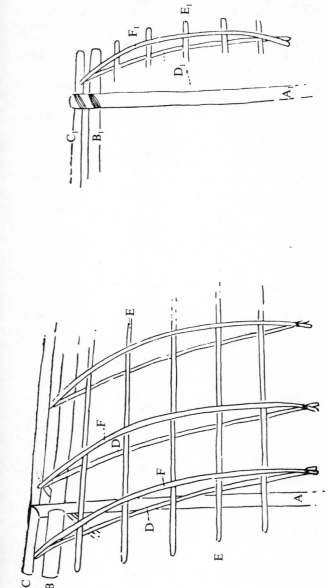

Fig. 6 Framework of the thatched roof

A, A₁. The two piles, which support the roof (*góragóra*). The front pile (A) is higher than the rear one (A₁).
B, B₁. Lower ridge pole (*dagira*).
C, C₁. Upper ridge pole (*o'úre*).

D, D₁. Ribs or rafters of the inner framework (*dáeló'u*).
E, E₁. *Dereána*, roof battens.
F, F₁. Outer rafters (*ló'u*).

Through two pairs of holes cut in both platforms the two roof-supporting poles (*góragóra*) are passed and sunk into the ground. Standing on the upper platform, the men can construct the framework of the thatching. In the loftier houses, however, it is necessary for a man to stand on a thick log of wood – about a metre high – in order to fix the two main ridge-poles of the roofing. The upper ridge-pole (*o'úre*) is much slenderer than the lower one (*dagíra*). Both poles are passed through the front pile and are lashed to the rear one (fig. 6). The front pile is as a rule higher, hence the sloping profile of the roof. The *dagíra* (lower and stouter ridge-pole) is passed through a hole cut in the front *góragóra*, the *o'úre* (upper ridge-pole) rests on a concavity in the top of the front pile. Both ridge-poles are very close to each other, some 10 to 20 cm. only, separating them. The two poles are, however, not fixed simultaneously. After the *dagíra* is put in, and before the *o'úre* is fixed, the inner frame of the roof is constructed.

This consists of a set of transversal ribs (technically rafters, *dáeló'u*) running from the *dagíra* down to a longitudinal pole, parallel to the *dagíra*, which is fastened to the main poles about a metre or so below the upper floor (this pole is also called *abába* – the general name for long, thin mangrove poles). The rafters lie close to each other, and I counted fifteen in a house of average size. On these rafters longitudinal poles (technically roof battens, *dereána*) are fixed, running, of course, parallel to the *dagíra* and *abába*. There were five *dereána* in the same house in which I found fifteen *dagíra*. This framework of rafters and roof battens, made of fairly thin, flexible poles of red mangrove, constituted the inner skeleton of the thatching. The *raison d'être* of this double frame for the roof is, as far as I am able to judge, to give an additional strength to the sago thatch, which has often to stand a considerable stress of wind. It is also this form of construction which enables the natives to give the Gothic arch profile to their houses. It would be impossible to fix the first (inner) set of rafters giving them the full curvature; indeed they are much less bent than the outer set of rafters (called *lóu*). These are attached on top between the *dagíra* and the *o'úre* (i.e., between the two ridge-poles), and to the *abába* below. Thus they start and end at the same points, as the inner rafters, passing on the outer side of these. Hence the greater curvature. The thatching (*ato*) made of sago palm leaves, folded half length and stitched together, is attached to the outer rafters. The men begin at the top, and for this work again require to stand on some elevation (usually a log of wood). Thus the slopes (*déri*) of the roof are made. The two gables (*babágu*) are made subsequently, the thatch being fixed to a framework of rafters and battens, the former radiating from the top of the gable, the latter being placed obliquely (as in the diagram). The rafters are attached at the top to the ridge-poles and at the bottom to a horizontal pole (*babágu ána*).

The front of the house (*itsári*) is, as mentioned, higher than the rear (*díni*). The front is also ornamented. Access to the house is usually gained through the front, on which side the facilities are much better.

In very small houses access to the lower platform (verandah) is gained directly by means of a sloping log, which serves as a ladder. In all the larger houses, however, there is an intermediary platform (*aúna dóu*), or there may be two, in which case the sloping log leads to the first and lower one. Such platforms rest on four piles (called *aúna dóu dogóta*), which are usually thick and not very well finished or deeply sunk. In some houses, though not in all, an oblique stake, serving as a ladder, is also placed at the rear of the platform.

The access to the upper compartment is gained from the verandah by a trap door (*urunóga*), an opening in the roof of the verandah or upper floor some two to three metres from the front, a ladder leading from the lower to the upper platform. The ladder (*orábo*) consists of a board with pear-shaped holes cut out.

The house decorations consist of carvings done on parts, of pendants hung along the eaves, especially on the front gable, and of pigs' jaws or fish tails bound to the front roof pile and to the front *babágu ana* (horizontal pole running along the thatch eave in the front). The carvings are done on the front end of the *o'úre* (top ridge-pole) which projects beyond the front gable, as well as on the ends of the *dereána* (longitudinal roof battens). The carving resembles, roughly, fish tails and snakes' heads, but the natives do not so identify them, saying that they have no meaning, and are only traditional designs. The outer sides of the six main piles are carved, the pattern consisting of several parallel rows of four-sided pyramids. The same 'crocodile skin' pattern is carved on the roof of the verandah (under aspect of the upper floor). In two or three houses in Mailu village, in one house in Kurére, and in one house in Dérebai there were large crocodiles carved at full length of some two to three metres in very deep bas-relief.

The pigs' jaws and other remains of feasts are perhaps the most characteristic decoration in all Western Papuo-Melanesian tribes.[10]

Kinship

In the house the members of the agnatic 'greater family' live in close contact. The parents are extremely fond of their children, nurse them carefully, fondle them and play with them. The communism in the supply and preparation of food and in the common meals, the communism in objects of daily use – all these contribute to the establishment of bonds of kinship between the members of the household – i.e., between the members of the agnatic or greater family. Brothers living together, or a paternal uncle and his nephews living in the same house were, as far as my observation goes, on much closer terms with each other than relatives of similar degrees living apart. This was evident whenever there was a question of borrowing things, of getting help, of accepting an obligation, or of assuming responsibilities for each other.

The paternal authority over the males soon becomes very weak, but I was not able to ascertain to what extent this was conditioned by the pre-European custom of sending the boys to live in the *dúbu*. The father's rights over the female children persist even after their marriage in the form of the gifts of pigs which he receives regularly, and which entail the obligation of returning them.

The bonds of kinship find at the same time a very strong expression and enhancement in the custom of *vevéni*, which entails an extensive communism in food.

The classificatory terms of kinship are very similar in their main features to those found among the Koíta by Dr. Seligman.[16] In the following table I have adopted the mode of presentation recommended by Dr. Rivers in the 'Notes and Queries'. The letters in parentheses are to be read:– m.s. = man speaking; w.s. = woman speaking.

Father = *abá'i*.
Mother = *adé'i*.
Son or daughter (m.s. and w.s.) = *oeva*.
Elder brother (m.s.) = *uíniégi*.
Elder brother (w.s.) = *uíniégi*.

---

[16] *Op. cit.*, pp. 66 and 67.

Elder sister (m.s.) – *uíniavétsa*.
Elder sister (w.s.) = *uíniavétsa*.
Father's brother (elder or younger) = *abá'i*.
Father's brother's wife = *adé'i*.
Father's elder brother's son = *uíniégi*.
Father's elder brother's daughter = *uíniavétsa*.
Younger brother (m.s. and w.s.) = *raú'égi* or *nábu*.
Younger sister (m.s. and w.s.) = *raú'avétsa* or *nábu*.
Father's younger brother's son = *raú'égi* or *nábu*.
Father's younger brother's daughter = *raú'avétsa* or *nábu*.
Father's sister (younger or elder) = *aíbo*.
Father's sister's husband = *aúe*.
Father's sister's son = *naî'égi*.
Father's sister's daughter = *naî'avétsa*.
Mother's sister = *adé'i*.
Mother's sister's husband = *abá'i*.
Mother's sister's son (elder) = *uíniégi*.
Mother's sister's daughter (elder) = *uíniavétsa*.
Father's father = *ová'i*.
Father's mother = *ová'i*.
Mother's father = *ová'i*.
Mother's mother = *ová'i*.
Mother's brother = *aúe*.
Mother's brother's wife = *aíbo*.
Brother's child (m.s. and w.s.) = *oeva*.
Husband's brother's child = *oeva*.
Wife's brother's child = *oeva*.
Sister's child = *oeva*.
Wife's sister's child = *oeva*.
Mother's younger brother's child = *nábu*.
Son's child (m.s. and w.s.) = *natáni*.
Daughter's child (m.s. and w.s.) = *natáni*.
Great grandfather (pat. and mat.; m.s. and w.s.) = *goína*.
Husband = *eme* ('my husband' = *inéme*).
Wife = *avétsa* ('my wife' = *inavétsa*).
Wife's father = *evai'égi*.
Wife's mother = *evai'avétsa*.
Husband's father = *evai'égi*.
Husband's mother = *evai'avétsa*.
Daughter's husband (m.s. and w.s.) = *botsía*.

Son's wife (m.s. and w.s.) = *táma*.
Wife's brother (elder or younger) = *naivágu*.
Wife's sister (elder) = *uíniavétsa*.
Wife's sister (younger) = *nábu* (not *raú'avétsa*).
Sister's husband (elder or younger) (m.s.) = *naivágu*; also sometimes called *goîna* (term applied to great grandfather).
Elder sister's husband (w.s.) = *uîniégi*.
Younger sister's husband (w.s.) = *nábu*.
Husband's brother (elder) = *uîniégi*.
Husband's brother (younger) = *nábu*.
Elder brother's wife = *uíniavétsa*.
Younger brother's wife = *nábu* (not *raú'avétsa*).
Husband's sister (elder and younger) = *naivágu*.
Elder and younger brother's wife (w.s.) = *naivágu*.
Wife's elder and younger sister's husband = *itsigoîna*.
Husband's elder and younger brother's wife = *múnigoîna*.
Son's wife's parents = *veáni*.
Daughter's husband's parents = *veáni*.

These are the classifactory terms of relationship of the Mailu.[11] It must be, however, noted that although the term for elder brother, *uîniégi*, for instance, comprises more people than we would design in our so-called descriptive system, it is by no means comprehensive of all the members of the village community, or even of the clan, which would, were it possible to trace their kinship, fall into the classificatory category of 'elder brothers'. In other words, if we should take the village community, or the clan, or even the subclan, and ask our informants (*ex hypothesi* a member of this group) to classify those men according to their relationship to him, he would be unable to do it. He would pick out a certain number of men and design them by appropriate kinship terms. Of the rest he would say that they are no relations of his. The 'classificatory' system of kinship does not classify the man's community nor his clan, nor even his subclan, according to their degree of relationship. Only such people as a man is actually able to place in his pedigree are designed by kinship terms. As the Mailu man is not able as a rule to trace his genealogy beyond his grandfather, the range of the classificatory terms is not very wide.

It is true that in addressing each other the natives use the terms of kinship within a much wider range, comprising practically the whole community and, *a fortiori*, the subclan and clan. Whoever is not addressed by one of these terms is spoken of as *gaîdi* – a word corresponding to the Mailu *turágu* and meaning 'intimate friend'. It must be noted, however, that the terms of relationship used in such a broad sense are really 'terms of address' merely. The difference between their strict use and their broad use as 'terms of address' is essential. In the first case they express an actual social relationship, which is rooted in the mode of living (membership of the household and of the subclan), in the economic relations (e.g., the *vevéni* custom, inheritance, forms of work, etc.), and in certain ceremonial duties and obligations (e.g., mourning). As terms of address, the classificatory terms of kinship are only the expression of a certain feeling of étiquette, which compels two people engaged in a friendly conversation to exaggerate the intimacy of their relationship and to consider the use of personal names as a disrespectful act.

Again, it must be emphasized that even within the narrower limits of their application – i.e., as far as they are traceable genealogically – the terms of kinship do not imply that the native's attitude of mind and his social relation to all the people designed by the same term is exactly identical. Both in the ideas and feelings of the natives, and in their customary regulations the 'own' brothers or parents occupy quite a different position to the cousins or uncles, although the former are designed by the same words as the latter. Thus, for instance, in the customs referring to mourning the 'own' brothers would be the more important of the chief mourners, and they have also the whole benefit of the native rules of inheritance. The expression used in Motu to design the actual relationship by blood, in opposition to the purely titular terms of address, and also to discriminate the 'own' brothers and sisters from the collateral ones, is:– *bóga* (belly) *támona* (one), meaning 'born of the same woman'. I was told by my own Mailu informants that exactly the same expression is used in Mailu: *tsînai* (belly) *omubúa* (one).

The general expression for kindred, corresponding to the Motuan word *váravára*, is in Mailu: *emegi* (men), *goîna* (great grandfather), which might perhaps be translated: 'people belonging to the ancestor'. The relatives by marriage are called *múnimúni* (marriage) *aúra* (side) *emegi* (men).

The real, or own, father is designed by the expression *abái* (father) *gubîna* (chief or master), which may be translated 'the chief or main father'. This expression would be used to answer or put a question: 'Who is this man? Is he your *real father*?' It would never be used as a term of address. The father's elder brother is spoken of and addressed as *uîniabá'i*; the younger one *raú'abá'i*. Those terms would be used only when stress is laid on the distinction, both in speaking of the father and uncles and in addressing them. If the father and one of the uncles were present the father would be addressed as *uníbá'i* or *raú'abá'i*, according to whether he was the elder or younger of the two.

A concrete example, illustrated by the following genealogy, will make it clearer:–

If Romári, Puána's father, and Bará'u, Romári's younger brother, were present, and Puána were to call out '*Inabái*, my father!' both would answer. If Puána wanted his father he would then specify his call, and say, '*Uíniabá'i*!' (and not '*Abái gubîna*'). But if he were asked by someone present, 'Who is that man?' he would say, if Romári was designed, '*Abái gubîna*'; if Bará'u was meant, he would say, '*Raú'abá'i*'.

I asked several of my informants who were a man's nearest kinsmen, and all agreed without hesitation that the man's own brothers (the sisters were not included) were his nearest – his real – relatives; speaking in Motu, they used the expressions: '*váravára gaubádabáda*; *váravára kórikóri*'. This view, held privately by individuals, is entirely in agreement with the 'customary or social view', as it might be called, embodied in the rules of inheritance and in the mourning customs.

Some of my informants, though not all, also said that the mother is the nearer relative of the child than the father, pointing out that the child is born of the mother. This view is also endorsed by some of the customs (e.g. mourning customs), though it stands in contrast with the fact that the man is undoubtedly at the head of the household.

Certain relatives cannot be addressed by their own names, and their names are taboo when they are not present. Thus the names of the father and of all his brothers are taboo (*góra*). The same is the case with the mother and her sisters. In general, the names of all the relatives of all the previous generations (grandfathers, uncles, aunts: *ovái, aîbo, aúe*) are *góra*. Nobody would address them with their personal names nor pronounce them in public. The same étiquette is applied also to the other members of the community who belong to generations older than that of the speaker. It was considered very discourteous to address such a person by his, or her, personal name. A classificatory term of relationship would be used in such cases. Again, if the man was a stranger, some term of respect was used. The Motuan, and generally Melanesian, word, *taúbáda* (great) is now used all along the coast as such a term of respect.

The brothers, sisters, children, and grandchildren were called, addressed, and spoken of by their personal names.

CHAPTER III
TRIBAL LIFE

1 DAILY LIFE

Division of daytime

The natives divide their day into several periods, determined, of course, and mostly named, by the position of the sun.

Morning is called *dába*;[17] the time at, and after, sunset, *valavítsa*; evening, *vagarútsa*; night, *gárugubáre*. The other periods are called after the respective position of the sun (*nína*, in Mailu).

Thus, to summarize all the names in their consecutive order:-

1. *Dába aioíetsa* or *dába kívonai* = early morning.
2. *Dába* = morning.
3. *Nína atsanaravaína* = time before mid-day.
4. *Nína atsá'i* = mid-day and early afternoon – that is, whilst the sun is high.
5. *Valavítsa* = late afternoon, about sundown.
6. *Vagarútsa* = evening, early part of the night.
7. *Gárugubáre* = deep night.

The *dába* and *valavítsa* times are the busy ones. The natives do not like to do any work during the hot hours of the day, and even during the feasts the mid-day hours are devoted to siesta. This is, of course, not a hard and fast rule.

Sleeping

There are no fixed times for going to sleep or for rising. As a rule, the natives go early to bed and are early risers. But when there is dancing or night fishing, or any other nocturnal occupation, they remain up till late into night.

---

[17] The same term as in Motu.

They sleep, during the cooler season, in the upper part of their house, under the sago palm thatch. During the change of the south-east trade wind into the monsoon (October to December) they spend the hot nights on the lower open platforms, and very often they sleep under small shelters erected near the houses. There are no bedsteads in their houses, only mats spread upon the floor. For pillows they use short, and rather thin, logs. I never saw any of the carved wooden pillows, as used on the north-eastern coast.

Toilet, dress, and cleanliness

They have, in general, no regular times for washing or making their 'toilet', but they bathe fairly often in the sea (coastal natives) or in creeks (inland Mági). They also wash with *dehoro*, fluid prepared by moistening scraped coconut and squeezing out the mess, which also plays a very important rôle in native cookery. The bathing in the sea or creeks seems to be generally due to the desire to get cool rather than to a craving for cleanliness. But undoubtedly they often bathe in order to cleanse themselves, as, for instance, when they remove the mourning or ceremonial dirt. Besides these occasions there is no ceremonial bathing, or no presumption of cleanliness on ceremonial grounds, but the natives generally rinse their hands and mouths with sweet, or salt water after every meal. As a rule, the natives are fairly clean, and they hardly ever shock the eye or the olfactory sense, except when they are obliged to keep dirty, as in the cases just mentioned.

They have, of course, a characteristic smell, but this is by no means strong or unpleasant. In the way of artificial scents they use several kinds of aromatic herbs, which they put in their armlets. The most popular of these has, to the European nose, a strong and decidedly offensive smell. Some of these herbs are cultivated by the natives in their gardens, and they are used indiscriminately by both sexes. The testes of the cuscus are also used as perfume, and are placed in armlets or necklets.

As mentioned above, they use the coconut to anoint themselves, and this gives to the natives one of the predominant, but by no means unpleasant, smells. They never use pigs' fat for anointing themselves, and indeed they seem to have a certain horror of getting greasy with this fat.

The care of the hair is one of the most important toilet activities with the natives, and squeezed coconut, which is smeared all over the body, is especially used as a shampoo.

In mourning the men shave their hair. Otherwise they let it grow until it forms the large, mop-like *chevelure* which is so characteristic of the Papuo-Melanesian.[12] This mop is left with its natural contour, except when they dress up for dancing, on which occasions it is bound and decorated in various ways. Individuals with wavy hair are exceptional, and I never saw in the Mailu district any person with the woolly, close-cropped hair characteristic of the Papuans. Nor is their hair ever plaited with mud or grease, as is done in some parts of the Territory.

To keep the hair in order they employ a comb, which they normally carry in their hair (except when in mourning), thus using it as a decoration. The comb (*pé'e*) consists of a piece of wood (from 15 in. to 30 in. long). It is split at one end into several teeth, which are kept apart by a string passed between them. Another piece of string tied round their base keeps them together. The other end of the comb serves as a handle, of which the most usual forms are a plain long one, in which case the comb is called *pé'e gági*; and a shorter carved form called *pé'e úru*.

There are other and more ornamental forms of handle (coming probably from the eastern culture area), having a long elastic handle-end and decorated with banana seeds[18] (*gúdu*) and pandanus leaf pendants, or with the handle covered with string. But these are very

Fig. 7   Native Comb With Plain Handle (*pé'e gági*)

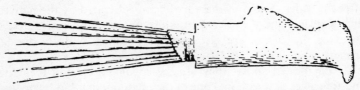

Fig. 8   *Pé'e úru:* another very common form of native comb, showing a characteristic motif in the shaping of the handle. ('Bird's head' motif imported from the Southern Massim?)

---

[18] Wild banana (*Musa ensete*).

seldom seen, and then only on festive occasions. The comb is put into the man's thick hair close to the temples, in a horizontal plane, the handle usually pointing forward or slightly to the side. The comb is so solidly fixed in the hair that it sometimes serves to support a considerable weight of feather ornaments during the violent exercise of native dancing. The feather ornaments worn by the men, as shown in pl. 9, are attached to combs.

Ordinarily the *pé'e* is used to comb the hair and keep it in order, though the men occasionally use it to scratch the scalp.

Depilation is done by pulling out the facial hair and by shaving the scalp. The pulling out is done by means of a small pumice stone (*imúta*; in Motu, *dahúru*); the hair, being gripped between its rough surface and the thumb, is pulled out by a jerk. Another way to perform the operation is by means of a fibre (*bóra*; in Motu, *répo*) of a garden plant.[19] A loop of this fibre held close to the hairy surface is

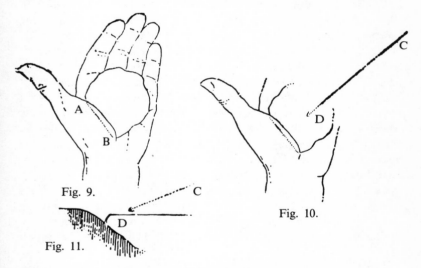

Fig. 9.

Fig. 10.

Fig. 11.

Showing method of making obsidian flakes
Fig. 9 The line A B indicates the position of the edge of the piece of obsidian, resting against the palm.
Fig. 10 The line C D shows the direction in which the striking-stone moves.
Fig. 11 Shows the obsidian core in section, with the trajectory (C D) of the striking-stone, which moves towards the edge D.

[19] The Motu of Hanuabada bring the *répo* from the gulf as one of the goods acquired in their annual trading expeditions (*híri*) to the west.

twirled round so that the hair gets tangled, and can then be jerked out. No hair on the body was removed by the Mailu.[20]

The shaving is done with thin, sharp obsidian (*nabúa*) flakes, obtained in the following way. A piece of obsidian is placed in the hollow of the left hand with an edge pressed against the palm, near the commencement of the wrist. This edge is struck with another stone in a plane perpendicular to it and at a rather sharp angle.

The obsidian splinters and yields, usually, several small, sharp, thin flakes. These are used as razors, and with them shaving is performed apparently with ease by the barber, and comfort to the person shaven. No equivalent for soap is used. Recently the introduction of bottles has greatly reduced the demand for obsidian, which has to be traded from the north-eastern coast.[21] Conservative experts, however, praise the superior sharpness and elasticity of the obsidian razor as compared with the best flaked bottle glass.

Women, when in mourning, shave their hair, but not otherwise. In that sex there is a greater variety in the methods of arranging the hair; for besides being left to grow as it will, in which case it forms the characteristic mop, it is plaited with mud and grease. Some women wear it plaited all over, when their head presents a kind of *caput Medusae* – a style called *urubatúna*. Others leave it alone on the front and top, plaiting only the occipital locks into curls, which hang down over the neck. This is, however, a fashion introduced from the Massim, and is called *dóio*. The plaiting into locks seems to be the correct way of treating women's hair when it grows long, and it is connected with the fact that the women do not wear a comb, nor have I ever seen a woman using one to comb her hair or to scratch her scalp. With the locks plaited the comb is, of course, unnecessary.

The natives do not use lime for discolouring their hair, nor are there any other methods of imparting to it an artificial hue.

The nails are clipped with a sharpened shell, or else are bitten off.[[13]]

The piercing of the septum of the nose is done with a sharp shell, though they sometimes use a broken ring of tortoise-shell, which, when made to grip the septum, acts like a spring and works its way through the soft cartilage by force of elasticity. This last-mentioned

---

[20] The body hair was not removed by the Motu, but the natives of Hulá'a, Kerepúna and Aróma, occupying the coast between the Motu and the Mailu, remove their pubic hair by means of pumice stone.

[21] See chap. iv., sec. 4.

method is used when the child is quite young.

The ear lobes are either perforated with a sharpened shell, or by the tortoise-shell ring method. In the latter case one ring is first fixed on the lobe, and when this has worked through more are added till the opening is fairly large. Should the lobe break they pare the two ends and join them.[14]

The operation of ear-piercing is performed on all individuals of both sexes without exception; the nose-piercing, however, is largely neglected. For neither practice was I able to find out any support in the native beliefs.

The hole in the nose septum is used for the insertion of the nose stick (*góvi*), made from the shell of the giant clam, and from other shells, and sometimes of tortoise-shell. This nose ornament (now nearly in disuse) was apparently worn on festive occasions only.

The perforated lobe of the ear (called *ope*) is decorated with split tortoise-shell rings, strung into the lobe one after the other, thus collectively forming a cylindrical body hanging beneath the ear conch. Sometimes these tortoise-shell rings are alternated with perforated discs of the red ground shell, well known as 'native money of the Pacific'. These are placed with their plane perpendicular to that of the tortoise-shell disc, so that they present their broad surfaces to the eye. Rather uncommon is a fairly large white shell-disc, with a serrated external border placed in the lobe.

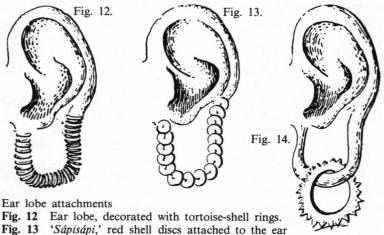

Fig. 12.   Fig. 13.

Fig. 14.

Ear lobe attachments

Fig. 12 Ear lobe, decorated with tortoise-shell rings.
Fig. 13 '*Sápisápi*,' red shell discs attached to the ear lobe by means of tortoise-shell rings.
Fig. 14 White, serrated shell disc, used as a decoration of the ear lobe.

All of these ornaments, the tortoise-shell rings (*gebóre*), the shell-discs (*agéva*), and the white, serrated disc (*Kúre*) are of local manufacture.

The teeth are sometimes artificially blackened to a jet black colour. To effect this they mix the decayed root of the *badila* tree with the green leaves of some other kind of tree. This mixture they apply to the teeth with a piece of bast, allowing it to remain overnight. The process is repeated from time to time.

All the women tattoo the face and the body in a pattern identical with that of the Massim, and undoubtedly borrowed from them. The tattoo is done by pricking the skin with a thorn of the sago palm or of the lawyer cane, and introducing by this means a substance made of charcoal and some other materials. The tattoo marks show deep blue on the brown skin. The design is done in a fixed order, as in the Motu tribe,[22] though apparently the order is not the same in the two tribes. The first tattoo, which takes place at the age of four or five, is done in the lower abdominal region and round the vulva. Then the left hand and forearm are worked over; after that the right hand. Both upper arms follow. Then, just before the swelling of the breasts, this part of the body is tattooed, and next in order comes the legs. The ornamenting of the face is connected with a small feast, in which women only participate. Taro is brought into the house and the girl sleeps on it. The next day the girl's face is tattooed, and in the afternoon the food is eaten. The shoulders of a woman are tattooed after marriage, and the faces and bodies of the men are never tattooed.

The dress and ornaments varied with the occasion. Broadly, one may distinguish three typical forms – the normal form of dressing, the mourning, and the festive, attire. In the case of a man the essential article of clothing, the perineal string or cloth, remains unaltered, the ornaments only being changed; these are removed during mourning and increased on festive occasions. The women have different kinds of grass petticoats for each of these occasions.

The man's perineal band consists either of a piece of native rope (called in this case *ivári*), or a piece of cloth (*lámoa*), beaten out of the inner bark of the paper mulberry tree. Both are worn in the same way, the cloth automatically rolling up into a rope-like shape. The string is passed round the body and between the legs, lying over and

---

[22] Cf. C. G. Seligman, *op. cit.*, p. 74.

between the testicles and displacing the penis to the left. The prepuce is extended and passed under the rope, the penis being thus kept in position. This arrangement of the genitals is called *bú'i*.

Nowadays the natives have practically abandoned their old form of dressing under the stress of missionary influence, and are clothed in European rags of often indescribable filthiness, so that one only sees the *bú'i* arrangement on old people or at feasts, when the natives revert to their ancient fashions. The man's dress is completed by a pair of armlets and the comb as described above. The armlets (*tsáriba*; in Motu, *gána*) were plaited with a kind of fern vine, which has a very fine brown colour in the finished article. The better class of armlets had on them designs interwoven with the golden-yellow cortex of an orchid (*gaíle*), the two most usual designs being in the one case a zigzag line (called *gaíle túri lóbo lóbo káo*), and in the other consisting of three or four lines parallel to the edge of the armlet (this is called *gaíle túri lauróro*). The armlets, the belt, and sometimes the perforated lobes of the ears are habitually used as receptacles for trade tobacco, plants, sticks, string, and other small articles. Whenever bulkier things have to be carried for a long distance both men and women use baskets.

The women wear 'grass' petticoats, and this dress is still universally in use, though it is sometimes supplemented by a singlet worn on the upper part of the body, or, exceptionally, by a ragged,

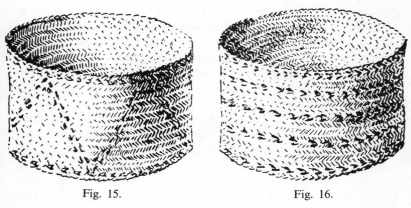

Fig. 15.   Fig. 16.

Native armlets
Fig. 15 Plaited and ornamented with yellow orchid straw in a zigzag line.
Fig. 16 Decorated with yellow orchid straw.

shapeless cloak put over everything. The so-called 'grass' petticoats are made of coconut palm leaves, which are cut into narrow strips with a small sharp shell. The narrower and finer the strips the better the quality and the more festive the garb. The very best examples are very supple, and have the flexibility of a fine fabric. After the leaf has been split into a number of strips it is inserted between two bands of the same kind of native bark (*varu*) as is used for making native rope. These form the top of the skirt. The bottom is cut into a straight line. Several of such petticoats are worn one over the other, and the greater the gala the more petticoats are used, so that a fully-dressed native girl invariably suggests the effect and associations of the crinoline. The women wear the same kind of armlets as the men.

Meals

There is only one substantial meal in the twenty-four hours. It is eaten in the afternoon, at sunset, in the *valavítsa* hours. What remains over is eaten next morning, but this does not constitute a substantial meal and is eaten cold. There is no meal at mid-day, except during the period of the change of the south-east trade wind into the north-west monsoon, when this is eaten. I was not able to find out the reason for this change of mealtime, but it was stated as a fact, and I was able to verify it by observation in December and January.

Nowadays a number of natives have served their terms as plantation boys, or have been in contact with the Mission, or served the white man in some other capacity, and the custom of eating substantially two or three times a day largely prevails over the old arrangement. I was, however, assured by all my informants that in the olden days a man would never eat much in the morning or think of eating before sunset.[23]

The inmates of each house eat their meal in common, sitting on the verandah. Relatives and friends from other houses are often present, and are invariably invited to partake of the meal. The men and women eat at the same time, sitting in one circle – the men in a group near the front of the house, the women on the women's side. The food is portioned out for everybody in a separate dish or basket (see below).

---

[23] This applies also to the Motu.

Although friends from the same village are not ashamed, or afraid, to eat with their hosts, strangers from another tribe would not partake of the food in the presence of others. Igua, a Motu of Elevála, who came as my 'boy' to Mailu, could never be induced to eat food given him by any of his numerous friends in the village. Whenever he happened to assist me at a native repast he took his share away to eat it in solitude at his own encampment. I was assured that this was the right thing to do, and that no native would ever eat publicly in a strange village;[15] if, however, there were several natives of one tribe in a strange place they would not be ashamed to eat in public.

In the olden days, when *dúbu* houses existed, strangers were entertained there, and there they got their food. The *dúbu* was also the eating-place of the bachelors and of such married and old men who chose to take their meals there. Their food was sent by their respective mothers or wives.

Vevéni custom

Besides supplying food for its inmates, every household is obliged to distribute a certain amount of food to other related families. The amount of food given away, and the number of households to whom it was presented, varies with the abundance of food cooked that day, but there is a certain minimum of people who must be thus treated every day. This custom is called *vevéni* (in Motu, *hierahía*), and as far as I have been able to ascertain it prevails among all the Papuo-Melanesians.

This *vevéni* food must, in the first place, be sent to the father's house, in the case in which the father and son do not live under one roof. Then come the 'own' (blood) brothers, and afterwards, when food is plentiful, the first paternal and maternal cousins and the uncle are presented with food. Of course, the same people return the presents to the donor in a corresponding degree of frequency and abundance. As a rule the natives, when asked to which houses they send the *vevéni*, give a definite number, which is usually some three to five, a fact which shows that normally there is a fixed number of people with whom the interchange of food takes place.[16] If food is scarce, and both his parents dead, he gives the *vevéni* to his elder and younger own brothers, and to his sister. If he has sufficient food he shares it with his half-brother and half-sister, of the same father but of different mothers. In cases of exceptional abundance he sends food to his paternal and maternal cousins (tribal brothers) in equal shares.

Food: raw materials and preparation

The animal food of the natives consists of game, such as pigs, wallabies, kangaroos, rats, bandicoots, cuscus, and various birds, and of fishes and shellfish. The inland Mági had a better supply of land game and the Toulon islanders had a greater abundance of fish, but all the villagers are both hunters and fishermen. Moreover, fish seems to be a much more easily and regularly accessible form of food for those natives who live near the sea than game is for the inland natives. Pork is derived from two sources – the wild boar, which is hunted, and the pigs that are bred in the village. The village pigs, which are more valued, are killed only on the occasions of important feasts.

Vegetable food is undoubtedly far more important in native households than animal food. In the Mailu district, as in all wet regions of Papua, the predominant vegetable food consists of bananas and taro, bananas occupying the first place. Of these there are very many kinds indigenous to the country, and now there are, besides, several introduced sorts. There are four kinds of indigenous taro and four kinds of yams. There is another tuber, called in Motu *taítu*, of which there are several varieties. Sago grows in many places, and every village possesses its sago swamp and coconut plantation. Nowadays the introduced sweet potatoes and pawpaw constitute extremely important items in native housekeeping.

The bananas are eaten ripe as a fruit, but their chief culinary use is to be eaten as vegetables, for which purpose they are used in the green, unripe state. They are not peeled, but only cleaned and their ends cut off. The taro is cleaned, scraped, and, when it is very bulky, chopped into large chunks. The same applies to the yam and *taítu* roots, and to the sweet potato – a recent introduction to Papuan soil. The pawpaw is also used green, as a vegetable. The scraping of the taro, yam, and *taítu* is done with a *Cypraea tigris* shell (*gúna*) cut in half and sharpened. Taro and yams are chopped into pieces with a pearl shell (*Meleagrina* sp.; in Mailu, *oráva*) sharpened into a fine blade. The scraping of bananas is also performed with a shell, of which two kinds are used, one very small and called *ku'i'i*, and the other slightly larger and called *nika'i'i*; both are of the same shape.

A

Fig. 17.

Fig. 18.

Vegetable and fruit scrapers

Fig. 17 *Gúna*, a vegetable scraper, made of the top half of a *Cypraea* shell, sharpened into a blade at the end A.

Fig. 18 A small, naturally sharp-edged, bivalve shell, used as scraper; called *ku'i'i* (smaller species) and *níka'i'i* (larger species).

Cooking and dishing-up

If the food is boiled, both vegetable and animal foods are cooked in the same pot. There are three methods of cooking used by the Mailu natives: boiling, roasting, and baking with hot stones.

Boiling (*dáridári*; in Motu, *nadúa*) is done in one of the large earthenware pots, which are manufactured on Toulon Island and in its direct colonies (Domára, Oraîdo, and Kurére). Leaves, usually those of the banana, are put at the bottom of the pot, the food is placed on top of them, and is again covered with leaves. Some water is poured in, but not in sufficient quantity to swamp the whole contents of the pot, so that the process is rather one of steaming than of boiling. The result is generally very palatable, though not equally appetising at all times.

The process of boiling does not require more than about one hour at the outside. It is done on the verandah if there is no wind, or in the room, when there is too much breeze. The pot is supported by three stones of regular shape and equal size, the sticks of firewood being inserted radially into the spaces between the stones. Sometimes old damaged pots are used as supports instead of the stones.

After the food has been boiled the solid substance is distributed into wooden platters or baskets. There are two kinds of the former,

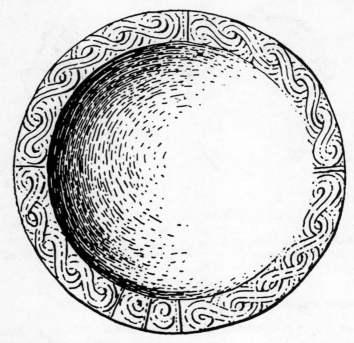

Fig. 19 Wooden dish (*gaéba*)

one circular and flat, with a scroll ornament on the upper border; this
is called *gaéba*, and is manufactured in the Massim area. The best
specimens, however, come from the Trobriands and Woodlark
Island, and they are also manufactured by the Southern Massim. The
other form of wooden platter, called in Mailu *abóma*, is oblong, and
may be described as boat-shaped. They are sometimes manufactured
locally, but their real home seems to be Hood Bay, where they are
made by the Kerepúna. They are also used by the Motu of
Hanuabada, who, however, do not themselves make them, but trade
them from the Hood Bay natives. Their Motu name is *Dihu*.[24] (See
pl. 11 and 12, where *abómas* of an exceptionally large size are shown.)

The baskets, called *no'obóea*, used at times for dishing-up solid
food, are rather roughly made of plaited coconut palm leaf.

[24] The circular wooden dishes do not reach as far as Hanuabada, where their
place is taken by the round earthenware plates called *kíbo*, or, if larger, *ná'u*,
which are manufactured locally.

Fig. 20 Oblong wooden dish (*abóma*)

The solid food is eaten with the fingers, or, if it is hot or bulky, with one-pronged forks, made either of wood or of a pointed wallaby bone.[25]

The liquid obtained by boiling, called *ríu* (in Motu, *vasiáhu*), is ladled out of the pot by means of the *bío*. This is the half of a coconut shell, with all the soft material removed from both the outside and inside, and sometimes with the brim serrated by way of ornamentation. There is also a slight prominence on one part of the rim, which serves as a rudimentary handle.

In the second form of cooking (called *gábu gábu*; in Motu, *gábua*) the food is roasted over the fire or placed in hot ashes.

The third method in use among the Mailu is baking by means of heated stones (called *ponúa*; in Motu, *amúdo*). In this a layer of stones (not heated) is first put on the bottom of a hole dug in the ground, and on these some heated stones, on which the food to be baked is placed; then on the top of the food more hot stones, and finally a layer of banana leaves.

It is to be noted that the three processes are by no means used indiscriminately, or side by side. Wherever and whenever the pot and

Fig. 21 Halved coconut shell, *bio*, used as a spoon.

[25] I did not make a note of the Mailu names for forks. In Motu the bone fork is called *díniga* and the wooden one *nébo*.

other requisites are available boiling is much preferred by the natives. Soup (*ríu*) is very highly appreciated, and boiled food is considered altogether superior. The method of baking between stones is said to have been practised formerly (before the white man's influence) by all, or nearly all, the inland Mági, especially by those on hostile terms with the Mailu islanders, who had the monopoly in pot-making. Nowadays, friendly relations and trading having been established between all the Mági-speaking people, boiling is the only method of cooking in use, except under special circumstances. Baking or roasting is resorted to in cases of emergency on hunting expeditions, or when on marches, etc., water is not available. There is also a series of taboos which, in certain cases, forbid the use of boiled food and only permit of roasted or baked nourishment.

Sago dishes and coconut cream

Although the native food presents a considerable variety, owing to the number of available plants, they have no different dishes, in our culinary sense of the word, and the food stuff retains its name after it has been cooked. The only exception to this culinary sameness is the sago, which can be prepared in several ways, thus yielding different dishes called by different names. The sago (*odei*; in Motu, *rúbia*) emerges from the manufacturing process as a dirty white mass of farinaceous nature, wrapped in leaves and tied up into long, sausage-like parcels about sixty inches in length and ten inches in diameter. This mass is sometimes eaten raw, but more usually it is prepared and cooked. If the finely crumbled material is boiled into a porridge with green coconut milk and brine it is called *patsíra*. In Motu, sago porridge is called *iára*, and is usually boiled in wallaby or fish broth. Slightly larger pieces of sago, similarly boiled in coconut milk and brine, are called *góda* (in Motu, *bákibáki*). Still larger sago dumplings are called *bína veláru* (in Motu, *mánemáne*, but the Motu do not use salt water in boiling sago); and meat patties made of sago are called *ubúbu*. To make these a taro or banana leaf is taken, some sago is put upon it, then a piece of fish or meat, this being again covered with sago, and the whole, wrapped in the leaf, is boiled. *Gúmi* is a dish prepared of scraped coconut and pounded sago, mixed together and kneaded into balls or sausages, which are boiled. Sometimes sago, wrapped in a taro or banana leaf, is simply baked in the open fire, in which case it is called *bómu*. Another kind of sago dish is called *néva*;

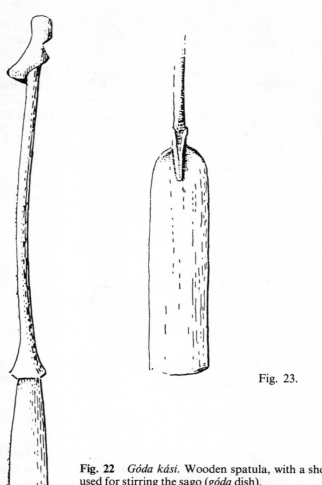

Fig. 23.

Fig. 22 *Góda kási.* Wooden spatula, with a short handle, used for stirring the sago (*góda* dish).
Fig. 23 *Patsíri kátsi*, wooden spatula, with long handle, used to stir the sago porridge (*patsiri*). Blade length, 25 cm. Total length, 120 cm. There are longer specimens in use (see. pl. 12).

Fig. 22.

two small parcels of sago, wrapped in banana leaf are made, and a large flat stone is heated in the fire. Then the sago parcels are put on either side of the stone, and the whole is wrapped up in a big banana leaf and left until the sago is cooked.[26] The cooking of sago in the methods first-mentioned is done in the ordinary clay pots, and in contrast with the boiling or steaming of the vegetables, which needs no stirring, the sago boiling requires the constant use of a spoon. For this purpose large wooden spoons, or, rather, flat spatulas, are used. Some of these are provided with very long handles, thus permitting the stirring well away from the fire (see figs. 22 and 23, and pl. 12).

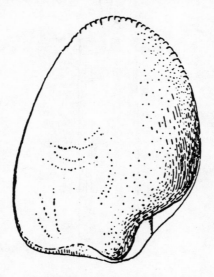

Fig. 24   Coconut scraper, *Kaikóa*, a shell serrated at the end. It is used as a coconut scraper.

Perhaps the most important seasoning and culinary ingredient in Mailu cooking, as well as in that of all the other coastal natives, is the coconut cream, *góro góro* (in Motu, *dehóro*). It is the only regular source of fat in the native's diet, and it renders his food both nourishing and palatable. To obtain it a ripe coconut is broken and the interior scraped with a piece of shell, which is usually cut into an oval shape and serrated on one side (see fig. 24). This instrument is

---

[26] The Motu prepare sago by boiling it with ripe bananas and call it *púrirári*. Small dumplings of ripe banana and sago (*dia*), wrapped in banana leaves, are boiled in water and eaten with *kétara*, which is boiled coconut cream (*dehóro*). Sago porridge boiled in *dehóro* is named *iára*, as just mentioned.

named *kaikóa*.[27] The scrapings are soaked with water and squeezed, or they are sometimes strained through a basket, especially when the coconut cream is manufactured on a large scale on festive occasions (see pl. 11), and is eaten as a sauce practically with all the solid food, except when the coconut taboo has to be observed (see sec. 5 of this chapter). Sometimes, as mentioned above, the food is boiled with *dehóro*.

The jungle supplies the natives with a certain amount of fruit, such as native mangos, mangosteens, a fruit called *gaméla*, and several others, the names of which I did not record, that are eaten raw.

Narcotics

As narcotics the natives use tobacco and areca nut. A native tobacco was used before the advent of the white man, but nowadays twisted trade tobacco – called universally in Papua *kúku* – is exclusively smoked, at any rate by the coastal natives. They use the often-described method of smoking through a bamboo pipe (*báubáu*), which is provided with a small hole to hold a cigarette. The tobacco, which is cut and kneaded, is rolled into cigarette form in a leaf, of which there are several kinds, called *ná'pera*. The cigarette is inserted in the hole, and by inhaling at the mouth end the *báubáu* is filled with smoke. The smoker then removes the cigarette and draws in the smoke through the hole in which this has been inserted.

As a rule one person – usually a young boy, and in any case the youngest member of the gathering – performs the function of filling the tube with smoke and of handing it round. Smoking is a social business, and whenever there is a gathering of any kind a *báubáu* is essential. There are at present scarcely any of the richly ornamented bamboo pipes in Mailu, as they belong to other parts of the territory. I was informed that the Mailu know how to ornament the *báubáu*, but evidently they are either only poor experts in the art or else they do not care very much for it, as I do not remember seeing a single carved or burned *báubáu* in Mailu, though they are plentiful in some other villages.

A social function analogous to that played by tobacco smoking is

---

[27] Besides the serrated pearl shell, other shells are used as inferior implements, notably a large *Venus*, called *eíra*. Nowadays natives often use large and complicated scrapers supplied by the white man's trade.

that of betel chewing. The ingredients here are: The areca nut (*wéni*; in Motu, *búatau*), the wood and bark of betel pepper (in Motu, *pópo*), some leaves (betel leaves?), and lime. The latter is carried about in the lime gourds which form one of the most characteristic accessories of a New Guinea native. The lime is used by stirring it up with, usually, a spatula – a kind of wooden knife – or sometimes with a pointed bone, from which the lime is licked off. Mailu natives, however, do not manufacture either the gourds or spatulas with any really artistic execution, though they possess some of the well-known ebony carvings of the Northern Massim which are used as spatulas. Not only are the spatulas manufactured in the locality poor and without characteristic features, but the Mailu, in contrast to their neighbours, the Massim of Bónabóna and Suá'u, do not really care for the finer specimens. These two groups, though as a rule unable to produce the fine carvings of the Trobriand islanders, import and value them, and are very loath to part with them.

2 VILLAGE LIFE

The seasons and their influence upon the social life of the natives

The village life varies with the seasons. There is a season for dancing and feasting; much thought is then given to these activities, and on their advent the whole character of the village changes. There are times when there is much fishing and times when hardly a native takes out a net, though women go out by night and search the reef with torches for *frutti di mare*. The trading expeditions are carried out at fixed times in the year, and the gardening activities are, of course, periodical, and regulated by the seasons. Thus it is necessary to give an outline of a native's year and the way in which it is divided. The special activities (feasts, economic activities, dancing) will be treated in subsequent chapters; in this section I shall speak of what may be called the normal village life, that is of the aspect of the village, as it is when there is nothing special going on.

Seasons; native division of the year

The Papuan year is naturally divided into two halves; the time when the south-east trade wind is blowing (May till November), and the summer, during which the north-west monsoon is prevalent (January till March), there being about a month's interval, during which the wind changes and there is very little breeze. The trade wind blows steadily, commencing every day before noon, reaching its climax at about four in the afternoon, and dying away at night. Any other wind at that season is exceptional, there being even very little land breeze at night. The monsoon does not blow steadily, but it occasionally comes down in violent gusts (called *guba* in Motu). There blows sometimes the southerly wind during the north-western season, and, as a rule, the land breeze is fairly strong at night.

All the coastal natives naturally regulate their social life with reference to this seasonal bipartition and divide the year into two halves, *viz.*, in Mailu, *bodéa*; in Motu, *laurabáda* (the south-east trade season); and, correspondingly, *avára* and *lahára* (north-west monsoon time, or summer). Besides these main divisions the Mailu natives have further subdivisions, distinguishing several seasons or times (*wána*) in the year. These are named after natural phenomena. The names of the two main divisions are also derived from the same source: *bodéa* meaning, in the first place, the south-east trade wind, from which both the south-eastern direction and the winter season have been named. *Avára* was originally the name of the north-west monsoon, and also means the north-western direction and north-western season. As wind names the two words are substantives; in direction and season naming they are used in an adjectival form: *bodéa aúra* meaning the south-eastern side or direction, *bodéa wána* the south-eastern season, *avára aúra* the north-western side or direction, and *avára wána* the north-west monsoon season.[28]

The Mailu seasons are not related to the changes of the moons, though some of my informants designated them as moons (*dovére*). This seems, however, to be due to the influence of the Motu language, which I used in talking with the Mailu natives, the Motuans having names for the thirteen moons (lunar months).[29]

The proper word to designate the Mailu year divisions is *wána*

---

[28] It is the same in the Motuan language. The substantives *laurabáda* and *lahára* mean the south-east trades and the north-west monsoon respectively; adjectively, the words are used in *laurabáda káha*, the south-eastern side or direction, and *lahára káha*, the north-western direction. Also *laurabáda* or *lahára néganai*, the south-eastern or north-western season; literally, in the time of the *laurabáda* or *lahára*.

[29] The Motu divide their year into 13 moons, the beginning of the year being somewhere in January. It is determined by the position of Pleiades, so that the first moon usually falls into its right place in the astral year.

(time, season), and not *dovére* (moon). These divisions are only loosely defined, being determined by winds, flowering of certain plants, and by other phenomena which, though regularly occurring, lack the precision of astronomical phenomena.

The Mailu natives seem to place the beginning of the year somewhere about the end of December and the beginning of January, at least they usually start the enumeration of their seasons with that time, which is the period when the first gusts of the monsoon set in.[30] The season is named after the wind *avára kíwanai*, which means 'small *avára*'. At that period there is little or no day fishing, but at night the reef is searched with torches. Some sailing and trading is done, the land breeze at night being favourable to voyages in any direction along the coast. If the big annual feast is belated it may fall within this period, in which case there is much trading and sailing done during the small *avára*. In any case, the natives sail at this season westwards to Léa to get sago and to Magaúbo (Table Point), where they get the *akai*, a small kind of areca nut. They come back home easily with the strong monsoon.[31] This season corresponds to our months of January and February.

After *avára kíwanai* comes the *avára agóda*, or big *avára*, so named after the force of the monsoon. This is also the real wet season, during which there is not much sailing or fishing, and the festivities as a rule are over. It comprises, roughly, the second half of March and April, and towards the end of it the gardens are being planted.

The next season is called *tsilówo*. It is subdivided into: *t. gogótsa*, which means the point, the front, or the beginning of *tsilówo*; *t.*

---

[30] This coincidence between our, European, beginning of the year and what I am calling here 'the native beginning' is hardly due to the influence of missionaries or of other white men. In the mind of the native there is good reason for calling this time the beginning of the year, for this is the time when they commence making new gardens – the most important activity among the majority of the inland tribes, who are agriculturists. Again, on the sea, this time marks the beginning of the monsoon; the shorter, but more interesting period. All along the coast this is also the period when important sailings take place. Thus among the Motu the *híri*, or great expedition to the gulf, returns with sago; the Hulá'a make their *híri* to Hanuabada and the Mailu make their departure for Aroma. Again, at that time the big feast is either over (Southern Massim, Mailu mainland) or (exceptionally, as in Mailu village) it is in immediate approach. This change of seasons (December-January) is decidedly much more likely to appeal to the natives' imagination than the other one (April-May).

[31] See Chaps. iv. and v., where native trading and its connection with native festivals are described.

ogóda, the big, or full, *tsilówo*; and *t. lóbo*, or the breaking up of the *tsilówo* season. This period is named after the high, rank *lalang* grass which covers the slopes of the hill on Toulon Island and many patches in the jungle of the district. The grass flowers at about this time (May and later). The beginning of the *tsilówo* season is marked by the appearance of the flowers; then these ripen into fruit and disperse their fluffy seeds, which marks the end of the season. On the mainland the natives are engaged with their gardens, and the Mailu islanders begin their fishing. They go to Magaúbo (Table Point) to catch the *ume* fish, which they smoke. During this season the monsoon subsides, there is a time of calm, and the south-east trade wind begins. The same season is also called after the phenomenon of the drying of the reef (*lagáru wúra* = dry reef). Another characteristic name for this season is *borówo bóuai*, which means blowing the petticoats awry, in reference to the effect of the first strong gales of the south-eastern breeze. The *borówo bóuai* overlaps the *tsilówo lóbo* – the breaking up of the *tsilówo* season, which occurs about the middle of July. After this comes the *viníu* season, named after a tree which sheds its leaves in the middle of winter (July, August). The next season (September) is called *bátu*. This is the name of the characteristic buds of the *viníu* leaves which begin to appear about a month after the tree has shed its leaves. The whole of this season is also called sometimes by the name of *aurári*. This would cover our months of July (second half), August, and September.

The spring is named after the *lióro* tree, which is flowering and fruiting at this time (October till December). This season is divided into *l. gogótsa*, the beginning of the *lióro*, and *l. ogóda*, the full, or big *lióro*. This is perhaps the most pleasant season, there being no rain or squalls, while the weather is cool, owing to the continuance of the south-east wind. It is the best time for sailing, as the prevailing wind will easily carry westward, and the return journey may be made with the land breeze, or with one of the first blows of the monsoon. It is the time for dancing and preparing for the big annual feast, and consequently it is also the time for love-making. Very often the big feast is held during the *lióro* , as well as all the preparatory sailing and trading. The natives consider the *lióro* as the pleasantest and most important time of the year, and the word for year is *lióro*. The last part of the *lióro* is named *obu*, after the fruit of the *lióro* tree, and it is just at the time when this fruit begins to turn brown and ripe that the *avára* (north-west monsoon) begins to blow.

Normal life in the village

As mentioned above, the villagers are busiest in the morning and late afternoon. The mid-day hours are spent in a siesta, unless work is pressing; then, as a rule, the village looks dead and deserted. Some exceptionally industrious women – and usually you see the same over and over again – will sit the whole day long on the sand under the house making pots. Or some men will finish making arm-shells, so as to have something to trade with. Again during the *lióro* and *avára* seasons, when there is much sailing done, the whole male population, at times, leaves Mailu village, and such villages as Kurére and Loupóm, where there are many canoes. The women and children follow the men in great numbers, so that the village is practically deserted. This is undoubtedly an innovation since, before the white man's influence, it would not have been safe to leave the village defenceless but for the presence of a few weak people. But even in olden days the intensity of village life must have varied greatly with the season.

Early in the morning the village is very busy. People eat their frugal morning meals and prepare for their day's work. The time at which they start for their gardens or other work varies with the distance. On Mailu Island the gardens are close at hand; in the mainland villages they are often fairly remote. The day is usually spent out of the village in one or other of the economic occupations (gardening, fishing, hunting, sailing), those remaining behind devoting themselves to siesta. In the afternoons the women return from the gardens, carrying vegetables and firewood, and water in water-bottles. An hour or two before sunset the meal is prepared and put on the fire. In the evening, if it be the proper season, there is some dancing in the village; otherwise the people sit in groups and talk. At such times the fronts of the verandahs are crowded, the men in some houses sitting on the verandah, in others the women gathering together on the front.

There is a marked separation of the sexes in the village life. At daytime, when at work, there is the man's end of the verandah – the front; and the women's – the rear end. Not that there would be any taboo or even customary restriction in this respect, but, normally, one sees the men in the front part and the women busy round the fireplace behind. If there is anything going on in the street there will be in some houses women in the front of the verandah; but usually they keep to themselves. The groups in the street, on the beach, behind the houses, and on the bush side of the village are formed by members of one sex only. Men and women converse freely in public and approach each other, but it is not the right thing for a boy and girl to talk together in public for any length of time, and husband and wife do not associate in the street. When I approached a group of women my native interpreters and informants usually drifted away, or sat discreetly at a distance, never freely joining the circle of women. There is, in fact, a great deal of decorum in the relation of the sexes in public, a man never paying too much attention to a woman in public. There is also what might be called a distinct feeling of decency, without giving this term its strict, moral European meaning. My informants would not talk loudly of certain subjects on the verandah, for fear that women might hear from the adjoining houses, although hardly any woman was able to understand Motu, in which the conversation was carried on.[32] And once, in the course of inquiring about man's dress in olden days, I was warned not to talk loudly in public about the *bui*, or arrangement of the perineal band; in fact, I was asked not to say this word loudly, as everybody would be ashamed, and, indeed, I saw that my informants would feel seriously uneasy at such a breach of étiquette. I was told at one time that men would never mention before women any words or topics that would be considered indecent in our sense of the term.

The division into clans is quite marked in village life, members of the same clan associating much more closely than those of different clans. The people naturally keep to the neighbourhood of their houses when they go out into the street or on the beach, and squat down to work or gossip, or, as is most usual, to do both at the same time. Unless on business, it is not usual for people to intrude upon the grounds of another clan. The groups of women engaged in pottery-making, or the men in making arm-shells, etc., sit in the portion of street or beach adjoining the houses of their clan, and the dancers, who for months rehearse the dance before the feast, do so in front of the houses of the clan that is giving the feast.

---

[32]Men learn Motu when working in plantations, or when in jail, or when in contact with the native constabulary. The members of the latter all speak Motu, as they are recruited from all tribes, and had to adopt some common language. Women have none of those opportunities. Thus Motu has become distinctly a man's language. In Mailu few men, especially those under forty, do not speak it, but there is not a single woman who can speak this language.[[17]]

3 Sexual Life and Marriage

Sexual life before marriage

The love affairs of the Mailu youths and maidens are settled in the
manner typical to the Papuo-Melanesians, which has been described
by Prof. Seligman in the case of the Koíta.[33] As there are, however,
notable differences in details, the general tone of the whole
proceedings being perhaps slightly stricter and more decorous in
Mailu than amongst the Port Moresby tribes, it will be necessary to
give a full account of the erotic life of the Mailu.

The boys and girls have perfect freedom to please themselves in
choosing their lovers and in managing their intrigues. This does not
mean, of course, that there is anything like a promiscuous
intercourse or even anything approaching licentiousness in sex
matters. The stern correctness observed in public life penetrates into
the privacy of love-making. A girl who changes her lover often is
considered decidedly open to blame; a girl once betrothed is bound
to keep chaste, the same rule of conduct applying to a boy. And far
from being polite and easy-going towards strangers in these matters,
as is the case with the Massim,[34] the Mailu would never allow a
stranger to approach their women. This puritan feature is shown
nowadays in the fact that it is more difficult for a white man to
obtain favours from Mailu women than it is in any other coastal
districts; this was the verdict of all the competent white Papuans I
consulted on the matter. And when, a few years ago, a beachcomber
persuaded a married Mailu woman to elope with him, public opinion
was so strong that the Mailu village constables handcuffed the man,
and had to suffer afterwards for thus exceeding their powers.

The prenuptial sexual relations are subject to the rules of exogamy,
and clan exogamy regulates both marriage and extraconnubial
intercourse, though not with strict rigidity; in fact, there are to my
knowledge two cases, one in Mailu and one in Kurére, of
endogamous marriage – endogamous not only with reference to the
clan, but even to the subclan. These two cases refer to rather old men,
who, so far as I could ascertain, had married before the white man's
influence had made itself felt. They are stamped[18] by the natives as
instances of wrong marriage, and it is said that such provoke both

---

[33]Cf., Seligman, 'Melanesians', chap. iv., p. 76.
[34]Seligman, 'Melanesians', p. 501.

indignation and derision. But apparently there has been no attempt at interference or punishment in these instances, and when things had settled down the men concerned seemed to enjoy their due share of public respect.

To return to prenuptial relations, the custom of having a sweetheart is called *uf'ui*. The young man calls his mistress *uf'ui avétsa (avétsa = woman)*. From the confidences of several young sparks [19] of the village of Mailu, I have been able to construct the course of native flirtation. It seems that the initiative comes from the young girl.[20] A girl who fancies a boy might ask him for a piece of betelnut or a bit of tobacco, when they meet casually on the way to the gardens, or during the dances, or on any other occasion when men and women come momentarily into contact without attracting attention, and the boy would naturally grant her request. After several such hints, the boy would seize the first opportunity of approaching the girl again on an occasion when he could do so without drawing the eye of public opinion upon them, and he would then spontaneously offer her a small gift of *kuku* (tobacco) or betel. At this the girl with 'natural astonishment' would ask, 'Why do you give me this?' to which would reply the boy, 'Because I love you'. And very likely they would arrange, then and there, for a further meeting. The rendezvous would take place in the girl's house at a time which would be sufficiently late to give an ample margin for all the other inmates to be asleep. The boy, seeing that all is dark and quiet, would climb up the verandah and try to find the girl in the appointed corner, and she would carefully ascertain by touching his face and ornaments that it is the right person. They would talk to each other in undertones, taking great care not be be heard or detected by the other inmates of the house or by any of the neighbours. There was some disagreement between my informants as to whether the girl's family and the neighbours really do not know – and must not know – what is going on, or whether they more or less admittedly wink at the proceedings. I should be inclined to think the latter. Anyhow, even in the case of detection there would be no punishment for the offenders, though some fuss and a bit of abuse might make the next evening unpleasant. The thing is, or ought to be, kept a secret from the other boys of the village, only the nearest friend (*gaidi*) or friends of the man concerned being in the confidence.

Kissing was, of course, not known by the natives of Mailu before the white man's advent. I was told, however, that the younger generation have acquired that habit from the Europeans, and that they seem rather to appreciate it. The usual form of flirting was for the boy to sit close to his sweetheart, holding her hand or her breast, and talking in undertones.[35]

It is very characteristic – and the emphatic consensus of all my informants leaves no doubt on the point – that in cases when the young man has serious matrimonial plans there is no sexual intercourse between the two. In that case the two spend the evening, often late into the night, merely talking. On the other hand, if the boy does not want to marry the girl, intercourse takes place, though even in such a case matrimony may evolve in the course of time. Anyhow, I was assured that the boy not unfrequently plans and suggests marriage when the first rendezvous is appointed, and that in such a case he would not make any sexual advances.[36]

Moreover, the boy would not pronounce the name of his *fiancée* in addressing her, which interdiction obtains also between husband and wife.

A girl who has had many intrigues is said to be less desirable as a wife; at any rate, she could not be married by betrothal (see below).

If the boy wishes to marry (whether he has treated his sweetheart as *fiancée* or as mistress) he makes his appearance at her house one evening in a noisy and ostentatious manner. He goes straight to the fireplace, and does not try to conceal his presence or to keep quiet; good form, however, requires that the girl's people should feign sleep. Next day the girl's parents go to the house of the father of the boy and, accusing him of intruding into their home, allude to

---

[35] Among the Motu the right conventional attitude whilst courting was for the boy to sit on the knees of his mistress (*sîhári*).

[36] This version is confirmed by the identical state of things to be found among the Motu, Koíta, and Sinaughólo. The boy would never cohabit with his sweetheart if she was betrothed to him by the *máo-héni* (Motu language) form of marriage (this form of marriage is called in Sinaughólo, *kílakau*). If originally he did not overtly declare his matrimonial intentions, a boy might have an intrigue with his mistress (Motu, *sihári*; Koíta, *sivári*; Sinaughólo, *kologhána*). He could in course of time make up his mind and marry her, in which case the marriage form is called in Motu, *heráhe*; in Koíta, *iríri*; in Sinaughólo, *véga'raghoréma*. At any rate, the fact that the time of engagement is free from prenuptial intercourse stands above doubt in these tribes as well as in the Mailu. I had exceptionally good information on this point in the Sinaughólo, as I was admitted into the confidence of a smart and fast set of Ligo young men, who discussed matters among themselves and told their experiences in my presence in Motu, whïch they all speak as a second mother-tongue.

marriage. As the boy's behaviour is an indication of his willingness, there is no difficulty in settling matters.

Besides these settled relations between a girl and a boy there seem to be at times general flirtations amongst a group of boys and girls, but, so far as I am aware, they only talk, though they possibly form preferences and arrange for meetings; no licence, however, is incidental to such gatherings. In such cases some of the girls assemble in the house of one of them, and the boys try to find it – a search in which they do not, of course, meet with great difficulties. The elders, in all probability, assemble in the upper thatched room while the young people meet in the verandah.

The only time when there seems to be any licence beyond the *ui'ui* relationships is during the big annual feast; in fact the dancing, which takes place with increased intensity during the few days of the feast, seems to be associated with opportunities for short-lived intrigues, and occasionally there even seem to be features of licentiousness, groups absconding together; but on this point my informants do not agree.

I have been told by Mr. Greenaway that the observation by women of taboos before the feast is associated with the idea of the preventative properties of those taboos. The young girls and young married women, as well as the men, abstain from drinking fresh water and eating boiled food, eating only roast food and drinking the milk of roasted green coconuts. They also drink and rinse their mouths with salt water. This, I am told, is supposed to prevent conception, to which accident the licence associated with the feasts is thought to predispose.

Thus the connection between cohabitation and conception seems to be known among the Mailu, but to direct inquiries as to the cause of pregnancy I did not obtain emphatic and positive answers. The natives – of this I am positive – do not clearly grasp the idea of the connection between the two facts, just as they do not grasp the connection between illness, bodily decay, and death. From several informants I got the answer that possibly the two things are connected; but, like Prof. Seligman among the Koíta, I found the firm belief that it is only continuous intercourse – for a month or more – that leads to pregnancy, and that one single act is not sufficient to produce the result.[21] This may explain the ideas and practices of the preventative taboo just mentioned.

Neither do the natives seem to trouble very much about the causal connection in point. Ignorant of the physiological knowledge we possess, they approach in this connection the standpoint of the Arunta and the many other aboriginal tribes of Australia, amongst whom Prof. Spencer and Mr. Gillen have found a complete ignorance on this point, associated with a belief in totemic incarnation.[22] I was, however, unable to discover any beliefs in supernatural causes of pregnancy or magical means to produce or prevent it.

It must be noted that even the taboos before the *Madúna* (feast) do not mean so much that the natives know the connection in question, as that they are afraid of conception during the feast time – a fear which might as well be based on an original belief in supernatural incarnation as on a knowledge of the real association.[23]

The state of affairs in sex matters seems also to accord with slackness of native induction. There are very few virgins among the grown-up marriageable girls, and yet illegitimate children are rare, if not altogether absent – a somewhat mysterious state of things, which has been found by Prof. Seligman to exist among the Southern Massim.[37] With the assistance of a white resident in the district of over twenty years' standing, who is himself married to a native woman of Mailu village, I inquired into the matter as carefully as I could. My friend informed me that, in spite of his strenuous attempts to discover a native preventative of conception, he failed to find any, and that the natives always told him that they knew of none. Abortion is undoubtedly practised by both married and unmarried women; but, as among the Massim, it is not frequent, especially in the case of the unmarried. It would seem, therefore, that the women have some means of guarding against an undesired conception. Thus the matter is obscure, and needs explanation.

There is no licence on the part of married women in any form or under any circumstance, and adultery was in all cases considered a serious offence, which was sometimes punished by death (see chap. iii., sec. 5).

During the menses (called *laro*, which means blood) the woman is

---

[37]'Another puzzling feature of the licence undoubtedly permitted throughout the Massim area is the very small number of illegitimate births which take place. Wherever the confidence of the natives was gained it was admitted that abortion was induced, but the most careful inquiries failed to produce evidence that the practice was as frequent as might be expected considering the prevailing liberty'. – Seligman, 'Melanesians', p. 500.

isolated, and she usually sleeps in a small temporary hut erected near the house or in the woman's corner of the house. She is never sexually approached during the period. I was told by one of my informants, a very intelligent and trustworthy man, that menstruation only takes place just about new moon. When, however, I tried to check this statement by inquiry of other men, it was neither corroborated nor denied, they saying that they did not know anything about this purely feminine subject. But I have reasons to assume that the statement represents the woman's view. I could not, of course, ascertain the actual truth; but even if this be merely the belief of the Mailu women, it is of great interest. Not one of my informants was aware that pregnancy can be diagnosed by the stopping of the menstrual flow; they were, in fact, very much astonished and genuinely amused at the idea. This seems to confirm the view, expressed to me directly by some white men, who were fairly well acquainted with native women, that much secrecy and reticence obtains between man and woman in sex matters.

General remarks about marriage

The marriage institution among the Mailu possesses distinct and, more or less, independent aspects. It is – in its essential and universal quality – a contract between two individuals, involving sexual relations, community of daily life, mutual services of various kinds, and, last but not least, community of economic interests in the fullest sense of that word, as applicable to the native conditions. On the other hand, marriage involves a series of mutual obligations between the husband and the wife's family. They consist in the exchange of gifts – in the main of pigs and native ornaments – which form the substance of the annual feast. This aspect is a prominent Mailu feature of marriage. The same state of things seems, however, to obtain among the other Papuo-Melanesians and among the Massim, though perhaps not with the same distinctiveness. The regular exchange of gifts is one of the main features of the Papuo-Melanesian and Massim cultures, as has been fully recognized by Prof. Seligman.[38] Now, it is beyond doubt that this exchange is in nine cases out of ten initiated as the original price of the bride paid by the bridegroom at marriage, and subsequently returned to him. Then, in

---

[38] 'Melanesians', *passim*.

turn, he has to give a pig when the next opportunity offers, and so on.[39] Although the balance seems to be always in favour of the girl's family – in the sense that they get more – there is no doubt that this system differs strongly from marriage by purchase pure and simple, and that one should speak of bride-price, etc., only in a qualified sense. Under this aspect, marriage in the Mailu (and other coastal tribes east and west) acquires a much wider social significance than it would otherwise possess. It is essentially connected with, and regulates, the gifts of pigs at the big annual and funeral feasts, and thus enters as an essential component into an institution which governs half the public life of the natives. The two aspects of marriage – individual and public – will be described separately.

Marriage in its individual aspect; marriage ceremonies

Referring to what has been said above concerning the prenuptial relations, it may be stated that there are two forms of marriage in the Mailu – marriage by early betrothal, and marriage evolving from a preconjugal intrigue (*uí'ui* relationship). I was not able to ascertain whether the natives distinguish sharply between these two forms by special names and differences in the ceremonial.[40] At any rate, there is a clear distinction between the engagement (*veáni*), when marriage is in view and during which no sexual intercourse takes place, and the intrigue (*uí'ui*), when the two cohabit without intention to marry.

The following account refers to the marriage by betrothal, and I unfortunately failed to inquire what modifications take place when the second type of relationship evolves into marriage. One thing is certain, however, namely, that the conspicuous gift, forming the substance of the marriage contract, obtains in both modifications.

---

[39] The subject is discussed under the next sub-heading.
[40] As stated in a previous footnote, there was a sharp distinction between the two forms in the Motu, Koíta, Sinaughólo. The *máo-héni* form (marriage by betrothal) could be contracted only by a girl who had no previous sexual experiences (called in Motu, *rámi hebóu*; 'having her grass petticoats unparted'). A girl who has previously had *síhari* (lovers) could contract only the *heráhe* form of marriage. The *máo-héni* marriage was carried out with more preliminaries and much more ceremonial. The girl was promised when fairly young; in the Sinaughólo tribes, further inland from the Lígo district, quite small girls might be betrothed when not more than three to five years old. The decision in, and the formalities of, the betrothal were mainly left to the care of the older generation, this being obviously necessary in the case of very young girls. But with the elder girls, consent seems usually to be essential. The final, and most important, part of this form of marriage is the presentation of gifts of

The girls are betrothed at an age not earlier than seven or eight, but usually at about fourteen or fifteen. In the betrothal, in its proper form, the initiative always rest with the parents, and very often the inclination of the girl plays no part in the arrangement. The first agreement is accompanied by a small gift, called *odi'egéri*, usually consisting of some five sticks of tobacco, or, before the advent of the white man, a corresponding amount of betelnut, some feathers, etc. There would also be a small feast accompanying the *odi'egéri*. At the same time the previously described tattooing of the girl's face is performed. This tattoo was a performance necessary for marriage, and it is always done when a girl is betrothed; many girls, however, have their faces tattooed without being promised in marriage. After the preliminary gift there is a mutual exchange of food presents, in which the balance seems to be maintained fairly equal on both sides. If the girl's clan celebrate a *Madúna* (big feast) during this period, the boy's father supplies the girl's father with a pig, in account of the marriage gift to be paid. It may be also added that such small feasts as that connected with the *odi'egéri* gift are usually performed in connection with a *Madúna*. Such a feast is held before the men set out on their trading trip west to fetch pigs.

As mentioned above, both the young man and his *fiancée* do not, as a matter of étiquette, cohabit during the time of their engagement, neither must they have other intrigues; a girl would even refuse to marry a boy as to whose infidelity she had got positive knowledge.

After a period of time, varying in length according to the girl's age and other circumstances, the actual marriage takes place. The marriage gift, in the form of pigs and some articles of native wealth, may have been given during one of the previous feasts, but according to native custom pigs are given only at feast time. The actual

---

food and native valuables. These are presented by all the boy's relations in amounts proportional to the closeness of their relationship. The *heráhe* form of marriage, called also *headáva-henáo* – marriage by stealing – is certainly the less decorous form, though it was the more frequent before the white man's advent. It derives its second name from the circumstance that a girl thus wedded had usually been previously promised to another boy. Hence also the difficulties often attending such marriages. The preliminary ceremonies of betrothal and exchange of gifts are absent, and only the final one of bridal price takes place. It is identical with that which occurs in the *máo-héni* marriages. (This short outline is a very much abridged account of the excellent information obtained on this subject from a committee consisting of Ahúia, a Koíta man, a Motu of Gábagába, and several Sinaughólo men. It will be published in full in another place.)

marriage consists in the girl's coming to the bridegroom's house and eating with him – an act called *tuíni daba*. The girl usually brings with her a few native valuables in repayment (probably only partial) for the bridegroom's gifts. She prepares some food – vegetable and fish only, no pig being boiled on that occasion. The food is placed on a dish between the two, and they both partake of it, *bon ton* requiring them to be bashful, and not to look at each other. It is this eating in common (*tuíni daba*) which constitutes the essence of marriage from the ceremonial point of view.

The marriage is, however, not consummated immediately after the *tuíni daba* ceremony. The girl returns to her parents' house for another week or so, and only after this interval has elapsed do they cohabit. The two are now married, but the mutual exchange of gifts survives the consummation of marriage, and lasts indefinitely.

Relations between a man and his wife's family as established by marriage

This, as said above, may be summarized in the man's duty to provide pigs when the clan of his wife's family holds a *Madúna* feast and in their duty to return this gift in a more or less adequate form, when the man's *aúra* (clan) gives a feast. The importance of this state of things lies in the fact that it throws a new light on 'marriage by purchase' in general. There is really no element of barter in the whole proceedings, for it is understood that the gift by the bridegroom, or by his father and family to the girl's family will be returned later on – at least partially. Again the psychological aspect of the 'payment' – the term here is, of course, not quite correct – is also noteworthy. The girl is not estimated as worth so much, and the corresponding value exacted; in fact, I think that an insufficient marriage gift to the girl's parents would be accepted without much fuss, though I was not able to get satisfactory evidence on this point.[41] On the other hand,

---

[41] In this respect I am in possession of much better information concerning the Motu-speaking people of the Central Division, owing to the fact that I could talk to them in their own language, for to both Koíta and Sinaughólo the Motu is a second mother-tongue, and also to the fact that my informants were exceptionally intelligent. I was assured by Ahúia, Maganiméro – an exceptionally clever Lígo man – and other authorities that there never were any quarrels about the final gift offered for a bride. On the other hand, when the price (*laráha*) given for a widow to her deceased husband's brothers was paid, there was usually considerable amount of quarrelling, and even fighting.

the man and his family were extremely eager to give as much as possible for the wife, knowing that by so doing the ambition of his future partner would be gratified, and that his own prestige in the tribe would be enhanced. This view would also apply to all his subsequent gifts. Nevertheless, I think that the real decorum is observed by givers and receivers only on the occasion of the first gift. At the feasts there is always some quarrelling about pigs, though this does not mean that a man is not eager to do his best in giving them. One of my friends in Mailu failed, through no fault of his own, but through the accidental death of his pig, to bring the necessary gift to a member of his wife's family; he was genuinely mortified by this, and he was ashamed to go to the houses of the Maradúba clan, which was to give the feast. He told me that no reproaches, still less any quarrelling or punishment, awaited him, but that he was sorry and ashamed for his own and his wife's sake. This is an illustration of what I gathered from the general accounts and concrete examples of all my informants. Everyone was proud of having given so many pigs, and everyone was eagerly anxious to procure as many animals as possible for the approaching feast.

If a man wants to behave like a gentleman he gives at least one pig a year. The first goes usually to the girl's father, and as a clan very seldom gives a feast every year, the next pig goes to some other relation of the girl. When a girl's clan is again making a *Madúna*, the bridegroom gives a pig to his eldest brother-in-law, and so on. All these individuals are supposed to return his presents, though it seems that, as a rule, a man never gets back the same amount of pigs as he has given to his wife.

In order to complete the account of the relationship obtaining between a man and his wife's family, the custom called *liá'i* must be mentioned. It comprises a series of taboos observed by the man, which entail a general avoidance of some of his relations-in-law, and forbid him to mention their names. The taboo upon the names of these people is analogous to the taboos upon the personal names of the parents and grandparents, mentioned above (chap. ii., sec. 4). It is to be noted that the two sets of taboos – the one referring to the 'own' relatives and the other referring to relatives-in-law – are distinguished by different names. The first is called by the general term *góra*, applied to things tabooed or forbidden; and the second by a special name, *liá'i*. The father-in-law (*evai'égi*) and his son-in-law (*botsia*) do not address each other by their names, nor do they pronounce them. Their names are *liá'i* to each other, but they may talk to and approach one another. The same restrictions apply to a man and his mother-in-law, and also to a woman and both her parents-in-law. The strongest *liá'i* restrictions, however, obtain between a man and his wife's elder sister (*uini'avétsa*), this being the same term that a man applies to his own elder sister. A man is not allowed to approach her, nor even to touch any object belonging to her, and, especially, would a man avoid touching her *rámi*, or grass petticoat, if it were lying about the house. He may talk to her, but only from a distance, and, of course, he does not address her by name, nor does he pronounce it in her absence. A man can approach his wife's younger sister (*nábu*), but her name is equally tabooed to him. So are a man's wife's brothers' names. The sanction of *liá'i* consists in the first place of a general reluctance to, and intense fear of, infringing the étiquette and doing the thing in a way that is essentially wrong and unacceptable by social rules and by the code of manners inherent in all human beings. This fear is very pronounced among the natives; they are extremely anxious to do the 'right thing', in which respect they do not differ essentially from the civilized white man. In order to understand the psychological background of such purely customary – I might say such *mondaine* sanction – one ought to compare it with that of our own rules of *savoir faire*, and I think that most men would much more readily commit acts of extreme folly than behave in an outrageously incorrect manner in a drawing-room or ballroom. To transgress the *liá'i*, or any kindred rule, would be for the native an act as improper as for a society man to appear in flannels at a ball or to omit his necktie at a formal garden party. We very often press the native for an explicit sanction or reason for some of his customary rules. 'What, for instance, would happen if a man broke the *liá'i*?' No wonder the native can given no answer, or simply says, 'Our fathers did so, and so do we.' This will appear much less obscure and specifically 'savage' to us, if we remember that the natives live in very small communities, and that in consequence the quality and intensity of their public opinion or social censure is very much the same as that of a social circle of mutual acquaintances in our own society. The fear of being ridiculed, of being *gauche*, or eccentric, the keen desire to be correct, to do always the right thing, to be smart and *dernier cri* – all these feelings actuate the natives as they do the white man in reference to his social *milieu*. A white man would be just as much puzzled if he were asked to adduce the reason, origin, and sanction of the rigidly observed custom of wearing a white necktie with his full evening dress and a black one with his dinner jacket. 'Everybody does it; it is the right thing to do', is alike the answer both of the brown and of the white man, and neither can produce any other sanction than that it is the rule of his social circle. When pressed, my informants said that a man transgressing the *liá'i* unwittingly, for intentionally nobody would dream of doing so, would expect some kind or other of illness to befall him.

It is to be noted that *liá'i* taboo on relatives-in-law is much more stringent than the *góra* on the names of parents. Several of my friends did not mind mentioning in my presence the names of their fathers and grandfathers, acting on the principle that 'New Guinea custom has little bearing upon one's behaviour towards a white man'. But they would not apply this principle to their father-in-law's name. Wishing to ascertain the extent of their reluctance, I tried to tempt Píkana, a particularly greedy and sophisticated middle-aged Mailu – with the elder and more genuine gentlemen, such as my friend Papári, I would not have attempted the experiment – by offering him successively increasing quantities of tobacco. It was only at five sticks that he began to waver, which means that his reluctance was very great indeed.

The parents-in-law belong to the circle of relatives who receive the *vevéni* gift of food.

Essentials of the marriage contract

Besides its ceremonial side and its conditions of validity, and besides the general duties which are imposed upon a man towards his relatives-in-law, marriage establishes a personal relationship between husband and wife. And perhaps the most essential data concerning marriage are those bearing upon the reciprocal duties and privileges, the general character of their feelings towards each other, and all the facts characteristic of their respective status. In this place I shall state those details very briefly, as several of them are described in other sections.

Marriage is in Mailu patrilocal; the woman moves to her husband's house, lives with his parents and with his brothers and their families. In all her domestic duties she has to co-operate with her mother-in-law and with her sisters-in-law, and thus she becomes, in this respect, a member of her husband's house; and becomes its co-proprietor, in so far as she continues to live in it, even after his death, especially if she has children and does not think of marrying again.

She works in her husband's garden, and becomes, in fact, a co-proprietor of this also, since after her husband's death she continues to use the garden for herself and her children. She even shares her husband's economic magic, which is a form of property that is greatly valued. Whatever he acquires by hunting and fishing, and whatever she acquires, go to their common household, and is used by them in common, subject to the deduction of the *vevéni* and other portions communistically distributed among various people. They have their meals together, except when in olden days the man occasionally ate his food at the *dúbu*. The two belong to each other exclusively in sexual matters, though, of course, for adultery the crime and punishment are much greater in the case of the woman. But it must be noted that there was no opportunity for a married man to enter into an intrigue without incurring the blame of public opinion and without setting at naught his domestic peace. And, as far as my knowledge goes, the unmarried men would be very keen to find him out and to set in motion against him all the adverse forces of offended public opinion for thus encroaching upon what they considered to be their own exclusive right. In public the married men shun the other sex even much more rigidly than the bachelors.

Husband and wife sleep together round the same fire, except, again, in those cases when a man slept in the *dúbu* in order to observe sex taboos, or when the woman has her period, or for some other reason.

In the matter of marital authority there seems to be a great independence on the part of both partners. I was unable to hear of, or to observe, any evidence that a man ever tyrannized over or bullied his wife, neither do the men appear to be often 'hen-pecked'. During the many times I sat and talked with the natives in their houses I observed that the women kept apart, especially if other men besides the owner of the house were present. But if a woman approached there was never the slightest sign of shyness or fear in her manner towards her husband, and I never saw any one of them as much as rebuked or spoken to unkindly by her husband. On the contrary, there were present all the signs of friendly and unconstrained relations between them. And this was, if anything, more pronounced in the case of old couples. As to the scope of real authority, *i.e.*, of the limits within which a man could impose his will upon a woman, I think that these were very restricted. All the services required by a man from his wife were strictly regulated by custom, and even the sphere of their mutual personal contact was defined. Whether a woman desired it or not, she was usually free from her husband's presence, his bad tempers, and of his possibly arbitrary wishes for the greater part of the day.

The question arises to what extent is the mutual affection and regard which undoubtedly obtains between the two partners, due primarily to erotic love. It seems to be beyond dispute that this feeling exists among the lower races, though neither in their art nor in incidents in their lives could I find signs of its expression. Nor could I find evidences of what may be called romantic sentiment. I know, however, of several instances of acute dislike, in which girls had either to be actually forced to submit to the affianced husbands or to run away in order to escape a distasteful match.

On the other hand, strong and decided inclinations exist of which I could record several instances. So also the intrigues of married women, which occur fairly frequently, point to the existence of passions willing to run considerable risks and able to overcome substantial obstacles.

As it is evident from previous passages, sexual jealousy is very pronounced, and this sentiment is not based only upon the sense of ownership established by marriage, since it exists very markedly in respect to the *ui'ui* relationships.

Polygamy is very infrequent; I have only one polygamous marriage to record amongst the total number of marriages in the pedigrees of Mailu village. One very strong obstacle to polygamy would be the duty of providing pigs for the wife's family. This duty is onerous enough for a monogamist, and the obligations of polygamy would be surely beyond the powers of an average man.

4 CHILDREN AND THEIR PLAY

Birth and infancy

The information available on this heading is unfortunately very scanty. I was not able to speak with any woman, and men are not good informants on the subject.

What I know about native ideas concerning conception has been said in the last section. During pregnancy the woman has to observe a general fish taboo (*oribe tóra*). If she did eat fish the child would be injured. She can, however, eat boiled food and drink fresh water. The pregnant woman (*amara orá'i*) sleeps in the house near her husband, but they do not cohabit. Sexual connection during pregnancy would kill a woman. At the birth no man may be present, not even the husband. He would be too much ashamed to see it. The mother and the mother-in-law of the puerperient, as well as her sisters and sisters-in-law, are present, and they act as mid-wives. There are no specialists in this art in the village. If twins are born, one, usually the second, is killed as a rule. The reason given is that a woman cannot properly feed two infants, and that to carry them about, etc., would give too much trouble. Infanticide would be practised in the case of illegitimate children – which, as said before, are extremely rare. It would be done also in the case of a man deserting his wife. If a woman had a series of girls, or a series of boys, and she wanted a child of the opposite sex, she would kill a newcomer if it were of the undesired sex. If the mother dies in childbed the offspring is buried alive alongside the mother. The form of infanticide is, as a rule, strangulation of the baby.

In Mailu, as among all the races on that level of culture, suckling goes on long after the child is able to eat other food – till about three to four years after birth.

In infancy children are carried about by their mothers and very often by their fathers. The method of carrying children by the women is to seat them astride upon the protruding upper edge of the petticoat, the child clasping the mother's body with both its legs and the mother holding it with one arm (see pl. 14). Both parents nurse the child and fondle it. The operations of nose and ear piercing are performed in infancy.

Childhood and initiation of boys

Children live with their parents. They are very independent, the parents interfering little with their games and inclinations. In fact, I observed, and my observation was endorsed by Mr. Saville, that the elders hardly ever give commands to their children, preferring to ask them to do what they wish, in fear lest refusal should compromise their authority and prestige. Chastisement, in any form, seems never to be used to children, except perhaps in a fit of impatience.

The stages of childhood and adolescence are marked by few

incidents. At the age of about three to four the girl gets her first grass petticoat. At a slightly later stage the process of tattooing begins and ends with the tattoo on the face which coincides with the marriageable age.

The boys go about without any garment for a much longer time. They get their perineal band at the age of about eight to ten years, and there is a small initiation ceremony (*u'au'áu*) connected with this event. The eldest boy is given his *síhi* (Motu name for perineal band) by his maternal uncle (*aue*), with whom the boy's father exchanges some gifts. The younger boys get their *síhi* from the first-born, and there is no exchange of food. The initiation ceremony seems to have been more elaborate in former days, when the *dúbu* existed and when the white man had not yet suppressed the institution of head-hunting, with which this ceremony was apparently connected in some way. I was told by Papári, a fairly old man and the best informant in Mailu, that in the olden days the initiation was more elaborate, being performed when there was an enemy's head available. In the preparation of the head, the boy to be initiated used to lend a hand, and this formed part of the initiation ceremony. On such, and only on such, occasions would the ceremony take place in the *dúbu*. The boy spent about a fortnight in the *dúbu* previously to the ceremony, and was not allowed to leave the place. He had to keep the typical taboo – *i.e.*, abstention from boiled food and fish – and his food was handed to him by men. If the boy wanted to leave the *dúbu* house for any necessity he could do so by night, or if he did so in the daytime he had to cover himself completely with mats; neither was he allowed to comb his hair.

The boys who were thus undergoing the initiation taboo used to remove the skin and flesh of the enemy's head, which was part of the process of preparing it for the collection in the *dúbu*, and very likely boys at the suitable age would wait until there were a few heads ready for the head-hunter's collection. On the other hand, if such were at hand some boys might be invited to undergo the initiation, so that the two performances might coincide.

The ceremony itself was performed after the period of the taboo in the *dúbu* itself. After that the boy was no more called *támaru*, but *u'áu*, which corresponds to 'young man'. On the day of the ceremony there was a dance.

At other times the adoption of the perineal band usually took place on one of the *oró'u* (big canoes). In such cases the ceremony would be connected with the big feast (*Madúna*), and take place just before, at the time when the canoes had returned from Aróma laden with pigs and betelnut for the feast. The ceremony is always accompanied by a small feast, for which a pig was killed. The pig is previously given by the boy's father to the maternal uncle. In the case of the perineal band being given by the boy's elder brother the pig is killed by the father.

At the exchange of gifts which takes place between the father and the maternal uncle it is the latter who profits.[24]

Games and amusements

As said above, the children's life is fairly free. From the age of about five they play and roam at will, and the bigger boys and girls may go some distance away from the village. Even at that stage the separation of the sexes is marked, for the boys and girls roam in separate groups, hardly mix in their play, and very often have altogether different ways of playing.

Many of the children's games have a clear educational value. They consist very often in the imitation of the activities of their elders, and the children often use toys and implements made, *ad hoc*, with a considerable amount of labour. The elders, usually parents, take part in the play and teach the children, with evident interest and care, how to sail a toy canoe or use a toy net or fish spear. On Mailu Island these educational games refer mainly to sailing and fishing, as might easily be expected in a community of sailors and fishermen. But imitation of native dancing – which becomes a very important activity in the later life – and imitation of spearing belong to the class of educational play.

These are children's games having an educational aspect. Children also join their parents in their activities, first in play, then more and more seriously, thus imperceptibly acquiring the arts of mature life. The girl sits near her mother and watches her making pottery; or, with a small stick, imitates her actions in digging the ground, or helps her in peeling the vegetables and preparing the food. Small girls join also their mothers in searching for *frutti di mare*.

The boys join their fathers on hunting expeditions, and when they go with them to sea they observe and lend a hand in managing the big canoes.

Besides these games with an educational aspect there are a few games pure and simple. Thus catscradles, played all the year round, especially by women, form a very favourite pastime. There are also a few games like tug-of-war, etc., played by boys and girls separately late in the afternoon and on clear moonlight evenings. As these correspond in a way to dancing, the older boys do not take part in them; but full grown-up women enjoy them side by side with small girls.

Toy boats and sailing games of the boys

The play with boats must be described more fully. There are two kinds of boats made for the special benefit of boys – small models of the large, crab-sail double canoes (*oró'u*), and small out-rigger canoes (called *káro*), so small that no grown-up man could sail in them, but large enough to support one or two urchins. In these the boys sail, usually within the reef which runs not far from the beach. But sometimes they venture further out, even in fairly rough weather, in a way that, for skill and daring, arouses wonder and appreciation even in the unfeeling breast of a field ethnographer.[25] The time for these escapades is usually at the break of the seasons, when the south-eastern wind changes into the monsoon, and undoubtedly they afford the means of learning how to manage a canoe and a sail, which latter is very often used. They also learn how to bail out a dug-out when it has sunk by water-logging.[26] They all swim very well.

The models of the *oró'u* are used in play. Whole days are spent in shallow water by boys in following their canoes as they sail across the small bay in front of the Mailu village (see pl. 15 and 16). This play with models of the large boats, called *ede'edé'i*, is done during the north-west monsoon season, as at that time the Bay of Mailu is absolutely calm. The models are fairly accurate, even in the ornamentation, with one exception: the big *oró'u* consists of two boats joined by a platform and lashed together, while in the model one of the dug-outs is replaced by an outrigger float. In this way the boys get acquainted with the construction of the *oró'u*, though the models are made by the elders.

Another sport very much enjoyed by children is fishing with a miniature of the *távita orá'i* net (called *t. o. kínovoi*, which means a small net of that name), the father showing the boy how to use it. Small fish are caught this way, to the great delight of the boys. Over and over again I saw boys playing at fishing in this way for hours together. Miniature models of the other small nets (*gébi orái*) are also made. The fishing corresponds, on a small scale, to the fishing done by the men with these nets (see chap. iv., sec. 3).

Small fish spears (*udi kínovoi; údi* meaning fish spear) are made for boys. They are taught how to use them, and they often set out by themselves for fishing expeditions. Those toy spears are about two-thirds the size of the real ones, and they are used by boys eight to twelve years old.

Some skill in throwing spears may also be possibly acquired by a game (Motu name, *kíki*) in which two boys try to spear soft thick twigs planted in the sand with small pointed sticks (about 40 in. in length).

During the dancing season groups of boys, using small bamboos as drums, sometimes perform for hours in imitation or caricature of the grown-up men's dance. The nearer the feast the more zealous grow the boys, who in this respect follow the lead of the grown-up men.

The children used also to play a kind of tug-of-war and several other games, the details of which I failed to record, though I saw them performed several times. In one a line of girls 'wind themselves up' into a sort of tangle, which is afterwards unravelled; in another two rows of girls face each other and join their hands. A small girl is taken by the arms; she is balanced on the joined hands of two girls, and then has to spring on to the next pair and so on. These games are accompanied by songs.

5   REGULATION OF PUBLIC LIFE: LEGAL INSTITUTIONS: *GÓRA* (TABOO)

General remarks

When dealing with abstract conceptions referring to social life, such as law, religion, authority, etc., it is necessary to be extremely careful not to project our own ideas and associations into native life and thought.[27] One must consider how far our terms – law, legal, criminal and civil law, etc. – are applicable to native conditions. To use these terms in the strict sense in which they are defined in jurisprudence would be an obvious mistake. To use them loosely and without troubling as to their meaning would be essentially unscientific, because, in the case of the field ethnologist, it would show that he has not been considering very carefully where to look for his facts and how to group them.

It will be desirable to explain the manner in which the legal aspect of native life was sought for, without, of course, pretending to give a satisfactory and universally valid definition of law, etc. A field ethnographer has to describe facts in their essential aspects; that means to select. And selection implies the possession of theoretical principles of classification – definite criteria as to what is essential and what is not.

In collecting facts about law and legal institutions the following considerations have afforded the guiding principles. In every community there exist fundamental rules which must be observed. The infraction of these rules is a lurking temptation, and there are always individuals who succumb. As a preventative, or reaction, to this there exist some measures of restriction and redress; broadly speaking, some restraining forces. To discover the rules, the possibilities of infringement, the restraining forces, to classify them, following as closely as possible the conditions of native social life, and to find out the natives' own point of view in these matters – all this constitutes the ethnographer's task under the heading of law.

Broadly speaking, the most elementary of the social rules are identical in all societies: they protect a person's body from injury and they guarantee a certain amount of personal freedom. Murder, bodily hurt, assault, rape, and other attempts on person or liberty are considered to be wrongs in all human communities at the top as well as the bottom of the scale of development. Again, there are everywhere some rules protecting a man's personal property. The infringement of any of these rules is resented by the injured person and by the social group to which he belongs – family, clan, village.

This is one source of criminal law. The other springs from the public resentment which follows the violation by the individual of the essential rules which constitute the given social structure, as, for instance, the rules of exogamy or of religion, etc.

These facts constitute the basis of criminal law. In this broad sense the conception can be applied to native societies, and the distinction between civil and criminal law can be maintained. Under civil law in a native society we can understand the set of rules regulating all the normal relations between persons, as kinship, marriage, economic co-operation and distribution, trading, etc.; and between persons and things, property inheritance, etc. Civil law being thus a set of rules regulating the social mechanism in its stationary, normal course; criminal law being the safety arrangements, putting things aright whenever there is any hitch in their normal course.

Collecting and describing facts from this point of view an ethnological inquirer is not likely to violate the conditions of native life, because the ideas and principles of classification used are sufficiently broad and plastic, though not loose, to be adapted to any social conditions, and they are not borrowed from European jurisprudence.

But although this might do justice to native institutions, and might inform the reader as to the legal aspect of native sociology, it would give no information about native legal ideas. By discussing matters with intelligent – sometimes extremely intelligent – natives, and by letting them compare native social rules with the introduced European system of administrating justice, I came to the conclusion that the conception of criminal law, or of civil law, or of the distinction between the two, could not find any counterpart in native ideas, not even in a rudimentary form. Nevertheless, the natives use words for forbidden; they have their systems of taboos, which possess a distinctly legal aspect, though this is mixed with others as well. In order to do justice to explicit and fundamental native ideas about rule, prohibition, and sanction, it will be necessary to describe their system of taboos and try to distinguish between its legal and non-legal aspects.[28]

Rudimentary measures corresponding to criminal law

The data concerning law will not be described in this section. Civil law comprises all the rules governing social life. Those rules, so far as they are known to the writer, are stated, *passim*, throughout the description of the activities and institutions. I have tried also to state their stringency and universality; to describe the function and the mechanism by which they would be maintained if infringed. It would be mere repetition even to enumerate these details in this place.

In collecting facts relating to criminal law one is confronted with serious difficulties. It is clear from what has been said above that the ethnographer cannot put his questions direct, but has to procure a certain number of actual, concrete facts, draw from them his own inferences, and describe them in his own terms. Now it is especially difficult to get authentic facts referring to crime, such as murder,

rape, theft, etc. The white man's influence has been operating in the
district for over thirty years, and the younger generation of natives
are at present imbued with European ideas of justice – individual
responsibility, value of human life independently of tribe, clan, etc.
And crime, from the point of view of the native conditions, is
certainly less frequent now than it was before. On the other hand, the
native thinks that these topics had better be avoided, and is extremely
careful not to talk too much about them without obvious necessity,
especially to a man whom he knows to be on good terms with the
local missionary and resident magistrate. Thus accounts of the little
crime that is still going on and tales of the good old times are not
willingly communicated.

For such reasons I was unable to learn much in the way of
authentic stories about murder, adultery, and theft as they happened
in olden days, and about the way in which these crimes were
punished and avenged. I obtained a few hints, however, which allow
me to give a broad outline of the existing state of things. Murder
within the village was uncommon, but there are cases on record.
There were quarrels at feasts about pigs, and sometimes also over
women. There were resentments in the village, in the clan, and in the
family. Thus, not long ago, an influential and fairly intelligent native
killed his own mother, being extremely worried about a matter with
which she had nothing to do, and somewhat annoyed by her request
that he should stay at home and not enter the white man's service.
This modern Orestes got three years in prison. The natives did not
approve of his action, but when I inquired what would have
happened in the olden days, it was clear that no punishment would
have been inflicted, there being no man or social body whose
business it would have been to punish the offender. Cases of such
murder within the family or village, undoubtedly closely allied to the
running *amok*, seem to have occurred in the past. In a case like that
just mentioned, when the victim belonged to the man's own family,
and when there was nobody to resent the loss and the wrong done,
the murderer would have escaped scot-free. The public resentment
against him would not have been strong enough to ensure actual
punishment, and if the man had nerve enough to get over the shock,
and live down the subsequent reproachful attitude of his fellow-
tribesmen, he could continue his life in peace and quiet.[29]

As said, there was no central authority which would spontaneously
and automatically deal with the offender. The legal function did not

enter into the duties and privileges of the clan chief; but if the injured person belonged to another clan, or even to another family, the relatives and clansmen would take things into their own hands. If they were strong enough, they would kill a man of the offender's clan or family. It seems, however, that this sort of justice did not interest the clan so much as the family in the narrower sense of the word – the brothers, in the first place, the father, and the first cousins. If those were not strong enough, they could 'hire' a man or men by payment of pigs, arm-shells, and food, to do the business in their place. I gathered that in such a case matters would be considered as squared, and that it would not be followed by an everlasting *vendetta* within the village.

Adultery on the part of the woman was punishable by death, if the couple were caught *in flagrante delicto*, or if the husband felt strongly about the matter. Under such circumstances he would have been considered to be within his rights, and would not suffer retaliation. In less flagrant cases of adultery the whole affair might be settled by payment, the woman possibly going over to the co-respondent. In that case the bridal price would have to be repaid to the former husband, in addition to an atonement gift.

Theft did not seem a very serious offence, except when things were tabooed (see below). Otherwise the man would be possibly chaffed and would acquire a bad name for stealing, which is considered rather in the light of a joke than as a serious shortcoming.

Perhaps the most important of criminal offences, in Mailu as in all other Papuo-Melanesian tribes, was the practice of evil magic. As far as I could ascertain, however, there were not many magicians in the Mailu district. Nevertheless, there were always a few men believed to possess powers for good and evil, but much more distinctly for evil. I do not think, however, that there would be any means of redress against their evil magic. If attacked by one of them, people would be much more likely to try to propitiate him by gifts. Whether these men, who undoubtedly wielded much more authority than anyone else in the village, were ever appealed to for the administration of justice, I am unable to say in the case of the Mailu, though I have very positive confirmatory evidence in the case of the tribes of the Central Division.

The nature of the punishment for crimes when the offender was from another village will be dealt with in the next section. In this case crime was nearly always evil magic.

Taboo *(góra)*

The word *góra* means *taboo* in its most general sense – *i.e.,* corresponds to the word *forbidden*. If one wishes to say that it is not allowed – as used to be the case in intertribal wars, for instance – to go to another village, one says this place is *góra*. Thus this word is not only applied to taboos with supernatural sanction, but to all interdictions in general, even if they be imposed by the nature of things and not by the will of men. The word *góra* is used also to denote the signs, usually consisting of coconut leaves, which were put up in connection with taboos. Such signs, however, do not in all cases imply a taboo. Thus the term *góra* has a wider range than the word taboo. On the other hand, the most important class of taboos – the food restrictions – are called *tóra*. Thus a spot is *góra*, the coconut trees are *góra*, fish is *góra* – as long as the interdiction refers to fishing. But the coconuts are said to be *tóra*, so is the fish and any other form of food. Thus *ama tóra* means coconut taboo; *oribe tóra*, fish taboo; *tsebére tóra*, a taboo on taro.

I shall first describe all the facts comprised within the native idea of *góra*, and then shortly discuss them.

The most important forms of *góra* refer to the coconut. The coconut stands also in an especially intimate connection with the *góra* institution, since it is used almost exclusively for the various *góra* signs, or, at least, it forms the most essential and characteristic element of almost all of them. As mentioned before, the term *góra* applies both to the condition of the coconut plantations for the time being and to the signs which indicate usually this condition. The coconut palms become tabooed and *góra* signs are erected on two occasions – death and feast.

For some time after the death of a man his own coconuts, those of his family, and, in certain cases, of the whole clan become taboo. But there was a strict distinction between the trees belonging to the man and his relations (the actual mourners) and the trees belonging to the other clansmen. In the first place, whereas the former became taboo under any circumstances, the latter were tabooed only in the case of an adult and influential male. And then there was a still more important distinction – the dead man's own trees and those of the mourners (the *nanáma* and *do'á'e* people; see chap. v., sec. 4) were tabooed automatically by the presence of the dead man's body. As will be described in detail hereafter, the body was buried either under the house of the deceased or among his coconut palms. The body and the grave were the symbols of the taboo. They protected the nuts magically, the dead man's spirit was angry when anybody touched them, and he punished the culprit by the same penalty which was attached to the other *góra* – the man became unlucky in fishing. It is very important to note that the taboo was called in this case *nebúru*, and not *góra*. Thus the dead man's coconuts were called *nebúru áma*, and the grave was said to be the *nebúru* sign. And it was emphatically affirmed that the presence of the body was quite sufficient to establish the taboo, and that never were any *góra* signs erected among the trees of the deceased or of the mourners. But the presence of the body was the *conditio sine quâ non* of the *nebúru*. Of this I was able to observe an interesting concrete case. About four months previous to my arrival at Mailu village, Bú'a, the former village constable and apparently by far the most influential man in the village, died in the jail at Port Moresby.[30] His body remained there. As he was a very important man, not only his relatives, but the whole clan – and many men from the other clans – observed coconut taboos on his account. Now, under normal conditions, his and his mourners' trees would have been *nebúru*, and no *góra* would have been placed among his trees. As his body was not there, however, a *góra* had been erected in the middle of his plantations, and these were said to be *góra*, and not *nebúru*. Thus his body, and his spirit, being far off, the *góra*, with its inherent magical sanction, had to be erected. When the body was buried, not in the coconut grove, but under the house, as was sometimes done in the olden days, it nevertheless acted as a *nebúru* token and sign of taboo, because it was nearby. As a matter of fact, the coconut plantations were never far away from the village.

A *góra* was put up by all the other people who mourned for the man (these were called *mágu ragu'ái*), but were not the chief mourners (*i.e.,* belonging to the *nanáma* and *do'á'e* groups). Also by all the other clansmen and tribesmen who were not mourning, but who wished to honour the deceased if he was a 'big man'. The *góra* sign consisted either of a vertical sapling or of a kind of gallows, composed of two verticals and one horizontal. Both used to be decorated with coconut leaves; in fact, they had to be young leaves of a small coconut tree. On coconut *góra* the young leaves are said to refer directly to coconuts. Thus I saw a mixed *góra* standing in the midst of a grove of mixed coconuts and betelnuts. On it were coconut leaves, which were said to refer to the coconuts, and betelnut stalks as a token of the betel. But it must be noted that some *góra*, having nothing to do with coconuts, are also decorated with coconut leaves.

When a *góra* is to be erected the owner of the palms gives away a quantity of nuts to be eaten by the young men and boys of his clan. Then the *góra* is erected, and the following spell is pronounced by the owner:–

'*Bó'i*	*éva*	*góra*	*émegi*	*óm*	*náma*	*áma*
spirit	this	gora	man	a	some	coconut
ítsi	*bána*	*bó'i*	*tseíba*	*bó'i*	*óre'óre*	*tseíba'*.
eat	time	spirit	do (act)	spirit	angry	act

Which in free translation would mean:– 'O spirit! When a man eats this tabooed coconut, O spirit, act; O spirit, be angry and punish him!' The spirit thus invoked would be one of the ancestral spirits of the owner. His rôle in protecting the tabooed coconuts is quite analogous to that of the recently deceased man towards his *nebúru* palms. The spirits in both cases get angry (*bó'i óre'óre*, an expression used often to design ill-luck in general; in Motu, *diráva díka*, spirit bad, angry), and prevent the offender from doing good fishing, particularly with the big nets (*gaúma*), but also with the smaller ones (*orá'i*).

Thus in both cases the taboo is enforced by a supernatural sanction – by the fear of the evil results, automatically following the offence. It is to be noted that no spells are uttered to the spirit of the deceased in order to make him protect his own coconuts; evidently he takes very good care that nobody touches those which are to be eaten at his feast, or are at any rate associated with his family's mourning duties. On the other hand, the spirit who is not personally interested in the proceedings must be invoked to play his part. The rôle of both spirits seems anyhow a very impersonal one; they are merely mechanical factors, bringing about, as an intermediate agency, the evil results inherent in the breaking of the taboo. They have no initiative in dealing out the punishment, nor is there anything left to their personal choice, and, on the other hand, a man violating the taboo would have no personal fear of the anger of the spirit. The natives are in general very little afraid of ghosts, though they dread darkness and its evil powers. The men are afraid to break the taboo purely and simply in order not to lose their fishing capacity, and from any other point of view the personal insult to the spirit, and its consequent annoyance, would not apparently matter. No man would with full knowledge violate a taboo, either a *nebúru* or a *góra*; if he unwittingly does so the punishment strikes him in the same form,

without regard to his motives. The culprit would, however, have no
other direct social punishment to bear; he would not be exposed either
to ridicule, contempt, or anger.

The *prima facie* object of the *góra*, admitted by the natives and
apparent in its most obvious function, is to prevent the coconuts from
being eaten and then to ensure a plentiful supply of nuts for the
mortuary feasts. It must be remarked, however, that the *góra*
arrangement overshoots its mark, as an enormous amount of nuts
become damaged and absolutely useless before the feast comes on.

So far we have spoken about the *góra* and *nebúru* – *i.e.,* taboos
imposed upon coconuts on the death of a man, symbolized either by the
man's body and grave, or by a special sign enforced by the man's own
ghost or by a spell-bound ancestral spirit – both of which, in a purely
mechanical and automatic manner, and unmoved by propitiation or
deflected by wrath or insult, work certain mischief upon the offender.

Similar taboos are imposed when there is a big feast, independently of
the death of anybody of importance. In that case there is no intrinsic
reason why the coconuts should be respected by the whole village or by a
clan, and a substitute for such a reason is created by erecting a big taboo
sign in the village. This sign is also a *góra*, called *tóna góra*. The erection
of the *tóna góra* is associated with the construction of a series of simple
góra in the palmgroves of the people who have to contribute to the feast.

When a big *Madúna* feast is to be held, a few months before the first
festivities – *i.e.,* roughly a year or more before the main feast, the *tóna
góra* is erected in the village street, in front of the house of the *Madúna*
master. He gives a small feast in his house, and then the trumpet-shell is
blown and an incantation is uttered. In this they utter the names of
different places, where coconuts are plentiful, and invoke the coconuts
to congregate and be plentiful in their village. This is the spell:–

'*Gadá' isiu áma ee –– e (long drawn)*
Bónabóna áma ee –– e
Gé' agéa áma ee –– e
Dahúni áma ee –– e

Gána áma tseri' áda
Evara aíba
Woyáu ligo woyáu láge'.

The first words in the first four lines are names of places; *áma* means
coconut; *gána áma tseri' áda* means all coconuts.

I did not obtain the full literal translation of the text, but the general meaning is obvious; the names of places rich in coconuts are called out – a kind of sympathetic verbal charm – and all the coconuts are invoked to congregate in order that the supply at the feast may be plentiful. Subsequently the other small *góra* are erected in the bush in the same manner, and the same invocation is addressed to an ancestral spirit, as is described above for the death *góra*.

The *tóna góra* consists of a fairly high vertical pole, to which several coconut leaves are fastened.

It is to be noted that the *tóna góra* is not erected on every occasion when a feast is given; in fact, it does not seem to be a very frequent feature. Whenever there is a fairly important death in the clan, or in the clans, giving the feast, and whenever the feast is at the same time one in the series of mortuary feasts, there is no *tóna góra*. For this the *nebúru* is sufficient. Nor is it erected on the death of a village notable.

Thus in the spring and summer of 1914 there were feasts in preparation in Kurére, Máilu, Loupóm, and Laruóro. Amongst these I only saw a *tóna góra* in Laruóro, where the feast was to take place in the summer of 1915–16. All the other places had *nebúrus*.[31]

It is obvious that the real sanction of the feast *góra*, governed by the main *tóna góra*, are of the same nature as the mourning *góra*, since the same invocation is uttered to the same agencies. But the *tóna góra* has no such sanction, and from the nature of its spell it is evident that its function is rather a magical one, to ensure a plentiful supply of coconuts. In this it is analogous to those other arrangements at a feast which aim at securing a plentiful supply of pigs for the feast.

Another form of *góra*, erected in the street in front of the master of the feast (*Madúna*) is the *móto góra*. It consists of a small square erection, composed of two sticks topped by a horizontal and covered with young coconut leaves, to which several of the large white shells (*Ovulum ovum*) are bound. This *góra* has nothing whatever to do with coconuts, except as to the leaves with which it is wrapped. Neither has it anything to do with any taboo or prohibition. It is simply a pledge, each shell representing a pig promised to the master of the feast by one of his relatives or friends. There is no spell connected with it, and it is only a forecast of the future splendour of the feast, which in its preliminaries and arrangements is full of such glorifications. When several clans arrange a feast a *mótu góra* is placed in front of the houses of head men of each clan.

Besides the coconut, several other articles of food may be *góra*'ed.

Betelnut (*wéni*) occupies a position in native life in many ways analogous to the coconut. At a man's death the betelnut palms are tabooed along with the coconuts, as has been already mentioned. As the groves of these two palms are usually contiguous, the same *góra* spell serves for both, its comprehensiveness being only expressed by the attachment to the *góra* sign of a piece of the areca palm.

The *wéni góra* (betel, or areca nut taboo) is, however, also used in another case. When the nut is deteriorating in condition and becoming 'soft like water', they try to improve it by putting a *góra* on the tree. This they do by tying a stick horizontally to the palm trunk and fastening some croton, or palm leaves to the point of junction of stem and stick. There is no spell, nor is there any taboo implied by the *góra*, which is obviously merely a kind of curative charm. It is simply a magical *góra*, and has no legal significance.

Quite similar in its essential is the fish *góra (oribe góra)*. It is put up in the water over the reef, and consists of a sapling with coconut leaves tied to it. This *góra* is erected upon the decision, or advice, of the old and experienced men of the tribe. When fish become scarce in any particular place on the reef or near it the old men, or the head men of the clan owning rights (purely nominal) over the reef, decide to erect a *góru* on this spot, and fishing there is tabooed for so long as the *góra* is up. It stands for some three to four moons, and when upon investigation it is found that fish are plentiful again the fishing is resumed. The *góra* would very probably be put up during a season when, in any case, there would not be much fishing done, as for instance in the seasons of busy sailing and trading. This *góra*, although it involves a taboo, has evidently no legal aspect, and is merely a magical and economic contrivance. There is a spell uttered when the *oribe góra* is erected, but I am not able to record it.

There are some minor *góra* attached to fruit trees, such as the native mango (*boróa*), a fruit tree called *gaméla*, and several others. They consist of a piece of palm leaf wound round the stem. They were said to be precautions against boys climbing the trees and eating the fruit before it was half ripe. The boys would be afraid to climb a *góra*'ed tree.

The men of Mailu Island make no sago palm *góra* in their sago swamps in Léa; but when the sago is not good, 'like water', the mainland Mági erect an *odei góra* (sago *góra*) on the path leading through the swamp. It is a pole with sago leaves bound to it.

I was informed that such a *góra* also constitutes a kind of mark of proprietorship, but on the whole my information on this point is defective.

Besides the *góra* there is another method of protecting property by means of a magical sanction. It is done by means of a conditional curse called *onága*. When an owner is afraid of his coconuts being stolen, or suspects that they have been interfered with, he utters a spell and binds the coconuts together (with a piece of their own fibre, torn off the husks). The man who has stolen, or who should intend to steal, gets boils and swellings all over his body, and dies from this complaint, which also is called *onága*. I was not able to record the spell, nor to obtain any details concerning similar protective measures which were said to be sometimes applied in the case of bananas and taro.

It is obvious that the native classification of facts embodied in the term *góra* is by no means adequate from a scientific point of view. It brings together those which are only superficially similar and discriminates between essentially kindred phenomena. But this very circumstance makes the adduced data rather interesting, for undoubtedly such a quaint, and obviously antiquated, mode of using words and classifying facts points to a previous state of things which differs from the present. And linguistic survivals are perhaps the most trustworthy, since a word may be used in a somewhat inadequate sense without practical inconvenience. On the other hand, a social institution, when its function changes, must either adapt itself fairly completely to its new form of existence, and hence vary in its essentials, or it withers and becomes obliterated. I will not speculate upon the nature of the survivals embodied in the Mailu conception of *góra*, and I wish only to point out briefly some of its peculiarities.

Góra, in its broadest and most abstract meaning, means taboo, rule, prohibition; it is distinctly the conception covering what we would call law in our society. In the more restricted and concrete sense, it implies a legal arrangement allowing certain goods to be protected against all consumption, and thus to be reserved for ceremonial religious purposes. It is never a symbol of proprietorship or a simple form of protection of private property, the latter function being performed by the *onága*. On the other hand, some *góra*, the *tóna góra* and the fish and betelnut *góra*, have a distinct magical function. One of them, the betelnut *góra*, has hardly any legal aspect; the fish *góra* involves a prohibition, and the *tóna góra* is, in its legal aspect, only a sign that there are prohibitory measures elsewhere. The *móto góra* has, again, neither legal nor magical aspect.

A few more words must be said about the previously mentioned food taboos, which the natives comprise[32] under another word, *tóra*. These taboos are met with on very many sides of social life – during feasts and economic activities; in some of the critical moments of human life, like initiation, puberty, and pregnancy; in relation to some sexual facts, and so on. These are mentioned in their respective connections, and will be only enumerated here in brief.

There are no tribal or clan *tóra* – *i.e.,* there is no food restriction imposed upon the whole village or the whole clan. There exist, however, individual, hereditary *tóra*; those descending in the male line, are closely associated with 'white' magic, and will be dealt with in chap. v., sec. 2; they were also obligatory for people practising 'black' magic and the healing art.

In addition there are a series of temporary taboos not attached to the person, to which all men and women are at times subject. Such are the taboos observed before and during the feast.

There are taboos connected with sex practised by women – the menstruation and pregnancy *tóra*, and there is the *tóra* of initiation.

As the headman of the clan has to undergo the most strenuous taboos, and to undergo them more frequently than anyone else (*e.g.,* at the feast), the *tóra* is also a means of social differentiation.

There are also some *tóra* observed during certain economic activities (chap. iv.).

6   WARFARE AND HEAD HUNTING[42]

The external relations of the Mailu villages with each other have been outlined in chap. ii., sec. 1. On the whole, they were not friendly. The

---

[42] The data covered by this section are very scanty and unsatisfactory. This is partly owing to the intrinsic difficulty in obtaining authentic concrete accounts about war and fighting in bygone days, and partly to the fact that I was more interested in the social constitution of the tribe, and that my inquiries about war, etc., were less extensive and thorough than on several other topics. The type of Mailu fighting seems to be identical with that of the Port Moresby tribes, of which there are some very good accounts collected by Prof. C. G. Seligman in his oft-quoted work: chap. ix. (Koíta), chaps. xli. and xlii. (Southern Massim). Broadly as far as I can judge, these illustrate the fighting methods of all the tribes of the southern coast.[33]

tribe was subdivided into sections, and each section, comprising several neighbouring villages, was waging a perpetual war against all the others. Their wars consisted either of systematically planned and prearranged raids, or of attacks on stray people whenever the chance offered. This did not occur very frequently, and though good care was taken by travellers, hunters, fishermen, etc., to make the opportunities as rare as possible, there was always the chance.

The mainland people, especially if a village was situated on the border of a 'confederacy', were obviously exposed to raids, for whenever the mainland people ventured from their fortified villages, which were pitched on top of fairly high and steep hills, down to the sea shore in order to get salt, fish, or shells, they were exposed to the danger of meeting the dreaded Mailu islanders, who were frequently sailing about, and would not for anything miss an opportunity of securing a head or two for their collection in the *dúbu*. On the other hand, the Mailu people, though practically safe on their own island, had to go to Léa, near Table Point, in order to procure sago. They used to hunt on the mainland near Magúbo (Greenaway Point), and to go on distant trading expeditions, when they might be blown ashore and wrecked. It was from the mainland also that they obtained their timber. Thus the occupants of all of the Mailu-speaking villages were more or less exposed to the risk of falling amongst their foes in greatly superior numbers and of being killed.

They used, however, to take their precautions, for when engaged in economic pursuits away from the village and within the reach of enemies it was customary to station sentries (*páiva*) in full armour and war-paint. This they did when felling trees in the bush, or when getting sago in an exposed swamp, as was the case when they went to Léa, where they were liable to be attacked by the Magóri.

The expeditions, or raids, might be carried out either by sea, which was the only way open to the Máilu, Loupóm, and Laruóro villagers, or they were made by land, as between the mainland Mági.

There were in Mailu special war canoes (*bobóre*). These were rather long dug-outs, longer than the usual *gébo* canoe, with an outrigger and float. The prow (called *bobóre itsána*) was decorated with wooden carvings; the stern (*aripara*) was not decorated. Each *bobóre* had its own name and each belonged to a clan or subclan. The following are the names of some of the canoes and the clans to which they belonged:–

Clan name	Subclan	Name of the war canoe
Mailu village –		
Bodéabo		Karokóko
Urumóga	{ Diadúbu	Dariábu
	{ Bánagadúbu	Reumánu
Maradúbu		Oíawáea
Moráu }		
Oraido }		Gominamánu
Loupóm village –		
Gobudúbu		Loubébe
Boimarai		Avareási

When it was decided to make a raid there was a feast and a dance – the *daúge* dance, as a rule. There were some men who had the decisive word in war affairs, and these were not identical with the clan headmen; and upon those going out to fight there was a taboo imposed called *góbu*.

For purposes of defence the mainland people had tree houses or platforms – I could not definitely settle which – called *lúmi*. The situation of the villages, which were invariably perched on the tops of hills, allowed the natives to control the approaches, and in order to make the defence more effective they built the tree fortifications on forked branches of the *báni* tree. In these they used to keep plenty of spears and stones, and, in cases of need, men, women, and children used to take refuge in them and hail missiles on their adversaries. The most effective way of attacking such a fortification was to cut down the tree. On the average there were about four such houses in a well-sized Mági village, which consisted of some forty houses. The villages were also stockaded.

Another form of fighting must be mentioned: the fights and quarrels which seem to have been invariably associated with the feasts. Squabbles over pigs and women and personal resentments, assumed naturally an acute form at feast times, when nerves were highly strung and passions on the alert. Unfortunately, my informants left me with general assertions, and I was not able to obtain any concrete instances.

The weapons in Mailu were identical with those of the coastal tribes in the Central Division. The heavy wooden spear, made of one piece, with the point barbed on one side with fairly large barbs. Sometimes there were two or three longitudinal barbed ridges running towards the point. There was also the stone club, but I was

not able to ascertain the specific forms used, as there are now no
clubs in the villages, all having been sold out to curio collectors.

A broad wooden shield, nearly a square, with rounded edges and
slightly tapering towards the base was used. It had a handle of ratten
cane and was ornamented in front with a rather broad belt of plaited
cane, ornamented with coloured feathers at the edges. The shield was
called *vétsi*, and was made of a soft wood (*una*).

An essential part of the war equipment, especially at times of
organized raids, was the war dress. Besides the perineal band, they
used to wear round the loins a piece of rattan (lawyer cane). The head
was decorated with a crown of cassowary feathers (*gúia*), or with the
feathers of *tsi'aí* (a bird of paradise). They used also to insert
cassowary feathers in their armlets and in the belt. The face was
painted all over, the left side red, the right white. A V-shaped
ornament of these same colours was painted on their breasts; a white
band passing from the front of the right shoulder down to the sternal
notch, when it met a corresponding band in red (the painting was
called *umu*). On the ankles and below the knees strips of pandanus
leaves were bound, and they wore the boar's tusk ornament (*má'a*)
suspended from a shell necklace (*kéma*). During fights, as during
dances, they put the boar's tusk into their mouth. Sometimes, as
amongst the tribes of the Central Division, the *musikáka* (Motuan
name) ornament – a flat piece of wood, inlaid with the red seeds of
jequirity, edged with boar's tusks, and with a pair of eyes made of
shell in the middle – was used as a 'mouthpiece' in fighting. This
ornament is well represented in many museum collections.

The Mailu were not cannibals and, except on their inland border,
where their neighbours, the Udáma, possibly practised
anthropophagy, they were not in contact with any cannibal tribe.[43]

They practised head hunting – that is, the killing of a human being,
man, woman, or child, solely with the object of securing the victim's
head. The body was left on the spot where the individual had been
killed, and the head was cut off and taken to the village. The
amputation of the head was done with a bamboo knife (*kápakápa*),

---

[43] On the west their neighbours were the Aróma people, who also were not
cannibals. On the east their immediate neighbours, the Bónabóna, were the only
Southern Massim who did not adopt this practice. The line of demarcation
between the anthropophagous Massim and the Bónabóna runs between Fife and
Farm Bays. The natives of the former did not eat human flesh, and the first
village in Farm Bay (Saváia) did so.

which the warrior carried suspended from a string round the neck, the knife hanging down the back. The head was carried to the slayer's *dúbu*, and there boiled in a pot, which was directly afterwards thrown into the sea. Then the skin and flesh were removed, and the skull, being thus roughly cleaned, was placed in the smoke and dried, so as to prevent the putrefaction of the incompletely removed soft parts. During this time the people used to prepare a feast, gathering bananas, taro, and cooking sago, fish, etc. When the skull was sufficiently smoked and dried it was prepared for hanging in the *dúbu* by drilling a hole in the top of the skull, through which a string was passed. Then the feast took place, during which a dance, called *ma'o*, was performed. In this the slayer, holding the skull under his arm, danced ceremonially.

The homicide had to undergo the usual taboo – that is, abstention from boiled food and fish – for a time after the act, and the violation of the taboo was believed to entail the complaint of abnormally enlarged testicles. During the feast he sang a special song, and he had also the right to wear white cockatoo feathers at the dances – a privilege which was highly valued, and which is now, in these degenerate days, impudently assumed by many a *miles gloriosus*, who has not even seen a man speared properly in all his life.

CHAPTER IV

ECONOMICS

1 LAND AND GARDENS

Land tenure

There are two forms of land tenure in the Mailu district. The Mailu
islanders (Toulon Island) possess only a very limited area for
agricultural purposes, and they have accordingly a modified form of
land tenure. Their gardening and their agrarian laws are of less
interest to them than to those of the mainland Mági, and, having
exceptionally good opportunities and capacity for fishing, they are
also much less dependent on the produce of their soil. On the
mainland, on the other hand, the question of land tenure is more
important, not only because the natives there are nearly entirely
dependent upon the produce of the soil, but because they have to
deal with the normal conditions of the agricultural Papuan –
abundance of land at the disposal of a fairly small community.

One has to use the legal conceptions of 'ownership' with extreme
caution when dealing with native conditions. Ownership in land
means with us the exclusive enjoyment of all the real economic rights
and all the privileges and pleasures one can derive from a certain
portion of land, subject to a very limited state of control, such as
forest and game protection, mining rights, etc. This form of
ownership does not, of course, exist in New Guinea, and it is not
exact either to use the term loosely or to try to find the nearest
approach to the European state of things in the native conditions.
The only correct course is to investigate all the rights enjoyed exclusively by an individual, or by a social group, with regard to a particular
portion of land. As a matter of fact, in most tribes those rights are not all
concentrated in one and the same 'legal person' (social body or individual man). Some of them are vested in social groups (village community, clan), others are apportioned to individuals.

This is the reason why the problem of native land tenure, so extremely interesting from the sociological point of view, and so important for the administration of the country, has not been often correctly treated.[44] And in the purchase of land from the natives there have very often been great and serious difficulties, leading to loss of time and money on the one side and to irritation and a feeling of wrong on the other.

The description of the mainland Mailu land tenure will be given first, as it is the more important. Land ownership, in our full sense of the word, involves among others the right to exclude the land from trespass, and the exclusive right to some of the produce of the soil – such as water, clay, and minerals. Among the Mailu natives these rights belong to the village community as a whole. Each village has around it an area which forms what may be called its sphere of influence. On this area strangers could not trespass, on pain of being immediately seized and killed. Friendly neighbours could go through to the village, but they might not loiter, for fear of being suspected of evil magic and similar crimes. A stranger, whether friend or foe, is not entitled to any of the produce of the soil; he could not use a waterhole, or take clay for pottery or red earth for painting, etc. In villages near, or on the sea shore, the adjacent beach and reef belong to this sphere of influence. The village community is the group in which these rights are vested, and, on the other hand, these general rights are not further apportioned and subdivided among the clans or individuals. This statement refers to the Mailu natives living on the islands (Toulon, Laruóro, and Loupóm), as well as to the mainland villages.

---

[44]Even in Prof. Seligman's treatise, where, as a rule, everything is stated with admirable accuracy and lucidity, land tenure is not dealt with in a quite satisfactory manner. Speaking of the Koíta he says, 'Each man has his share in the *iduhu* garden land, which descends to his children', etc. (p. 87). Further statements imply also the existence of individual land ownership in a fairly European sense of the word. Now the Koíta, as the Sinaughólo and Mági – and I think all the Papuo-Melanesians – make their gardens not individually, but jointly, the whole clan making one enclosure, and the ground inside being subdivided among the clansmen. There was no such thing consequently as exclusive individual claims to any portion of land for gardening purposes. There was no subdivision of land among individuals, save in the exercise of certain purely nominal over-rights. As the natives, however, attach a great importance to these over-rights, they very often mention the name of an individual as the real owner or 'boss' *(biagúna kórikori* – 'real boss', in Motu). Even the Motu, who possess very little land, have no individual garden land apportioned to a man hereditarily. This latter state of things (individual land tenure) I found only on Mailu Island. Among the Northern Massim, on Woodlark Island, I found a system of land tenure almost identical with that of the Koíta and mainland Mailu.

Between friendly villages their spheres of influence are divided by recognized boundaries; but between hostile villages there seems to have been belts of country where nobody would have liked to venture.[45] Again, there were some tracts of country, or areas of economic importance, where several villages tried to exercise their economic rights, either in harmony or in strife. Thus the small island of Abá'u, in Cloudy Bay (now the seat of the Resident Magistrate of the South-Eastern Division), has a stone quarry. This seems to have been used by the Mailu islanders and by the Loupóm people, and by several other villages near Abá'u (Domára and the non-Mailu speaking communities in Cloudy Bay). Again the sago swamps in Léa were used by the Mailu, the Loupóm, and the Magóri (a non-Mági village), who were not always on friendly terms with each other. So also the jungle near Greenaway Point (Mogúbo) was used by the Mailu for hunting and getting wood, and it was the garden land of the Loupóm.

Thus, in the use of the most elementary necessities (access to waterholes, use of wood and clay, and the right of free passage), the land is open to the members of a village community to the exclusion of all others. The right to make gardens is vested in the clan. Each clan makes its gardens collectively within one enclosure, and each clan has its own territory where it makes its gardens to the exclusion of the other clans. This seems to be the general form of garden land tenure. And my inquiries, made on several points on the mainland (in Dérebai, Bórebo, and Banóro), led to the same conclusion. As this is the general form of land tenure among the Papuo-Melanesians, it may be assumed to be also in the case among the mainland Mági. I had, however, such poor informants amongst these that I should have treated their data with extreme caution had they not been confirmed by other evidence.[46]

---

[45]Since the establishment of European rule things have been considerably changed in this respect, as the natives are no longer afraid of raids and ambushes.

[46]The facts obtained about the Papuo-Melanesians of the Central Division are perfectly convincing and clear. I have visited a number of native garden lands, discussed the ownership in many cases of new and old gardens, and drawn sketches of boundaries and garden sites. I tried the same method of concrete instances in Mailu district, but my informants spoke Motu poorly and could hardly understand what I wanted, or else they were suspicious. Mr. Armit, the Resident Magistrate at Abá'u, who has been brought up in Papua, and knows the natives and their customs intimately, gave me the same statement with regard to the land tenure in the Mailu district.

In Loupóm I obtained better evidence, but this instance seems to be exceptional. The members of the two main clans of the Loupóm – Boimarái and Gobudúbu – make their gardens communally, each clan making every year its own separate enclosure. But the soil is not divided between the two clans; it is used jointly and indiscriminately by both. It must be, however, understood that though one clan has for a time the exclusive use of a certain portion of the village lands, this must not be regarded as establishing a proprietorship. After two or three years the garden land reverts to the jungle, and thus again becomes at the disposal of either of the two clans.

Besides the general right to the soil vested in the village community, and the right to make gardens vested in the clan, there are some privileges vested in individuals. Such was, for instance, the right to give permission for hunting in a certain district, or to give the order for burning grass. There are many such privileges among the Papuo-Melanesians which, though absolutely devoid of any economic importance, yet appeal strongly to personal vanity, enhancing the sense of self-importance, and are, on that account, highly valued by the natives. It may be said, broadly, that at a native feast the 'master of ceremonies' does not derive any material benefit from it; but yet the privilege of giving a feast is highly valued by the master, as it greatly contributes to the raising of his social status.

There is, of course, individual, real property in land in the case of – first, a man's own house and the corresponding village site, and, secondly, his coconut and betelnut plantations.

Thus to summarize this paragraph it may be said that the village community possesses all the most elementary rights over its territory – thoroughfare, use of water, timber, clay, and minerals. The right of making gardens is vested in the clan, whose members make communal gardens on their own portion of land. Again, there are individual privileges, such as taking the initiative in hunting, burning grass, etc.

On Mailu Island the land is entirely subdivided amongst individuals, each man owning his own tract where he and his wife make the garden. When a man's children grow up he apportions to each male his respective plot of ground, which comes under separate cultivation as soon as the boy marries. In Mailu, practically all the rights to land are individual and hereditary. As long as the garden is not planted the natives walk freely on each other's ground. Firewood is collected by each woman on her husband's ground; clay and waterholes are used by the whole community jointly.

Garden making

It is difficult to give a description of gardening on Mailu Island as at the present day the gardens are very much neglected. Mailu village, which was always a trading community, has still further declined in this direction since the white man's rule (see sec. 4), and nowadays much vegetable food is imported from the mainland, with a consequent decrease in the interest taken by the natives in their gardens. Every man grows his coconuts on his own plot of ground, and cultivates part of it for bananas, taro, and yams. Low and slender fences are built round the plots in order to protect them from the wallabies, and as the soil has to lie fallow for a number of years only small patches are under cultivation. It would seem that in olden days, before the white man's advent, the island could not have been self-supporting, and this was my first idea, which was confirmed by the opinion of the Rev. W. J. V. Saville. But all my native informants, when questioned independently, contradicted this view categorically, all of them affirming that no trading for vegetable food was carried on with the mainland villages, and that the island was entirely self-supporting.[34] I feel convinced that the native information is correct, and it seems the more probable, as the fish supply on the island is plentiful and the soil very fertile. Garden making on the island was not so difficult as on the mainland, as there was neither the high jungle to remove nor the bulky pig-proof fence to construct. The only hard work in Mailu gardening was the clearing of the high, dense thickets of *lalang* grass (in Mailu, *tsilówo*). The grass is first burnt, and then uprooted. This latter was done by means of long, strong, and well-shaped sticks, pointed at the end. They were made of hard wood, and called *gebátsa*. The men drive the sticks into the ground with vigorous blows, and, using them as levers, loosen the soil and turn up the sods. A row of men, some eight or ten, each holding a *gebátsa* in either hand, work together, slowly moving backwards. In this way the ground is thoroughly broken up in a relatively short time.[47]

On the mainland the heavy work comprises the burning down of the scrub and the making of the strong palisade which protects the garden against the intrusion of bush pigs and wallabies. The big trees and the scrub are cut about mid-winter, in the *aurári* season. They

---

[47]I saw the process in the Koíta tribe. It is well described in the Rev. H. Newton's book *(op. cit.,* p. 123), from which I have borrowed some expressions.

are left to dry during the rainless season of *lióro*, and at the end of
this, just before the rains set in (December, January), they are
burned. The fence is made round the cleared area, and consists of
strong, round, vertical stakes, to which horizontal wooden bars are
lashed with lawyer cane. Within this enclosure the ground is
subdivided among the members of a clan, and the different plots are
so grouped that access to each can be obtained through the garden.
Diagramatically it may be represented thus:-

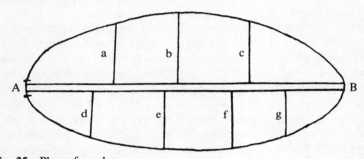

Fig. 25 Plan of garden
A. Stile over fence.
A-B. Main path.
a, b, c, d, e, f, g. Boundaries of plots.

The planting of the gardens begins in the *avára kívonai* season, at
the onset of the heavy rains. No special gardens are made for taro,
yams, and bananas.[48] There is only one name for garden – *madáva* in
the Mailu dialect, *iápa* in that of the mainland. Bananas and taro are
planted in one place, yams and sugar-cane in another, the bananas
and taro being planted first and the others afterwards. The garden,
and the taro in particular, had to be watched carefully and weeded.
The yams, and especially the newly introduced sweet potatoes, do
not require such care, and this is the reason for the great popularity
of the latter among the natives.

The clearing and fencing is done by men; the planting by both
sexes. But all subsequent work, such as weeding, etc., is done by
women exclusively. One result of this distribution of work is that an
unmarried man does not have a garden.

---

[48]In the Central Division each of the Koíta, Motu, and Sinaughólo clans makes
two, or even three enclosures, and special gardens, designated by special names,
are apportioned for bananas, taro, and yams.

A new garden is made every year, and the taro and yams are harvested during the first year. During the next year or two bananas and sugar-cane are gathered. The banana bunches are wrapped in leaves when they begin to ripen to protect them against flying foxes and birds. After three years the fence decays, the garden is open to wild pigs and marsupials, and the natives make little more use of it.

If the ground has proved fertile and the crops have been a success the natives make the next year's garden near by; but if the soil has proved to be unsatisfactory or 'unlucky' it is made at some distance in the scrub. I was not able to find that any omens were used in choosing the spot for the garden. The natives possess a great knowledge of the soil, and know, by the nature of the wild jungle, whether taro, bananas, or yams will succeed. The size of the garden depends *ceteris paribus* on the amount of yam eyes, taro tops, and banana seedlings available for planting. They also plant in their gardens some of the aromatic plants worn in armlets as perfumes and for decoration, as well as those yielding the poison used for stupefying fish. Of recent years they often plant the introduced pawpaw and pumpkin.

Magic used in garden making will be described in chap v., sec. 2.

When making new gardens sex taboos are observed, and in olden days, when the *dúbu* were in existence, the men slept in the *dúbu* and the women remained in the house. At the present time the men sleep in a bachelors' house, or else the men club together in one house and the women in another. It is considered that anyone not observing complete sexual abstinence when taking part in the making of new gardens would blight the crops.

Another important agricultural activity is sago making. There are sago swamps at the bottom of the deep valleys at the foot of the hills near the coast, on which the mainland Mági villages are perched. Thus all the mainland villages had their sago swamps. One such swamp might be used for sago-making by several neighbouring and friendly villages. For example, the villages of Bórebo, Dágobo, Unévi, and Pedíri make sago in the same swamp, which was situated in the valley at the foot of their respective hills. In the swamp there seem to be boundaries between the spheres of influence of each village, but I was unable by inspection to ascertain the existence and nature of these boundaries. At any rate, I was assured that trespass over these boundaries, or disputes between the villagers about sago have never occurred.

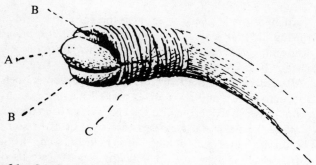

Fig. 26 *Ota*, Sago impelement.
A Stone blade. B, B – Wooden socket in which the blade rests; the upper portion is loose and the lower forms part of the handle. C – Lawyer-cane lashing, which keeps the two sockets together.

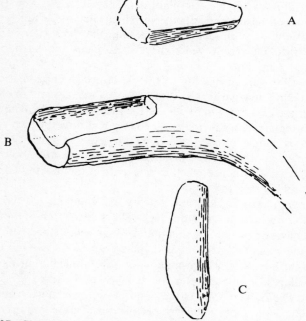

Fig. 27 Showing the *ota* taken to pieces, after the lawyer-cane lashing has been removed.
A, Upper, separable portion of socket; B, lower portion (made in the body of the handle); C, the blade, seen in profile. This is wrapped in a piece of coconut palm spathe (*núnu*) before being fixed in the socket and lashed with cane.

The Mailu islanders had their sago swamp near Magaúbo Point, the tract of country being called Léa. As mentioned above they had to be on the watch for the Magóri people, and while working the sago had to set scouts (*paíwa*).

The natives distinguish three kinds of sago palms – *tsíni*, a not very large tree, with many thorns on the bark; *rábia*, a big tree, without thorns on the bark; and *na'óta*, a tree of moderate size, also without thorns. The general name for sago is, in Mailu, *odé'i*; in Motu, *rábia*.

The process of making the sago is as follows: – After the tree has been felled and opened, the pith is pounded, washed, and shaped into more or less large cakes, or put into vessels. In Mailu the implement used for pounding the sago (called *ota*) consists of a small stone blade, fixed by lawyer cane into a bent handle (see figs. 26 and 27). After the pith has been pounded with this implement, it is washed in a trough formed by the hollowed-out palm trunk; then the women squeeze the water from the pulp and put the dry material into dishes, from which it is removed to be wrapped in broad leaves from trees growing in the swamps, so forming large, cylindrical, sausage-shaped bundles.

The coconut and betelnut

The coconut and betelnut palms were not planted in the gardens, but near the village. It is characteristic that the natives who, for reasons of a taboo or of a fast, will let hundreds of coconuts waste without making the slightest attempt to rescue them, and even without showing very much concern, are extremely economical when planting them. They never put the whole, intact nut into the soil, but use for planting nuts which have begun to sprout, and which have been treated in the following way: – They first remove the nut from the husk, so as to leave the upper part of this, with the attached sprout, in an intact condition. The nut is, with a great sense of economy, eaten, and the husk, with its sprout, planted, the result being that the plant grows much more slowly, bears fruit a few years later, and probably never becomes as robust a tree as if the whole nut were planted, for, under the native method, the young plant, in its early stages, is deprived of its natural nourishment. No work or care is subsequently devoted to the growing coconut trees.

The coconut palm is a plant of extreme economic value to the natives. The Rev. H. Newton, in the book so often quoted in this article, describes all its different uses among the natives on the north-eastern coast of New Guinea.[49] Exactly the same uses are made of the tree and its products among the Mailu, and I will briefly summarize Mr. Newton's list, adding only the specifically Mailu details. The leaves of the palm are used for plaiting mats (*tsináu*). A leaf is split in the middle and the two halves are plaited together, the split mid-rib forming a frame. Such mats are used as large trays, or as doormats and screens. The women's petticoats are made of palm leaves, and there is a form of basket made of the same material. Again, native brooms are made of the young leaves, and the dry leaf is used as a torch when fishing at night and collecting *frutti di mare*.

The spathe, or leaf sheath, which is astonishingly like an artificial fabric, is used for many purposes, such as wrappings for hafted stone blades and for making the large portfolios in which dancing feathers are kept, and it also has its use in making the sails of toy canoes.

The coconut, in its green, unripe condition, affords an extremely pleasant drink. In its ripe state it is used in the form of a coconut cream, and it is eaten raw. The hard shell of the ripe nut is used for waterbottles and spoons.

The operation of removing the thick outer husk preparatory to piercing the shell in order to obtain the kernel is by no means easy. To do this the native holds the nut between his feet and uses the long, heavy stick, sharpened at the end, called *gebátsa* (see above), with which the husk is chopped off. The husk, which is used as fuel, consists of a thick layer of fibre, covered with a polished skin. When burnt it yields an acrid smoke, which is used at the wet season for keeping off mosquitoes. It is used also for such cleaning and scrubbing as the natives require, and it affords the best painting charcoal. Mixed with salt or fresh water it contributes the black paint of mourning.

Use made of some jungle plants

Besides the cultivated plants, the natives utilize the wild jungle plants for many purposes. I am not able to give anything like a complete list of the forest plants which are used as food or for technical purposes, but a few examples may, however, be given by way of illustration.

The high timber was used for dug-outs, which were the most important structures in the construction of the large and small

---

[49] *Op. cit.*, chap. xiv.

canoes. Formerly a much softer timber (Mailu name, *móda*) was used for this purpose, as only stone tools were then available, but since they have possessed iron axes they make use of different kinds of harder timber. The same holds good with reference to the house-building material. The bush furnishes the native with an extremely strong and flexible lashing in the form of lawyer cane *(oro)*, which is used either simply stripped of its thorns or, when finer lashings are required, it is split.

Material for ropes (*váru*) and string (*tákoi*) is furnished by bush plants, and it is to be noted that the native always uses the name of the original plant to denote the finished article. Thus *váru* and *tákoi* are names of plants, which are, as stated, used also to denote the rope and string made from them respectively.

2   HUNTING

As mentioned above, hunting was carried on both by the mainland Mági and by the Mailu islanders, but there was not much done on the island itself. A few wallabies, which lived on the grassy slopes of the hills, were hunted from time to time, and at the end of the dry season, when the grass was burned, there was a bigger hunt; but there was not enough game to make it a serious business. The hunting grounds of the islanders were at Mogúbo Point, on the mainland, opposite their island, but they were not very good hunters; they did not use the big nets used for catching boar and wallaby, and they were thus deprived of the most efficient means of securing the game. The different clans of Mailu village are said to have had, even in the olden days, their different hunting grounds.

Thus the Bodéabo used to hunt in a district called Bódatúmu, the Urumóga in Gebédi, the Maradúbu at and near Mogúbo Point, the Morá'u on Magarída and the Oraído on Irúna. This statement does not mean, however, that the clan would hunt by itself, with the exclusion of the others from the sport and economic advantages; as far as I was able to ascertain it means only that individual clans used to take the initiative and invite the others to partake in the hunt on the clan's grounds.

Hunting was much more important for the mainland Mági, who could not depend upon fishing, and these used to hunt with the large nets. There was, of course, individual action as well in spearing the wallaby; but the most important method was a collective hunt with nets and drivers. There was only one name used for hunting, or, rather, two words used indiscriminately – *laíva* and *apána*. Hunting connected with grass burning was carried on, but not on a very large scale, owing to the restricted extent of grassland in the Mailu district.

The hunting of the larger game was done with nets, of which there were two kinds. The pig nets (*lóva*) were made of thin, but strong, rope (*váru*), with very large meshes, so that when a pig ran into them it got its head entangled in them. The wallaby nets (*eu*) were made of much thinner cord, and had fairly small meshes, just large enough to allow the wallaby to push its head through.

During the hunt the nets were set up by means of sticks attached to both ends, and there was usually a supporting stick in the middle. In order to make them more resistant, strings, passing from the tops of the end supports, were tied to a log or stone. The pig nets were set so that they joined each other, end to end, in a curved line, thus presenting a continuous barrier. The men, armed with spears and with the hand boar trap (*kóna*) stood on the inside of the curve, close to the nets, and the outer ends of the curve were closed by a line of men, who by shouting and making a noise drove the pigs on to the line of nets. Charging blindly, they usually did not see them, and ran right into the nets, which were set up just firmly enough not to fall down when first struck, and on the struggle of the pig to release itself the net collapsed and entangled the animal, which was immediately speared by the men standing nearby. Should the pig for some reason turn upon a man, the above-mentioned trap, *kóna*, was used. This consisted of a pear-shaped frame of strong cane, to which was attached a loose netting with very large meshes, made of thin, strong rope. The *kóna* was held by the man against the charging boar, which ran its muzzle and head right into its meshes. The man was able to wrestle with the animal for some time, but others, coming soon to his rescue, speared the pig.

The wallaby hunt is conducted in the same way as the pig hunt, with the exception that the nets are not joined up to each other, but a space of about one net's length being left between every two. In these spaces stand the hunters (see pl. 26 and fig. 29). The reason for this arrangement is that there is no danger of the wallabies charging through the gaps, as they are too much afraid of the men, whom a boar would not heed; moreover, the leaving of spaces between the nets allows the line to extend over a longer distance.

If such a hunt takes place on grassland, instead of in the jungle, the grass is burned along a curve, which with the line of nets forms a closed circuit.

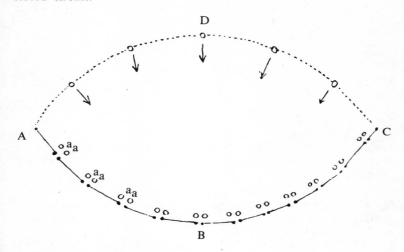

Fig. 28 Diagram of a pig hunt.
A, B, C. Line of nets.
A, D, C. Line of drivers.
a, a. Men with spears and *kónas* waiting for the pigs.

The season for hunting with fire was October and November (*lióro*), before the monsoon brought rain, when the grass was consequently dry. Hunting with drivers was mainly done in *lióro* and in *avára* – that is, between the fishing and the gardening seasons.

The nets, when stretched, are each about 15 m. long and just over 1 m. high.

Cassowaries were caught in traps made in the following way: – A long pole of the *tsuítsa* tree was cleft at one end, and the cleft forced open by a thin piece of wood (*odáva*) thrust into it (see fig. 30). Above the angle where the two jaws of the cleft diverged a young cassowary was tied. The mother bird, on seeing it, approaches and, pushing out the *odáva*, is caught by the neck in the cleft. When used the pole is held so that the arms of the cleft are in the horizontal plane and at the height of the adult bird's neck.

Cockatoos were caught by finding the hole in a tree where the birds were nesting, and by tying in front of this a small framed net

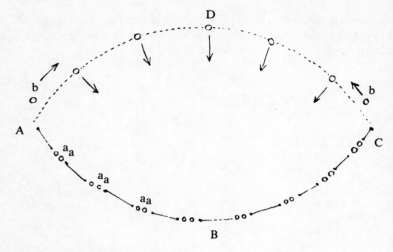

Fig. 29 Diagram of a wallaby hunt.
A, B, C. Line of nets.
A, D, C. Line of drivers or of fire.
b, b. Position of two men with firesticks who set the grass on fire in the direction of the arrows pointing from them.
a, a. Men waiting at the nets.

(*odi*), which is also used for hand fishing. The net was provided with a contrivance by means of which it could be slipped off the frame and closed. A man then goes round the tree and strikes it with a stick, and the bird, thus frightened, flies out into the net, which is immediately closed by another man. The white cockatoo (*oráma*), the red one (*uráva*), the small brown (*ero*), and the large brown *(bína)*, as well as the black *(begrému)*, were valued for feather ornaments.[35]

The bird of paradise (*tsiáke*) was caught in a snare (*onígo*) set on a branch of a native *Ficus (báni)*, on the fruits of which the birds feed. When the bird walks on this branch a man standing underneath pulls the snare and catches the bird.

The cuscus *(oúra)* is caught by cutting down the tree in which it hides.

A word may be said in this place about the breeding of pigs. As a rule, the sows only were reared and kept in the village, and they usually lived within the village enclosure. But they were allowed outside as well, where they mated with the wild boars of the jungle. This is alleged as one of the reasons why the pigs on the mainland in

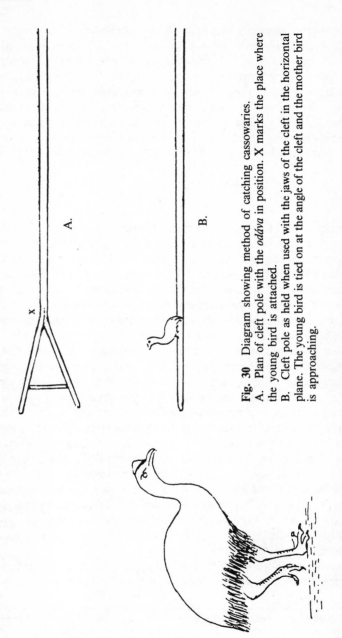

Fig. 30 Diagram showing method of catching cassowaries.
A. Plan of cleft pole with the *odáva* in position. X marks the place where the young bird is attached.
B. Cleft pole as held when used with the jaws of the cleft in the horizontal plane. The young bird is tied on at the angle of the cleft and the mother bird is approaching.

Mailu district were not nearly as good as those of Aróma, where the Mailu islanders, who did not breed their own animals, used to provide themselves with the material for their feasts. The Aróma pigs had much better food, as the large coconut plantations there were used for fattening them. Both sows and boars were kept in the village, thus precluding the admixture of the inferior, wild breed of the jungle. The Aróma people are also said to wash their pigs with coconut cream and bathe them, and they put some leaves as medicine into their food, but they do not utter any spells nor use any charms.

3 FISHING

In Mailu Island fishing is the most important economic activity, this industry having here reached a much more varied development than amongst the mainland Mági, and all that is said in this section applies to Mailu Island. The mainland Mági, who, in order to fish, had to venture down to the beach from their stockaded villages, and who had to be always on the alert, had much fewer methods of fishing in the past, although nowadays, when they live on the beach, they have probably adopted all, or nearly all, of the Mailu methods.

To the Mailu islanders the sea and its inhabitants are objects of the greatest interest. Several times I observed a great uproar in the village, shouts ringing from one end to the other, and people hurrying to the beach in the greatest excitement, the reason being that dugongs were seen in the shallow water near the reef. Often when I sailed in native canoes, or in launches, or paddled in a dinghy, I saw the excited and keen interest with which the boys watched fish moving in the sea. One evening, when I climbed to the top of the Mailu hill with several natives, they were exclusively interested in watching the fish which they could see with their keen eyesight in the water, some 200 m. below where we stood. When the women prepare for going out at night with torches, for the collecting of fish or shellfish, the excitement is evident during the whole afternoon and evening.[50]

Except the collection of *frutti di mare*, all the serious fishing is done by men, who often go out alone, or in twos or threes, with their fish

---

[50]The great excitement shown by the women in Bartle Bay whilst their fishing is in progress is described by the Rev. H. Newton *(op. cit.,* pp. 115, 116).

spears *(udi)*. This consists of a long shaft and of a crown-shaped set of slightly barbed prongs, forming a cone, which has its apex where the crown touches the shaft, and spreading out towards the points. They spear the fish, either from canoes or standing on the reef. This form of fishing goes on all the year round, and it is sometimes done by night with a flare. The real fishing season is *tsilówo*, at the change of the north-west into the south-east season, and during the first months of the south-east trade wind. At that time much of the fishing is done with nets.

There are several kinds of nets, adapted to the size of the fish and to the method of fishing. The smaller kinds are called *orá'i* and the larger *gaúma*. The former are made of string *(tákoi)*, which is made from thin fibres, twisted by the palm on the thigh. The *gaúma* are made of the native rope *(w'áro)*, which is prepared from the inner bark of the tree of that name. This is twisted into a very rough cord, which is wound round itself so as to form a very strong rope of double the original thickness. Thick kinds of such ropes are used in navigation, and a fairly thin sort for net making.

The different sorts of small nets are named after the kind of fish which is most frequently caught with them. Thus the net having the smallest mesh and width is called *távita orá'i*, after the small fish *távita*. The floats *(uto)* of this net are cut out of a very light kind of wood; they are not carved nor decorated, and have the shape of Bovril bottles. The sinkers *(boi'á'u)* are made of conical or spiral shells, which have been worn down to small, flat discs by the action of the waves. The length of the nets, which consist of separable sections, is of course variable, and sometimes several of them are joined together. The height of the *távita orá'i*, when set in the water, is about 40 cm. Slightly larger is the *lorowátu orá'i*, both being named after the two kinds of fish most frequently caught with them. The floats of the last-named net are identical in shape and material with those just mentioned, and their sinkers are made of a species of *Venus* shell, called *gíri*. Slightly larger again is the *gébi orá'i*, and still larger the *du'i orá'i*.

The large *gaúma* net stands in quite a different position in the community of nets, for there is some magic connected with it. The *orá'i* nets are private property, and they were kept in houses. The *gaúma*, on the other hand, is the property of the subclan, and it was in olden days kept in the *dúbu*. The *gaúma* have all their own names, which are here given:–

Subclan	*Gaúma* name[36]
Wáratsadúbu	Lágo'amúa
Aritsadúbu	Goítsie'amúa
Bódeadúbu	Batsu'amúa
Gáradúbu	Goítsie'amúa
Gónidúbu	Bánamúa
Díadúbu	Móguamúa
Boíladúbu	Bátsu'amúa
Bára'idúbu	Duámu'amúa
Bánagadúbu	Oi'amúa
Máradúbu	Agiu'amúa
Mótodúbu	Tówadá'e
Móraudúbu	Rúru'amúa
Morá'u	Ogobada'amúa

The *gaúma,* as said above, are made of thin *wáru* ropes. They had large wooden floats and heavy sinkers, made of fragments of large *Conus* shell (*a'i'a*), and when set in water the net might be from 2 to 3 m. high. There were two classes of this kind of net. The *umegaúma,* used for catching the big *ume* and other large fish, and the dugong net, *opi gaúma.* There was only one of the latter in the Mailu village, but there were several of them in Domára, at the western end of the Mailu district. These nets are held in most regard, and there are customs, taboos, and magic associated with them (see below). Each such net has got also its own individual name, but I failed to record that of the one in Mailu.

Various kinds of fishing, both by day and night, are done with nets, the smaller being used exclusively in shallow water.

1. Day fishing

Táea

This is done quite close to the shore, the men, of course, wading. A large heap of stones *(c)* is previously piled up in the sea, so that a number of small fish may find shelter and congregate. One man keeps one end of the net fixed on shore, and two, or more, others hold it at different points, while several men try to drive the fish into the net. By shouting and splashing the water they frighten the fish out of the pile of stones, and then, closing upon the net, they drive the

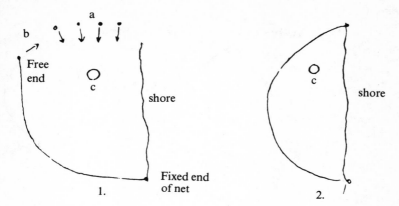

Fig. 31 Diagram of *Táea* fishing
a. Arrows indicating the direction in which the fish are driven.
b. Direction in which the free end of the net is moved.
c. Heap of stones.
In 2. the net is closed against the shore.

fish into it, swing its free end towards the shore, and the net, having been thus closed, the men take out the fish. For this form of fishing the *lorowátu* and *gébi* nets are used.

Gébi fishing, in which the net called gébi orá'i is used.

This method is similar to that just described, insofar that the fishing is done in shallow water and small fish are caught.

The difference is that one end of the net does not touch the shore. Two or three men hold it away from the land, while several others drive the fish into it by beating the water with sticks, screaming, etc. Then the net is closed by bringing the ends together, and the fish are taken out by hand.

Dú'i

This kind of fishing is done further out in the sea. Some four or five men paddle outside the reef, and when fish are seen two men get into the water and swim, holding the two ends of the *dú'i* net; others, also swimmming, make a noise, and so drive the fish into the net, and when they come in contact with it, it is rapidly raised and both net and fish are lifted out of the water together, without previous closing of the latter.

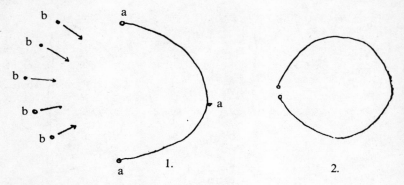

Fig. 32 Diagram of *gébi* fishing
a, a, a. Men holding net.
b, b, b. Men driving the fish.
In 2. the net is closed.

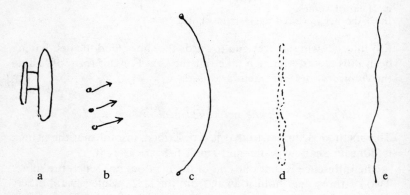

Fig. 33 Diagram of *dú'i* fishing
a, Canoe. *b.* Drivers swimming. *c.* Net. *d.* Reef. *e.* Shore.

In the *távita* form of fishing the net is also not closed, but is lifted as in the method just described. The nets *(távita orá'i)* employed for it have very small meshes, and are used in shallow water to catch very small fish.

The deep-sea fishing for big fish *(dóa)*, in which the *gaúma* net is used, is always conducted in the daytime and from a large canoe *(oro'u)*. These are sailed some distance outside the barrier reef which surrounds the island, and preferably towards an outlying reef. The men scout for the fish, one of them usually climbing the mast of the canoe to look out. When they are seen, the net is cast and is held by four men, or so, as they swim. A few other men, also swimming, drive the fish towards the net, which is closed upon them by bringing the two ends together. One end is then moved along the net, as shown in the diagram, so as to circumscribe the space in which the fish are confined, and these are then taken out. Sometimes, when fishing is done near the reef, the net men wade instead of swimming.

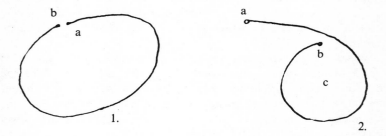

Fig. 34 Diagram of *dóa* fishing
1. Net closed.
2. The end *b* is then moved along the length of the net so that space *c*, in which the fish are, becomes gradually reduced in size.

2. Night fishing

Bóni

This is the form of nocturnal fishing which corresponds to the *táea*, day fishing. Stones are piled together in heaps near the shore, with the object of inducing small fish to seek shelter therein. *Lorowátu* and *gébi* nets, sometimes several joined together, are attached by one end to the shore, and the rest of the net is moved by one or more men. Several men, by holding torches of dry leaves, beating the water with sticks, and shouting, drive the fish into the net, which is closed against the shore and the fish taken out by hand (see diagram of *táea* fishing).

Aúaurúi

In this method the spear is used. A few men paddle out in a small canoe *(vao'na)*, in the bow of which one of them stands, holding a torch in one hand and a spear in the other. The fish, when they approach the light, are speared. The fish commonly captured in this way is the *aúau* (in Motu, *korabáda*).

A method of capturing fish which is still to be mentioned is that by which they are poisoned, or, rather, stupefied, by means of a plant which is called *tú'a*. For this the net is also used, as well as a heap of stones, to attract the fish. The leaves of the *tú'a*, which have been previously pressed between two stones, are bound in a big bundle, which is attached to the end of a long stick. The bundle is thrust into the heap of stones, and the men beat the water and shout. The fish, both frightened and stupefied, swim right into the net and are easily caught.

The dugong *(Halicore dugong)* fishing *(wálowúlo)* is always carried out in shallow water, either inside the barrier reef or near it on the outside. When the animal is seen, the men, to the number of about ten, enter the water and spread the dugong net. Other men drive the animal against the net, and when it is entangled its head is held down in the water until it is suffocated.

On the return of the fishing party to the village the men sing the following song, beating the time with the large floats on the dugong net:-

> *Pikana au ena vavíne*
> (name) man his wife
> *Ila gorila kaikai ai kaikai au*
> food cook eat
> *Ena vavíne ila gorila,* etc.

This song was said to be in the Aróma language.

4   TRANSPORT AND TRADING

Introductory remarks

Trading by land did not play a great part in the economics of the Mailu district, for on the Mailu mainland these people produced practically the same articles in all their villages, and there was no occasion for exchange between them. Moreover, communication was not easy in the direction parallel to the main range, as any village group would have to deal with hostile neighbours. Travelling along the beach in a direction parallel to the longitudinal axis of the continent, which is now regarded as the easiest way of communication, was also impossible for lack of personal security. There was, it seems, some trading done in the transverse direction between the mainland Mági and their inland neighbours, but I was unable to discover that any really important article was traded that way, and it seems also clear that there was no trading route across the main range. I was informed by Mr. Armit (Resident Magistrate at Abá'u) and by Mr. Higginson (Resident Magistrate at Samarai), who know the Mailu hinterland well, that there is a long gap between the Udáma (natives of the Mailu hinterland) and the tribes living on the other side of the main range.

Thus trading by land and transport on land do not play any part in the affairs of the district.

The Toulon islanders are the great trading community of this part of the country, and they carry out their business by sea. They possess well-proportioned sea-going canoes, provided with the well-known crab-claw sail, which form one of the most picturesque features on the south coast of Papua. I am told by sailing experts that the Mailu *oro'u* (called by the Motu *lugúmi*) are the best sea-going canoes in the territory. They are quite as fast and manageable as the Woodlark canoe *(vága* or *amuiúwa)*, and as they are able to sail close to the wind trading expeditions in either direction are possible. From the fact that they are built with two dug-outs instead of one (as is the case with the *vága)*, they are able to stand heavy weather better than the latter, and they are also able to carry more cargo.

Description of native canoes and of native sailing (see pls. 17, 18, 19, 20, 21, 22, also 3).

The hull of the *oró'u* consists of two dug-outs joined together by a set of poles, on which rests a platform. There is no differentiation between bow and stern, as it is sailed either way; but the hull is not bilaterally symmetrical, because one of the dug-outs is larger than the other, and it is on the larger one that the mast is fixed; there is also a small lateral platform on the same side. The dug-out on the mast side is called *tsébi*; the smaller one is called *lárima*, a name also given to the floats of the small outrigger canoes. The dug-outs are at the present time made of the wood of the *móda*, which is one of the tall, tropical trees with buttressed trunks. In olden days, before the white

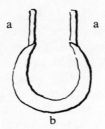

Canoe Making
Fig. 35 Transverse section of one of the canoes, which forms the basis
of the double canoe *(oró'u)*. It shows the planks *(a, a)* forming the
gunwale, and the dug-out log *(b)* forming the bottom of the canoe.

man's implements were in use, the *ilimo* tree, the wood of which is
much softer than that of the *móda*, was used for this purpose, as the
latter was too hard for their stone tools. The trees were secured in
olden days on the Baírebo River, which is on the mainland, opposite
Mailu, or in Léa, the district where they used to make sago.
Expeditions in search of this timber consisted of a number of men, as
it was necessary to be prepared for defence. The tree was felled,
dragged to the water, and brought to Mailu, where in olden days they
were hollowed out with stone tomahawks, but now the work is done
exclusively with steel implements. The log, after excavation, was
provided with a fairly high gunwale, made of two long planks, placed
one on each side, and two short ones at the ends. The gunwale *(oro'u
tsípa)* is lashed to the dug-out log by means of a fairly thin, but
strong, vine *(tsináre)*. Holes are made near the upper border of the
dug-out and in the middle of the gunwale plank, and the vine lashing
is passed several times through those two sets of holes and over the
top of the gunwale. These lashing strands are, nautically speaking,
'served' – that is to say, the vine is wound round them closely. Some
ten or twelve lashings are made on each side.

This combined structure – dug-out and gunwale – is strengthened
by a set of six ribs *(a'e)*, which are placed in opposite pairs in the
middle and at both ends of the canoe. The ribs are made of branches
of the *váru* tree, which are naturally bent to less than a right angle.
They are lashed to the canoe by the *tsináru* vine in three places, one
end being fastened to the upper edge of the gunwale, the knee to the
top edge of the dug-out log on one side, and the other end to the top
of the dug-out on the opposite side (see fig. 38).

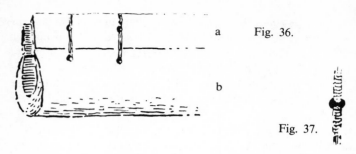

a   Fig. 36.

b

Fig. 37.

Fig. 36 Shows the manner in which the gunwale plank *(a)* is lashed to the dug-out *(b)*. The longitudinal strands of vine are shown passing through the holes.

Fig. 37 Shows the way in which the vine is wound round its longitudinal strands.

The gap between the gunwale and dug-out, as well as any holes, are caulked with the soft bark of a tree *(kaítsio)*.

The perpendicular planks *(birítsa)*, which close the canoe at both ends, are carved at the top with a more or less uniform design, but even the best carving done in Mailu is of poor quality, as compared with that of the Massim (see pl. 17). The dug-out ends in a pointed horizontal nose *(oró'uáre)*, which projects for some two or three feet under the carved part of the *birítsa*, and is sometimes ornamented.

The carving of the *birítsa*, which are made of *móda* wood, seems suggestive of the human face, but the natives do not endorse this interpretation. These are the essential parts of the two canoes, which form the hull of the compound canoe, the *oró'u*.

The two canoes are joined together by about ten horizontal poles *(iádo)*, passing through holes made in the four gunwale planks, and

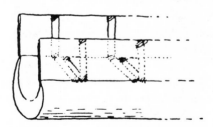

Fig. 38 Two pairs of ribs of a canoe. In reality the pairs are much further apart, as there are only three pairs in the whole canoe.

strongly lashed to them with *tsináre* vine. They project beyond the gunwales, so that they are easily seen on both sides of the *oró'u*, and their ends are usually ornamented with streamers of coconut leaf spathe (see pl. 17, 18). The platform *(vavá'o)* of boards rests on the *iádo*, to which it is solidly lashed, and it covers only the space between the dug-outs – that is to say, it does not encroach upon the latter.

The whole structure is still further strengthened by a framework of four strong poles. The two longitudinal ones *(o'aó'a)* run along the top of the outer gunwales of both canoes. The transverse poles *(abába)* are broad, flat, and board-shaped, and run outside the *birítsa*.

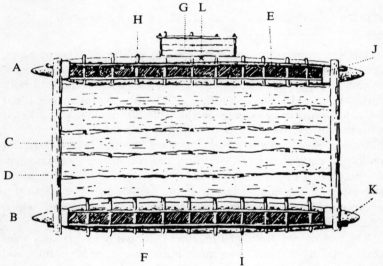

Fig. 39 Plan of an *Oró'u*
A. *Tsébi* canoe (mast side). This dug-out is the larger of the two.
B. *Lárima* canoe; it is as a rule the slighter one.
C. Platform *(vavá'o)*.
D. *Abába*.
E. F. *O'aó'a.*
G. *Tsébi wára* (in this diagram the *tsébi wára* platform is made exceptionally short; usually it is much longer).
H. I. *Iádo*.
J. *Birítsa*.
K. *Oró'uare*.
L. Place for mast.

On the outer side of the *tsébi* dug-out a small lateral platform *(tsébiwára)* is constructed, projecting above the water (indicated on pl. 3). Close to this, and sometimes partially upon it, the mast *(véa)* is erected on the *tsébi* dug-out. A short log *(dábi)* is lashed to two *iádo*, and a young *madáve* tree, about 8–10 metres high, is lashed to the *dábi* and to the two *iádo*. The ropes supporting the mast consist of a fourfold strand of untwisted rattan or lawyer cane (in Mailu, *nídi*; in Motu, *oro*).

This passes from one end of the *lárima* dug-out to the top of the mast, where it is looped and rests on a piece of wood stuck through the mast, and from here it descends again to the other end of the *lárima*. At both ends of the *lárima* the strands, which are ornamented with streamers of coconut spathe *(núnu)* are fastened by strong, looped knots. Similar streamers are sometimes attached to the top of the mast, and in some cases the latter is ornamented with cassowary feathers.

Fig. 40 Showing the manner in which the stays are fastened to the mast, near the top.

Each canoe has one mast and one sail *(déudéu)*. The sail is constructed of matting *(eba)* made from a freshwater reed. Narrow strips of this, about 40 cm. broad and 6–10 m. long, are stitched together with the bark fibre of the *váru* tree – the same bark as that from which the ropes are made – and needles made of the wood of a palm *(góro)*. The characteristic crab-claw form of the sail is conditioned by the convex form of both spars and by the curved line of the upper rim of the sail.

The boom *(itsá'u)* and the yard, or gaff *(atana'itsáu)*, are composed of two or more poles of *kóke* wood, which is very tough and elastic lashed together with thin *váru* ropes. The ropes (in Mailu, *déudéu ora'ora)* by which the sail is hoisted pass through a hole in the top of the mast and are made fast to an *iádo* at the base of the mast. Before hoisting the sail the rope is moistened in order to make it run easily through the mast hole. The sail is attached to the boom and gaff by lashings placed about every 50 cm. The gaff, when hoisted, comes to the top of the mast at about two-thirds of its (the gaff's) length. Both boom and gaff are attached to the bottom of the mast. The sheets (ropes holding the boom) are tied to the boom at about its middle, and they pass to the last rear *iádo* of the *lárima*. In moderately rough weather they scandalize *(bádi póa)* the sail by folding the bottom apex of the triangular matting so that the top of the sail comes much lower. In very rough weather they lower the sail, cast it off from the boom and gaff; then they highstop the task of the sail, putting a short spar across its belly to spread it out.

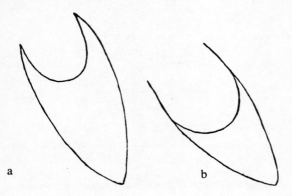

Fig. 41 *a,* Full sail; *b,* scandalized sail.

The rudder *(maréva)*, in most cases made out of an old leaky dug-out, is a broad board, about 4 to 4.50 m. long, tapering in width towards one end.

The rudder is lashed to the third *iádo* from the stern of the *tsébi* with a piece of *váru* rope, and it hangs down by the side of this canoe and parallel to its side, somewhat after the fashion of the steering oar of a Viking's galley. About 1 to 1.20 m. from the top of the rudder

Fig. 42 Mailu rudder

two holes are made in it, one under the other, and through these two loops of rope, called *maréva dó'i*, are passed. A stick *(maréva dóra)*, about 2.50 m. long, passes through the two loops and serves the purpose of a tiller in steering *(oma)*. This can be done by one man if the weather is not too rough. The steerer stands with one foot on the *tsébi* and with the other placed on the rudder half a metre below the lashing, in order to keep it submerged, as it naturally tends to rise when sailing. By the movement of the tiller he can rotate the plane of the rudder and so direct the course of the boat just as is done with an ordinary rudder, with this difference, that in the case of the Papuan boat the rudder, from its position not far from ''midships', serves to some extent as a leeboard, and so checks leeway.

As mentioned above, these boats are able to sail fairly close to the wind, making but little leeway. They cannot go about ship in the ordinary way, as the larger *tsébi* dug-out must always be to leeward; in fact, the smaller and lighter *lárima* acts more or less in the same way as the float in a catamaran, and if too much weight is put on this the craft capsizes.

In order, therefore, to go about ship, called *dóedóe*, the natives proceed as follows: – They unship the rudder, lashing it at the other end of the *tsébi*, and reverse the sail, the bows of the boat then becoming the stern, and they go off at right angles to their former course.

If there is no wind, or only a very little, they sometimes row, the oars being rather large and quite different to the paddles used for the small boats. The oar is fastened to an *iádo*, and they pull in a sitting position.

Ownership of canoes

There are usually two owners to a canoe, called *oró'u gubina égi* (canoe boss man) and *lárima gubína égi* (float boss man), meaning the 'man controlling the canoe' and the 'man controlling the *lárima*'.

The first is the chief owner. Nowadays, when there are at times as many as thirty to forty *oró'u* in Mailu (they are often traded and thus the number varies), a man and his younger brother usually own a canoe jointly. In olden days the *oró'u* were much fewer, and, as far as my information goes, there was only one in each clan, or, if this was big enough, one in each subclan. Each clan or subclan had its own name for its *oró'u*. Thus there were two *oró'u* in Loupóm, of which Oradoróm was owned by the Gobodúbu clan and Avareási by the Bo'imará'i. In Mailu I obtained the following names of canoes (though it is not a complete list):-

Clan or Subclan	Canoe name
Bodé'abo	Kóbu
Boiladúbu	Aru'ábu
Banagadúbu	Kilápu
Maradúbu	Lokóm
Motsodúbu	Vé'agú'ia
Morá'u	Aria'umóga

In Laruóro the following were the canoe names:

Clan or Subclan	Canoe name
Motsodúbu	Mogu'ánave
Dagedúbu	Oribegá'i
Waratsadúbu	Dunári
Bo'idúbu	Láeagá'i
Gúbaredúbu	Had no canoe

In this state of things, when each canoe belonged to a clan or subclan, the headman of the clan or subclan was also the chief master of the canoe, and his brother or uncle would be the second owner. As a matter of fact, ownership was in this case, as in many others, rather a question of a honorific title than of exclusive usufruct. A big *oró'u* could conveniently hold some fifteen or twenty people, and that was as many as were likely to set out on any expedition from one *dúbu*. On the other hand, the sailing – as far as course, dates of sailing, etc., were concerned – was a matter regulated by custom, so that there was really very little scope to exercise the rights and privileges of ownership in Mailu sailing.[51]

The crew of the *oró'u* consists, at the minimum, of six men, of whom it takes three to look after the sail in rough weather. One man can steer in fine weather, but it requires two or three when it is rough, and one of the crew is sometimes needed to use the *ivára* – a long pole used to push the boat off the shore or off the reef in the case of traversing a narrow passage.[52]

Besides the *oró'u*, some natives of the district use smaller double canoes, called *gébo*. These resemble the *oró'u*, but are only about half their size, less ornamented, and without carved *birítsa*. They are used for short journeys only.

The *vaóna* – a kind of catamaran, or dug-out, with float – is of the typical Papuan form. There are only a few peculiarities about the attachment of the float to the outrigger, of which, however, I have not made a record.

Very small dug-outs, used as playthings by boys, have been mentioned above.

Trading expeditions

The *oró'u* were the means of transport on water of Mailu, Laruóro, and Loupóm. As a matter of fact, however, as far as distant sailing was concerned, they appear to have been a monopoly of the Mailu islanders in the olden days.[53] Laruóro was a fairly recent settlement, and neither it nor Loupóm ever used the big canoes for distant expeditions or trading voyages. They used them in rough weather to reach their gardens on the mainland, where a small dug-out would not have been safe. They also made short coastal journey to Déreba, Bórebo, etc., but that was all. The real trading and distant voyages of the district were done exclusively by the Mailu islanders.

---

[51]If a man did not possess an *oró'u* he could borrow one (*gánade otsáutsa*). The price for the journey from Mailu to Aróma is: one *abóma* (long wooden dish), several coconuts, a couple of spears, and some food. This would be shared by the two owners.

[52]The platform of the *oró'u* could be covered with a mat roofing, and the boat was thus made into a sort of dwelling, habitable even in rainy weather, and affording protection against the sun. The boat was used in this manner when beached on some distant visit. The house-boat figured on pl. 3, remained thus beached and inhabited for weeks in Mailu village.

[53]Domára, in the west, may have been an exception. The Mailu also traded their canoes to the Aróma natives.

It was necessary that these should be good sailors, as they were obliged to import many commodities from abroad, and even to cross from
Mailu to the mainland in rough weather required a good deal of seacraft,
as the channel is about five miles in width and quite unsheltered from
either the south-eastern or north-western winds. On the other hand, the
short distance of less than a mile from Loupóm to the mainland was
fairly sheltered, especially in the south-eastern season.

The Mailu, in olden days, seem to have been self-supporting, as far
as food is concerned; but they had to procure the sago on the
mainland, without which there could be no feast and no certainty of
a sufficiency of vegetable food. They had also to fetch the timber for
building canoes and houses, and the sago palm leaves for thatching
their roofs. They had to go to the tropical jungle on the mainland for
the different fibres for their string and ropes, and for the reeds for
their matting and basketry. They had on their island no suitable
wood for making spears and shields, nor the proper stone for clubs
and stone axes. Further, they had neither wild boars on the island,
nor could they rear village pigs, and a Papuan without a pig is a very
incomplete human being. Thus they were, in their requirements, a
community entirely dependent upon resources from outside, and
they had to get the required commodities either by robbery, piracy,
or trade. As a matter of fact, in olden days they used to do all these.
But I do not think that piracy and robbery were ever important
factors in the economic life of the Mailu community, and at present
they have become absolutely harmless Philistines under the pressure
of law and the influence of religion.

Their own economic activities on the mainland (sago-making and
hunting) have been previously mentioned. There remains to be said a
few words about their trading. By their excellent craft, good training
in seamanship, and by their eminently favourable position, the Mailu
islanders were exceptionally well adapted to become a great trading
factor on the southern coast. They could leave their village without
approaching any hostile settlement, and they had no rivals equalling
them in seamanship anywhere within their sailing area. In this they
seem to have been better off than the trading communities of the
eastern end and the archipelago (Milne Bay, Engineer Group, and
Louisiades), which must often have met with disaster from hostile
tribes on their trading expeditions.[54]

---

[54]See C. G. Seligman, *op. cit.*, chaps. xli. and xlii.

The Mailu had a clear coast from Sua'u Island in the east, where their crab-claw boats met the oval-shaped *vága* (or *amuiúwa*, as they are called in that district) of the Massim, to Aróma in the west, where the native traders from the Hood Bay villages, and even the Motuans, met and carried westward their trading business.

The Mailu were traders in the true sense of the word; they not only exchanged their own products for the things they wanted, but they played the part of middlemen, obtaining some articles in the east and exchanging them in the west with a great advantage, and *vice versâ*.[55]

As the trading was done seasonally, it will be best to give an account of the several expeditions conducted annually and, as a rule, with reference to the native seasons and division of the year described in chap. iii. As mentioned there, the season of *avára ogóda* was spent at home, and so was *tsilówo*, which was the fishing time. It is in the *aurári* season (July-August) that they began the regular series of trading journeys and the expeditions preparatory for trading. From the convergence of the statements of all my native informants it appears certain that this series was usually carried out in the same order, and that in olden times it did not essentially differ from the present state of things, though the trade is now carried out more briskly than before, and, owing to the security from raids, a much larger number of natives venture to leave the village than would have been then possible.

As said, the first expedition leaves Mailu in the *aurári* season, going westward to Aróma, in order to bring home a supply of betelnut, which is plentiful at that time. I could not ascertain what was the article they exchanged for the betelnut, but I believe it was chiefly pottery. On this expedition they fish for the *Conus millepunctatus* shell all along the barrier reef from Mailu to Aróma, and they acquire unworked shells from the Aróma people. In fact, the collecting of these shells is undoubtedly the most important aim of this expedition, as it makes possible the subsequent manufacture of arm-shells, which again are the main article of trade with the Aróma.

In the *lióro* season (late September and October) they go to Léa to make sago, of which they produce much larger quantities than their own wants require. The surplus is traded to the Aróma people on a

---

[55]Cf. the description of similar communities in the Massim area, C. G. Seligman, *op. cit.,* pp. 526 to 528, and p. 536, *et seq.*

second expedition, buying this time small pigs and dogs. Aróma is
the chief centre, but on the way there they trade with the other
villages (Dómara, Vilerúpu, etc.).

After this second expedition to Aróma they sail in the *lióro ogóda*
season (November-December) eastwards to Bónabóna Island, the
villages round Mullins Harbour, and further along the coast as far as
Suá'u. There they acquire, in the first place, arm-shells in return for
the small pigs and dogs which they had obtained in Aróma. These
arm-shells are made in the Southern Massim district and in the
archipelago, the best ones being manufactured in the Trobriand and
Woodlark Islands. The Mailu make arm-shells themselves, and they
seem to be as good at that industry as any others. But it pays them to
trade the arm-shells down from the east to Aróma, owing to the
difference of prices between these two districts. The Mailu know also
some tricks by which the market value of a shell can be increased.
The value of an arm-shell is estimated according to the position it is
able to occupy on a man's arm. The higher up it will go and the easier
it will retain its position on a strong man's biceps the more valuable it
is, and to this end the Mailu very often grind down the shells in such
a way as to allow them to be slipped further up the arm.

Besides the arm-shells, the Mailu used to acquire several other
articles of the much superior Massim workmanship, particularly the
exceedingly fine ebony carvings of the Northern Massim, and the
fine, green polished axe blades coming from Woodlark or the
D'Entrecasteaux group.

As the trading routes of the east are essentially connected with
those of the Mailu, and as the general cultural influence of some of
the eastern people upon these natives is unmistakable, it seems
advisable in this place to say a few words about the trading lines on,
and round, the eastern end of Papua, as this is cut off by a line
touching Mullins Harbour on the east and passing through
Cape Vogel, including also those islands of the adjoining archipelago.

Prof. Seligman has given an excellent account of the Massim trade
routes, as far as they are contained within the Massim area proper.[56]
He shows how the main manufacturing area (the Trobriands and
Woodlark) used to be in communication with the D'Entrecasteaux
group, and with the trading centres in the archipelago, such as

[56] *Op. cit.,* chap. xl.

Túbetúbe, in the Engineer group.[57] Prof. Seligman also traces the lines of direct communication between Murua (phonetically spelt Muiú'a) or Woodlark Island and the Louisiades[58]; but this is less important in the present connection. He also shows how the natives of Milne Bay were in constant communication with the trading communities of the archipelago, and were thus provided with the products of the Northern Massim (Trobriands and Woodlark), as well as with those of Louisiades and the D'Entrecasteaux group. 'Lastly the hamlet-groups behind the head of Milne Bay had at least occasional intercourse with the people in the neighbourhood of the head of Mullins Harbour on the south coast, and there is reason to believe that there was formerly a trade route (never perhaps of great importance) from Mullins Harbour to the head of Milne Bay and thence to the north coast in the neighbourhood of Taupota'.[59] And again: 'Mailu canoes journey eastwards trading with a number of islands of the Massim'.[60]

The data collected by Prof. Seligman enable us to connect the Mailu trading routes with those of the Massim. The last quoted explicit statements bear directly upon our problems, and, in fact, they indicate the two main approaches of the Western Papuo-Melanesian world to the Massim culture area – Mullins Harbour and the coast between Bónabóna Island (entrance to Mullins Harbour) and Suá'u. As far as I know, the Mailu canoes seldom go beyond Suá'u even now, and they hardly ever went any further in the olden days, so that I do not think it can be said that they used to trade with a number of the Massim islands. Had they done so, it would have been undoubtedly the most important channel through which such articles as greenstone blades, ebony carvings, fine basketry, and other products of the Northern Massim and of the D'Entrecasteaux group would have found their way into the Mailu and other western districts. As matters stood, it seems that a much greater amount of articles was traded via Mullins Harbour. There seems to have been at least two, or even more, overland routes to Mullins Harbour from the Massim area. One is mentioned by Prof. Seligman in the statement just quoted. It leads from the eastern shore of the deep

---

[57]Cf. *op. cit.*, pp. 529–530, and pp. 537 to 539.
[58]*Ibid.*, p. 530.
[59]*Op. cit.*, p. 535.
[60]*Ibid.*, p. 540.

inlet to the head of Milne Bay, through an almost completely flat country. This route passes exclusively through Massim territory, and does not traverse any of the other tribes. But although this was a very accessible way, the journey from Mullins Harbour to Milne Bay being said to be easy, it was quite an unimportant route, as is correctly stated by Prof. Seligman. There was, however, another trading route, starting from the northern and north-western shores of Mullins Inlet, as well as from the villages on the eastern shore of Orangerie Bay, and going practically straight, northwards, to the villages of Bartle Bay. These villages must have carried on an extensive trade with the D'Entrecasteaux group, though on this head I did not obtain much information.[37] That concerning the overland trading route seems fairly reliable, as it was computed from data obtained independently at Mailu, in the village of Dahúni, Mullins Harbour, in and near Fife Bay (east of Mullins Harbour), and from two sets of inland people – *viz.,* several Magawáru men, whom I examined in the Sámarai jail, and a few Borowá'i men, whom I met at a *So'i* feast in Sílosílo (between Fife Bay and Mullins Harbour). The several items of information obtained from these sources harmonized perfectly.

Starting from the north, there is a place on Goodenough Island called Siriwáwu, which is – or perhaps it is better to say was – a great centre for axe-blades, for the industry and trade in stone implements are rapidly vanishing. I was emphatically assured by a great number of inmates of the Sámarai jail (belonging to all the different tribes of the eastern end) that Siriwáwu was the place were the stone blades were made.[38] Whether it was really another quarrying centre, like Sulóga on Woodlark, or whether it was one of the places where the blades used to be finally worked up and polished, or whether it was only a great trading emporium for stone axes, I am, for the present, unable to decide. Anyhow, it was mentioned to me as the most northerly point of the great Mullins Harbour trading route, where the stone blades were procured. Besides the stone blades, other articles, such as formed the usual trade circulating throughout the Massim area, were traded by this route.[61] It is to be remembered that this route connected, in the first place, two Massim districts – that of Bartle Bay and those of Bónabóna and of the southern shore of Mullins Harbour.

---

[61] Cf. C. G. Seligman, *op. cit.*, p. 536, where the main trade, as circulated by the Túbetúbe, is enumerated.

The articles which passed southwards this way were the fine ceremonial handles manufactured in their best form in the Trobriands and in Muiú'a (Woodlark), and called *diriwá'u* by the Massim of Bónabóna (the usual pattern of these is reproduced by Seligman, *op. cit.,* pl. lxi.), and *konawé'u,* the heavier form, which is more popular in Woodlark and the D'Entrecasteaux group (see pl. lxii. of the same work); the round carved wooden dishes; the ebony lime spatulas, and the carved wooden sword clubs *(kerépa)*; obsidian *(nabú'a)*, which was found only in one place on the D'Entrecasteaux group (Goodenough Island);[39] baskets of fine workmanship *(pópo)* made by the Northern Massim.[40] How these articles came to the villages in and near Bartle Bay I cannot say, but it appears from a remark of the Rev. H. Newton that the natives of that district did not do much trading themselves.[62] Thus it is very likely that the islanders brought them down.

The mainland people traded chiefly pigs and dogs to those of the D'Entrecasteaux group, passing on the articles which they had acquired from the inland natives, such as birds' feathers, fibre belts, etc. They used to get about four or five fine greenstone axe-blades for a pig, and for a big piece of obsidian they paid one plaited fibre belt.

The goods received from the northern islands were further traded by the Wedá'u and other coastal villages to the inland people. The latter exported to the coastal villages such articles as were not obtainable on the grassy seaboard, and which could be easily found and manufactured in the mountain jungle. Amongst these were spears *(aiera)*, fibre belts *(tairóro)*, cassowary feather stalks *(dziwéni)*, cassowary feathers *(waíge)*, and some kinds of baskets *(góba)*. These native words were given to me in Sámarai in the Wedá'u language. The *tairóro* belts consist of a number of strands of plaited, brown fern vine. They were manufactured by the inland tribes on the southern coast – that is, from Gadaísiu eastwards – and on the northern coast from Cape Vogel eastwards. As examples of prices it may be quoted that one belt was paid for a piece of obsidian; ten spears were given by the inland people for one clay pot made in Iási'iási, on the coast east of Cape Vogel; ten cassowary feather stalks were exchanged for one pot.

---

[62]'... Up the north-east coast there are no canoes that sail. At Taupota and Wedau they are just dug-outs, shaped stem and stern, with an outrigger ...' *(op. cit.,* p. 41).

I obtained the following names of villages through which the trading route passed, starting from Bartle Bay and its neighbourhood and going from north to south. The first inland village was Geláría – a community often mentioned by Prof. Seligman and the Rev. H. Newton in their works referred to. Then in succession came the Magawáru, Mainá'u, Dzibogána, and Borowá'i peoples. These lived inland, north of Mullins Harbour, and they traded directly with the Mailu. The Borowá'i are always mentioned in Mailu as the people from whom the greenstone axe-blades come, though it seems beyond doubt that they did not manufacture them themselves, but imported them from the great quarrying centres in the north.

At the point where the trading route reached the Mailu, around Mullins Harbour, certain complication takes place in the character of the articles traded. On the way through the mainland some of the inland produce (feathers, vine belts, articles of bamboo and other wood, etc.) have joined the articles sent down from the Northern and North-eastern Massim. Again, some of the north-eastern produce gets absorbed by the inland tribes; some is deflected to the east after reaching Mullins Harbour. It is a noteworthy fact, and it shows the great importance of the overland trading route, viá Mullins Harbour, that many of the coastal villages east of Bónabóna import the Northern Massim produce viá Mullins Harbour. Thus in Fife Bay, some fifteen miles east of Bónabóna, I was told that stone axes and ebony carvings came from the Borowái and other Mullins Harbour tribes. In this way the overland trading route feeds both the western and the eastern shores of the southern coast, reckoning from Mullins Inlet. And there takes place a distinct selection, some articles being much more appreciated by the Mailu and some by the Southern Massim. Thus, though the Mailu knew, and sometimes used, the ornamental axe-handles in their feast ceremonials, they never possessed them in any great number, used them extremely rarely, and did not appreciate them very much. Again, though one finds many of the fine Trobriand ebony carvings in Mailu, there is a very marked difference between the Mailu and the Southern Massim in the appreciation of these objects, the latter using them much more frequently, and parting with them much more reluctantly, in spite of the fact that they are numerous among them.

The main objects of trade which ultimately arrived at Mailu by this route were, as stated, greenstone axe-blades and arm-shells. As far as I am able to judge, products of the mainland hill jungle, such as feathers, bamboos, etc., also reached Mailu in considerable quantities by that route.

Again, some products of the Southern Massim (Bónabóna) were acquired by the Mailu on their expeditions to the east; amongst these were the best kind of baskets *(nóvo)*, round wooden dishes, and carvings in brown hardwood of a workmanship inferior to those of the Trobriands. From the Mailu the Southern Massim purchased dogs, small pigs (imported from Aróma), boars' tusks, shell discs, and clay pots (called by the Massim *guréva)*. The Mailu imported a number of netted string bags (Motuan name, *kiápa)* which they acquired in Aróma.

To return from this digression to the Mailu trading proper. The trading expedition to Bónabóna returned about the beginning of January, after which they set out for their final expedition to Aróma. On this occasion arm-shells – a number of which had been in the meantime manufactured in Mailu and others acquired in the east – were traded for full-grown pigs. These were brought back and were usually at once used for the feast.

Before the expedition started for Aróma a man – usually the chief of the subclan – used to make a charm and pronounce a spell *(u'úra)*, in order that the expedition should be successful and that they should sell the arm-shells in a lucrative manner and bring back many pigs.

The name of the charm was *mariwána déwa-réva* (see pl. 23, 24). The man who made it remained within his house for three days, and during that time observed the usual taboo – that is to say, he abstained from boiled food and fish, drank no water, and only ate roasted green coconut. The rite was performed immediately before the departure of the canoes in front of the house of every man who was about to sail, by the chief performer, who sometimes had an assistant.

The performers stand in front of the house and, singing an incantation, which I was unable to record, they sweep the platform with long green reeds with a slow swaying motion. Then they tie the reeds round the central, front post of the house, which proceeding is said to have some magical influence upon the arm-shells. The performer sails, as a rule, on the canoe.

With the return from Aróma the trading activities of the Mailu are finished for the year; but as there was a big feast in Mailu practically every year the trading was resumed in every *Aurári* season, and was intimately connected with all the preparations for the feast that are interwoven with the preliminary festivities – it thus absorbed the whole social life of the Mailu for the better part of the year. The trading was essentially seasonal and regular, each expedition forming a step in a consecutive series of ceremonial transactions and industrial activities (making of arm-shells, sago, pottery; see below), and everything leading up to the final expedition which brought back the all-important pig supply. The times of sailing adduced in the above description cover the case of a rather big feast. If it were a smaller one it would usually be held at an earlier date, sometimes as early as December, and the two expeditions to Aróma might in that case be reduced to one only.

On the mainland the feasts were held earlier, in the *lióro* season. Here the natives did not, of course, make all the preparations and trading expeditions. They reared their own pigs or collected them from the neighbouring villages, and they made sago from their own swamp. To this subject it will be necessary to return in describing the feast and the festive activities in chapter v. The importance of the feast in the native social life and the great interest they take in it cannot be overrated. The intimate association between the economic life of the Mailu islanders and their festive activities must also be fully realized if one wishes to form a right idea of their social life. Although my knowledge of the mainland Mailu is very limited, I think that their economic life – their agricultural activities – are also strongly interwoven with the feast.[63]

Among the Mailu the two special phases – the feast and the trading – are so interdependent that if the feast were abolished there would be no scope for trading; if the trading were suppressed the feast would be impossible.

To return from this digression to the trading pure and simple, it is

---

[63]Studying the *Tábu* feast in the Sinaughólo tribe I was able to see that it possesses distinct economic features; it is closely associated with the native gardening. This feature, however, is very much obscured among the Koíta of the Port Moresby District, who undoubtedly have accepted this feast from the Sinaughólo; see. C. G. Seligman, *op. cit.,* pp. 145 to 150 and p. 18, where it is stated that 'according to the Sinaughólo it was among themselves that the *dúbu* originated, being adopted later by the neighbouring tribes'. I should add that this opinion is shared by the Koíta and Motu of Gábagába, Gaile, and Tupuseleía, who acknowledge their indebtedness to the Sinaughólo. Further, the mythology of the feast and the knowledge of all its ritual is so much more flourishing among the Sinaughólo that it seems certain they were the centre from which the feast in its present form has spread, and among these it is undoubtedly connected with gardening activities.

certain that the Mailu community was one of the very important links in the great chain of intertribal trading which encircled the whole of Papua. There is no doubt, however, that articles from the Gulf seldom reached the Massim area and conversely, and it is also a fact that there was no absolute breach of continuity, no absolute impossibility that articles, ideas, and customs should travel from the mouth of the Fly River, and beyond, as far as Woodlark and the Trobriands and the north-eastern coast. Thus, for instance, the ceremonial blades of fine workmanship, made in Muiú'a and the Trobriands, were to be found all along the southern coast of the Territory, as far, according to Prof. Seligman, as the Fly River. Nevertheless, there does not seem to have been any great cultural influence carried by this stream of trade. The influence of the Gulf culture undoubtedly extended as far as Port Moresby, and beyond to Hulaa and Kerepúna; but it seems to me that it did not even reach Mailu. While some of the Massim objects seem to travel further, the general influence of their culture on the Papuo-Melanesians does not extend beyond the Mailu district.

5 FORMS OF WORK

General remarks

There seems to be no doubt that human communities, standing at different levels of culture and living under different conditions, differ widely and essentially in the quantity and quality of the work they are able to perform; but it is not easy to state, or adequately to characterize, these differences in terms of convincing facts. Mere general statements that the natives are lazy and slack, or that they are good workers, have really very little value.

On the other hand, in order to give facts which would speak convincingly for themselves, it would be necessary to observe the natives at work for a long time; to study the conditions under which they are capable of strenuous work; to see under what circumstances they work willingly and effectively; to investigate the stimuli to their work, aims, incentives, and so on. Such a task is, of course, beyond the capacity of an ambulant ethnologist on a short visit. Much valuable information on such points could be gathered by those who have to deal with natives on the plantations, especially as regards the way in which the natives are adaptable to European methods of working. More difficult, perhaps, would be the attempt to picture the native's way of working under his own natural conditions. Knowing how interesting and important are the problems of labour in modern sociology, it is possible to appreciate how much we could learn by studying these facts from the ethnologist's points of view.

Being unable to do the best under this heading, I must attempt to take the next best course, and, while avoiding mere generalizations, to make a few remarks embodying some of my observations about native ways of working. The natives are undoubtedly capable of strenuous and continuous exertion. They are able to dance for six hours at a time, and apparently to enjoy it, but it must not be imagined that they do it in a state of trance or that they work themselves up to a high pitch of nervous excitement. On the contrary, they dance the same figure over and over again (obviously rehearsing and practising it), they keep perfectly cool, and there are no signs of visible exhaustion, either immediately or the day after. I never had opportunities of watching the natives for any length of time at any prolonged hard labour, such as strenuous and continuous paddling or garden work, though I have seen them doing both in a manner which would not make one suspect them of slackness or of any lack of efficiency and endurance. I may, however, refer the reader to the remarks of the Rev. C. W. Abel,[64] and especially to the excellent account of men's work in the often-quoted volume of the Rev. H. Newton.[65] Both observers vouchsafe that at times the native does continuous work under his own conditions of life.

Some of the natives actually like work. One sees a woman sit day after day making clay pots. I saw perhaps about a score of women in Mailu busily at work, without any suggestion of compulsion, throughout hot, muggy days, when everybody else was trying to take a siesta. Again, one often sees men working strenuously, keenly, and continually at the manufacture of arm-shells and of other shell ornaments, or mending ropes or string. Some of them (both men and women) will work alone, absorbed in what they are doing – though, generally speaking, they like to work in groups. Much heavy, systematic, and tedious work falls on the native women. They have to bring in water, firewood, and vegetables, and to prepare the food,

[64]The Rev. C. W. Abel, 'Savage Life in New Guinea' (see chap. 'The Papuan at Work').
[65]'In Far New Guinea' (see chaps. viii and ix).

day after day, without respite or holiday. Their work is undoubtedly more monotonous than that of the men. Neither men nor women avoid actual hardship in work, for they will sit up all night fishing, and at times of need they do not mind working in the middle of the day, though, as stated above, they like to have a siesta at that time.

All this does not mean that the natives do not understand 'the perfectly aristocratic art of doing absolutely nothing'. On the contrary, I formed the impression that they have a great deal of artistic feeling for the beauty of the *dolce far niente*. At times they will sit about for hours talking languidly, looking with vacant eyes at the surrounding world, when no doubt they are not harassed by the unpleasant feeling that time rushes on steadily and inexorably. Whenever anything is done by one man there are usually a dozen looking on, though without keen interest. Whenever canoes return from a journey the whole village looks on and watches. Sometimes several natives will leave the village, perhaps with fish spears in their hand, perhaps on the way to their gardens, and they will sit down on the beach for hours slumbering or talking, or gazing in front of them.

But it would be quite inadequate to call this 'laziness'. This term would be either a flat truism, if it meant that in a hot, enervating climate, with no incentive to spur him on, and with all his needs easily satisfied, man does not develop a feverish activity and keen strenuousness; or it would be an obviously false statement if it meant anything more or less. Lazy is an adjective having a meaning or value on a moral background only, and as such ought to be strictly excluded from scientific language.

Communal labour

Besides these avowedly general remarks, there are a few other tangible facts as to native ways of working that may be adduced. Working single handed, without adequate tools, the native is often unable to perform some specially hard tasks. Some such he might be able to do, but it would take him so long a time that the work would be rendered tedious or the results be impaired by the action of the weather, etc. Again, in olden days, it was sometimes necessary, for reason of safety, for the natives to do their work in rather large numbers. It is no wonder, therefore, that communal work was a prominent feature of native economics, and that hardly any of the more difficult and bulky tasks were performed without appeal to the community for help, or, at least, to a part of it. Communal work is also well in keeping with the general communistic character of the native economics (see below). Exactly as in the consumption of goods the benefit to the owners very often lies in the honorific title rather than in the amount of his own individual consumption, so in the labour the owner often seems to organize the communal work and subsequent feast, and not so much to bear the burden of the greatest amount of work done.

In olden days, when a big *ilimo* tree had to be cut on the mainland in Baíreba, in order to make a dug-out canoe, a strong force of men used to help the owner of the canoe. Not only his own relatives *(emegi goína;* in Motu, *váravára)*, but a number of the clansmen and villagers from other clans as well joined in the work. They helped in the cutting down of a tree, which in the old days, when stone axes were exclusively used, must have been a rather heavy task. The dragging down of the tree to the shore was done by a number of men who, as they hauled on the log by means of strong vines attached to the trunk, sang the refrain *'Deuoo, deuoo, aí'.* Other men acted as scouts and kept watch over the safety of the working party.

After the log was dragged into the village there was a feast given by the future owner of the canoe to all those who had helped in the work, for which a pig was killed.

The scooping out of the canoe was done by the owner, helped by a few of his friends only,[66] but at the final trimming of the double canoe *(oro'u)* a larger number of people took part; that event also was accompanied by a feast.[67]

Again, at some stages of garden making, collective labour is used. On the mainland each man clears his own portion of the communal garden, as far as the cutting down of the small scrub is concerned, but in the clearing of the heavy timber the work is done collectively, all the clansmen working together and their friends joining them. There is a big feast, given by the owners, in which all the workers participate. On Mailu Island the hard task is the clearing of the strongly-rooted *lalang* grass *(tsilówo)*, which is done with long sticks. The friends and relatives of the owner of the garden (which on Mailu

---

[66]See canoe-making on pl. 20.

[67]When the sail is sewn together from single strips of matting a number of men help in the work, who are entertained at a feast by the owner of the *oró'u* (or owners, see chap. iv., sec. 4). The workers are not decorated at the work or at the feast.

Island is not communal, but private, property) join and do the work. In this case there is, of course, also a feast as a kind of payment for the work done. Both at work and at the feast the workers wear festive adornments *(láo)*, though not of a very gaudy nature. They insert *pépe* (pandanus streamers) – which look like long white paper tapes – into their armlets, and cockatoo feathers are stuck in the hair, which is bound up with *pépe* so as to form a *chignon*. No face or body painting is done. The feast, for which no pig is killed, is, as a rule, held at the garden, the owner (or owners, on the mainland) providing bananas, taro, sago, and fish, if this be available, and making everything succulent with *dehóro* (Motuan name for coconut cream).

There was also a good deal of communal labour done in connection with the building of a house.[68] The big piles forming the main framework were brought from the mainland by the owner, assisted by his family. Then, a great number of people – practically all the men available in the village – are summoned to help in the erection of the piles. On this occasion the *láo*, or ceremonial dress, is put on. There is, of course, a feast, consisting of fish and vegetables, and the future house is decorated. Several of the subsequent stages are done by the owner himself, assisted, as usual, by one or more of his family and near friends. In this way they bring lawyer cane for lashing, sticks and poles for the thatch frame, and the sago leaves used for the roof. The latter work is done by collective labour. The complete house is decorated and a big feast *(urúma itsítsi*, 'house-making feast') takes place, but for this also no pig is killed.

When one of the big nets *(gaúma)* was made, all the men of the *dúbu* (subclan), of course, participated, as the *gaúma* was collective property – *i.e.*, was used in common by all the members of the subclan, though the headman had a normal over-right to it. The men do not make any *láo* (adornment). There is a common feast, in which fish is an essential item.

Sexual division of labour

It is a well-known fact that among practically all the native races the domain of man's and woman's work is very definitely marked off, and that no one ever thinks of encroaching upon the sphere of action of the other sex. This feature is, I think, quite universal. Among the

---

[68]See the description of the house and house building, chap. ii., sec. 4.

Papuo-Melanesians and Massim even the details of the division of labour seem to be identical throughout the whole area. My inquiries, however, into this matter have not been sufficiently careful for me to be able to bring any very interesting facts to light. From my notes, however, as well as from what I remember having seen, the state of things in Mailu seems to be, in this respect, identical with what obtains among the natives of Bartle Bay. These have been described by the Rev. H. Newton, to whose account the reader may be referred.[69]

6   PROPERTY AND INHERITANCE

Introductory remarks

The question of the tenure of property, or real law, is so important that it has been necessary to allude to it on several occasions in preceding paragraphs.[70] In this place some general remarks will be made and the scattered facts stated elsewhere will be summarized. What has been said before, in connection with land tenure, must of course be borne in mind – namely, that 'property' or 'ownership' are terms which are used here not in our (modern European) legal sense, but as short expressions for the sum of the customary right a man, or social body, enjoys with respect to a material object.

Communism

This term is often applied with reference to the mode in which goods are used by natives of the same general stage of culture as the Papuasians. Here again detailed, concrete facts must be given, and the general conditions of native life kept in view, if the term is to have any meaning at all. The natives of Mailu live in small village communities, the members of which are in constant mutual contact and entirely cut off from the outer world, so that there is no possibility or opportunity of exchanging the majority of goods in

---

[69]*Op. cit.,* chapters on Men's Work and Women's Work (chaps. viii. and ix.).
[70]Thus in sec. 4 of chap. ii. the rights of a man to his house were discussed, and again in describing the *góra* and *onága* institutions the problem of property and rights to things had to be touched upon. The most important form of 'ownership' – land tenure – was described in sec. 1 of this chapter.

common use.[⁴¹] On the other hand, these goods are quite abundant;
food, materials for clothing, firewood, common implements are
neither scarce nor difficult to prepare for use. There is then no room
for very strong individual appropriation, and the natives are
certainly extremely liberal and 'communistic', in the sense that a man
in possession of food or objects of common use readily gives them
away temporarily, and, in the majority of cases, even permanently; so
also a man in possession of any privileges will freely share them with
others. On the other hand, it must be emphatically stated that there
was no 'communism' in the sense of all men having equal, free, and
unconditional access to all goods and privileges. From many details
previously given the reader will be aware, both that objects of
common use, whether food or implements or what not, did belong to
certain men, who had the right to give them away, and also that
certain privileges, like participation in a hunt or in a fishing
expedition, or a passage on a canoe, had to be granted by the
'owner', or master, of the given privilege, though these were granted
very easily indeed.

And this right to give away things, to grant access to privileges,
was undoubtedly highly valued by the natives. At a big hunt, with
grass burning, in which I took part, inland of Port Moresby, on the
Laróge River (usually but incorrectly called Lalóki by Europeans), a
curious ceremony took place. In the morning, before daybreak, all
the men in the camp assembled, and one man, the traditional 'owner'
of the privilege of communal net hunting and grass burning on that
tract of country, pronounced in a loud voice certain ceremonial
words in a Koíta language, which were answered by the loud
acclamation of all the men. I was told afterwards by Ahúia – an
excellent informant – that the trend of the harangue was simply: –
'My great grandfather and my grandfather and my father used to
make big hunting on these grounds. Now I give the order for the
hunt. We will hunt to-day'. I did not take notes of the original text in
Koíta, but Ahúia's information is quite reliable, even when he gives a
free version. I was also told by him that such a formal opening of a
hunt was absolutely essential for its legal constitution. Should any
group of the natives burn grass and hunt that tract of country
without having obtained such a formal consent from the master – for
which the master's presence was, of course, also necessary – the
master's clan would seriously resent such breach of étiquette, and, in
the olden days, even fights might have resulted from it.

I am quoting this incident, which I observed among the Koíta, because I was told in Mailu that a similar state of things obtained there, though I failed to record any of the details, and I had no opportunities of observing any facts of that type. The incident quoted is quite characteristic of the point at issue. The natives indeed have a keen sense of clan privilege, or village community privilege, which as a rule is vested in one man – the headman of the village or of the clan, as the case may be. Thus the man giving the order for the hunt was a *idúhu róhi*, a headman of a clan. In Mailu the *dúbu gubína* would have to decide when a net *(gaúma)* should be used, or when a canoe should sail, and who should take part in the operation. It is characteristic that there is only one word for owner, and for headman, chief, or master (in Mailu, *gubína*; in Motu, *biagúna*). The main psychological element in this form of 'ownership' seems to be rather the craving for social prominence than desire for a greater share of material goods. The chief at the annual feast, the man who makes a big catch of fish, the owner of a pig which is slaughtered – these do not get a greater share than their friends; indeed, in many instances they get much less (see, for instance, sec. 2 of the next chapter, concerning the taboos inherent in dugong magic). But they play a prominent part in the performance; in the first place they divide the goods to be distributed, and they formally give them away. And this form of using and enjoying wealth is immensely valued by the natives.

Another set of facts must be referred to in discussing native views concerning property and real rights to things. I mean the magical rights of an economic nature, appertaining to fishing, gardening, and hunting, which are owned by individuals and used for their own benefit. It is clear that the natives regard those rights as being of economic value, and the fact that, under modern conditions, they barter them shows that they even treat them simply as 'goods' – as interchangeable privileges.

Native view of economic value

When discussing inheritance and marriage gifts with the natives, I was struck by the fact that I had a tendency to attach the greatest importance to certain classes of goods, whilst the natives seemed to pay much more attention to others. In other words, I was impressed by the fact that the natives have a scheme of values different from our own. Thus, as land on Mailu Island was allotted to individuals and inherited in the male line, I used to pay the greatest attention to inheritance in land. The natives, however, used to pass quickly over this subject and give me only few details with reference to it, treating it as altogether unimportant, and dwelling much more upon the distribution of coconut palms and native ornaments.

Consequently I inquired into the subject, and obtained very clear, definite, and unanimous answers, with which a number of independent witnesses unhesitatingly concurred. In the native's mind, the native ornaments form the most important class of property. Over these there is most concern and discussion when dividing a dead man's property among his heirs, and on other occasions when property is divided or exchanged. Arm-shells, shell discs, boars' tusks, dogs' teeth, bird of paradise feathers – these form the class of goods which loom as the most desirable form of property in the mind of the native. Pigs come into the same category, though it must be remembered that the natives of Mailu Island did not rear pigs extensively, and that these animals were usually disposed of at a feast, immediately after they had been acquired on the trading expedition to the west. On the mainland, where they were reared by the villagers, they were highly valued. Dogs were also a highly esteemed form of property. After the native jewellery and the domestic animals, the ownership in coconut palms was most highly valued. The garden land had, in a sense, no value on the mainland, where each individual possessed, by the fact of membership of a clan, the right to acquire as much garden land as he desired, or, rather, as much as he and his wife were able to cultivate. The lack of value in this sense was due to the fact that there was no limit to the land which might be taken by any individual, and that no rights in land were ever acquired or exchanged; in fact, such a proceeding would have no object, and it would only have been a breach of custom. The land had, however, value in the sense that the members of a clan, as one social unit, would essentially resent and oppose any encroachment upon their territory on the part of outsiders. In spite of this, on Mailu Island, where land was parcelled out among the individuals, it does not stand as a very important item in the native ideas of value. As a matter of fact, there is plenty of ground on the island, and the main difficulty lies in working it rather than in obtaining the rights to it.

The ornaments or native trinkets are displayed at feasts, both on the person and on the house. They are sometimes produced and

shown to friends, and visitors, and people in the village usually know
who has specially fine arm-shells or shell discs, necklaces, etc. The
natives are by no means churlish and close about lending their
ornaments, and at dance or feast time one often sees ornaments
borrowed from relatives and friends.

Inheritance

The most desirable part of a man's property, the personal ornaments,
his wealth (*babadá'u*; in Motu, *kóhu*), are inherited by his 'own', as
opposed to his classificatory, brothers only. They share, roughly, in
equal parts, though the eldest brother seems sometimes to get the
first pick. The parents, the sisters, the widow and children of a man
do not get any share in his jewellery. The coconuts are divided among
a man's brothers and sons. If the latter are young they do not get very
much at the time of death, but they receive their share later on. The
house is inherited in the male line, as stated above, so that if a man
dies his eldest son becomes the 'master' or 'owner' *(gubína)* of the
house. If he is a small child at his father's death the title is latent (the
father's younger brother being considered 'owner' or 'master' for the
time being), but as soon as the boy is grown he comes into his rights.
The right to the gardens, as frequently stated, is hereditary in the
male line – being on the mainland implicitly included in the clan
membership, or on Mailu Island referring explicitly to the paternal
garden land.[42]

A few concrete examples, accompanied by pedigrees, will illustrate
these general rules. The following is the account, given me by
Omága, one of the Mailu village constables, of what happened after
the death of his father, Onága, and the pedigree shows the
relationship of the persons concerned:-

Omága's father, Onága, died, leaving two younger borthers, Bania
and Tsára, and two younger sisters, Boítse and Mádo; as well as five
children: the boys Kávanai, Omága, and Woná'i, and the girls Dígu
and Dagáea. At the time of Onága's death all his children were
young, and his brother Bania was regarded as 'master' of the house,
this being then tenanted by Bania, his wife and child (not mentioned
in the pedigree), Tsára, and Onága's widow and children.[43]

All the coconut trees left by Onága were also taken over by Bania,
who subsequently gave some of them to his younger brother Tsára.
Bania also took charge of the garden land for as long as the boys

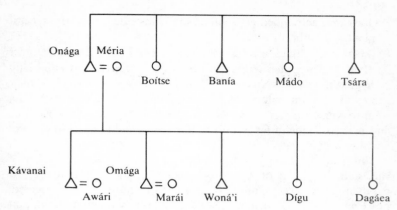

Fig. 43

remained young. When Kávanai married and thus became a grown man, Banía gave him over the whole land left by his father and all the coconut palms, except Tsára's share. When Omága, Kávanai's younger brother grew up and married, the latter gave him his share, both in garden land and in coconut palms. Again, when the youngest boy, Woná'i, becomes grown up he will receive his share from both his elder brothers.

The native ornaments, however, all went to Banía and Tsára. Neither Méria, Onága's widow, nor his sisters, nor his children, received any share in his native ornaments.

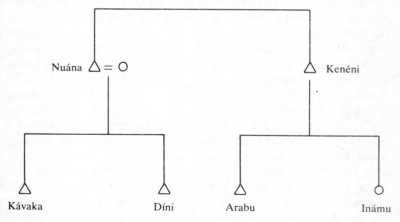

Fig. 44

One other actual pedigree will serve to illustrate further the general principles of inheritance.

When Nuána died, not his sons, Kávaka and Díni, but his younger brother, Kenéni, inherited his wealth. Moreover, as Kávaka and Díni were grown up when Nuána died, and had by that time received their shares in coconut palms, all the remaining coconut trees of Nuána went to Kenéni. After Kenéni's death, however, part of the coconuts, and perhaps some of his wealth or jewellery would return to Kávaka and Díni.

This state of things would lead apparently to a congestion of riches, in the form of native ornaments in the hands of the last survivor of a large family of brothers. It must be remembered, however, that native ornaments were constantly manufactured, that they were exchanged or distributed in connection with feasts, ceremonies, marriage transactions, etc., and that native wealth often changed hands, and so never could accumulate to any large extent. Thus the inheritance of native ornaments by the deceased man's brothers – with a very small share sometimes falling to his paternal first cousins – did not entail any serious strain in the economic equilibrium in the village.

There was no special legal mechanism to enforce all the transactions connected with inheritance. Thus the brothers had to agree upon the division of the wealth; the children had to come to an understanding with reference to the coconuts and garden land, etc. When the children were minors at their father's death, and all their gardens and coconuts were under the care of their paternal uncle, it was of his free accord that the latter gave them their due shares, so that they were consequently entirely dependent upon his good faith. When I asked Omága what would have happened if his uncle Banía would not give him and his brothers their due shares he was not able to answer. He dismissed the hypothesis, and said a man would always give his nephews the garden land and coconuts which belong to them by right. As a matter of fact, it must be remembered that a man had always enough coconuts and garden land for his own use. Again, Banía lives in the same house with Omága and Kávanai, and their mutual relations are, to my knowledge, very intimate and extremely good. So that there was no reason, and no psychological likelihood, why any quarrels should arise among the natives in matters of inheritance in land and coconuts. As to the division of wealth among brothers, I received the impression that the customary rules for division were very definite, in the sense that all had to receive more or less equal shares, and that the only deterrent was the fear of incurring the contempt that would inevitably be shown for any manifestation of cupidity or act of rapacity.

7 INDUSTRIES

Introductory remarks

In this section I shall enumerate and briefly describe what may be called the industrial products of the natives, the most important objects in use, and the articles of trade manufactured locally. The building of native houses – a very important native craft – has already been described. The native canoes, especially the large double canoes with a platform *(oró'u)* are, as has been pointed out before, both objects of extreme importance in the tribal life of the Mailu islanders and articles of trade exchanged for pigs in Aróma. Their construction has been described in a previous section.

We will complete the series by saying a few words about the following articles:- (1) Pottery – The Mailu pots were essential both for use in their own households and as articles of trade. (2) Arm-shells and other shell ornaments. – These were indispensable for the Mailu islander as means of acquiring pigs; in fact, they were the standard article given in exchange for pigs, canoes being paid over only when arm-shells were short. Though a considerable number of these articles were imported into Mailu, the local manufacture was very important, and the Mailu also made other shell ornaments. (3) Baskets. – These, some of which were acquired from the Southern Massim, were traded to a limited extent; they were very important in native life as being the only means of carrying foodstuffs, firewood, and objects in daily use, when on a journey. (4) Stone implements were to a great extent imported into Mailu, though some were locally manufactured, and a few are still made and used in Mailu. (5) Carvings were never a speciality of the Mailu, and only very rough and inferior work is produced.

The technological side of the industries here described is very unsatisfactory, as throughout my work I was concerned with the social life of the natives rather than with technology. The following account is meant chiefly to be a survey of those main economic activities which are directed towards the production of objects of use and trade.

Pottery

This art was the exclusive monopoly of the inhabitants of Mailu Island, but I am not able to say whether this was owing to the fact that there was no clay available anywhere else in the district, or whether this is an example of the extreme inertia of the natives towards the alteration of a tribal status sanctioned by tradition. The natives of the district always state that suitable pottery clay is only available on Mailu, but this means merely that they do not know of any other place.

On Mailu Island the clay is obtained in many localities from deep holes dug in the alluvial flat, behind the village. It is fairly clean, does not contain many small stones, and is used without any previous treatment. It is brought into the village in baskets, plaited of coconut leaves, and it is wrapped in leaves to keep it moist. It is usually brought in the morning and used the same day.

The accessories of pottery consist of a ring of banana leaves, half a coconut shell, a shell of a species of *Venus*, and usually a large melon shell *(Melo diadema)*, or, in place of the latter, another coconut shell, which is used as a receptacle for water.

The method of pottery making may be described as a 'method of coiling', an expression used by Prof. Seligman with reference to the technique of the Southern Massim.[71]

The clay, as it is brought from the pit, is fashioned into long cylindrical 'fingers' or 'sausages', by rolling between the two palms (comp. pl. 27, the woman on the right-hand side). The worker (always a woman) takes a large handful of clay, kneads it a little, and rolls it into the desired shape. The 'sausages' are about the thickness of a finger and some 40 cm. long. The first sausage is coiled on the rim of a half coconut shell, which thus acts as the nucleus of the pot. The shell is placed in the ring, made of banana leaves (see pl. 27). After the first sausage is coiled, the woman joins another to its end. The coiling is done in the following manner: – The free end of the clay sausage is held in the left hand, the right hand joining it to the rim by the pressure of thumb and forefinger (see the woman on the left of pl. 27). At this stage of the process the successive coils, though joined to each other and flattened, are to be seen plainly, as well as the finger marks. The unfinished pot looks, in fact, as if it were streaked horizontally and grooved vertically.

---

[71]*Op. cit.,* p. 25, footnote.

The successive coils being placed in broadening circles, the pot is first shaped into a roughly conical form, and this can be called the first stage in the process. (See the pots on right and left on pl. 27.)

The next stage consists of the smoothing of the rough surface, in which process the fissures between the adjoining coils are obliterated, and in the imparting to the pot its final form and ornamentation. The pot is first smoothed and scraped. This is done by using both the palm and fingers of the hand and the *Venus* shell referred to. Usually the shell is handled with the right hand on the outer surface and the left hand passed inside. The scraping and smoothing by means of the shell being done upon that part of the clay surface, which is supported by the open left hand (comp. pl. 27; the woman in the middle).

By the same means (shell and open palm) the final form is imparted to the pot. About one-third of the distance from the top of pot the original, simple conical shape is altered by the formation of a waist, immediately below which the pot bulges, while towards the top it opens out in a conical form. This last conical portion forms what might be called a broad rim or lip of the pot (cf. pl. 27; woman in the centre).

After the completion of the upper part of the pot it is taken out of the coconut shell, which so far has served as its bottom, and a few coils are put in to cover the hole. These are smoothed down by tapping the surface of the pot with the hand and scraping it with the shell. It may be mentioned, by the way, that the Mailu technique in pottery does without the heating or tapping which among the Motu forms the longest stage in their manufacture. In consequence of this the Mailu pots are said to be of inferior quality and durabilty.

The pot is now ornamented. Its rim is covered with one of the traditional ornaments, of which there are some eight or nine in use among the Mailu, but I failed to record them. The engraving is done in the soft clay with a thin piece of wood.

The third and last stage consists in the burning of the pots, which is done in the afternoon. They are laid on the sand upon the beach, usually several at a time, the mouth of the pots being turned to windward. Dry sticks are laid all round them individually, the greatest amount of fuel being placed on the weather side, so that the heat may penetrate well inside the pots.

As mentioned above, pots are made by women exclusively, who, during their manufacture, are stated to observe a strict taboo; that means that they do not eat anything from the moment they begin their work until the time they have finished burning the pots. Whether, considering that the natives hardly ever accepted food during the day, this taboo is very important, I was unable to ascertain. At any rate, several informants asserted that it was so, and I received the impression that pottery is considered to be a serious, and perhaps even to some extent a sacred, activity.[72]

Arm-shells[73] and other shell ornaments

The arm-shells, with the exception of the strings of shell discs, are the most highly valued articles of native ornament, and they form one of the principal means of exchange. They are made of the shell of *Conus millepunctatus*, and Mailu was one of the chief centres of their manufacture. I have heard native *connoisseurs* pronounce those made here to be the best, though possibly this statement may only mean that the best arm-shells come from the east and that the Mailu were the middle-men who imported them and sold them to the natives of the Central District (see chap. iv., sec. 4).

The *Conus* shell *(opi'ópi)* is, in harmony with its name, of an almost perfectly conical shape, and the armlet is made out of a ring formed by a transverse section of the shell cut near the base. The 'cutting' is done by means of a stone. For this purpose any stone of a fairly small size (about that of a child's fist) can be used, provided it has a blunt point. With this point the manufacturer (always a man) taps the shell with light blows in quick succession, under which its rather soft calcareous substance is, one might say, worn away along the line where the blows are struck. In this manner the base of the cone is first cut off. Then another similar cutting is made, parallel to the plane of the first at a distance from it of about one-third of the total length of the shell, and this second section forms the ring.

The next stage consists of the removal of the outer surface of this ring and of the polishing of its internal surface. The former must be rubbed quite clear of all colouring matter, even to the removal of the punctiform pattern, in order that the arm-shell should be quite white when finished. The ring is then polished on the inside, as far as may be – that is to say, so long as it is not made too thin and weak. The

---

[72]This is also the opinion of the Rev. W. J. V. Saville, to whom I am indebted for having drawn my attention to the pottery taboo.[[44]]

[73]See the description of arm-shells in Seligman, *op. cit.,* p. 513, and pl. lix., where several of them are figured.

object of this process is to give the arm-shell the biggest possible aperture, for the larger this is the larger the arm which the arm-shell is able to fit, and consequently the greater is its value.

The polishing of the outer surface is done on a broad, flat piece of sandstone, and a piece of the same kind of stone, shaped into cylindrical form and pointed at each end, is used to polish the inside by inserting it within the ring and working it to and fro. During the polishing process of both inner and outer surface the shell is kept moistened.[74] The same name, *urú'a*, is given to both the flat and the cigar-shaped sandstone, the name denoting the material and not the form, as is always the case in native technological nomenclature. The polishing process is called *urúru*. After the arm-shell is ready it is perforated in two or three points, near the lateral opening formed by the lip of the *Conus* shell, and is ornamented with shell discs *(sápisápi*, a universal Papuan term, probably originally Motuan) and with the black wild banana seeds.[75]

Besides the arm-shells, the Mailu also manufacture the shell discs called *sápisápi*, and another kind of red shell discs, which differs from the former in that they are coloured on one side only. The *sápisápi* are worn strung on a string like Chinese perforated coins, when they collectively form long cylinders.[76] The Mailu red shell discs are worn fixed by their flat surfaces to a string, thus showing one side only. Large white shell discs are ground down from the base of the *Conus millepunctatus*, and the pearl oyster shell is used to manufacture an ornament shaped like a half-moon, which is worn as a breast ornament by men and women, but I failed to record the technical details of the manufacture of these last-named objects.

In former times the *Conus* shell was used to make small axes *(oba'úa)*. After the upper ring had been detached in order to make the armlet, the residual cone was split longitudinally, and small blades could thus be made. This use of the *Conus* shell has, however, now been abandoned, and I was unable to purchase any old specimens, though a few were made for me in the old fashion.

Baskets

Several forms of baskets, all of local manufacture, were used in

---

[74]See pl. 28.
[75]See the two arm-shells on the left side of pl. lix. in Seligman's book.
[76]See pl. lx. in Seligman, *op. cit.*

Mailu, but I was not able to grasp and record the technological principles of their manufacture. Consequently I can only give a general description of their basketry and mention the varieties.

1. *Apáka* – In this, the rudest form, the basket is simply plaited from a coconut leaf. The midrib is split longitudinally and the leaflets interplaited in such a way that the pieces of rib form the rim of the basket. To this a rough handle is sometimes attached. This form is known all along the southern coast as far as Port Moresby, and I was told that the same kind is used in the Gulf and on the Fly River. Among the Motu it is seldom used, as there the universal use of the string bag *(kiapa)* eliminates all need of other receptacles. Among the Mailu the *apáka* is used for carrying clay, sand, wood, shellfish, and all sorts of coarse and dirty materials in general. It is very easily made, and its manufacture does not require more than half an hour, but it only lasts for a short time and is readily thrown aside.

2. *Réva* – This kind is similar to the foregoing, being also made of coconut leaves. It is used chiefly for catching fish and shellfish in the *rú'i* form of fishing, for which women go out at night with torches of dry coconut leaves *(karéta)*. It is never used for carrying things.

3. *No'obóea* – This is a circular-shaped form of basket, made of coconut leaves, in a much more elaborate fashion than is the case with the two preceding kinds. It also is never used for carrying things, but it often serves as a platter, solid food taken out of the cooking pot being placed on this, or on a wooden dish. The *no'obóea* is also used sometimes as a strainer in the preparation of coconut cream *(dehóro)*.

4. *Nóvo* – This basket, which is solidly made of some kind of cane, is the most important form, serving as the general carrying vessel of the Mailu. It is more or less flat, and has an oval-shaped mouth. Two strands, attached to one side, pass through two holes in the opposite side, and are joined by a broad band of bast. The woman carries the basket with this band across her forehead, the basket resting on her shoulders. In these baskets, and in these alone, heavy loads of native vegetables and firewood are brought into the village from the gardens. It is also used on journeys, when the woman carries her own, and her husband's, personal belongings *(tóba)*. This form is

made in Mailu, but it is also imported from the east, from the Southern Massim of Bónabóna, and from the neighbouring coast, where they are apparently more skilful in the manufacture of the *nóvo* than are the Mailu. The *nóvo* form of basket is not known to the west of the Mailu district.

Stone implements

At the present day, when steel axes, adzes, and chisels are used for felling trees and scooping out canoes, the natives no longer make stone implements. It is therefore not possible to give an account of this subject from personal observation; I was only able to question the natives, a proceeding which is particularly unsatisfactory when material objects have to be enumerated and described. The natives, however, gave me the names, with some details, of the following implements.

U'a – Stone axes used for felling trees and scooping out canoes. The stone blades, made of dark-green volcanic tuff, were imported from the east, and those used for the first-named work were very large and strong, and were permanently fixed to their handles. For scooping out canoes smaller blades were used, which could be turned in their sockets and thus be fixed at any angle to the striking plane. This adjustment permitted them to be used for hollowing out canoes through a fairly narrow opening.

When a blade broke they took it out of the handle and sharpened it on a broad flat sandstone. Thus in the course of time the large blades became reduced in size.

Ota is the small blade used in the sago pounder. This blade was manufactured locally, and it is still made and used. Unfortunately, I was not able to observe the process, as the necessary stone comes from Abá'u, and there was none of this in the village during my stay.

The sandstone implement used for polishing the arm-shells and axe blades, and the implement used for grinding down the arm-shells from the inside, have been described.

Obsidian flakes, obtained in a manner described above (chap. iii., sec. 1), were used for shaving and as chisels for finer carvings, such as those of limesticks.

Carvings

There were a few objects regularly carved by the Mailu. Amongst
these were the carvings on the vertical boards closing the dug-outs of
both sides in the large double canoes. So also those on the boards
forming the verandah roofs of the houses, and on the outside of the
piles. The fine carvings on smaller objects made in Mailu were, in
imitation of those of the Southern Massim, but were quite inferior to
the latter.

CHAPTER V

MAGICO-RELIGIOUS ACTIVITIES AND BELIEFS

1 DREADFUL BEINGS; SPIRITS; SORCERY

Fear of darkness

It is important to study not only the ideas of the natives concerning ghosts and spirits, but also their emotional reactions towards such ideas – not only how they picture in their minds beneficent or maleficent beings, but how they behave, and emotionally comport themselves, towards these imaginary beings which to them are so real.

Of the natives of Mailu it may be emphatically stated that they hold in great fear the terrors lurking in the shadows of night. Nothing would induce a man to venture out alone at night, even for a few hundred yards from the village. I observed that at dusk the men became very nervous and hastened towards the village, so that darkness should not overtake them when alone in the gardens. One of the oldest and wisest men in the village – in fact, the greatest authority on native lore and custom – Papári, was quite as unprepared for such risks as any of the boys and young men. I offered to some young men who had been much influenced by the white man's teachings the, to them, large reward of ten sticks of tobacco if they would walk alone at night about a quarter of a mile from the village to the Mission Station, but they smilingly declined the offer. Their fear is greater on a dark than on a moonlit night, and they are also afraid of darkness in their houses; hence the custom of keeping the fire going during the night. If a man has to leave a house in the night to satisfy a necessity of nature, he arouses another person to keep him company on his walk to the garden or to the seashore, a statement which is confirmed by Mr. Greenaway, who has lived for a long time amongst and with the natives.

I believe that in this respect the natives of Mailu do not differ from the other Western Papuo-Melanesians, all of whom share this intense dread of darkness. On the other hand, it is interesting to note that the general fear of the night[45] is not an essential characteristic of this stage of culture or even of this type of human society, for among the Northern Massim of Muiú'a (Woodlark Island) I found an entirely different state of things, the men volunteering quite readily to go alone at night for long distances out of the village.

Nature of the dreaded beings; the *bará'u*

Returning to the Mailu, the next problem is of what kind of maleficent beings are the natives afraid? We modern Europeans are so accustomed to associate all dreadful things definitely with the idea of death, to treat them as ghosts, visitors from the other world, or supernatural beings, that the idea that living men should be the object of a superstitious and annihilating fear seems to us nearly incredible. This was, at least, my own attitude of mind towards the facts I found in Mailu. Yet it seems absolutely beyond doubt that the Mailu and, as far as I know, all the Western Papuo-Melanesians, are exclusively afraid of evil magicians, as constituting the one and only dreadful danger threatening them out of the darkness of the night.

The *bará'u* (the exact counterpart of the *váda* of the Central District) is to the natives a living man, endowed with the knowledge and powers of making himself invisible, and of working evil magic with the help of the night and of his own visibility.

The *bará'u*, as he prowls about at night, invisible, able to kill his victim and desirous of doing so, is always thought of as some individual man from a neighbouring village, in body, not in spirit, nor as his double. When the *bará'u* leaves his abode to go on his nefarious errand, his place in his house is empty – he goes away bodily.[77] The *bará'u* smears himself all over with some magical herbs, and mutters some spells and becomes invisible. Some people say, however, that he is only invisible from his front aspect and that he can be seen from behind, and this is the reason why people see often mysterious shadows moving in the dark. He can be heard, however, as he moves about. The *bará'u* travel great distances; they come like the wind, quickly and invisible, but as to the exact method of these

---

[77]I have dwelt on the subject of the *bará'u*'s bodily wanderings, because there are several statements about New Guinea sorcery, showing that there is a kind

aerial flights my informants were unable to give me any details, saying that this was entirely the concern of the *bará'u*, and referring me to such a one for further information. This, of course, was hopeless, since a *bará'u* is extremely careful in preserving his *incognito*, especially to white men. I knew, however, the names of some men in Mailu who were suspected of belonging to the craft, and these were precisely the men who would not even give the popular version of the problem.

There was some lack of precision in the statements, and lack of agreement between my informants, when I came to inquire about the details of the method used by the *bará'u* in securing his victim. In broad outline, the version universally approved by my informants corresponded exactly with the description given by Prof. Seligman of the Koíta.[78] The *bará'u* comes to Mailu and finds his victim asleep in the house. He kills the man and restores him to life again; or he touches him with a magical substance, when he pines away and presently dies. Or else a *bará'u*, fixing upon two or three men fishing or walking in the gardens, stuns them with properly administered blows of a club, but the victim never knows he has been operated upon by a *bará'u*.

In general outline this is the belief universally held. There were, however, discrepancies among my informants' statements in respect to details. Thus some said that the *bará'u* opens the man's body and

---

of emanation, or 'sending', projected from the sorcerer and attacking the victim. Thus, Prof. Seligman describes the 'sending', emanating from witches, as it exists in the belief of the natives at Bartle Bay and inland from there *(op. cit.,* pp. 640–643). It is very important to call attention to such differences in belief as exist between that recorded by Prof. Seligman and that found in Mailu. Prof. Seligman's statement is extremely detailed and concrete, and seems to me to be as well established as anything we know about the Papuasian natives. What I am about to say, consequently, does not refer to that statement. I have found a remarkable tendency among the white observers to introduce into native ideas 'spiritual agencies', 'emanations', etc. Thus, some white men, who knew Mailu perfectly well, informed me that *bará'u* is an evil power, projected by the sorcerer. *Bará'u* is, indeed, the name for the sorcerer's evil power, but his never wanders about without its receptacle, and there is nothing of an 'emanation' in the native belief. Again, in Port Moresby, one of my friends, a resident of long standing in Papua, and a high authority on the natives, maintained in an argument with me, that *váda* was a 'sending' from a sorcerer. A careful subsequent inquiry carried out under the patronage of Ahúia, finally convinced both my friend and myself that *váda* was no 'sending' in any sense of the word, that it was the sorcerer in his own person, and that when he went out to kill a man, he had to leave his own abode and actually make the journey.[46]

[78]*Op. cit.*, pp. 170 and 171. Cf. also pp. 187 and 188 and pl. xxxi.

takes something out of it, or puts something into it – a version identical again with that obtained in more detail by Prof. C. G. Seligman among the Koíta. Another of my informants told me that the *bará'u*'s method consists in the touching of a man's body, or even his footprints, with some leaves, and then in putting the latter into a preparation also called *bará'u*. The ingredients of this mixture are salt water, wild ginger roots, and *góbu*, the bark of the native cinnamon tree. Yet another informant said that sometimes the *bará'u* simply touches the victim with his mixture.[79]

Again, one of my informants – a very reliable man – assured me that whenever a *bará'u* comes to the village and enters a house with the intention of killing a man, he always tries to have connection with some female member of the household in her sleep – the man's wife, or his sister or daughter. The man, bewitched by the *bará'u*, does not remember the fact after he awakes; but the woman is always aware of having been interfered with in her sleep, and much valuable information as to the crimes committed by sorcerers, and even as to their identity, is supposed to be obtained in this way. As to the questions whether the *bará'u* is invisible to the woman, and, if so, how she can recognize him, my informant could not give me satisfactory answers, though he did not on that account waver in his belief.

I wish to add that although I was not able to obtain many esoteric details with reference to the Mailu sorcery, I have had exceptionally good opportunities of grasping the general attitude of the native mind towards the question of night-terrors and sorcery, and of laying bare certain psychological features of their beliefs, which mere inquiry could not have elucidated. For some time I was staying in a disused mission house, not far from the present Mission Station. Somehow the news spread about that there were ghosts in the house, and both my cook-boy and some village boys, who used to come and sleep there, refused to continue to do so, leaving me to sleep alone. Finding this state of things convenient on account of the protection it afforded my belongings when I went with my boy to the village at

---

[79]This also corresponds with what Dr. Seligman found to be the practice amongst the *bará'u* of the Milne Bay natives *(op. cit.,* pp. 638 and 639). As the influence of the Southern Massim is strong in Mailu, I am inclined to think that the two above-mentioned versions concerning *bará'u* may be the outcome of the Massim beliefs superimposed upon the original doctrines derived from the Western Papuo-Melanesian stock of ideas.

night, I did not discourage the belief, nor did I betray any scepticism with regard to it. One evening, while sitting with my boy and some Mailu men, I listened to their conversation, carried out in Motu. I found that they were discussing the question of the ghosts that haunted my house. Seeing that they took the matter very seriously and expressed views extremely valuable to the ethnologist because they exemplified the native beliefs on a concrete basis, I joined the conversation and asked their opinon and advice with regard to my case. They certainly were under the impression that I was concerned for my safety, and they gave me their *bonâ fide* view of the matter. I asserted emphatically that, as a white man, I was afraid only of ghosts, but I added that, not knowing the habits of the local evil powers, I would like to know what I had to fear and how I should best protect myself. It was these questions which elicited most of the information given above – information which had until then been withheld from me. I need not add that I was not satisfied with one conversation, but subsequently had several interviews with various informants, asking for their expert advice in my difficult position.

I was told, unanimously and emphatically, that ghosts *(bó'i)* are absolutely innocuous; because they are like a shadow they cannot hurt. That people should fear beings with no power to hurt, my informants could not believe, indeed they seemed amused by the idea. They asserted that the ghost could not have been a *bó'i*, because a spirit can neither talk nor make a noise, and it was a public fact that in my house some noises, as of footsteps and voices, had been heard. My men advised me, in the first place, not to sleep in the house, and if I had to remain there not to sleep alone. I remarked that nobody was likely to risk his life so lightheartedly, whereupon they warned me of the extreme folly of putting out my hurricane lamp at night, as I was known to do, which was a plain invitation to the *bará'u* to come and do his horrible work. The most hopeful feature of the whole affair, however, was that as a white man I was to a great extent, and perhaps completely, immune from the evil attempts of even the most skilled and malicious *bará'u*. The future has shown that my Mailu friends were right, since all the attempts of the *bará'u* have failed, so far as concerns myself.

As in all other tribes, the *bará'u* are considered in the Mailu tribe to be the real cause of death. Using Prof. Seligman's words: '... except in the case of very old folk, death is not admitted to occur without some obvious cause, such as a spear thrust. Therefore when vigorous and active members of the community die, it becomes necessary to explain their fate, and such deaths are firmly believed to be produced by sorcery.'[47] In Mailu a *bará'u* from another village, always a hostile one, is suspected of having been the cause of the evil deed. There are, of course, *bará'u* in all villages, even in Mailu, as mentioned before, though no one will openly admit it. But these, or even those from a friendly village, would never be suspected of an attempt against a Mailu citizen. To the west there were no evil sorcerers, a fact which coincides also with the generally friendly relations between those people and the Mailu. On the other hand, the eastern neighbours of the Mailu were greatly dreaded as highly maleficent sorcerers. All the villages east of Dérebái are simply swarming with dangerous *bará'u*. These villages had been on hostile terms with the Mailu in the olden days, and, curiously enough, the villagers between Port Glasgow and Gadaísiu, in Orangerie Bay, are considered to be the most atrociously criminal and the most virulent of sorcerers. As far as it was possible to ascertain, I found that in the past these villages had not been on terms of intense hostility with the Mailu; whereas those nearer Mailu (from Dérebái to Port Glasgow), which were on terms of acute hostility with the Toulon (Mailu) islanders, are considered less skilled in sorcery.

The villages most prolific in *bará'u* are also remarkable from the ethnologist's point of view on account of their mode of disposal of the dead, which will be described in sec. 4 of this chapter. The method of discovering the culprit *bará'u* at a man's funeral will also be treated in that section.

When there is a death in the village, the natives are always very much affected. They do not leave their houses after dark, and they sleep up in the room and not on the verandah. I was inclined to see in this the proof that the natives are, after all, afraid of the ghosts, despite the emphatic denial of the fact by the natives themselves. On further consideration, however, I am inclined to trust the direct native information. After all, the natives may be instinctively and emotionally frightened and impressed by death, but their ideas need not take the shape of fear of ghosts; seeing his work done so successfully, they may only realize the more intensely the danger of the prowling *bará'u*. This is, however, only speculative, and further inquiry is necessary before the question can be settled. I wish to draw attention to an interesting passage in one of the works of Spencer and Gillen, which throws some light on the problem under discussion.

Speaking of the Warramunga natives of north-central Australia, the authors say:- 'They have a very firm belief in the existence of evil beings, who are commonly known as *kurdaitcha*, and are supposed to prowl around with the object of killing their enemies by means of magic'. 'The time that immediately follows upon a death in the camp is one during which the natives are very excited and very imaginative'.[48] And at one time, when a death had recently occurred in the camp, the authors witnessed an armed party setting out to ward off the malignant sorcerers.[80]

It may be noted that the *kurdaitcha*, like the *bará'u*, are always living men who practise sorcery. The excitement in the camp, psychologically due, if I am right, to instinctive fear of death, reflects itself in the native mind in ideas of increased danger from prowling *kurdaitcha*.

Spirits of the dead

From this somewhat theoretical digression let us turn to the beliefs of the Mailu. As pointed out above, the question whether or not the natives are afraid of the spirits of the deceased, at least immediately after death, must be left open. The burial practices with reference to the spirits of the deceased will be discussed later, but I must confess that I failed to ascertain the meaning of these practices with respect to the placation or propitiation of the ghost. In the same measure as I am confident of having grasped clearly the general outline of the native mind with reference to sorcery, I feel that I was unable to penetrate deeply into their eschatological beliefs. My experience is that direct questioning of the natives about a custom or belief never discloses their attitude of mind as thoroughly as the discussion of facts connected with the direct observation of a custom, or with a concrete occurrence, in which both parties are materially concerned.

The natives use the following terms covering the connotation of the words *spirit* and *vital principle. Aiaigáve* is the breath, respiration, and it is considered to be the vital principle of the living man. Its seat is in the breast, and it ceases to exist at a man's death.

---

[80]Spencer and Gillen, 'Across Australia', vol. ii., pp. 394–5. I am indebted to Prof. Spencer's kindness for additional information on the passages quoted. He informed me that the case described bears directly upon the question discussed in the text.

The 'spiritual part' of a man which wanders to the nether world (Biúla; see sec. 4) is called *bauegéne. Bó'i* is the spirit which dwells in the severed and preserved skull. It is this spirit which is invoked in all incantations *(u'úra),* and in the formulas of protection for the *góra.* This also is the spirit with which the family communicates when the severed head, kept by them in the house, is consulted or addressed in terms of endearment. It seems obvious from the fact that the skulls are kept in the houses, carried about and, so to say, fondled, that the *bó'i* cannot be considered to be a dreaded being. The expression *bó'i óre óre* (corresponding to the Motu *diráva díka),* which means the 'spirit is bad' or angry, is very often used, but it distinctly does not imply the feeling of personal fear or awe on the part of the natives. It is an expression used to denote ill-luck pure and simple.

Karavéni; O'o

There is a belief in maleficent female beings called *karavéni.* These are women from the eastern villages, about Gadaísiu and O'ibáda. They are associated with shooting stars, and whenever such a star falls over a village a *karavéni,* bent on mischief, has landed there. Whether the woman assumes the form of a star, or whether she merely travels by means of this aerial locomotion, was not clear to my native informants, nor, I must confess, to myself; but one cannot expect clearness or consistence in beliefs, whether savage or not. When a *karavéni* enters the body of a person, this latter becomes *o'o.* Such a person, without any provocation, without being angry or sorry, simply because the *karavéni* was inside him or her, might be guilty of any conceivable mischief. Such people in olden days would kill a man, woman, or child; they would destroy property, burn a house (which would mean the whole village as well), chop up a canoe, throw spears at a house, etc. Sometimes they would come running along to the gardens, frighten people they met on the way, return in their frenzied state to the village, and fall down exhausted.[49] Next day they would be quite well again, as if nothing had happened. Thus I was informed by the natives about the *o'o.* As is usually the case, in the perspective of native narrative and information, things assume larger dimensions just as they are removed in time. When I asked about concrete examples of *o'o,* several cases were mentioned, amongst which one was fairly recent. A Laruóro woman, named Vaíla, used to have *o'o* fits regularly. At such times she dressed up fantastically, decorating her head and body with leaves and weeds, and seizing a spear or a drum, she performed a dance of her own, of which the natives were very much afraid, but she did not commit any of the crimes attributed to the *o'o* of 'olden days'. It is, however, quite possible that the *o'o* were not always so harmless. There occur instances of murder done simply to give vent to a man's disturbed state of mind, these being undoubtedly related to the *amok* psychology. A case in point is the murder of his own mother by Owáni, a native of Loupóm, which occurred quite recently (mentioned above, chap. iii., sec. 5). Though the natives were doubtful whether this was a case of *o'o* – very likely there was too much white man's fuss about the matter to make it an *o'o* pure and simple – still, all agreed that an *o'o* man would behave just like that, and the *karavéni* and *o'o* belief undoubtedly covers this region of native psychology.

2 MAGIC

Black magic

The only black magic I was able to trace among the Mailu is the sorcery of the *bará'u* described in the foregoing section. There is, as far as I could detect, no minor black magic. None is practised with the remains of food, hair and nail clippings, or with objects long associated with the human body. I saw people in Mailu carelessly throwing away the shaved off, or pulled out, hair, and I was told that nobody would be afraid of doing so, though on the mainland, especially towards Gadaísiu, a Mailu man would take precautions, and burn his hair clippings and throw the remains of his food into the sea.[81]

---

[81] I know, though on this point my information is only superficial, that the inland natives practise the magic of remains. Thus, in Abá'u jail I watched a number of prisoners from the various inland tribes at a meal. After they had finished eating one of them took the food remains, peel, etc., mixed the whole lot carefully, and threw it away. My attention was directed to this fact by the Resident Magistrate, Mr. Armit, who also informed me that this act was a measure of precaution, for when the remains were mixed no one was able to pick out those which belonged to a hostile tribe, and perpetrate magic against him. Again, I was informed by an ex-Resident Magistrate from the north-eastern coast that there was a sharp line of demarcation between the Papuans and Papuo-Melanesians, the latter not practising the magic of remains, while the former were addicted to that habit.

White magic apportioned to individuals

Though there was no minor black magic, there was plenty of white magic wrought among the Mailu tribe. There were two classes of it, quite distinct from the ethnologist's point of view, though I do not think the natives trouble in any way to classify their magical store. The first class can be described as the individual, private, and hereditary magic; this being a form of individual property of distinctly economic value in the eyes of the natives. The second class is of public character, consisting of spells and practices known, if not to everybody, at least to many, and practised more or less publicly, and more or less for the general benefit. In both classes I found that economic magic – *i.e.,* magic done to advance gardening, hunting, fishing, and trading – is by far the most important, though healing ranks among the magic of the first class, and some spells, not directly economic, concerning wind and weather, are to be found among the second.

Let us describe the magic of the first class – the individual magic. This form is either entirely, or almost entirely, universal, in the sense that every grown-up man has his own monopoly in that line, one man knowing how to make bananas grow well, the other how to make coconuts thrive, or another how to make one or other kind of fishing successful, etc. Thus, while this form of magic is, in a way, universal, it is at the same time entirely specialistic. But it is not a speciality in the usual sociological sense of the word, because, as a rule, a man would not perform his magic for anybody but himself. Thus it by no means represents a professional capacity. Being at the same time private property, it is inalienable, though now the sophisticated natives would attempt to trade in magic, as will be illustrated below. This magic is transmitted, hereditarily, from father to son, and the husband always initiates his wife into his own magic. On the other hand, women never inherit magic from their fathers, except when there is no male issue in the family. It should be remarked that brothers, especially those living in one and the same house and forming one household, practise their magic in common. Thus it would be perhaps more correct to speak of household magic than of individual magic. On the other hand, as each of the brothers keeps a nominal overright to one of the formulas, allowing the other or others to use them freely, the term 'individual' may be used (cf. the concrete example given below).

This is the sociological aspect of the individual magic. Turning now to its technical side, it possesses three essential elements – the condition of the performer, obtained by the observation of certain permanent taboos; the use in it of certain material objects, which, in Mailu, are always leaves or herbs (except in one case, to my knowledge, noted below); a magical spell, pronounced by the individual during the performance of the magic. All three elements are absolutely and equally essential for the satisfactory result of the magic. The magical substance (leaves) must be properly handled and the spell recited during this performance, and in this consists the magical act. Again, if the man dared to break his taboo *(tóra)*, not only would his magic be ineffective, but serious illness would be his punishment. A man who ate tabooed food would suffer from an outbreak of sores all over his body, which was the universal form of punitive illness, except in the case of the dugong charm to be shortly mentioned, when swelling of the belly would be the penalty befalling the wrongdoer. The taboos observed by the various men are not a secret, and I was able to learn those of a number of men in the village. But the magical formulas and the names of the ingredients are kept absolutely secret, and I owe it to the special kindness and confidence of one of my native friends that I obtained the esoteric information concerning two magical procedures. These I shall describe, as well as another case, in which, though I did not actually obtain the intimate details, I took part in the negotiations going between my cook Igua and Píkana with reference to a powerful dugong fishing charm. In this way I obtained an insight into the way in which the natives regard the whole affair from the economic point of view.

To begin with the last-mentioned case, Píkana, the owner (or, more correctly, *gubína*, master) of the only dugong net in the village, is also the possessor of a dugong magic which he has inherited from his mother. His maternal grandfather had no male progeny, so he gave it to his daughter, the mother of Píkana, who afterwards transmitted it to her sons, Píkana and his younger and less energetic brother, Máru. The dugong net and the dugong charm are inseparable and, from the manner in which the natives looked at things, I felt convinced that the charm was by far the more important element of the two. Another net could have been easily made, but what would be the good of it – if the charm was to be kept secret? And so Píkana has the monopoly of the net – a monopoly which is much more a question of honour than of economic advantage. In order to be competent for his magic, Píkana has to observe the dugong and turtle taboo permanently, and he is thus debarred from the very privilege which his monopoly bestows on his family, his friends, and, undoubtedly, on many other villagers, since a dugong catch would afford a feast for many. I am strongly under the impression, however, that Píkana places immense value on his privilege or monopoly, and that he would not easily part with either of his properties – the net or the charm. And this was also the opinion of the other natives.

This reluctance would, however, apply only to the other Mailu men. When my boy, Igua, a Motu of Elevála, came to the village, Píkana did not hesitate to enter into negotiations with him with reference to the charm, knowing well that the Motu have plenty of dugong nets, and charms as well. Píkana's charm, which is said to have been imported somewhere from the west (Domára and Aróma) a few generations ago, is the only one, as I was asssured by several informants, in which the magical substance consists of stones instead of herbs or leaves. Píkana has got three stones, which are put in contact with the net, and then a spell is uttered. One of these stones, and an incantation as well, was to be sold to my cook-boy for ten shillings, for which sum of money he applied to me one day, explaining the whole matter. I expressed my doubts whether a Mailu charm would act in Elevála, to which Igua replied by pointing to the frequent cases in which charms are brought to the Port Moresby villages from the west, where they act perfectly well. Again I tried to point out the inconvenience of not eating either dugong or turtle, and of being exposed to the terrible danger of a 'big belly' should one's appetite prove stronger than one's good sense. This seemed to make a greater impression upon Igua; still, I think he would have purchased the charm had I not suggested that Píkana would be very likely to fake a spell and give him a false stone, and thus avoid the danger of having his magic spoilt, while at the same time he got money. This conviction prevailed, and Igua desisted from this negotiations.

The danger of spoiling the magic by letting anyone else know the formulas and the nature of the charm is clearly present in the minds of the natives. Thus, as a rule, nobody would dream of selling his magic, and indeed my other informants told me that Píkana's be-haviour was quite incorrect and exceptional. One of these, whom, before I quite appreciated the situation, I had unwittingly pressed for details of his magic in the presence of other Mailu men, told me afterwards that, had he disclosed anything in the presence of others and had they practised his magic, his previously charmed banana crops would have been blasted by such an interference, his own magic having become quite useless. This view was afterwards confirmed by others. Thus the individual rights to a form of magic derive their importance, not only from the actual economic value of the charm, but from the fear of its being spoilt altogether by divulgation.

I shall also adduce a concrete instance of the hereditary way in which charms are transmitted, in order to illustrate the general principles laid down above.

This is the genealogy of Omága, one of my informants:-

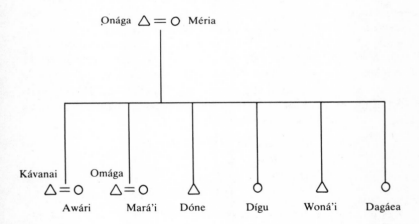

Fig. 45

The father of Omága, Onága, knew two forms of magic – a banana charm and a coconut charm. When the eldest son (Kávanai) had grown up, Onága taught him the former. He had previously taught his wife, Méria, how to make both charms. As Onága died before his other children were adult, it was the mother who imparted to Omága the knowledge of coconut magic, which is now his own magic. It is to be noted, however, that the two brothers, Kávanai and Omága, who live in the same house and keep a common household, have also their magic in common. Omága knows and recites his brother's formula when planting his bananas. Kávanai uses Omága's charm for his coconuts. Again there is a small brother left, Woná'i, who will be taught both formulas when he grows up. The two females of the family, Dígu and Dagáea, are not instructed in the family magic. As soon as they marry they will be taught the magical charms of their husbands. Of course, both brothers have to keep the two respective taboos *(tóra)* if they want to practise the magic. Again, Píkana and his brother Máru, who share the same house, have the same rights to the dugong and turtle magic, and they both observe the same taboo.

Omága communicated to me the text of his incantation, as well as the magical substances and procedure, which I will give here, with certain omissions immaterial from the ethnological point of view, which will prevent the charm from being misused by divulgation among the natives through some white man.[82]

The taboo of Omága's own magic is a fish called *urá'o*, which he is permanently forbidden to eat. The magical substance used by him consists of leaves of one of the native trees growing on the island, the name of which is taboo *(góra)* to Omága. A coconut about to be planted, with the young leaves sprouting, is then doctored by the magical leaves, the latter being wrapped round the young sprout of the coconut *(cf.* planting of coconuts in sec. 1 chap. iv). Then a handful of the magical leaves is taken, and the spell is chanted into them. In a free translation, this charm runs thus:-

> Many coconuts they come out;
> The blossom is breaking forth;
> The fruit is swelling;
> The fruit is breaking forth.[83]

After that the palm will grow very quickly and bear many fruits.

Again, the banana spell, belonging by title to Kávanai, but used by Omága, is performed in a very similar manner. The taboo to be observed with this spell also refers to a fish, called *báe*. Leaves of a

---

[82]This may seem an unnecessary precaution. Nevertheless, this pamphlet might fall into the hands of a white man passing through the district, and unscrupulous enough to divulge the charm among the natives. There is a class of white men only too eager 'to put down the native superstitions'. I remember myself a man boasting of having spoilt the results of a series of important magical ceremonies by publicly violating the drum taboo in an inland village. He was firmly convinced that he had thus done a great deal for the cause of the enlightenment of the natives.

[83]I am in possession of the original Mailu text, but I only give the translation for the reason just mentioned.

special kind of tree are also used in this magic. They are put into a bamboo, which is tied to the mother tree of the banana sucker about to be planted, and remain there over night. The next morning the man comes to the garden and digs a hole for the young plant. Holding this in his right hand and some of the leaves in the palm of the left, he chants a spell into the latter, then puts the charmed leaves into the hole and plants the banana sucker over them. The leaves in the bamboo are not thrown away, but always brought back to the village and used over and over again.

The formula recited in this case seemed more obscure than the previous one. After having translated it verbally into Motu, and then into English, I made the following version:-

> Trembling (or shaking) of banana leaves, come!
> Banana flowers hanging down, come.
> Big fruit, come!
> Many fruits, come!
> All the bands of bananas, come!
> Much food comes.

Whether the whole of the invocation, or part of it only ought to be translated in the imperative I do not know, but I think it is certain that all the single words are correctly translated. It is obviously a 'sympathetic' invocation, enumerating all the various things which are hoped to be obtained by the recitation of the spell. Needless to add, that if the magic is properly performed and the taboo strictly observed the banana crop is splendid.

I have been told by Omága and other informants that nearly all the individual magic of this description refers to economic objects, the only exception being the faculty for doctoring possessed by some men, which is also a kind of individual magic. These men also observe some taboos on that account, know certain spells, and use herbs. But I was unable to obtain any satisfactory information on the point, nor do I know whether such doctors would exert their powers on behalf of others for a remuneration, or whether, as the others do, they would keep their magic to themselves.

Magic of general usage

We may now refer to the other class of minor white magic – to the spells not monopolized by individual men.

Here belong in the first place the simple spells or prayers uttered on many important and critical occasions, as, for instance, when they set out on a sailing journey, or when caught by a stiff gale, during an economic enterprise, as in the arm-shell selling expedition to Aróma, or when fishing or hunting.

Such spells, or prayers, were always, as far as I know, accompanied by some magico-religious performances.[84]

Thus some betelnut (*wéni*), wild ginger root (*aráva*; Motu, *pópo*), and native cinnamon bark *(góbu)* were usually chewed and spat out. At times some manipulations were performed.

It is very important to note that all the formulas include an appeal to a spirit *(bó'i)*. I think that the natives never knew, nor troubled themselves, as to what spirit it was exactly. It was, however, always an ancestral spirit, and, as far as I was able to gather, the spirit of some recently dead ancestor, such as the father or grandfather of the man reciting the spell.

The spell *(u'úra)* recited when the natives go to catch fish and get sago for a small feast, runs as follows:-

'*Bó'i Oo ...*   *útsi éloébo*   *tsibilá'i*
Spirit O!   Do good   to me

orebe   *vamá'i bilá'i*   *oba*   *vamai*
fish   make catch me   shell   make catch

bilá'i   *ganalei'á'i*   *déma*   *odei*
me   your dance   because   sago

vamai bilá'i   *gana*   *oï'o*   *odei*   *déma'*.[85]
make me   your   mourning feast   sago   because

Which, in a free translation, would run:-

'O spirit! Make me successful in fishing! Make me successful in getting shellfish! Make me successful in making sago, because of your mortuary feast.'

I was not able to ascertain in a conclusive manner whether this

---

[84]I am trying to introduce as few theoretical preconclusions as possible, and to avoid any definite decision, whether the facts described ought to be regarded as magical or religious. Following Dr. Marett's advice in the 'Notes and Queries', I will call them magico-religious.[[50]]

[85]I am indebted for this and for the following *verbatim* translations to the Rev. W. J. V. Saville.

u'úra would be recited only when setting out for fishing, for making sago, for a feast, or on all occasions, but I should think the latter was the case.

Again, a pig *u'úra* was recited to me:-

'Borá'a	*áva*	*máraratsíba*
Pig	two	tame me

pitsóro	*dá vatseíba*	*gána*	*oí'o*
restless	not make be	you	funeral feast

borá'i	*déma*	*vaú'i*	*gonigoni*
pig	because	to-day	gentle (soft)

tsíba	*itsítsi*	*vatseíba*	*bó'i*	*dá*
be	food	make be	spirit	not

útsi	*óreóre*	tsíba	*gána*	*unári*
do	evil	me	your	mine

goníni	*déma'.*
gentle	because.

In a free translation:- 'Tame my pigs, cause them to keep still in consideration of your funeral feast pigs! Make the food (meat) to be soft to-day! Do not be angry with me, O spirit. Your mind is gentle!'

Unfortunately I failed to inform myself as to the occasions at which this *u'úra* was recited. It was, however, a general pig charm, made whenever pigs were ill or difficult to manage. Very likely it was recited, when pigs were brought to feast. The references to the funeral feast of the spirits made in this and in the preceding formula, do not mean necessarily that the pigs were brought for the man's funeral feast. It means merely that the spirit was reminded of his feast in order to pay more attention to the *u'úra*.

Again, when the men are sailing, and the sea is very rough, a charm is uttered. A man stands up, and, taking hold of the rigging with one hand and waving the billows down with the other, utters the following incantation:-

'*Oiá...*, *oia...* (the terminal vowels being long drawn out); *lailaié...*, *lailaié; dagana tara ai loeba avavaí loela kiavanaí audamini biraié oaimoru morue moru bidaaié.*'

This incantation is in the Bónabóna language, and I was not able to obtain a *verbatim* translation. I was told, however, that it also includes an appeal to an ancestral spirit. The incantation was recited to me in a rhythmic sing-song, the rhythm coinciding with the movements of the hand, everything expressing the calming, smoothing influence which the spell was supposed to exercise upon the waves.

When the men are sailing, and they are afraid of heavy rain, they say, holding both hands close to the mouth, with open palms and stretched fingers:-

'Rigirigi eé... (terminal vowels long drawn); *gareva boubou eé...; ibina rima de'ua reva é...; guiva lamunama de'ua reva é....'*

Then they say *tfuú...* (long drawn), and spread out the arms to disperse the rain clouds. This incantation is also in the Bónabóna language. I was told by my informants that the men between Gadaísiu and Bónabóna, and thereabouts, are also great wind and weather experts, as they are also learned in sorcery, and also that the Mailu men never learn, or purchase, these charms from them. All of these were, as stated above, uttered with chewing and spitting of betel, ginger root, and cinnamon.

There are also some incantations against snake bite. Mr. Greenaway knew a specialist at Dedéle Point who used to utter some spell over a stone and then throw it into the grass, which was said to prevent snakes from biting.

The *marivana de'ue reva*, or charm, for causing the arm-shells to be well sold, has been mentioned in sec. 4 of the preceding chapter (see pl. 23, 24).

There is a magical ceremony performed in connection with the big nets *(ume gaúma)*. A number of people go to some place on the barrier reef – usually to the part called Arié'u (north-western end of island). Two men hold a pole (made of the *ana* tree), round which one end of the *gaúma* is tied. A third man comes and strikes the *ana* with another stick *(laúna)*, and says:-

Orebe	vamá'i	bagiá'i			
Fish	cause to come	here			

gaumára	gugouvói'a	tsáde			
the net	we get	down			

boi	do	tseíba	órebe	míni	gabiá'i
spirit	not	comes	fish	give	here

orebe	*vamá'i*	*bagiá'i*
fish	cause to come	here

a'a'ma	*vatóra*	*óde*
water	is	taken

mari	*dadamaná'i*	*vatséna óde*
village	inmates	are glad

eu	*vagogo óde.*
the	firewood is cut

This translation (which I obtained through Motu) may be rendered in a free version:-

'O spirit, cause the fish to come! The net has been sunk; (angry) spirit keep away; let fish come to us; the water is ready (for boiling) and so is the firewood; the villagers are glad (hoping to get a good catch).'

Here again the natives were emphatic that this incantation is directed towards a spirit in order to appease the angry spirit and to make him favourable.

This charm is connected with divination. After the incantation has been uttered, they watch the *ana* pole, which supports the net and is held by two men. If it moves the spirits are well disposed. If the *ana* does not stir the fishing is not undertaken, and the men return to the village. This custom is known in the Bónabóna and Suá'u villages.

The magical practices, made in preparation for a feast, and described in the next section, also belong to the same class of magic as the spells just mentioned.

3   THE FEAST (*MADÚNA*)

Sociological importance of the feast

It has been necessary to make mention several times of the great annual feast of the Mailu, as it is associated with so many aspects of native life. It has also been stated that the feast forms a central feature in the social and mental life of the natives. In this respect the Mailu do not differ from the other Western Papuo-Melanesians of the south coast, and, as far as I was able to ascertain, from the inland people.[86]

By the expression that the feast is a *central feature* in the native social life, I wish to indicate that it occupies a great part of the activities of the native, both economic and social; that it is the main object, or, rather, the culminating point in his life's interest, and that it is a mainstay of the native's social organization. At the feast and during the feasting season there is an enormous display of all that the Papuan native really cherishes – drums, ornaments, dancing, fighting, women, and, above all, pigs. Again, the feast and its preparatory stages are connected, as was shown above, with marriage and sexual life, with trading (on Mailu Island), and with agricultural activities (making of sago and making of gardens on the mainland). Certain forms of *góra,* or taboo, are exclusively practised in connection with the feast. Again, as was stated in chap. ii, the organization of the clan is strictly connected with the feast; the main characteristic differentiating the clan from the subclan being that the former was a feast clan, *madúna dúbu.* These features will appear still more clearly in the course of the following description. In order to see the native life in the right perspective it is essential to realize this paramount social importance of the feast, as well as to realize that for the native the feast is one of his main objects of life – one of those things that 'keep him going', that make life worth living for him.

The description of the proceedings at, and the preparation for, the feast given in this section, is not all of the same degree of accuracy. Certain ceremonies and parts of the preparations I have seen, but unfortunately I was not able to witness the main feast in Mailu; and this makes the whole difference in the description of ceremonial

---

[86]Cf. C.G. Seligman, *op. cit.*, chap. xii., where the Koíta feast (called *Tabu*) is described. Prof. Seligman states also that the big annual feast plays an extremely important rôle among the Sinaughólo, who live inland from Gábugábu, some 30 miles east of Port Moresby. The Sinaughólo and kindred peoples stretch as far east as inland of Cloudy Bay. In Cloudy Bay I had the opportunity of talking with a native of Kevéri valley, in the main range, who told me that in their tribe there is an annual feast of much the same kind as among the coastal Mailu. Again going east, festive ceremonies of the same type were stated to exist among the Udáma, inland of Amazon Bay and Port Glasgow, and among the tribes living inland of Orangerie Bay. At the big *Só'i* feasts I witnessed, among the Southern Massim between Farm Bay and Mullins Harbour, the inland people, belonging to a non-Massim stock (the Borowai, Magawaru, etc.), performed a big *raú'a* dance. And it was said that they know more about the sacred dances, *góvi, ráu'a,* and *kóbiai,* than the coastal people of that district.

proceedings, for even the best native informants are essentially unable to give any consecutive details, and the detailed information of the white man on such a subject is completely worthless as long as he has not observed the facts for the purpose of study. This, I venture to say, is only possible for a trained observer. I have witnessed the most important preparatory feast in Kurére (Mailu district), and I have seen the whole series of preparations in Mailu village and different stages of it in several places on the mainland. I have also witnessed two big *Só'i* feasts in Isudá'u and Tsílotsílo, and one in Nawuápu in its last stages of preparation. Though the *Só'i* differs from the *Madúna* on many essential points, I was able to trace both the similarities and differences, having several Mailu boys with me. In this way I received a much clearer and more concrete impression of the Mailu feast than I would have been able to obtain from mere narrations. In the course of my account I shall carefully point out all the deficiencies in my information and shall also indicate what I consider to be well established.

The feast is usually called *Madúna*, which means distribution, the allusion being to the distribution of food which forms an essential feature of the proccedings. The word *maúru*, or wealth, is also used at times to denote the big feast. The smaller preparatory feasts are generally called *kanáre* or *gátsi*, each having besides its own specific name. *Oí'o* is the name of a mortuary feast, which will be described in the next section.

Connection between a feast and the dance performed at this feast

The whole character of the feast, especially in its magico-religious aspect, depends upon the dance, which is performed at its main phase. The most sacred and appropriate dance, and that invariably performed when an important *Madúna* takes place, is the *góvi*. For this dance the great ceremonial platform is created, on which it is performed, and with this dance are connected the taboos and magical practices, called *udíni*. Again, this dance, and this dance only, entails a series of preparatory feasts. The decoration of the houses also varies when the *góvi* is given.

Much less ceremony and taboo are associated with the dances *raúa* and *kóbiai*. These two imply certain taboos on the part of the master of the feast. He, and perhaps two or three other men, who act as his associates, abstain from boiled food, fish, and fresh water, eating only roasted food and drinking the fluid of roasted green coconut. The same holds good with reference to the *tsélo* dance, which seems, however, to be of more recent introduction and less often performed than the two just mentioned.

Practically at all the feasts the women perform their own dance – the *damoréa* – whatever others there may be. All the women who are to take part in the performance are required to observe the same taboos as the master and his assistants; there is also the curious observance previously mentioned *viz.*, the drinking of salt water by all those men and women who observe the taboos.

The name for the taboo, and for the tabooed people, is, in the case of *ráua, kóbiai, tsélo,* and *damoréa: gábugábu*, which corresponds to *udíni* in the case of the *góvi*. But the fasting does not begin with any feast, as is the case in *udíni*; the *gábugábu* people have a good drink of salt water after the sago is brought home and the houses have been decorated with the big sago sausages, and henceforward they observe the taboo.[87]

Again, when the *bára* is danced there is no taboo whatsoever, no preliminary feasts, no observances of a magico-religious character. I have reason to believe that this dance has been introduced comparatively recently from the west; it originates from Kerepúna, and from other tribes round Hood Bay, and has made its way, in recent times, eastwards as far as Mailu and westwards to the Sinaughólo, where I had the pleasure of meeting its pioneer and introducer into the tribe, the Motu and Koíta. It is a lively and varied dance, accompanied by extremely poor and uninteresting music, and, in spite of its apparent variety, it is to the European critic both decidedly monotonous and greatly inferior to the other dances. But it is at present immensely popular with the natives, being much preferred to any other dance; in fact, one may say that it is the fashion in Papua nowadays.

Changes in village life when the feast approaches

Whatever dance is performed, and whatever may be the differences

---

[87] All these dances have been introduced from the east – the more sacred ones from the inland tribes of Orangerie Bay and Mullins Harbour, the less sacred *(tsélo* and *damoréa)* from the coastal Southern Massim. For the description and general characteristics of these dances, as well as of the others, see next chapter, sec. 1.

in the preliminary stages of the feast, they are in all cases accompanied by an immediate and general quickening and brightening of the village life. The men, who rehearse the dance every evening, when they are not away on food gathering or trading expeditions, decorate themselves more and more sumptuously and completely. Their numbers increase, the older men gradually joining in. Drums are hung on the front parts of the verandahs, and so are arm-shells, necklaces of *sapisapi* and of other shell discs, with pendants of boars' tusks, large shell discs, and plates inset with jequirity (the *musikáka* of the Central Division). These ornaments appear on the dancers during the performance. It is to be noted that when the *góvi* is performed the drums are hung in the house of the headman of the clan, who is also the master of the feast. The houses are also decorated with streamers of dry pandanus, twigs and palm-leaf ornaments, which at certain dances are stuck into the belt and armlets. When the *góvi* is danced, the *oá'u* leaves, which are also used in the *udíni* magic (see below), are used to decorate the houses.

A very characteristic feature of the approaching feast is the display of food, in which the houses of the headmen of all the subclans are hung with sausages of sago. In the case of a big *Madúna* this decoration is put up as many as four to six months beforehand. Thus I saw the houses in Kurére, where a big feast was about to take place some time in March, decorated with sago in October. The sago, as packed and prepared in the Mailu district, goes bad in about four weeks, and the packages fall to pieces in two months or so; thus, as the final display ought to be edible, the decoration has to be renewed three or four times, with the result that immense quantities of valuable food are wasted. In Mailu village, where the feast in February 1915 was to be a very small one, the sago appeared at the beginning of January, and would have to be replaced once only – or even the half-rotten material might be distributed. A short time before the feast, the bananas are hung up in long rows in front of the houses of the clan, or clans, giving the feast. As the bananas are very perishable in the hot tropical atmosphere, many of them rot before being used, as I have myself seen in Mailu.

This wasteful display of sago and bananas is parallel to the accumulation and partial waste of coconuts connected with the various coconut taboos (*góra*) described in chap. iii. The coconuts are brought together in the palm groves, and arranged in neat rectangular figures under the coconut trees, covering the ground at times for a couple of square metres. Before their time comes many of the nuts have sprouted to an extent that they are no longer edible, and the waste consequently, in the opinion of the Rev. W. J. V. Saville, is quite considerable.

Again, the display of pigs during the feast corresponds also to the same psychological attitude of the natives.

The quickening of life in the village is manifested also by the increase in the intensity of sex life, and by the frequency of small feasts, of a more or less private character, which are in preference held at that time (see what has been said about small feasts, preliminary to marriage, chap. iii., sec. 3, and during the initiation ceremony, chap. iii., sec. 4). During the last few weeks before the advent of the feast one frequently sees men boiling sago and preparing coconut cream, and groups of women unusually busy at cooking, etc.

Series of minor feasts and preparations for a Góvi Madúna

These general remarks will furnish the broad background to the details which follow, and they will enable the reader to sift from the account the features common to all feasts from those peculiar to the *Góvi Madúna*. The latter is by far the most important in the native's own eyes and in that of the ethnologist. It has, therefore, been chosen as the subject of the following description. The other forms of *Madúna* can be easily realized by the reader by the suppression of specific details.

As mentioned in the section on taboos, the coconut *góra*, and especially the specific festive *góra*, the *tóna góra*, are erected a long time before the feast begins, and, as far as I know, this is the first step in the series of preparations for the feast. When the coconuts are tabooed in virtue of death – *i.e.*, when they are *nebúru* – the state of things is to be considered as preliminary to a feast.[88]

The real preparations and the series of preliminary feasts begin with the *kanáre* or *gátsi* (small feast), called *maúru amáta*. It is held at the beginning of the *aurári* season (midwinter); that is, roughly, about six months before the main feast will be given.[89]

---

[88]Of the connection between the ordinary feast and the mortuary feasts I failed to obtain a clear idea. The little I know will be said in the next section.

[89]For the description of the native seasons see chap. iii., sec. 2.

At this the *damoréa* is danced, as, in fact, it is danced at practically all the smaller feasts. Women only take part in it, and they are decorated with strings of shell discs and wave, as they would wave a fan, the *eláki*, or folded mat of pandanus leaves.[90] The dance begins, as is always the case at a small feast, in the afternoon *(valavítsa)* and is continued till daybreak, and at daybreak several pigs, to the number of twenty or thirty, are killed. If there is a big *Madúna* in preparation they are carved on the verandah of the house of the *Madúna* master *(madúna gubína)*, and the meat distributed amongst those present, each *dúbu* or subclan of the villages which had been invited receiving its share. After this distribution the men of the clan giving the feast bring some stones and pile them in front of the master's house. This is one of the preliminary signs that a *góvi* feast is about to be held, and the erection of the heap of stones seems to be the main ceremonial function of the *maúru amáta* in the series of preparatory feasts. But as I have not witnessed this feast my information may be defective, though I observed the heap of stones in front of the *madúna gubína*'s house, close to *móto góra*.

This latter sign *(móto góra)* is erected at another small feast, called *móto bádi*, held at the end of the *aurári* – in the *viníu* season. At this feast the men come dancing into the village from the bush. They perform a dance identical with that danced during the feast coming next in the series. As it was in this latter connection that I saw it I shall describe it presently. They also sing the same song and, as the whole proceedings are identical, they very probably bring something – some leaves used in the construction of the *móto góra* – to the village; but, unfortunately, I did not press that point, and my informants might very probably have omitted one of the details of the feast. At any rate, the most important ceremonial rôle of this feast is the erection of the small gallows, ornamented with the large white shell called by the natives *móto (Ovulum ovum)*. This is a sign that the *góvi* dance will be performed at the *Madúna*. As previously stated (chap. iii., sec. 5), this *móto góra* is also a token that as many pigs are already pledged for the feast as there are shells on the *góra*, each shell representing one pig promised by a man to the *madúna gúbina* (master of the feast).

---

[90]In Mailu district women do not use the ceremonial stone axes, which are an essential accessory of the *damoréa* further east, among the Massim of the southern coast.

Whilst they erect the *móto góra* they sing the following incantation:-

> *Dári   apua'í*
> dog   bite
>
> *borá'a   apua'í*
>   pig   bite
>
>   *nára   ónima   apua'í*
> a kind of   shellfish   bite
>
>   *dá'í   ónima   apua'í*
> another kind   of shellfish   bite
>
>   *bóia   ónima   apua'í*
> mother of   pearl shell   bite
>
> *a'í'a   ónima   apua'í*
>   shell   bite
>
> *apu   gáru   rua'í*
> bite   then   shake
>
>   *apu   góra   e'a'í*
> Tfe!!   Tfe!!   Tfe!!

It was stated that the object of this spell was to make people from other villages bring much food and many pigs to the feast. The significance of the individual words was obtained by making the natives translate them into Motu and so into English. It is impossible, however, to interpret them into any meaning, and especially into that given by the natives.[51] As this, however, is the normal state of things with reference to customary spells, incantations, and songs, there is no reason to dismiss any part of the information as spurious. At any rate, several natives were, independently, quite emphatic that the ultimate aim of the incantation is to increase the pig supply. Possibly the incantation invokes some calamities on those who would not keep their pledges.

After this comes the *oílobo* feast, apparently the most important preliminary one, which certainly contains the greatest amount of magico-religious element, and probably even more than the main feast. It marks the beginning of the fasting or *udíni* period, and is held some two months before the main feast. The *oílobo* I saw at Kurére was held just before Christmas – *i.e.,* at the very end of the *lióro,* or the beginning of the *avára kívonai* season – and the main feast was, both according to the natives and to my own calculations, to be held at the end of February or the beginning of March. This feast also is called *boróa evauré, boróa* meaning mango. In the morning of the feast-day a dance called *laíge* is performed in the village, both men and women taking part in it. The women hold the previously mentioned *eláki* in their hands, the men beat the drums and blow the conch shells while dancing. The ceremonial part of the feast takes place in the afternoon, during *valavítsa* hours; the men dress ceremonially and go out into the bush. Their decoration includes, in the first place, the ceremonial blackening incidental to all strict taboos, as well as to mourning. This blackening is done by the master (or masters, if more than one clan is giving a feast) of the *Madúna* and by several other men, who play a part in the feast arrangements and who join, at least partially, in the fasting. These men also have their heads well decorated with feathers and ornaments of boars' tusks, shell plates, etc., suspended from a shell-disc necklace. All the other men taking part in the ceremony are also decorated, but less profusely, and none of them are blackened. They all wear armlets and anklets of dry pandanus strips, a sign that they take an active part in the performance. These men bring back from the bush the mango saplings and the *o'á'u* creepers, which form part of the pig magic. They come in state, forming a procession, which is headed by a man blowing the conch *(bogígi)* made of a *Triton* shell. He is followed on both sides by two men, also with conch shells. Behind this triangle are brought the mango saplings, as many of them as there are clans performing the *góvi* dance, or what comes to the same thing, as many as the platforms that are to be erected. The saplings are carried by assistants of the *Madúna* masters, who take part in the *udíni* taboo. From the top of each there descend two streamers of the *o'á'u* creeper, the free ends of the latter being held by men. The master, or masters, of the feast *(madúna gubína)* follow the mangoes, each walking behind the bearer of his sapling. In the feast I witnessed there were two saplings and two *gubína* following, as two clans were to perform the *góvi* dance at the feast.

This group is followed by a number of men with drums, who all sing and dance to the beats. Both song and dance are, as is always the case, called by the same name, *boróa evauré laíge – boróa* meaning mango. The song runs:-

> *'Lá'upa'ápa*   *aí   gurí*
> The pole on the   platform it falls

> *arau'oí   oí   rei'ó*
> *modíri   bátsi   avaná*
> mango   mango

> *arau'oí   oí   rei'ó*
> *aílopulopo   aí   gurí*
> Tree on platform it   falls

> *arau'oí   oí   rei'ó*
> *modíri   tsáui   tsaúió*
> mango

> *gisóa   tsaúe   tsaúoí.'*

This song undoubtedly refers to the mango pole erected on the *góvi* platform; but the mango saplings which were then being carried were not placed on the platform, and I could not get any information as to the reason why this song is sung at that time. As it is, however, sung during a previous feast *(maúru amáta,* see above), there seems to be no doubt that it is a ceremonial song of special importance, and that it points to the great part played by the mango in the feast, though this part, in Mailu at least, seems to be distinctly of the nature of a survival.[91]

There is a characteristic and somewhat wild dance, to the accompaniment of the song and drums, in which they take long, elastic

---

[91]For the benefit of those readers who have never done ethnographical field work, I may add that it is in almost all cases quite impossible to obtain from the natives the direct meaning of, or the reason for, a song or incantation. The answer is always, 'Old custom, handed down by our fathers.' Again the literal translation of a song is very often impossible. Natives use obsolete words and phrases; some words here and there are translated, and these serve to the ethnologist as the clue to the general meaning of the incantation. Compare, for instance, the songs of the Central and Northern Australian aborigines given by Spencer and Gillen. The claims of the German missionary Strehlow, who gives full and extremely consistent translations of songs that the originators were unable to translate, must, as far as my own experience goes, be received with some reserve. Natives who have been long under the white man's training, as Strehlow's mission boys undoubtedly were, possess a wonderful ability of adapting the incongruities of traditional custom and belief to the necessities of an untrained, and hence too consistent, a white man. In Mailu there is the additional reason for allowing for a certain margin of obscurity and ignorance on the part of the natives, as the *góvi* dance and the connected ceremonies are undoubtedly introduced from abroad (see below, chap. vi., sec. 1).[[52]]

strides, leaping from one foot to another. At times they bend the knees and body and dance in an almost squatting position, in which position they look rather demoniacal. Again, at times the chiefs get in front of the mango trees, turn round, and dance backwards, looking up to the mangoes – a movement which, to the observer, seems to express a kind of adoration of the plants.

The song ceases for a short time, and the men dance to the rhythmic beat of the drums. Then the foremost men blow the conch shells and all the others join in a long-drawn O – o – o – in tune with the shells, the two sounds blending perfectly. Then the song is resumed.

Thus, singing and dancing, the men enter the village, where they are met by a group of women, decorated with diadems of white cockatoo feathers, and with necklets of shell discs, in the form of the *bági* and *samarúpa* of the east end.[92] The women dance and wave at the men ceremonially with folded pandanus mats and pieces of native bark cloth (I also saw a few pieces of calico), which action is called *tagábu*. The women wait until the men join them, then they dance backwards, and the whole *cortège* thus enters the street and comes right in front of the house of the most important *Madúna* masters.

Two of the large pandanus mats *(eba)* are next spread in the middle of the street, and all the men participating in the ceremony squat down. The innermost circle is formed by the two masters of the feast and by the bearers of the mango poles and of the *o'á'u* creepers, as well as by the old men of the village. This is the preparation for the cutting up of the mango saplings, *boróa pétapéta*. It begins by a ceremonial eating of betelnut, accompanied by a betelnut incantation *(wéni u'úra)*. Some betelnut is produced, and small parts of it are distributed in an earnest and solemn manner. The men, holding the pieces of nut in their hand and looking at them carefully and, one might say, tenderly, and swaying their bodies rhythmically, sing the following song. After they have finished it they eat the nut slowly.

1. | *Rogéa* | *bedána* | *bédasoní* | *toninamó* |
    | Island of Rogea | betelnut | licking the | lime spatula |

    | *bedaió* | *aitserí* |
    | betelnut | cut into pieces |

    | *tsabúbu* | *A-a-a ...* (long drawn) |
    | shake him | |

---

[92]Figured on pl. 1x. in Prof. Seligman's treatise.

2.   *Maivára   bedána   bédasoní...*
      Maivára, (in Milne Bay)

      (continued as above.)

3.   *Durubi   bedána,* etc....

Thus several localities, all from the extreme eastern end of New Guinea, are mentioned, and then the song ends with the last stanza:-

> *Taukuripokapoka   amubéda*
> (personal name)   your betelnut
>
> *bedaió   aitserí   tsabúbu*
> betelnut   cut into pieces   shake
>
>   *aitserí*
> cut into pieces
>
> *Kumakarakedakeda   amubéda*
>   (personal name)
>
> *bedaió   aitserí   tsabúbu*
> Aitserí

This song is addressed to the two legendary men, provided with the somewhat long names of Kumakarakedakeda and Taukuripokapoka, who have claims to the first introduction of betelnut. They lived in Maivára (a community in Milne Bay, at the eastern end of New Guinea). At that time there was no betelnut in the country. Then Kumakarakedakeda and Taukuripokapoka made a big feast, for which all the villages assembled. They gave betelnut to every village, and are the patrons of this article.

The song is intended to please these two legendary persons, and at the same time to make the nut plentiful. It is essential that it should be eaten during the performance. The natives were, as is usually the case, somewhat vacillating in giving the *why* of the custom. But the song is obviously a betelnut incantation, and all my informants were agreed that, should the ceremony be omitted, the nuts would suffer.[53]

After the betelnut ceremony is finished there comes the ceremonial cutting of the mango saplings, called *boróa gábi-gábi*, in which they sing a song referring to the cutting of the mango. During this performance two men take the two young mango trees in one hand, and small axes (iron ones in the performance I saw) in the other, and at each phrase of the song they mark the sapling with an axe cut. As the singing goes on – the same phrases being repeated over and over again, as is usual in native songs – the performers increase the energy of the blows. After the song is finished they cut the mango stakes into pieces about 30 cm. long. These, together with the *o'á'u* creepers, are wrapped in the mats on which the performance took place, and in this way form the pig charm, the use of which will be described directly. The song, as well as the cutting of the mangoes and the wrapping of the pieces in the mats, is called *oílobo*, which name is equally applied to the whole feast.

The song, of which I unfortunately failed to obtain the translation, runs as follows:-

1. *Oiauguro baiwa ewaiogodo baiwa*
2. *Ewaoi gera gerai a-a-a...* (long drawn)
3. *Ewaoi dagobe a-a-a...* (long drawn)
4. *Oiau gisoa boi guri*
5. *Oiau modiriva modiri auea*
6. *Eoiguri a-a-a...* (long drawn)

The numbers indicate the single phrases, which form distinct musical units in the singing. The song contains allusions to the mango *(gisóa modíri)*.

During the singing of this song, as of all those previously quoted, one old man took the lead. He was not one of the masters of the feast, and I was told afterwards that he was the greatest authority on the subject in the village. In the ceremonial songs the men look at each other, sing with much deliberation, and have the air of acting under a kind of inspiration to improve the song. The tune of all those I heard, as well as of the incantation in arm-shell magic that I heard performed on another occasion (see sec. 2 of this chapter), is identical, and, as compared with the tunes of some dancing songs, is strikingly melodious. It ascends in the scale within an interval approaching about a small terce or augmented second, and then descends again. The whole proceedings are very serious and solemn, but there is nothing esoteric about them. Both women and children of the whole village look on, though, prompted by their *savoir faire*, they keep at a distance from the circle of men, squatting round the mat. But although not esoteric, the ceremony is nevertheless extremely serious and important in the eyes of the natives, and not to be in any way lightly treated. As it was performed late in the afternoon I was unable to take any snapshots. I offered the natives exorbitant prices (six sticks of tobacco to each of the chief actors and three to all the others) if they would rehearse the performance next morning. I tried also to exert a certain pressure through the village constable, but all in vain. The natives did not want to profane the ceremony and risk the evil results of trifling with a magical performance.

After this there begins the fasting and general taboo on the part of those who are going to play any rôle in the subsequent dance and feast. As mentioned above, the general taboo – *i.e.,* abstention from boiled food, fish, and fresh water, as well as the drinking of salt water from time to time – is observed by both men and women; that is to say, by all the men who will dance and assist the master at the feast, and by all the women who will play a certain ceremonial part (such as that played in the dancing to receive the men during the *kanáre*), and by those who will dance the *damoréa*. A specially strict taboo, called *udíni*, which is also connected with the feast magic, is undergone by the master of the feast and a few of his nearest assistants. Thus at the *Madúna* in Kurére, the *udíni* was undergone by the two masters of the clans which danced the *góvi* (the third clan, as mentioned before, danced the *bára*); also by two men called *borá'a eva mini*, which means givers of pigs. These men carried the two mango saplings and cut them up at the *oílobo*. At the main feast they will help in carrying out the distribution of pigs. All these men are called *udíni* men *(udíni égi)*. These, besides observing the above-mentioned food taboos – and that certainly much more strictly than the other fasters – blacken their bodies all over; they have to practise complete sexual abstention, and they sleep in a special place, called *varatséva*. In former days, when the *dúbu* were in existence, the *udíni* men slept in these; nowadays they sleep in the upper thatched apartment of a house. In this room there is a corner set apart, and it is *góra* (tabooed), nobody being allowed to enter it.[93]

---

[93]While I was visiting Nawádu, in Farm Bay (in the Suá'u district of the Southern Massim), I inspected a recently-built house in which the master of an approaching feast used to sleep. The natives did not like my entering it, and whilst I approached one corner which was partitioned off with a plaited coconut mat and decorated with arm-shells and *bági* (heavy necklaces of ground-shell discs), I was earnestly requested to keep away. I did not know at that time the *udíni* customs, and I was not aware that the corner was tabooed.[54]

The most important element in the arrangement of the *varatséva* is the folded mat *(eba)* containing the cut-up mango and the *o'á'u* creepers. Besides these, some additional leaves, possessing magic properties, are usually inserted. Of such a nature are the leaves of a fruit-bearing tree *gaméla*, of a large tree called *i'o*, and some aromatic herbs, called *gáu*. All these plants were emphatically affirmed to be *borá'a iápa* – pig charm. The *Madúna* master sleeps on the mats. I was not able to ascertain for certain whether, or how, the articles of native wealth are displayed in the *varatséva* place, though I was informed that it was decorated with native ornaments. The three analogous arrangements that I saw in the Southern Massim district, where the taboo arrangements (called there *sobó'i'o)* are almost identical with those of the Mailu, were all richly decorated, or, rather, hung over with all sorts of native jewellery (arm-shells, strings of shell discs, ceremonial stone axes, etc.).

It is clearly and unanimously understood that the whole *udíni* proceedings are a charm for attracting pigs to the feast. Now, pigs are at the present time reared in all the villages and brought to the feast, so that it would seem as if the magic ought to be supposed by the natives to act upon the owners of the pig, rather than directly upon the animals themselves. Careful inquiry, however, proved that this is not the case. The charm is a pig charm, ensuring that plenty of pigs shall be brought to the feast. The questions as to the *modus operandi* of the charm were dismissed as useless sophistications. Again, a native in the course of discussion pointed out to me on his own initiative that some pigs in the coastal villages are practically living in the bush, and that they have to be caught by their owner before they are brought to the feast. This informant simply hinted that things are not so simple as I implied, but he refused to draw any conclusion. It is, therefore, clear that the natives universally believe that the *udíni* magic will secure plenty of pigs, and hence a brilliant feast, but they do not try to imagine how the magic is acting.[55]

The main feast

As already stated, I have not witnessed the main feast in the Mailu district, though my ideas were greatly helped by the observation of the big feasts in the Bónabóna district. I am also convinced from what I saw and heard that the main magico-religious elements are contained in the events above described – that is, in the preliminary

302 Magico-Religious Activities and Beliefs

feasts, preparations, and taboos. There is obviously less *belief* embodied in the practices of the feast itself.[94] The *Sói* feasts which I saw, and which were undoubtedly identical with the *Madúna* in the main outlines, had much less of the character of a silent and concentrated feast than the *oílobo* which I saw in Kurére.

As mentioned in a previous paragraph (chap. iv., sec. 4), the natives of Mailu Island, in anticipation of the final feast, go on expeditions to Aróma in order to bring back pigs, and shortly after their return the feast takes place. The last days are spent in collecting as many vegetables, coconuts and other fruits as possible. Word has previously been sent round fixing approximately the date of the *Madúna*, and great numbers of natives arrive from various villages. Those living at the greatest distances – even in olden days people used to come from as far as Bónabóna and the Massim villages beyond – usually arrive the earliest, as they want to make sure that they will not miss the feast. For those at hand this margin is not necessary. In the Massim district I witnessed both the arrival of a large number of native canoes for a feast and the departure of some, and both events were picturesque and impressive. When the natives leave their village for a feast they blow the conch shell and shout loudly to announce the event. The pig, suspended from a pole by its bound feet, is carried in a procession and put on board the canoe.

When the feast is imminent the canoes assemble, the whole horizon being dotted with crab-claw sails, with the oval sails of the east, and with small dug-outs propelled by paddles or small mast sails. The long-drawn, penetrating wail of the conch shell reverberates over the water, and is periodically interspersed with the wild scream, thrice repeated, with which the natives wind up the music of the shell. The voices from the sea are answered from the bush, and the sound of parties coming from a distance, with the weird O-o-o! of the shell and the shrill Iii! Iii...! Iii...! of the excited men, growing more and more distinct as they approach, is singularly impressive.

---

[94]These remarks are, of course, only statements of fact. How far the feast is to be regarded as a mere social revelry, as a magical ceremony, or else as a religious ceremony, is a theoretical question, which it is not necessary to discuss in this place. I need scarcely add that in this question, as in many others, I have tried to be as unbiassed as is possible for an ethnologist, though, of course, having theoretical problems constantly in mind I tried to read in every fact an answer to a general query, which does not necessarily mean 'the confirmation of a preconceived idea'.

When they arrive the various parties camp in groups, usually associating fairly well according to their geographical distribution. Notwithstanding the ceremonial peace which should prevail during a feast, the natives seem in olden days to have been always on the alert and very apprehensive of possible contingencies, and I believe with good reasons. After all were assembled the feast began. If I may conjecture from what I saw during a *Sói* feast and from what I was told by the natives, the first proceeding would be some dance not of a ceremonial character, such as the *damoréa* of the women and the *tsélo* or *daúge* of the men. After that the great ceremonial dance – which in a solemn *madúna* is always the *Góvi* – would take place, and on the next day the slaughtering of the pigs and distribution of the food. But as I never witnessed a feast it will be safer for me not to attempt a detailed account, but to confine myself to the enumeration of its essential elements.

1. *Ceremonial Elements* – The feast is the climax and the object of the fast and of the magical practices embraced by the native term *udíni*. The *udíni* is formally brought to a close at the feast by the *udíni* men washing in the sea and partaking of food. The *góvi* dance is also a ceremony in itself, but unfortunately I was not able to obtain any details on this point.[95]

2. *Dancing* – Besides the ceremonial dance, others are performed; I am inclined also, to think that, whatever it be, the principal ceremonial dance may, after it has been danced for a short time, degenerate into a mere pleasure dance. The distinction between the two is based upon the fact that the former is performed by men specially prepared, who would have been subject to some taboos. As far as I was able to ascertain, the *góvi* is not danced by the master or by any of the *udíni* men. The non-ceremonial dances would be performed by both sexes, while the ceremonial *góvi* would, in Mailu, be danced by men only.[96] At the dances in which both sexes take part there is undoubtedly a strong erotic element.

3. *Distribution of Food* – This takes place after the dance, usually on

---

[95]In Mailu the *góvi* is an introduced dance. I hope to be able to obtain some more precise information concerning it by the study of the natives inland of Mullins Harbour.[56]

[96]Though, according to Prof. Seligman's and the Rev. H. Newton's descriptions, the same dance is, in the Massim district, performed by men and women.[57]

another day. It is, as far as the interest of the native goes, undoubtedly the most important part of the feast. The food (sago and
bananas), as already mentioned, is displayed even at the preparatory
stages of the feast, and the pigs form the general topic of discussion,
comparison, admiration, and boasting. Groups of men and women
stand for hours round the rows of these animals, which, living and
bound, with their feet lacerated by the cruel mode of transport, and
bleeding freely from the wounds, lie in a pitiful conditon. To prevent
their untimely death, the owners sprinkle them with water. I saw all
this at the *Sói* feasts, and as Motu was the language spoken between
some of my boys and the villagers I could follow parts of the conversation. The above broad features are, of course, common to the
tribes I observed as well as to the Mailu.

The display of food is further augmented by the piling up of
vegetable food in the street, in front of the houses of the feast-giving
clan, immediatley before the distribution, every man contributing his
own share. The coconuts, sago, *taitu*, yams, taro, and bananas are,
in that order, piled in heaps upon the ground.

The pigs are killed on platforms, erected on the bush side of the
village, and both their flesh and the other food are distributed
amongst those present, the *Madúna* master calling out the names of
the clans which are to receive their respective shares.

These are, so far as I was able to ascertain, the principal features of
the main feast, and in spite of the imperfection of my account I do
not think that any matter of importance has been omitted. There are,
however, some general remarks still to be made. As previously
mentioned, the food aspect of the feast is extremely important to the
natives. Whenever I discussed the subject with a new informant, and
asked him what the feast was and how it was conducted, I usually got
the long ménus, in which marked enthusiasm was shown in respect to
the beauty of such a collection of fine, large fat pigs from Aróma.
The natives would also speak of all the toils that must be undergone
in order to procure the cherished pigs and the sago. Again, when,
with a number of Mailu boys and with Igua, my Motuan valet, I was
watching the *Sói* feasts in Tsílotsílo and Isudáu, my companions
were indignantly contemptuous of their poverty and plainness, and
when pressed to justify their criticism, they pointed out that the
quantity of pigs and of other food killed and cooked and given away
was ridiculously small. 'In Mailu', they said, 'the feast is beautiful,
lots of pigs are killed and distributed'.

So also the importance of the food is manifest in the ornamental display of bananas and sago, and in the fact that all the ceremonial and magical activities connected with the feast are directed towards the increase of food at the *Madúna*.

Perhaps almost equally fascinating in the eyes of the natives are the dances. A native dance, with full ceremonial decoration and, what is still more important, with full ceremonial setting, is something to be seen and remembered. I shall never forget the impression I received from a *raúa* dance, performed by some inland people at the feast in Tsílotsílo, and not the least striking accessory was the great excitement, mixed with feeling of real fear and awe, on the part of all those present. The artistic needs of the native are satisifed by the non-ceremonial dances.

Besides the ceremonial ornamentation of the dancers and of the master of the feast and his assistants, there is at each a general display of finery. Even on its approach, in Mailu, all the native ornaments were displayed, and in this way there were revealed also more than ordinarily fine lime spatulas, elegant decorated combs, armlets, belts, ear-shells, etc. In this respect the *Sói* feasts I saw were real 'Vanity Fairs', the native dandies swaggering about with ebony swords and sticks (useful in the case of scrimmage), wearing fine necklaces, and with their faces and bodies painted red, black, and white, in a more or less fanciful manner.[58]

Another general feature of the feast was the fighting, which seems to have been very frequent, though perhaps not usually resulting in much bloodshed. Fights were almost on the point of taking place at the feasts I witnessed, though the district was quiet and fairly civilized, and my presence undoubtedly acted rather as a deterrent. I was told by Mr. Greenaway, who has been present at many *Madúna*, that fighting was a regular feature of the feast, and the Rev. W. J. V. Saville informed me that at a feast in one of the Mailu villages of Orangerie Bay (eastern part of the Mailu district), at which he was present, a serious fight very nearly took place between the men of two usually hostile villages, who faced each other ready for the fray. It was only the presence of two white men, and their conciliatory efforts, that prevented an actual outbreak of hostilities. The cause was a quarrel over a woman, who left her husband and went to her own community to live with another man.

In a quarrel I witnessed among the Massim, it arose in one case out of a heated discussion over a pig, two parties laying hold of the unfortunate animal and nearly tearing it to pieces in their struggle while each asserted his right to the squealing victim. As I had to act as an arbiter in this case, I learned that the original owner of the pig sent it direct to the master of the feast, whilst the other party maintained that it ought to have been given to him.

On a second occasion the quarrel broke out over a curious custom. When the men bring the pig, carrying it on a long pole, to present it to the master of the feast or to one of the submasters (in the Massim area, where this occurred, there are secondary masters at each feast, though in the Mailu district there are no such persons), they run at a great speed and bump the post against the trunk of a young tree, in preference a coconut palm. They do this as often as they can, to the great annoyance of the owner of the tree (and, judging by its squeals, no doubt to that of the pig). Their object is to uproot the tree and knock it down, and though this is an acknowledged custom fights over the performance seem to have been the rule in olden days. I adduce this Massim custom as it adds to the general characteristics of the feast, and indicates channels through which fighting might enter into the apparently well-regulated course of the feast.

It must be added that all the participants in the feast, and especially the master and his assistants, are in an extremely high pitch of nervous excitement. To this contribute the long fasting, the great consumption of betelnut, and, primarily, the very atmosphere of the feast and the strong feeling of responsibility, to which the master is undoubtedly subject. All the ceremonial speeches I heard at the two *Sói* were spoken with great frenzy, with a quivering voice, foaming mouth, the muscles of the face twitching, and the whole frame shaking. It looked as if the man wanted to goad the apparently amazed crowd to some wild and desperate act. The effect, especially at night time, was so strong that I felt distinctly impressed, in spite of my complete sense of safety and of my good personal relations with all the performers.

I must say that I did not see any sign of quickening sexual life at the two *Sói* feasts, and it should be noted that the Southern Massim are distinctly more lax in sexual matters than the Mailu. In the light of what has been said in chap. iii., this means only that, in public, decorum is maintained right throughout the excitement of the feast.

Parts played by different social divisions in the feast

Finally, it seems necessary to sum up in a few words the sociological aspect of the feast – *i.e.,* to show what social groups come into contact on such occasions, and how they interact among one another.

The feast is, in some communities of the Mailu district at least, an intertribal event. Thus at the big *Madúna* of Mailu village, people of the Southern Massim district, from Bónabóna, Dahúni, etc., used to come, even in olden days, and I was told that people from Aróma, in the west, occasionally used to come as guests of the Mailu for the exceptionally sumptuous feasts. On the mainland the range of invitations was much more restricted, a few neighbouring villages only being invited. I failed to ascertain whether the inland people (Udáma, etc.) were accustomed to come to the mainland *Madúna*.

The village community amongst which the feast took place acted collectively as the host – even if the feast was given by one or by a couple of clans only, and not by the whole community; the latter, however, always had a great deal of work to do in the way of helping the feast-giving clan, and they would, moreover, undoubtedly share in its glory.

In the larger communities, such as those of Mailu, Kurére, Domára – I think even Derébai – the feast is given by one or two clans. Thus this year (1914–15) the *Madúna* in Mailu was given by the Maradúbu and Moráu clans; the previous year by the Urúmoga; two years ago by the Bodéabo; three years ago, again by the Maradúbu and Moráu, and so on, by one or two clans in turn. The smaller clans, Maradúbu and Moráu, which have been weakened by recent emigrations, naturally combine to give the feast jointly, but I was told that in olden days, when they were strong, the custom was to give the feasts independently of each other, just as the two stronger clans do now. I was also told that when a very big feast took place in those days the Maradúbu and Moráu, on the one hand, and the Bodéabo and Urúmoga on the other, used to combine in giving it.

As the Maradúbu and Moráu formed the western half of the village and the Bodéabo and Urúmoga the eastern, the local contiguity of these clans was reflected in their association as feast-givers.

Again, in the small mainland villages the feast was always given, not by a clan, but by a village community. This was quite natural, because some of these villages were composed of some ten to twenty houses, whereas Mailu has, roughly, eighty houses at present, and must have had more in the past.

Thus the friendly villages, which in the past lived on the hills about Port Glasgow, Millport Harbour, and Mayri Bay, used to hold their *Madúna* in turn, one or more of the communities each year officiating, independently, as the feast-giver. In this manner the villages of Bórebo, Dágobo, Unévi, Pedíri, Géagéa, and Banóro acted towards one another in respect to the feast just as the clans in Mailu village do, though among the Mailu villagers the solidarity in the preparations to the feast was undoubtedly greater than among the members of these different communities. I was told, in fact, that this year three villages (Pedíri, Unévi, and Dágobo) were holding the feast independently of one another. A few years ago Bórebo gave the feast; two years ago Banóro, and so on. It is to be noted, however, that though the whole village performed the *Madúna* at the same time, the single clans acted as independent units in its ceremonial aspect. Thus in Bórebo five platforms used to be erected for the *góvi*, and there were five masters and five sets of *udíni* arrangements. In Géagéa, where there are six clans, three platforms were erected, two clans using the same platform: – Oraído with Waratsadúbu; Uda with Arúme; and Danáwa with Baráu. Although, taken as a whole, a village community acted with relation to the other communities, in a manner analogous to the clan in the Mailu village, yet the clan structure within the village remained, and the part played by the clan and by its master was to a certain degree the same as in Mailu village, modified only by the fact that the other clans were active as well.

There was, as a rule, one master of the feast for each clan giving the *Madúna*. Thus, in the foregoing description, mention has been made of three masters of the feast in Kurére, though two only underwent the *udíni* and performed the preliminary feasts, as if it was only those two who made the *Góvi Madúna*. Again, in Mailu this year Doúna is the master of the feast for the Maradúbu clan, and Váru for the Moráu clan. In Mailu, however, when a single big clan performed the feast, there were always two masters – headmen of two of the subclans – and no one but a headman of a subclan could act as the master. Thus at the *Madúna* of last year, given by the Urumóga clan, both Papári, the headman of the Banagadúbu subclan, and Atsiló'i, the headman of Boiladúbu subclan, acted as masters. Again, when the same clan (Urumóga) made a feast a few years before, Dagáea, headman of Gónidúbu, and Api, headman of Garadúbu, were the masters. As there are six subclans in Urumóga, there were three changes of masters for the feast. Analogous conditions obtained in Bodéabo, and in Maradúbu and Moráu before they were weakened.

The master of the feast has to direct and supervise the preparations for it; he it is, as we have seen, who plays the most important part in the proceedings, and who also undergoes the ceremonial hardships. During the feast also he plays the most prominent rôle, calling out the names of the clans to whom food is given and delivering speeches. These he has also to make during the preparations. He is, in consequence, called *obása maímai égi*, 'the speech-making man'. As all the details of the feast are strictly regulated by custom, there seems to be for the master no scope for much initiative. In fact, his function seems to be to give utterance to decisions and orders, which would naturally arise from common consent as well as from normal routine. But the natives hold in great appreciation the right of being prominent in the public eye, and the function of the master is consequently highly valued by a man. Again, there is no doubt that if the master be influential, his exhortations to the villagers to make and gather plenty of food (sago, bananas, etc.), his personal power to make many outsiders bring plenty of pigs, and his personal distinction would make the feast much grander and more successful than in the case of an insignificant person, and the master, for his part, would certainly reap the main share of the glory resulting from the success of the feast. But it must be noted that the master of the feast does not by any means receive the lion's share of the food. As far as I was able to ascertain and observe during the *Sói* feasts, the master is much less occupied with eating than the others, and if there are many people to whom some food must be distributed his final share in its benefits may be next to nothing.

The whole task of the clan at the feast consisted in the accumulation of the food (sago, garden produce, coconuts, portions of pigs). The clansmen had to join in the ceremonial proceedings and observe some light taboos, the strict ones being assigned to the master and to the men who acted as his assistants. So also it was the duty of the members of the clan to watch that the people received their dues in the form of pigs at the hands of those whose duty it was to give them.

It has been said (chap. iii., sec. 3) that the pigs killed at the feast were for the most part given on account of marriage connections. On

the one hand, all those who had married a girl of a clan were bound
to give pigs when her clan gave the feast. On the other hand, the
clansmen received pigs from their fathers-in-law or brothers-in-law
in return for the pigs given before as payment for their wives. At any
rate, the bulk of the pigs consumed at a feast came from outside the
clan, and I doubt if more than one per cent came otherwise than
through marriage connections.[59] I have inquired into several cases,
and drawn up lists of the pigs given, the result being that I found that
all the pigs were given in 'payment' for a wife or 'gift'. Some vegetable food is also brought with them by the men from other villages.

All the food accumulated by the work and care of the clan, of the
village community, and of the members of other communities who
are present at the feast, is divided between those present. The division
is formally directed by the master, but I think his decisions are regulated by custom and étiquette, though I failed to inquire into this
matter.

Looked at from our standpoint, the feast, in its economic aspect,
might be described as a kind of picnic, organized by the clan or clans,
concerned, the expense being more or less equally shared by all those
present, and the credit for success by the organizers, who have also
undoubtedly been put to the greatest amount of trouble in the
proceedings.[97]

4   DEATH, BURIAL, AND MOURNING

General remarks

Reference has been previously made to the attitude of the native
towards death and the dead, and in this connection mention has been
made in sec. 5, chap. iii., of the rôle of the dead man's spirit in protecting the *nebúru* coconuts, and of a similar part played by an
ancestral spirit in reference to *góra*. Again reference has been made
to this subject throughout the first two sections of this chapter,

---

[97]The data given in this chapter ought to be compared with Prof. Seligman's
description of the *Walaga* feast (*op. cit.,* pp. 589 to 606). Prof. Seligman's
information will throw much light on many points I was obliged to leave
obscure. I had, of course, at the time to confine myself entirely to what I
observed and to what I could learn from the natives, and it was only on
working up my notes that I realized how many are the correspondences between
Prof. Seligman's facts and my own. I am convinced that the Mailu *Góvi Madúna*
and the *Walaga* are varieties of the same ceremonial institution.

especially in the first. I shall now give an account of death and burial as I have been able to reconstruct these events from the information gathered from the natives, for I have never witnessed the scenes occurring after death, nor the burial, nor the first stages of mourning. Many, indeed, of the old customs, as they are described in this section, could no longer be seen by a white man, as they have been abandoned, either in reality or in pretence, owing to the influence of Government rules and missionary teaching.

I have seen, of course, all the later stages of mourning, and I have watched the posthumous wailings in another district (Northern Massim, Woodlark Island). I am also convinced that I succeeded in obtaining an entirely trustworthy account of the facts as the result of independent discussions with several of my best native informants, who agreed perfectly in their concrete details. In this I was greatly helped by the kind suggestions of the Rev. W. J. V. Saville, who directed my attention to several customs carefully avoided by the natives. I am also indebted to Mr. Alfred Greenaway, who, later on, actually forced the natives to tell me truthful details by shaming them in my presence for their pretended ignorance, thus allowing me a share of the unlimited confidence he enjoys among them.

It is a well-known feature of the 'savage' outlook that he is not satisfied with what we called natural causes of death. This means, strictly speaking, that whenever a death occurs there is the belief that some sorcerer has been the cause of it. This mental attitude was mentioned when black magic and sorcery were discussed, and it also influences certain details in the native burial customs.

When a man, woman, or child dies the death throws a more or less large section of the community into mourning, and consequently upsets the course of normal village life. In the case of a child, woman, or insignificant man, the disturbance is slight; but in that of a full-grown and influential man his death puts its stamp on many aspects of tribal life. It has been mentioned above (chap. iii., sec. 5) that the system of taboos imposed on coconuts varies in name and general character, according to whether there was an important death in the clan or not. Again, after the death of a man, a series of feasts are held, and these are undoubtedly connected with the big feast (see below). Again, the mourners undergo certain food taboos which modify the tribal ceremonies, and so on. Broadly speaking, a death entails more essential changes in a savage community, relatively to its size, than it does in those of a higher level of civilization.

The mourners

As the principal features of burial and mourning are the same in all cases, being only in the case of an influential adult more elaborate and entailing more social activities, I shall describe such a case, illustrating the general statements by a concrete example – that of Bú'a, the recently deceased, influential Mailu village constable, and, according to my conjecture, the chief *bará'u* or sorcerer. The genealogy given below will serve as a basis for the kinship designations.[60]

The chief mourners are called *nanáma*. This class consists of the elder brothers *(uíni'égi)* and sisters *(uíniavétsa)*, and of the younger brothers *(raú'égi)* and sisters *(raú'avétsa)* in the classificatory sense of the term, which implies the inclusion of the man's own brothers and sisters and his first cousins, male and female; or, as the term cousin is not unequivocal, the children of both his father's and mother's elder and younger brothers and sisters. But it must be emphatically remarked that in the case of the *nanáma* the classificatory relationship is not extended beyond this limit. I was assured that the grandfathers or grandmothers (paternal or maternal), brothers' or sisters' grandchildren (= second cousins) would not be *nanáma*, and if they were not so in the case of such an influential man as Bú'a, it settles the matter.

In the case of Bú'a, his *nanáma*, or chief mourners, consisted of:-
(1) His four brothers – Kopére, Iári, Gíra, Tamára; (2) his father's younger sister's (Tóro's) children – Búdi, Naría, Goíbo, Vága, Aváre; (3) his father's younger brother's (Bóru's) children – Gíla, Garuboí, Vaíneri, Tagábu; (4) his mother's elder brother's (Dóbi's) two daughters – Oíni and Pó'i; (5) his mother's younger sister's two sons – Kaváka and Díni. The paternal and maternal uncles, as well as the brothers' or sisters' children, are not *nanáma*.

The widow also assumes deep mourning, though she is not called a *nanáma*, but a *doá'e*. The man's children do not assume the deep mourning of either category, nor would a man mourn for his children. A mother is subject to deep mourning for her children, but I failed to record in my notes whether she belongs to the *nanáma* or *doá'e* class, though I remember having been informed that the latter is the case. The name of bereft parents is *o'evaétsa*. A husband performed also the *doá'e* mourning for his wife, and the children mourn for their mother, as far as I remember, though I again failed to record the fact.

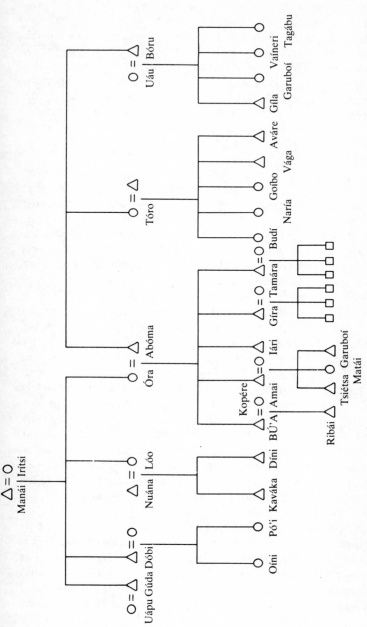

Fig. 46 Genealogy of Bú'a

Manái Iritsi Uápu Gúda Dóbi Nuána Lóo Óra Abóma Tóro Uáu Bóru Tagábu Vaíneri Garuboí
Gíla Aváre Vága Goíbo Naría Budí Tamára Gíra Iári Kopére Bu'a Amai Díni Kaváka Pó'i Oíni
Garuboí Matái Tsiétsa Ribái

Besides the chief mourners – the *nanáma* and *doá'e* – there is the class of *mágu raguá'i* people, who keep the *nebúru* coconut taboos, perform certain duties during the mourning feasts and at the burial, and contribute essentially to the mortuary feasts. The *mágu raguá'i*, in the case of an influential man like Bú'a, comprises all his clansmen, and many other people as well. In the case of a less important man the *mágu raguá'i* would be some of the members of the subclan and some of his other friends and relatives – *emégi goína*.

The mourning

The first period of mourning, during which the sorrow is expressed by loud wailing, weeping upon the dead, and by other acute symptoms of grief, is called *ini* (to cry). During this first phase the *nanáma* and *doá'e* are in the deepest mourning dress, their hair shaven, their skin deeply blackened, and the body covered all over with mats, which are also drawn over the head and conceal the face. If they require to move they walk about very slowly in a crouching position, with the mat kept over the head.

The second, much longer, period is called *mágu*. This is commenced by the deep mourners some time after the man's death, and it is also observed for some time, though not very strictly, by the *mágu raguá'i*. The *mágu* people – *i.e.,* the deep mourners in the later stages – smear themselves all over the body with black (*gurúma*; in Motu, *míro*), which is usually burnt coconut fibre, moistened with water and kneaded into a paste. This pigment is never completely washed off the body for any length of time during the *mágu* period. But in order to maintain its brilliancy and blackness it is periodically renewed. This is always done at some 'social' opportunity, such, for instance, as during a visit to a neighbouring village, or when assisting at a small feast or ceremony, or when returning home from an expedition. Otherwise the pigment would not be kept quite up to the mark, and the brown of the skin would be seen through it, making the man appear dirty rather than black.

It has been mentioned (sec. 1, chap. iii.) that in mourning the hair of the head is shaved and that on the face allowed to grow. This is continued by the deep mourners throughout the *mágu* period. The armlets of plaited fern vine, plain, or ornamented with yellow orchid straw, are thrown away, and in their place less ornate armlets of plaited string or of plain white fibre (called *kue-kue* in the mainland

Mailu dialect). Again, all the finer ornaments made of red shell discs are removed from the body; a man might also wear a necklet of string, with one or more white cowrie shells (*Ovulum ovum*) suspended from it. The right thing to do was to make up a necklet comprised of various relics of the dead man; his hair in the first place, his perineal band, his comb, shell-disc ornaments, etc. All such articles were bound together with strings and formed a fairly bulky ornament. So also plain strings, called *navanavára*, were worn across the breast.

During deep mourning a man might not dance, nor fish; he could, however, work in his garden, and he might do some hunting, but not much. The coconut taboo observed by the mourners has been dealt with above in sec. 5, chap. iii.

Weeping for the dead, and burial; mortuary feasts

After this general outline of mourning and of the mourners, let us turn to the details of the events that occur after a man's death, immediately and later. After a man dies his nearest relatives, friends, and acquaintances intone the wailing. This is a weird sound, very highly pitched and monotonously regular – first a long howl, then three short ones, terminating in a long one again. I heard this sound once only, in Dikóias village, Muiú'a (Woodlark Island), and for a while, until I guessed what it was, I was quite puzzled as to whether it was an extraordinarily loud wailing of children or some strange howl of Papuan dingoes, or what not. The lamentation of the nearest relations goes on for a considerable time, though that of the others soon ceases. The *nanáma* and *doá'e* sit round the corpse and embrace it, wailing and exclaiming, '*Ina nábu ee...!*' (long drawn) – 'O my younger brother (or sister)!' or '*Ina uíni ee...!*' (long drawn) – 'O my elder brother (or sister)!' They are also said actually to cry and to be very sad.

During this time the mourners *(mága raguá'i)* supervise the business side of the mortuary proceedings. I was informed definitely that these, rather than the deep mourners, manage things during the first stages of mourning. Thus, immediately after the man's death, they bring a certain quantity of coconuts to be distributed amongst all the houses of the village. This custom is quite analogous to the small coconut feast, given by the owner when he wishes to establish a *góra* over his nuts, and this small distribution of nuts after a man's death is the beginning of the *nebúru*, or mortuary taboo on coconuts, kept when a man dies. Before distribution the coconuts are piled in front of the dead man's house. This coconut feast is called *léle báu*.

The burial took place very soon after the man's death, and it was never done at night. Thus if a man died in the evening, or so late in the afternoon that there was no time for all the preliminary proceedings, he was buried next morning. If, however, a man died before noon, or soon after, he would be buried the same afternoon. In the case of an important man there might be greater delay in the burial, as there was more to be done in the way of preparations.

The corpse was washed with *górogóro* (coconut cream) and decorated, the more valuable ornaments being removed before burial. After a time, when the interment was about to take place, the body was placed upon a *tsiná'u*, or large tray of plaited coconut leaf, and as a rule two such trays were placed underneath and one above the body. A plaited mat *(eba)* of the same kind as is used for making sails is used to cover the body, being placed between the *tsiná'u*, and the whole of this arrangement is wrapped in a pandanus mat *(elaki)*. The bundle so constituted is now again put between two *tsiná'u*, and thus placed upon a board – usually one obtained by breaking up a worn-out canoe. The corpse is laid upon two poles, to which it is tied, and it is carried by four men, each supporting one end of the pole. The men who carry the body (called *gábi aíai tsiá'u*) are kinsmen of the dead man *(emegi goína)*, belonging to the *mágu raguá'i* class; but they do not include any of the deep mourners. The body, thus carried, is brought out of the house and placed in the middle of the street, the four men holding it on the bier. The principal *nanáma* man – the eldest surviving 'brother' (own or classificatory, as specified above) – addresses the departed by his name:-

> *'Matáu ga aiéni*
> *gana urúra aiéni!'*

which means, in a free translation, 'Matáu come!' They also exclaim, 'Where are you? Are you here? Are you present?' On this the body rocks and sways, which is the sign that the spirit, *bó'i*, is there, and that it is paying attention to the address.[98] Then comes the important part of the invocation – that in which the spirit reveals the name of

---

[98]Cf. sec. 1 of this chapter where the different 'spiritual parts' of a man are enumerated.

the *bará'u* (evil sorcerer) who has killed the deceased. The chief *nanáma* again addresses the *bó'i* (spirit) of the dead man, enumerating a number of villages of bad repute for harbouring evil sorcerers:-

> 'Borowai   bará'u   bá (long drawn)
> village name   evil   sorcerer
> *Dobuopu bará'u gabá* (long drawn)
> *Manubada bará'u má*
> *Gadaísiu bará'u má*
> *Bína bará'u má*
> *Géagéa bará'u má.'*
> etc., etc.

A long list is thus named – these, of course, being only *bará'u* villages – *i.e.,* such as were on bad terms with the Mailu. When the name of the village that was guilty of the murder by sorcery was called out, the man's *bó'i* gave sign, and the body swayed violently.[99] The name of this proceeding and of the address to the dead man's spirit is *vága*.

Then the body is buried *(gúri ṭsiáu).* As there are some differences in the mode of burial, or, rather, of the disposal of the dead in the various groups of villages in the Mailu district, it is necessary to speak of these separately. On Mailu Island, as well as in the adjoining villages of Laruóro and Loupóm, and on those of the mainland from a point opposite Mailu westwards, the body, wrapped up as just described, was buried, extended on his back in a shallow grave, either under his house or among his coconuts.

Over the spot, if the grave was dug in the garden, a small mortuary hut *(kápa)*, about two metres long, 1.50 m. high, and 1 m. wide, was erected, but as such huts are no longer made on Mailu Island, or, at least, very rarely, I did not see one. On showing to my informants the grave hut of the Suá'u natives, as reproduced on the plate facing p. 608 in Professor Seligman's book, they said the Mailu *kápa* was exactly like that, except that its roof was made of *tsináu* (plaited coconut leaves), and the upper ridge of the roof was straight and not

---

[99]Though this is only a conjecture, I wish to add that it is probable that the people holding the body were taking a *bona fide* part in the ceremony. The nervous tension at such a time must have been intense indeed, so that it is not surprising that at a certain moment the men swayed the body and believed it moved by itself.

curved, just as the horizontal ridge line of the Mailu house is straight and not concave, as it is in the Massim house. Sometimes a small fence *(gána)* only was made over the grave. If the grave had been dug under the man's house the place was marked by two pieces of wood.

The mode of burial was to a large extent determined by the man's social position, the important men only being interred under their houses; but it was also influenced by the season. As the deep mourners had to keep watch near the man's grave (see below), it was essential to secure them a certain minimum of comfort. Thus, in the very hot and dry season, at the end of *lióro* and beginning of the small *avára*, when the heat is at its greatest and the rain has not yet come, the body would in any case be buried among the coconuts, and the small *kápa* hut constructed; but if it was the wet season the corpse would be placed under the house. As the mourning was only very strictly kept in the case of important men, it is natural that in other cases the natives should prefer to bury the dead in the gardens.

As the presence of a dead man in the village was always a source of some discomfort, it was preferable, for superstitious, not hygienic, reasons, to have as few burials in the village as possible, and I think, though I am not quite certain on this point, that the *kápa* (small mortuary house) was made over the graves of important people, and the *gána* (fence) over those of all the others. Again, I was told that on the islands (Mailu, Loupóm, Laruóro), which are considerably drier than the mainland, the garden burial prevailed, while in the villages, on the mainland opposite Mailu, such as Dérebai, Wowuóro, Kurére (which is a Mailu settlement), and in others to the west, the reverse is the case. The mainland villages to the east, beginning with Bórebo, Dágobo, and Unévi, as far as Géagéa, also practised the forms of burial as described, though without the mortuary hut, burying their dead for the most part under the houses.

They sometimes used to dispose of the bodies on platforms in crevices of the rocks, in a manner that I will now describe. This was the exclusive burial practice of the few Mailu villages situated at the western end of Orangerie Bay, between Port Glasgow and the village of Gadaísiu, which marks the boundary between the Mailu and the Massim. I saw such a burial-place, called Dório, where the three small villages – Oibáda, Nobá'i, and Ori – used to lay their dead. It is situated at the mouth of a creek, quite close to the seashore, where a rock about 50 m. to 75 m. high rises above the sloping bank of the creek, which is clothed with a thick undergrowth that shelters the crevice. At the top of the bank, where the rocky wall rises, there are several shallow, but wide, cavities, with a front of about 30 m. or 50 m. In these there are several ledges and niches, and, as the rock is overhanging, anything placed under this shelter is protected from the weather. Here I saw several small platforms of very frail construction no higher than 150 cm. to 200 cm., about 100 cm. long, and about 60 cm. wide. On these were placed bundles of human bones, wrapped partly in the *elaki*, or pandanus mat, and partly in fibre petticoats, and I was told that the kind of wrapping denoted the difference between the sexes. The bundles were short, so that if they were made whilst there was flesh on the bones the body must have been wrapped in a squatting position, and this my informants said was actually the case. Some of the platforms were falling to pieces, and the bundles were on the ground which was strewn with bones, and a score or so of skulls were deposited on the ledges. Unfortunately I had only a few minutes to spare, so that I could neither take a photograph nor make a careful study of the place.

It is interesting to note that this mode of burial of the extreme eastern Mailu cannot be attributed to contact metamorphosis induced by the influence of their eastern neighbours, for the Massim of the eastern half of Orangerie Bay either bury their dead or dispose of them in half a canoe – the latter form being apparently the exception. These bury the corpses, not extended in a supine position like the Mailu, but in a squatting attitude, with both hands joined over the feet, the body being laid on an *elaki* mat spread on the bottom of the grave and covered with two other mats. Burial took place under, or near, the house, a small hut being erected over the grave.[100] If the body was buried in a broken boat it was laid supine.

To return to the Mailu burial practices. After the body has been laid in the ground, whether under the house or in the garden, all the people disperse except the mourners. The deep mourners – the *nanáma* and *doá'e* – are bound to remain by the grave for a fortnight to a month. The *mágu raguá'i* do some wailing, but they move about, and can remain, or go and come as their grief and other necessities bid them. The deep mourners, however, must never move from the place. If the grave is under the house, they sit there, and at night only move to the room above or to the verandah. So also, if the grave is in the garden, the mourners sit there the whole day, arriving at

---

[100]See Seligman, *op. ci.,* pls. lxx. and lxxi.

daybreak and returning to the village at sunset. As previously mentioned, they sit during the first days of mourning with mats drawn over their heads, they walk slowly, with their bodies bent, and move from the spot merely when compelled by natural necessities. They wail and cry and address the deceased by kinship terms, not by his personal name. They also talk to him, expressing grief:-

'*Aiéni íne; ónióni déma; gána urúra; baíbai déma; gána nabu; éna varóra; aúri loitsaítsi; dábae kaókáo otsíba*'.

Which, in a free translation, means:- 'Don't go; let us go together to your house (return); come back to your younger brother; if you go, let us go together to another house'. These and similar expressions are used, all showing the great grief and the desire of the bereft ones to keep the deceased with them.

Some three days or so after the burial the first small feast (called *bá'u* or *baívara tséitse*) is given. It consists of vegetable food, coconuts, bananas, taro, sago, etc., the coconuts being supplied by people who do not observe the *nebúru*, and the other food by the mourners. The latter, however, do not partake of the feast, but only give the food away to others.

After this feast the mourners pull the mat from over their heads, though they still wear it on their shoulders.

At the expiration of the next eight days or so another small feast, *déni bá'u*, is held, similar in its social aspect and in the food eaten to the previous feast, and at its close the mats are thrown away altogether, the wailing ceases, and the expression of grief becomes less acute. I am inclined to think that the number of these small feasts which are held depends upon the status of the deceased person, and that very probably the one just mentioned is normally the last. Names, however, for one or two more small *bá'u* feasts were mentioned to me by my informants, which seem to me to have been observed only in the case of important men. There was, for instance, the *baíba'e bá'u* or *baíba'e tseítsei*, after which the mourners were said to leave their watch by the grave and to return to their usual occupations. So also the *ariari tseítsei*, after which custom demands that the deep mourners should leave the village for a time and sail to other places. This custom was mentioned to me by several informants, and it was said to have been in the past rigorously observed in the case of deceased notables.

The account of these feasts is, I fear, not satisfactory, for I failed to ascertain what are the beliefs underlying them. I was, however, told by one of my native friends that the feasts were in some manner meant to feed the spirit, but my informant was not clear on the matter, and, indeed, confessed that he did not understand it himself.

After life

I also failed to obtain a satisfactory account of the beliefs concerning the doings of the spirit *bó'i* during the wailing and the period after the burial, though I obtained some hints on the subject and on that of a future life. On the whole, however, I am not very confident as to the accuracy of these facts, as I obtained them from one informant only, and that a Mission boy.[101] This informant told me, with reference to the doings of the spirit at and about the time of death, that when a man is sick his soul wanders on a 'bridge' towards the Biúla – the place of future life. All the other spirits try to frighten it away, and if they succeed and the intruder turns back from the Biúla, then the man does not die. If, on the contrary, the spirit succeeds in entering the Biúla, the man expires. The Rev. W. J. V. Saville kindly gave me another account of the Biúla:- 'The spirit goes to the south-western end of the Island of Mailu, and sails away towards the horizon. There is a ladder there, and the soul descends'. This account, apart from the high authority of my informant, is borne out by the fact that similar ideas concerning an after-life are entertained by the Motu.

There seems to be a certain amount of doubt as to whether the idea of Biúla is native or due to missionary influence.[102] I have inquired carefully into this subject, and though I was not able to obtain details concerning the Biúla, my native informants, without exception and independently, agreed that both the word Biúla and the belief in it were indigenous, and that Biúla was situated below the earth. One very good informant told me that it was a big native village on an underground river called Bómu. Slight variations, or even substantial differences, in the accounts of such a matter are not, however, astonishing. An ethnologist from another planet, for instance, might find it a matter of considerable discussion if he inquired where we located our heaven or hell. But though the spirit goes to the Biúla, it

---

[101] I have to thank the Rev. W. J. V. Saville for having helped me in obtaining details about this difficult subject.[61]

[102] Several persons interested in Papuan ethnology and knowing the natives, expressed this doubt to me personally.

is not altogether apart from its body, as both the post-burial wailing
and the following practices testify.

Final mortuary feast and treatment of the skull

Some two or three months after the burial the body was unearthed
and the head cut off, this custom being called *léa bó'o*, or *bó'o*
The soft tissues that remained were removed by boiling the head in a
native clay-pot, which was done in the bush by the man's wife or
mother, and the head was then dried and placed in a basket, called
tóba. The baskets were kept in the houses, on shelves under the
thatch.[103] Such a basket, covered with a piece of matting, was
sometimes taken out of the house and placed near the relatives. A
mother would do so with her child's skull, or a wife would keep that
of her husband in front of her whilst making pottery or plaiting mats.
Or, again, a brother's skull might thus keep company with a man at
work or at rest. Mr. Greenaway tells me that in olden days, before
the natives were scared by Government rules and Christian
preachings, people might be often seen sitting and looking at these
relics with evident affection, and that they might even talk to them.
This was primarily only the expression of love for the deceased
relative, but sometimes the advice of the deceased in matters of
importance might be sought from his skull, though in what way the
natives believed the answer could be conveyed Mr. Greenaway could
not tell me, nor could I ascertain from the natives.

As previously mentioned, the spirit which went to the Biúla is
called *bau'égene*; the spirit which remained in the head is called *bó'i*
That would explain the *dédoublement* of the man after his death. It is
evident from the facts given in the first two sections of this chapter
that the prayers *(u'úra)* were addressed to the *bó'i* exclusively, and the
bó'i also watched over the *nebúru* and *góra* (see sec. 5, chap. iii.).

To return from this digression concerning the spirit and after-life
to the series of funeral feasts and practices. There remains one more
stage to be described – the big mortuary feast *oí'o*, which concludes
the lesser mourning of the clansmen, etc. *(mágu raguá'i)*, the *nebúru*
state of coconuts, and the deep mourning of the *nanáma* and *doá'e*.
These latter, however, continue the blackening of their bodies and the

---

[103]See chap. iii., sec. 6, in reference to the preparation and preservation of the
skulls of enemies. These were placed in the *dúbu*, whereas those of relatives were
kept in the house.

shaving of their hair for a considerable time longer. The *oi'o*, or main mortuary feast, may take place some six months or a year after the death, whereas the blackening and hair-cutting is maintained, by the deep mourners, for two or three years. The date on which the *oi'o* is held depends very largely upon the season in which the death has taken place, upon the importance of the individual, and upon other feasts. I have unfortunately failed to obtain quite conclusive information on the point, but I think that an *oi'o*, as a rule, coincides, or, rather, is identical with either the big feast *(Madúna)* or with the first preparatory feast *(maúru amáta)*. However this may be, it seems that if a man died in the wet season his *oi'o* would be performed in the next *aurári* – *i.e.,* about six months later. If the death occurred in the south-east monsoon season the feast would be performed in the following *avára*. Sometimes, however, a year was allowed to elapse, as will be the case with Bú'a, the often-mentioned late village constable, who died some time in August, 1914, and whose *oi'o* will be performed in the winter *(aurári)*, 1915.

The most important ceremonial element in the mortuary feast is the dance, called *má'o*, which is performed by the mourners. In this the main part was taken by one of the nearest relatives, either male or female, the brother or the sister; sometimes it was the mother, but never the father or the widow. This performer dances the *má'o* holding the dead man's head under the arm, and, at the conclusion of the feast, the mortuary hut was also destroyed.

After this feast the chief mourners still do not relinquish their black paint, nor do they cease shaving their hair. The end of their mourning coincides with some feast of the clan, when, by the performance of ceremonial work, the mourners finally cast off their signs of mourning.

CHAPTER VI

ART AND KNOWLEDGE

1   ART

Decorative art

Judged by the average Papuasian standard, the artistic productions of the Mailu, like those of the Western Papuo-Melanesians in general, are distinctly unimportant and unoriginal.[104] Their decorative art is limited to a few unpainted carvings, of which the designs of the carved wood *birítsa* are, to my knowledge, the only original motives (see pl. 17). The carved decorations on some of the house-posts are common to all Western Papuo-Melanesians; the motive universally found in the Mailu houses – the parallel rows of pyramids – being also one of the typical elements in the carvings on the *dúbu* of the Central District.

The tattoo on women is practically the same as that found among the Southern Massim of the southern coast.[62] The same holds good with reference to the decorations on the pottery. Now, the designs used in tattooing and on the pots have names among the Southern Massim of which the meaning can be usually explained; moreover, they are used in the various other artistic productions of these natives, such as the ornamentation on lime spatulas, wooden swords, paintings on houses, etc. The designs have, therefore, evidently been

---

[104]The decorative art of the Southern Massim is definitely superior, and the Northern Massim produce really artistic carvings. So, also, amongst the tribes of the Papuan Gulf their artistic efforts are far superior to those of the Western Papuo-Melanesians and much more interesting. See Dr. A. C. Haddon, 'The Decorative Art of British New Guinea'. Prof. Seligman says, 'The Motu and cognate tribes ... are the poorest artists in the Possession' (*op. cit.,* p. 37). I think this statement may be extended to all Western Papuo-Melanesians, and the Mailu are inferior to the Motu even in their tattoo. Cf. what Prof. Seligman says about the Motuan tattoo on p. 38.

imported to Mailu from this district, and not in the reverse direction. This view is confirmed by the fact that the Mailu natives, when asked as to the meaning of a pattern, frankly admit that it is 'a Bónabóna pattern,' and beyond this they know nothing about it.

Again, all the wood carvings done in Mailu, such as the lime spatulas, sago spoons, and wooden dishes, are evidently copies, in much inferior workmanship, of the fine carvings imported from the east, consequently the decorative art of the Mailu should be studied in connection with that of the Massim, but as this cannot be done here I shall limit myself to the above remarks.[105]

Dances and songs

In these arts the Mailu seem equally unproductive and unoriginal. All their dances and songs come either from the east – from the Southern Massim and the tribes inland; or from the west – from the tribes around Hood Bay, and chiefly from the village of Kerepúna, a great centre of choreutic art. One or two of the dances have been borrowed from the inland tribes of the Mailu district. A short survey of the dances and songs performed at present in Mailu must here be sufficient, as an adequate description could only be given after studying them in their own respective homes. Many of the dances and songs are simply taken over without taking any trouble as to their meaning, and it would be interesting to study the process of such borrowing. This would involve an investigation of the original version, as performed and interpreted by the people who originated the dance, and of the copy, as performed by the borrowers.

The Mailu, when speaking of their dances and songs, distinguish between the *Madúna* dances and the *bára* dances, although, as mentioned, the *bára* may be also performed at the *Madúna*. All the former, which comprise the *góvi, raúa, tsélo, damoréa*, come from the east. *Bára* is the collective name given to a group of dances of a similar character, and introduced from the west (see chap. v., sec. 3, where the difference in the preparatory ritual of the various dances has been stated).

---

[105]In order to describe and analyze the decorative art of Eastern New Guinea, it would be necessary to study it in its two main *foci* – that is, in the Trobriand Islands and in the Louisiades. As I have as yet been unable to study either of these areas, it is impossible at present to undertake the survey indicated. There is, however, no doubt that both areas mentioned have had paramount influence on the art of the whole extreme east of New Guinea.

Góvi As mentioned above, this is the most important and most sacred of the *Madúna* dances, which must always be performed at a really big and important feast. I never saw it, and I am consequently unable to describe even its general character, but from native descriptions and demonstrations of the steps I may give the following particulars. It is always performed on a platform, at the middle of which stand the men with drums, who beat the time and sing the song. The dancers perform their dance on the four raised beams, laid on the four sides of the square platform. The dance consists of steps of a somewhat acrobatic character, the performer assuming a squatting position and then springing up, and in Mailu I was told that the movements are in imitation of the hopping of the kangaroo. In the Southern Massim district, however, I was informed that the dance represents the bird of paradise, and this view seems to be borne out by the fact that the dancers of the *góvi* wear wigs of the feathers of these birds. As the home of the *góvi* is neither Mailu nor the Southern Massim coast, but the mountain tribes inland of Orangerie Bay (eastern half) and of Mullins Harbour, it is only the study of the latter that would enable one to grasp the real significance of the *góvi*.

Raúa In this dance, which comes from the same inland people as the preceding, the dog is said to be mimicked. I once saw it performed ceremonially at the *Só'i* in Tsílotsílo. Men wearing large crown-shaped feather ornaments on their heads, three or four of whom acted as chief performers, advanced slowly in a large procession. One of the four, who was said to personate the dog, ran hither and thither with short steps among the other dancers. The beat of the drums was slow and regular, and the accompanying chant very monotonous and unmelodious.

Tsélo This is derived from the east, though the Mailu natives were unable to give me the exact locality of origin, nor could I ascertain this on my visit to the east. I saw this dance performed several times in Mailu, but never ceremonially – that is, with full decorations and scrupulous adherence to all the details of strict performance. The dancers stand in a circle, all holding and beating drums, and one of them begins a chant, in which the others join. The drums are beaten, not in a simple, regular rhythm, as is the case in the majority of dances, but the beats are varied and include fairly complex rhythmic figures. The song also is exceptionally melodious and musically interesting, showing rudiments of part singing, inasmuch as the initial melody is repeated by various singers, whilst the others sing a monotone in unison, so giving a harmonic background to the melody. Two of the dancers, who face each other in the ring, raise their drums and dance towards each other, in imitation of birds, as I was told.

Damoréa This dance, which is also an introduction from the east, is perhaps the most popular dance among the Southern Massim. At any rate, it was that most frequently performed during the *Só'i* feasts I witnessed on the southern coast. In its strict ceremonial setting, it is danced by women only, though when it is danced for entertainment only the men join in the singing and drum beating. The decorations for the *damoréa* are sometimes very various. The women wear crowns of white cockatoo feathers and have the lower parts of their faces painted white (see pl. 34). Sometimes the women wear small boards made of some light, soft wood, painted red, black, and white. They put on, as a rule, all their most valued ornaments – the arm-shells, the strings of shell discs, and other necklaces, and in their hands they hold a pearl shell or a piece of pandanus mat *(elaki)*. In the Massim district the correct thing is to hold one of the ceremonial axe blades, but these are not used by the Mailu. The dance is performed by two, four, or six women, who usually dance in couples. The 'band', consisting of women who beat the drums and sing, stand in the middle of a large circle of spectators, between whom and the band the dancers move. The music of the *damoréa* is like that of the *tsélo*, though simpler and less interesting from the European musical point of view. I was not able to ascertain the meaning of the songs or of the dance, though the latter had certainly a pantomimic character. The various figures were performed with slow, languid movements, the women, in one, looking down upon the ground as if searching for something, in another examining each other's ornaments.

Daúgé This is a dance of the inland people of the Mailu district, with whom it was a war dance, and by my native informants was not considered to be a *Madúna* dance. I never saw it performed or demonstrated.

Kóbiai Imported from the eastern end, and at present very seldom danced. I was unable to see it performed or to get any particulars concerning it.

All these dances have certain common characteristics, which differentiate them from the *bára* class of dances. The performers all dance to very slow beats of the drums, and usually move within a circle or a closed geometrical figure (a square in the case of the *góvi*). Again, in all of them animals seem to be imitated, and I was told that this was so in the case of the *kóbiai*, though my informants could not say what animal was imitated. The *damoréa* may be an exception. In all of them, again, as far as I know, there is a band and a few performers, who dance the steps with pantomimic movements. Usually the dancers are specially ornamented and have no drums.

The *bára* is quite different. It consists of a succession of very quick dances, performed to the accompaniment of a loud beating of drums, without the song, as well as of much slower dances with a song. Some of the latter are distinctly pantomimic, and represent such actions as felling a tree, building a canoe, making sago, rowing a boat, and the representation of a thunderstorm, etc. Both the motives and the character of the pantomime are rather artificial and theatrical. Some again of the slower figures consist merely of songs, sung to a rhythmic sway of the body and to a slow beat of the drums (see pls. 29, 30, 31, 32, 33).[106]

2 KNOWLEDGE

Knowledge of stars and weather

The Mailu natives have a good practical knowledge of the sea, of its tides and currents, and of the wind and weather. They are good seamen, as the sailing of their double canoes requires a certain degree of seamanship, and this was especially true in the olden days, when it was often more dangerous to approach the coast and beach the canoe than it was to face rough weather. They have a very good local knowledge of the reefs, and native boys are very useful in the sailing of the white man's craft; some of them even are in charge of small

---

[106]I have had very good opportunities of studying the *bára*, as it was danced practically every evening for weeks before the day of the *Madúna* – which, in fact, was to take place in Mailu a few days after I was obliged to leave. The *bára* I saw danced on the mainland in Kurére and in Gómoredúbu, in the Sinaughólo district. As I am at present ignorant, however, as to a number of its essential features, and as I hope to be able to see it in its proper home in Hood Bay, I prefer to leave my description for a future publication.[63]

sailing vessels and motor launches. The Mailu are in that respect quite as skilful as the Motu and the Hulá'a people.

They do not, however, take any theoretical interest, if I may so put it, in their surroundings. They have, for instance, neither 'explanatory myths', nor any other theories as to the origin or nature of the sea and land, or sun, moon, and stars. There is, however, a legend concerning the origin of Mailu Island, which asserts that it was hauled up out of the sea during a big fishing expedition from Aróma.[107]

Very few stars are differentially named, and among these the morning star is called Laráni, and the evening star Gamovanováno; but they do not know that the same star (Venus) shines at times before sunrise and at times after sunset. I also think that when another large planet – Jupiter, for instance – is on the western sky in the evening they give it the same name. Nothing is known about the nature of the morning and evening star.

The Pleiades are called Uniára. They are said to be women, and the three stars of Orion's Belt are named Borá'a'éva. These are said to be a man, a pig, and a child. There must have been some explanatory tale connected with these constellations, but if so the natives in Mailu have forgotten it completely, because even the oldest and wisest men knew nothing about the subject.

The natives are acquainted with many of the features of the tides. They know the spring and neap tides, and their connection with the moon; also the fact that the differences of level between high and low water is not the same in the two daily tides, and that, according to the season, this is greater in day time or at night time. One of the names by which the south-eastern season (the winter) is known is *lagáru wúra*, which means dry reef. It is remarkable that the natives have different names for the reef by day *(lagáru)* and by night *(múma)*. The *múma* appears in the north-western season (summer), and during this period the fishing and collecting of shellfish is done by night. The season for day fishing is when the *lagáru* is dry; that means during the winter or south-eastern season.[108]

---

[107]This legend, with several others, has been recorded by the missionary of Mailu, the Rev. W. J. V. Saville; these, I hope, will be shortly published by him.[64]
[108]For the information about the tides and the reefs I am indebted to the Rev. W. J. V. Saville, whose thorough familiarity with the language, and his long contact with the natives, has given him an excellent knowledge of many aspects of native life and psychology.[65]

It has been said that the natives are well acquainted with the seasonal sequence of winds; in fact, they name the seasons after the prevailing winds (see chap. iii.). The directions are also named after the winds. Thus, as mentioned above, the south-eastern direction is called *bodéa aúra* – the side of the trade wind; the north-western direction, *avára aúra* – the side of the monsoon. Again, the north-eastern direction, from which comes the land breeze, *tséba*, is called by the same name; the southern is called after *gabína*, a light southerly wind which blows in spells between the monsoons.

There are also weather experts in the village, particularly an old man, called Papári, who I very often found foretold the weather quite correctly.

Knowledge of disease and doctoring

My information on this subject is very imperfect. The natives seemed particularly reluctant to discuss such matters, perhaps because I was known as a *dógeta* (doctor), in whom they suspected a tendency to interfere with their own practices, or perhaps on account of some other form of *jalousie de métier*.

The general term for illness is *mará'i*, but there are besides some other names for minor ailments. Thus, *vára iáia* is the name for headache; *inigógu iá raítsera* designates an aching above the eyes, which is believed to be a very bad complaint. *Tsére raítsera* is an ailment in which the whole body is sore – the legs are sore, and the sufferer is not able to walk in a straight line. This is, however, by no means a native classification of ailment, which I was very anxious to obtain; but it is a difficult subject, and I was not successful.

The name for a doctor is *u'úra*, which is also the name for a magical incantation. A cure is called *auráro*, and there seems to be only one cure for all ailments. The doctor chews the bark of the native cinnamon tree *(góbu)*, some betelnut, and wild ginger root; an incantation is uttered, and the mixture is spat out. Massage *(pápapápa)* is always practised upon the sick person, its ultimate aim being the extraction of foreign bodies, which, as a rule, are considered to be the cause of all illness. When the 'doctor' feels that the foreign body has been brought near enough to the surface by his treatment he sucks the affected part, and then, with a retching sound, he expectorates the object which he is supposed to have sucked out of the patient's body. Stones, pieces of bark, small bones, etc., are thus extracted from the affected part of the patient, who in consequence is cured. The doctors are usually recruited from the male section of the population, and I only heard of one female doctor of repute. The price paid for a cure is considerable. In olden days it was one large arm-shell – a piece of native jewellery extremely valued by the natives. Nowadays the natives will pay as much as ten pounds (English money) for a good arm-shell, and the average price is one or two pounds.

With better opportunities it would have undoubtedly been possible to obtain more complete information, but these are often a matter of good luck in ethnological field work.[66] On the whole, I think that the art of healing does not play a very important part in the tribal life of the Mailu natives, just as their sorcery and magic, to which native medicine is so akin, are also not very highly developed.

Editor's Notes

1 Two later ethnographers who knew Ahuia Ova, F.E. Williams (1939) and Cyril Belshaw (1951), have also written appreciative comments about his life and work. Shelley (1978) examines local oral evidence for Ahuia's considerable reputation as a sorcerer. Ahuia's photograph appears in Seligman (1910: plate III).

2 I invited my colleague Dr Tom Dutton, an expert on the languages of Papua, to comment on this passage. He wrote:

> 'The "now" in this sentence is interesting in view of other evidence about the existence and use of a "Pidgin Motu" as a lingua franca in British New Guinea (Papua) before the time at which Malinowki was writing. The modern form of this language is known officially as Hiri Motu although it is more widely known as Police Motu. It took this name from its association with the first police force in British New Guinea, the Armed Native Constabulary, established by Governor MacGregor in 1890. Perhaps the "now" in Malinowski's sentence ·is to be read as referring to the spread and use of this language to Mailu, or that the language had hitherto been so variable that it was only then beginning to stabilize into a regular form.'

For a detailed history of Police (or Hiri) Motu, see Dutton (1985).

3 Although it was well known to Seligman (1910: 25), Malinowski does not mention the fact that Mailu (or Magi) is a Non-Austronesian language, and therefore unrelated to the Austronesian (or Melanesian) languages which predominate along the coast of southeast Papua. According to Dutton, Magi is 'the second largest best known Non-Austronesian language in Papua' (1971: 20). It comprises nine dialects spoken by approximately 5,500 people, of which the principal one (with about 2,000 speakers) is common to Mailu island, Kurere, Loupomu, Boru, Magaubo and Laluoro (Thomson 1975b). Several vocabularies, grammars, and other studies of Magi have been published by Strong (1911), Saville (1912), Ray (1938), Lanyon-Orgill (1944), Dutton (1971), and Thomson (1975a; 1975b). Saville (1935) left an unpublished vocabulary which Lanyon-Orgill incorporated into his own compilation

(1944). Abbi, who learned Mailu, commented briefly on the orthography (1975: xiii–xiv).

4   These statements are misleading for the Mailu area is in a transitional zone and rather prone to drought (as Saville's letters over the years well testify). Rainfall for the year 1914–15 recorded at Abau (close enough to Mailu to be an approximate guide) was 74.84 inches (PAR 1914–15: 65). But less than one inch fell during the last three months of 1914, so Malinowski's personal experience of the weather was probably of a long dry spell, despite his assumption of 'good rains even at other times'. Abbi (1975: 5) gives a few figures: the average rainfall for the four years 1956–9 at a nearby mainland plantation was 85 inches, with a range of 61.54 to 115.48. Thus, 'wide variations occur from month to month and year to year' (ibid).

5   Abbi (1975: 11) states that Duramu and Domu are not Mailu-speaking communities; this is confirmed by Thomson (1975b).

6   Saville (1926: 297–311) gives some information on the inland Dimuga people and their trade with Mailu. See also Abbi (1975: 11).

7   Abbi (1975: 57) and Saville (1926: 24, 206–8, 213) give more detailed accounts of this event.

8   Compare Saville's (1926: 31) more comprehensive plan of Mailu village (unfortunately undated, but certainly made within ten years of Malinowski's). Abbi (1975: 117) gives a sketch map of the village in 1962, and Irwin (1986: 51) a scaled plan of the village as he found it in 1973. Although the arrangement of the houses was markedly different in 1973, they were still grouped into the same four named 'clans' (Abbi's 'wards').

9   The original typescript reads: '...the subclan consists of a few houses, one of which is the "chief house" of the subclan; it is the house of the *dubu* headman'. By the insertion of a possessive, Malinowski's editors erroneously imply that the subclan has a 'chief'.

10 Saville (1926: 38–45) gives a less technical but far more lively account of housebuilding.

11 Saville (1935: Appendix 1) gives a few extra terms, but Abbi's list (1975: Appendix A) is probably the most reliable. The emphasis on relative age distinctions in ego's generation is perhaps the most remarkable feature of this kin terminology.

12 'Mop-like *chevelure*' is Stirling's substitution for the original typescript's 'halo-like mop'. Malinowski's phrase is more apt, judging by the photographs. Saville also used 'halo-like mop' (1926: 56).

13 The original typescript has a less ambiguous, active construction: 'They clip off their nails with a sharpened shell, or else they bite them'.

14 Malinowski had 'trim', not 'join'.

15 The original typescript has 'foreign village'.

16 At this point a sentence in the original was deleted by Stirling, but

only if it is restored does the passage make good sense: 'Thus one of my informants told me that he sends food to five houses'. Saville (1926: 49–50) gives a case of *veveni* distribution showing how it might be more complex than Malinowski's example indicates.

17 Again, Malinowski is referring to Police (Hiri) Motu (see note 2 above) and not to Motu proper.

18 For 'stamped' the original has 'branded'.

19 For 'young sparks' the original has the curious phrase 'brown nuts'!

20 For 'young girl', the original has 'bashful young lady'.

21 The omitted reference to Seligman is 1910: 84.

22 Malinowski probably had in mind Spencer and Gillen (1899: 265), where they mention 'the idea firmly held that the child is not the direct result of intercourse'.

23 Malinowski amplified this argument in his *Baloma* essay (1954 [1916]: 232–3 and n. 74), admitting that his 'statement about the Mailu is incomplete'. Despite what his informants told him, he seemed determined to find that the Mailu, like Trobrianders (though without their doctrine of 'virgin birth'), were ignorant of physiological paternity.

24 See Saville (1926: chap. XI) for a more informed account of Mailu initiation ceremonies.

25 Malinowski's unedited sentence is more homely: 'But sometimes they venture further out, even in fairly rough weather, a picture that would make any white mother or aunt faint, and which arouses wonder and appreciation for skill and pluck even in the unfeeling bosom of a field ethnographer'.

26 'Water-logging'; the original typescript has 'being filled with water'.

27 '[A]ssociations'; the original typescript is more accurate with 'categories'. The next sentence in the original begins with a stronger formulation: 'It is necessary always to consider how far our own terms...'

28 On Malinowski's rather confused and confusing uses of the term 'law', see Schapera (1957).

29 The original typescript has an additional sentence here which was unaccountably deleted by the editors: 'It seems, however, that in such cases the man would have been quite as likely to commit suicide, as to dismiss the incident. The Rev. C. Abel relates a case in which suicide by hanging actually occurred under identical circumstances'. Malinowski undoubtedly had in mind Abel's (n.d.: 88–90) account of a double suicide in Logea, though the circumstances were far from 'identical'. A woman committed suicide after quarrelling with her husband, and the following day he hung himself, possibly as an act of self-vindication, though Abel suggests he did it to evade the vengeance of his wife's kinsmen. In an early letter, Saville commented on the frequent occurrence of suicide ('mostly women, hanging themselves') in the Mailu area (SML 1.10.1902).

30 Given that Bu'a was 'by far the most influential man in the village', who later figures in the text (pp. 312–14) as the most important of Malinowski's 'concrete examples' (measured by the size of his genealogical coverage), one must wonder not only why he died in jail (in August 1914) but what put him there in the first place. Malinowski must have known, but he does not tell us. According to Abbi (1975: 69), Bu'a had been sentenced early in 1914 to six months' imprisonment for stealing another man's wife – a blatant abuse of his position as a village constable. But about the same time (February according to Saville's correspondence), Bu'a had been involved in another scandal. Together with two other village constables, Bu'a had arrested a European for the identical offence he had been (or was about to be) charged with: stealing another man's wife (see p. 174). Outraged at the indignity of being handcuffed by black men, the white man brought charges against them (and incidentally blamed Saville for inciting them); but on being allowed by the Magistrate to marry the woman, he withdrew the charges. While this does not explain how Bu'a came to die in the jail at Port Moresby, it does suggest he was in some sad way a victim of the colonial law he had been recruited to enforce.

31 The text (and typescript) had 'autumn and winter of 1914' and 'winter of 1915–16'. Clearly, Malinowski was mistakenly thinking in terms of Northern Hemisphere seasons.

32 For 'comprise' the original has the more correct 'subsume'.

33 Saville (1926: chap. XXI) gives far more detail on Mailu warfare.

34 Equally categorical is Irwin's statement: 'Mailu Island's carrying capacity was far too small for its population. Unlike other [Magi] villages, it was supported largely by specialized industry, a maritime culture and regularly-serviced trade networks' (1985: 15). Later in the text (p. 240), Malinowski spells out the extent to which Mailu was not self-supporting.

35 The page containing the two preceding paragraphs is missing from Malinowski's typescript and is replaced by an insertion (as printed) in Stirling's handwriting.

36 Malinowski does not mention that the suffix-*amua* of all but one of these net names means fish hawk or sea eagle, which Saville (1935) had called 'the totem of the Mailu tribe'.

37 See Newton (1914: 234) and Jenness and Ballantyne (1920: 34–5) for brief accounts of this trade.

38 The name Siriwawu is unknown to modern Goodenough Islanders, and there is, to my knowledge, no evidence whatever for the previous existence of any such 'great centre for axe-blades' on that island. Authorities are still agreed that the only axe-blade quarry in the Massim was Suloga on Woodlark Island.

39 Again, Malinowski's information was defective, for there are no deposits of obsidian on Goodenough Island. The 'one place on the D'Entrecasteaux group' is in fact Kukuya, southwest Fergusson

Island (see Jenness and Ballantyne 1920: 34–5).

40   In the original typescript, the last part of this sentence reads:
     '...the baskets of finest workmanship as the three tiered basket
     (*popo*) made by the Northern Massim'.

41   The puzzling phrase '...entirely cut off from the outer world' is
     sheer hyperbole, and Malinowski's own data on the Mailu's
     extensive trading voyages amply contradict it. See above, where he
     had concluded that 'they were, in their requirements, a community
     entirely dependent upon resources from outside [original typescript
     has "abroad"]...' (p. 240).

42   Saville (1926: 169) refers to two categories of property in additon
     to land: *ona* ('permanent'), and *babadau* ('transitory', by which he
     appears to mean 'alienable'). *Ona* comprises the house and its
     flooring boards, fruit trees, fishing nets, dance feathers,
     headdresses, canoes and pigs. *Babadau* (which Malinowski says is
     'the most desirable part of a man's property') consists of armshells
     and other ornaments, and stone axes (in Mailu Island only,
     because they were used for barter). It is worth noting that
     Malinowski does not give house planks or flooring boards their
     due as valuable property, though he does indicate how much
     labour was involved in their production (pp. 138). Each of the
     two house platforms required ten or more hardwood planks, each
     about 10 feet long, 2–3 feet wide, and up to 4 inches thick; Saville
     says a man would pay a pig for one (1926: 38, 40). Resident
     Magistrate Armit also remarked on flooring boards as wealth
     items 'handed down from father to son': a Mailu man 'treasures
     them like he does his pig and canoe' (PAR 1914–15: 59).

43   In the version of Onaga's genealogy given below at p. 281, he is
     shown as having six, not five children (Done being the third son)
     Curiously, Done is not mentioned in the text, though he certainly
     appears on the sketch of this 'pedigree' in Malinowski's fieldnotes
     (MPY 198).

44   Saville (1926: chap. xv) also gives an account of Mailu pot-making
     and illustrates pot forms and rim designs. Irwin's (1985) study,
     however, is by far the most comprehensive analysis of past and
     present Mailu pottery.

45   The original has 'this universal fear of darkness'.

46   Cf. Saville's brief account of *bara'u* (1926: 271). More to the point
     is Fortune's critical discussion of *vada* type sorcery in Dobu and
     elsewhere in Papua (1963 [1932]: Appendix II).

47   The citation is from Seligman (1910: 297).

48   The two quotations as given here by Malinowski reverse the order
     in which the sentences appear in Spencer and Gillen's text.

49   The original typescript has 'enchanted', not 'exhausted', though it
     is clear from his fieldnotes that he did mean the latter (MPY 194:
     240–1).

50   The reference is to Marett's section on 'The study of magico-
     religious facts' (NQ 1912: 251–61).

51   Obviously, Malinowski was to change his mind about the
     'meaninglessness' of incantations, and he was to write much about
     them and the difficulties they presented for translation in vol. ii of
     Coral Gardens (1935). The awkward phrasing, 'impossible... to
     interpret them into any meaning', occurs also in the original type-
     script.

52   In light of his subsequent work on the Trobriand language of
     magic this entire note seems prejudiced and ill-considered; one
     suspects he would have recanted these views by the end of his first
     year in Kiriwina. 'To sing' in Central Australia is virtually 'to
     create', to bring things into existence: hardly a meaningless act for
     the singers (J. Morton, personal communication). Spencer and
     Gillen (1899) give songs without even attempting to translate them;
     or perhaps Malinowski had in mind their sequel volume, where
     they refer to Aborigines 'chanting songs of which they do not know
     the meaning...' (1904: xiv). Roheim commented: 'Song, myth, and
     ritual are exactly co-ordinated – a connection which Spencer
     naturally missed, since he could not translate the songs and
     therefore simply maintained that they were unintelligible to the
     aborigines themselves' (1934: 86). Malinowski's criticism of Carl
     Strehlow (1913) is gratuitous since the latter knew the Aranda
     language well; his publications appeared in German between
     1907–1913 and would have been known to Malinowski. Carl's son,
     T.G.H. Strehlow, himself a speaker of Aranda since childhood and
     latterly a Professor of Linguistics, has published a massive work
     on *Songs of Central Australia* (1971); one has only to dip into it
     to be convinced that Aboriginal songs can be sensitively translated
     to yield rich meanings. T. Strehlow maintains that Spencer and
     Gillen 'were forced by their ignorance of aboriginal languages to
     omit the texts of the songs sung on these [ritual] occasions' (ibid:
     xvi).

53   See Saville (1926: 256) for a similar version of this ceremony; he
     too found the betel nut spell 'unintelligible'. According to Dr
     Martha Macintyre (personal communication), this song or spell is
     in the Logea (Rogea) dialect of the Southern Massim and is
     'slightly mistranslated' by Malinowski. *Bedaio*, for example, is the
     plural of *beda*, betel nut; *Rogea bedana* = 'betel nut of Rogea';
     aitseri = 'we cut into pieces'. The 'personal names' of
     Taukuripokapoka and Kumakarakedakeda are the names of
     reknown shell valuables (*bagi*) as well as of culture heroes.
     Gumakarakedakeda ('Monitor Lizard on the Road', a fabulously
     long necklace) appears in Malinowski's Trobriand text of the myth
     of Kasabwaybwayreta (1922: 322–4), and is discussed by Fortune
     (1963 [1932]: 218–23) and Roheim (1950: 185–93). In view of this
     double identification of hero and valuable, it is likely that the aim
     of the incantation was not only to increase betel nut, but also to
     attract famous *Kula* items such as these to the singers' community.
     In this connection it matters little that Mailu people had

'borrowed' the song from Massim neighbours, or that, not being in the *Kula* circuit themselves, their chances of getting their hands on such celebrated valuables were virtually nil. These names probably epitomized for the Mailu, as they did in the mythology of the Massim, the coveted wealth objects to be found in the *Kula* ring. Malinowski is almost certainly mistaken in assuming that introduced or borrowed songs or spells must be devoid of meaning in their new environment.

54   Malinowski mentions this event in his *Diary* (1967: 50); it is note-worthy for his remark about the tabooed corner: 'an important discovery – the only form of religious ceremonial'.

55   The original typescript has 'aiding', not 'acting'.

56   Presumably Malinowski meant the people of Borowai, whom he had planned to visit on his next expedition (see Young 1984: 12, 14).

57   Malinowski does not give precise references, and it is not clear it is 'the same dance' (i.e., *govi*) that Seligman and Newton describe for Bartle Bay (which is hardly to be identified with the 'Massim district' at large!). One of the descriptions in Seligman (1910: 595–6) was actually provided by Newton, while the other is of a dance witnessed by Seligman himself (ibid: 603–4). Although both dances were associated with the *Walaga* pig-killing feast and the raising of mango poles, no name is given for them. Newton (1914: 147) elaborates the account he gave to Seligman, but still does not name the dance. Malinowski's point is perhaps only half-correct and can be more accurately re-phrased thus: 'A dance similar to the *govi*, as performed in Mailu by men only, is danced in Bartle Bay by both men and women'.

58   The original typescript has 'Vanity Fair', a literary reference which is muted by the editor's shift to the plural. Malinowski was reading Thackeray's novel during his first weeks in Papua, and finished it after settling into Saville's mission house on Mailu (1967: 16).

59   The original typescript has 'one present', changed to 'one per cent' in Stirling's hand. Malinowski does not say how many pigs were killed at a *Madúna*, but since it would have been considerably less than a hundred, 'one per cent' (i.e., less than one pig) is an unlikely estimate for him to have made.

60   I have redrawn Bu'a's genealogy (Fig. 46), since the printed one is badly set out and contains a critical error (such that Bu'a's father appeared also to be his mother's brother). The mistake was doubtless due to Malinowski's confusing sketch in the typescript.

61   Saville (1926: 290–1) also has a little more to say about the under-world Biula.

62   The only detailed account of tattooing in the region is by Barton (1918).

63   Just why Malinowski was 'obliged to leave' Mailu 'a few days' before such a crucial event is not clear. His *Diary* gives few clues

(1967: 74; referring to 24.1.1915). He was glad to get away, and had presumably been waiting for some boat to call for him, but he says nothing about the impending *Madúna*. It does not appear to have been any extraneous pressure that obliged him to leave Mailu that particular week, and he was not due to go 'South' until late February. He might well have had a firm arrangement to work in Rigo with Ahuia, but it strains credulity to suppose that Malinowski (in this colonial era) would have foregone the chance to witness an important feast in order to keep an appointment with a 'native' informant, however intelligent. I suspect that, during these final weeks, witnessing the *Maduna* was less important to Malinowski than keeping to the schedule of his expedition. Concerning the *bara* dance, Malinowski did not subsequently see it in Hood Bay, nor did he ever publish what he knew about it. Saville (1926: 263) described it, however.

64 See Saville (1926: 196–8) for this and a few other legends. One of Malinowski's notebooks contains the outline of an 'explanatory myth' concerning the 'male' sun and 'female' moon, and why they do not shine at the same time (MPY 194: 287); he had probably forgotten about it. Malinowski's pronouncement on the Mailu's lack of 'theoretical interest . . . in their surroundings' was ethnocentric and too hasty, for he had only scratched the surface of local knowledge. Saville judged Mailu 'general utilitarian knowledge' to be 'fairly wide'; he says he was given ('without any trouble') the names of 117 trees, 191 fish, 69 edible crustaceans, 49 flowers, 27 varieties of banana, 46 birds, etc. (1926: 191).

65 See Saville (1926: 68–9) for more complete information on reef and tides. Saville also gives other interpretations for the naming of the stars (ibid: 194–6), and considerably more detail on ethnomedical knowledge and curing practices (ibid: 214–21). There are many discrepancies in this chapter between the Mailu terms given by Malinowski and the ones in Saville's work. These are revealing, no doubt, of Malinowski's ignorance of the language.

66 There is a slight difference in the phrasing of this sentence in the original typescript: 'With better opportunities it would have undoubtedly been possible to obtain better information, but opportunities are often a matter of good luck in ethnological field work!' Note the exculpating exclamation point, which the editor, insensitive to irony, would not allow!

References

Abbi, B.L. (1975), *Traditional Groupings and Modern Associations: a Study of Changing Local Groups in Papua and New Guinea*, Simla, Indian Institute of Advanced Study.

Abel, C.W. (n.d.), *Savage Life in New Guinea*, London, London Missionary Society.

Ardener, E. (1985), 'Social anthropology and the decline of Modernism', in J. Overing (ed.), *Reason and Morality*, ASA Monographs, no. 24, London, Tavistock.

Armstrong, W.E. (1920–21), 'Report on Suau-Tawala', *Papua Annual Report*, pp. 32–45.

Armstrong, W.E. (1927), Review of W.J.V. Saville, *In Unknown New Guinea, Man*, vol. 27, no. 41.

Barton, F.R. (1918), 'Tattooing in south eastern New Guinea', *Journal of the Royal Anthropological Institute*, vol. 48, pp. 22–79.

Belshaw, C.S. (1951), 'The last years of Ahuia Ova', *Man*, vol. 51, no. 230.

Boon, J.A. (1982), *Other Tribes, Other Scribes*, Cambridge University Press.

Clifford, J. (1983), 'On ethnographic authority', *Representations*, vol. 1, pp. 118–46.

Clifford, J. (1986a), 'Introduction: partial truths', in J. Clifford and G.E. Marcus (eds), *Writing Culture: The Poetics and Politics of Ethnography*, Berkeley, University of California Press.

Clifford, J. (1986b), 'On ethnographic self-fashioning: Conrad and Malinowski', in T.C. Heller, M. Sosna, and D.E. Wellbery (eds), *Reconstructing Individualism*, Stanford University Press.

Dutton, T.E. (1971), 'Languages of south-east Papua: a preliminary report', *Pacific Linguistics*, Series A, no. 28, Department of Linguistics, R.S.PAC.S., The Australian National University, Canberra.

Dutton, T.E. (1985), *Police Motu: Iena Sivarai (its story)*, Port Moresby, University of Papua New Guinea Press.

Ellen, R. (1985), 'Poles apart: some reflections on the contemporary image of Malinowski in his homeland', *Anthropology Today*, vol. 1, no. 1, pp. 24–25.

Firth, R. (1952), 'Notes on the social structure of some south-eastern New Guinea communities', *Man*, vol. 52, pp. 65–67.

Firth, R. (1957a), 'Introduction: Malinowski as scientist and as man', in R. Firth (ed.), *Man and Culture: An Evaluation of the Work of Bronsilaw Malinowski*, London, Routledge & Kegan Paul.

Firth, R. (1957b), 'The place of Malinowski in the history of economic anthropology', in R. Firth (ed.), *Man and Culture*, London, Routledge & Kegan Paul.

Firth, R. (1981), 'Bronislaw Malinowski', in S. Silverman (ed.), *Totems and Teachers*, New York, Columbia University Press.

Forge, A. (1972), 'Normative factors in the settlement size of neolithic cultivators (New Guinea)', in P.J. Ucko, R. Tringham and G.W. Dimbleby (eds), *Man, Settlement and Urbanism*. London, Duckworth.

Fortes, M. (1957), 'Malinowski and the study of kinship', in R. Firth (ed.), *Man and Culture*, London, Routledge & Kegan Paul.

Fortune, R.F. (1963 [1932]), *Sorcerers of Dobu*, New York, Dutton & Co.

Gellner, E. (1985), 'Malinowski go home: reflections on the Malinowski centenary conferences', *Anthropology Today*, vol. 1, no. 5, pp. 5–7.

Gross, F. (1986), 'Young Malinowski and his later years', *American Ethnologist*, vol. 13, pp. 556–570.

Groves, M. (1954), 'Dancing in Poreporena', *Journal of the Royal Anthropological Institute*, vol. 84, pp. 75–90.

Groves, M. (1963), 'Western Motu descent groups', *Ethnology*, vol. 2, pp. 15–30.

Haddon, A.C. (1894), *The Decorative Art of British New Guinea: A Study in Papuan Ethnography*, Dublin, Royal Irish Academy.

Haddon, A.C. (1901), *Headhunters, Black, White and Brown*, London, Macmillan & Co.

Haddon, A.C. (1937), *Canoes of Oceania*, vol. ii, Bernice P. Bishop Museum, Special Publication 28, Honolulu.

Irwin, G.J. (1974), 'The emergence of a central place in coastal Papuan prehistory: a theoretical approach', *Mankind*, vol. 9, pp. 268–72.

Irwin, G.J. (1978), 'Pots and entrepôts: a study of settlement, trade and the development of economic specialization in Papuan prehistory', *World Archaeology*, vol. 9, pp. 299–319.

Irwin, G.J. (1985), *The Emergence of Mailu as a Central Place in Coastal Papuan Prehistory,* Terra Australis no. 10, Department of Prehistory, R.S.PAC.S., The Australian National University, Canberra.

Jenness, D. and Ballantyne, A. (1920), *The Northern D'Entrecasteaux*, Oxford, Clarendon Press.

Kaniku, J.W.T. (1975), *The Epic of Tauhau*, Port Moresby, Institute of Papua New Guinea Studies.

Kubica, G. (1986), 'Bronislaw Malinowski's years in Poland', *Journal of the Anthropological Society of Oxford*, vol. 17, pp. 140–54.

Kuper, A. (1983), *Anthropology and Anthropologists: The Modern British School,* London, Routledge & Kegan Paul.

Landtman, G. (1927), *The Kiwai Papuans of British New Guinea*, London, Macmillan & Co.

Langham, I. (1981), *The Building of British Social Anthropology*, Dordrecht, D. Reidel Publishing Company.

Lanyon-Orgill, P.A. (1944), *A Dictionary of the Mailu Language*, London, Luzac & Co.

Laracy, H. (1975), 'Malinowski at War, 1914–18', *Mankind*, vol. 10, pp. 264–8.

Last, P.M. (1986), 'Stirling and the biology of the family: 47th Edward Stirling Memorial Lecture', The Medical Sciences Club of South Australia, Adelaide, TS.

Macintyre, M. (1983), 'Warfare and the changing context of "kune" on Tubetube', *The Journal of Pacific History*, vol. 18, pp. 11–34.

Malinowski, B. (1912), 'The economic aspect of the *Intichiuma* ceremonies', in *Festskrift tillegnad Edvard Westermarck*, Helsinki.

Malinowski, B. (1913), Review of B. Spencer and F. Gillen, *Across Australia, Folklore,* vol. 24, pp. 278–9.

Malinowski, B. (1918), Evidence given on Pacific Labour Conditions, 27 October 1916, Melbourne; in *British and Australian Trade in the South Pacific*, Report No. 66, Parliamentary Papers, Commonwealth of Australia.

Malinowski, B. (1922), *Argonauts of the Western Pacific*, London, George Routledge.

Malinowski, B. (1926a), 'The Papuo-Melanesians', in *The Australian Encyclopaedia*, vol. 2, Sydney, Angus & Robertson.

Malinowski, B. (1926b), *Crime and Custom in Savage Society*, London, Routledge & Kegan Paul.

Malinowski, B. (1926c), 'Foreword', *In Unknown New Guinea*, W.J.V. Saville, London, Seeley, Service & Co.

Malinowski, B. (1927), *Sex and Repression in Savage Society*, London, Routledge & Kegan Paul.

Malinowski, B. (1932 [1929]), *The Sexual Life of Savages in North-Western Melanesia*, 3rd Ed., London, Routledge & Kegan Paul.

Malinowski, B. (1935), *Coral Gardens and their Magic*, vol. i, London, Allen & Unwin.

Malinowski, B. (1954 [1916]), 'Baloma: spirits of the dead in the Trobriand Islands', in R. Redfield (ed.), *Magic, Science and Religion*, New York, Doubleday.

Malinowski, B. (1967), *A Diary in the Strict Sense of the Term,* London, Routledge & Kegan Paul.

Masson, E.R. (1915), *An Untamed Territory*, London, Macmillan.

Mulvaney, D.J. and Calaby, J.H. (1985), *'So Much that is New': Baldwin Spencer, 1860–1929: A Biography*. Melbourne University Press.

Nelson, H. (1969), 'European attitudes in Papua, 1906–1914', in *The History of Melanesia*, Second Waigani Seminar, Port Moresby and Canberra, U.P.N.G. & R.S.PAC. S.

Newton, H. (1914), *In Far New Guinea*, London, Seeley, Service & Co.

Norick, F.A. (1976), An Analysis of the Material Culture of the Trobriand Islands based upon the Collection of Bronislaw Malinowski, Ph.D. thesis, University Microfilms, Ann Arbor.

Notes and Queries on Anthropology (1912), 4th edition, B. Freire-Marreco and J.L. Myres (eds), London, The Royal Anthropological Institute.

Paluch, A. (1981), 'The Polish background of Malinowski's work', *Man*, vol. 16, pp. 276–85.

PAR *Papua Annual Report*, Port Moresby.

Parsonson, G.S. (1967), 'Torres and the discovery of southern New Guinea', *New Zealand Geographer*, vol. 23, pp. 132–56.

Payne, H.C. (1981), 'Malinowski's style', *Proceedings of the American Philosophical Society*, vol. 125, pp. 116–40.

Quiggin, A.H. (1942), *Haddon the Head Hunter*, Cambridge, University Press.

Ray, S.H. (1917), Review of B. Malinowski, *The Natives of Mailu*, *Nature*, vol. 100, pp. 335–6.

Ray, S.H. (1938), 'The languages of the Eastern and South-Eastern Divisions of Papua', *Journal of the Royal Anthropological Institute*, vol. 68, pp. 153–208.

Roheim, G. (1934), *The Riddle of the Sphinx*, London, Hogarth Press.

Roheim, G. (1950), *Psychoanalysis and Anthropology*, New York, International Universities Press.

Saville, W.J.V. (1912), 'A grammar of the Mailu language, Papua', *Journal of the Royal Anthropological Institute*, vol. 42, pp. 397–436.

Saville, W.J.V. (1914–15), 'Report of London Missionary Society', *Papua Annual Report*, pp. 64–5.

Saville, W.J.V. (1926), *In Unknown New Guinea*, London, Seeley, Service & Co.

Saville, W.J.V. (1930–31), 'Are the Papuans naturally religious?', *Papua Annual Report*, Appendix C. pp. 24–5.

Saville, W.J.V. (1935), 'A short English-Mailu vocabulary, with appendices', unpublished mimeo.

Schapera, I. (1957), 'Malinowski's theories of law', in R. Firth (ed.), *Man and Culture*, London, Routledge & Kegan Paul.

Seligman, C.G. (1910), *The Melanesians of British New Guinea*, Cambridge University Press.

Shelley, R. (1978), 'Ahuia Ova: new insights into the life of a prominent Papuan', *Oceania*, vol. 48, pp. 202–6.

Spencer, W.B. and Gillen, F. J. (1899), *The Natives Tribes of Central Australia*, London, Macmillan & Co.

Spencer, W.B. and Gillen, F. J. (1904), *The Northern Tribes of Central Australia*, London, Macmillan & Co.

Spencer, W.B. and Gillen, F.J. (1912), *Across Australia*, London, Macmillan & Co.

Stevens, H.N. (1930), *New Light on the Discovery of Australia as Revealed by the Journal of Captain Don Diego de Prado y Tovar*, London, The Hakluyt Society.

Stirling, E.C. (1896), 'Anthropology', in B. Spencer (ed.), *Report of the Work of the Horn Scientific Expedition to Central Australia*, vol. 4, London, Dulau & Co.

References

Stocking, G.W., Jr. (1974 [1968]), 'Empathy and antipathy in the heart of darkness', in R. Darnell (ed.), *Readings in the History of Anthropology*, London, Harper & Row.

Stocking, G.W., Jr. (1983), 'The ethnographer's magic: fieldwork in British anthropology from Tylor to Malinowski', *History of Anthropology*, vol. 1, pp. 70–120.

Stocking, G.W., Jr. (1986), 'Anthropology and the science of the irrational: Malinowski's encounter with Freudian psychoanalysis', *History of Anthropology*, vol. 4, pp. 13–49.

Strathern, M. (1981), 'Culture in a netbag: the manufacture of a sub-discipline in anthropology', *Man*, vol. 16, pp. 665–88.

Strehlow, C. (1913), 'Die Aranda und Loritja Stämme in Zentral Australien', *Veröffentlichungen aus dem städtischen Völker Museum*, Frankfurt-am-Main, J. Baer & Co.

Strehlow, T.G.H. (1971), *Songs of Central Australia*, Sydney, Angus & Robertson.

Strong, W.M. (1911), 'Notes on the languages of the North-Eastern and adjoining Divisions', *Papua Annual Report*, pp. 207–13.

Symmons-Symonolewicz, K. (1982), 'The ethnographer and his savages: an intellectual history of Malinowski's diary', *Polish Review*, vol. 27, pp. 92–98.

Thomson, N.P. (1975a), 'Magi phonology and grammar – fifty years afterwards', in T. Dutton (ed.), *Studies in the Languages of Central and South-East Papua, Pacific Linguistics*, Series C, no. 29, Department of Linguistics, R.S.PAC.S., The Australian National University, Canberra.

Thomson, N.P. (1975b), 'The dialects of Magi', Papers in New Guinea Linguistics No. 18, *Pacific Linguistics*, Series A, no. 40, Department of Linguistics, R.S.PAC.S., The Australian National University, Canberra.

Thornton, R.J. (1985), '"Imagine yourself set down...": Mach, Frazer, Conrad, Malinowski and the role of imagination in ethnography', *Anthropology Today*, vol. 1, no. 5, pp. 7–14.

Urry, J. (1972), '"Notes and Queries on Anthropology" and the development of field methods in British anthropology', *Proceedings of the Royal Anthropological Institute*, pp. 45–57.

Urry, J. (1982), 'From zoology to ethnology: A.C. Haddon's conversion to anthropology', *Canberra Anthropology*, vol. 5, no. 2, pp. 58–85.

Urry, J. (1984), 'A history of field methods', in R.F. Ellen (ed.), *Ethnographic Research: A Guide to General Conduct*, London, Academic Press.

Verma [Abbi], B.L. (1964), The Mailu: a Study of the Changing Structure of Local Groups. Ph.D. thesis, The Australian National University, Canberra.

Wax, M.L. (1972), 'Tenting with Malinowski', *American Sociological Review*, vol. 37, pp. 1–13.

Wayne [Malinowska], H. (1984), 'Bronislaw Malinowski: the influence of various women on his life and works', *Journal of the*

Anthropological Society of Oxford, vol. 15, pp. 189–203. (Reprinted, *American Ethnologist,* vol. 12, pp. 529–40.)

Williams, F.E. (1939), 'The reminiscences of Ahuia Ova', *Journal of the Royal Anthropological Institute,* vol. 69, pp. 11–44.

Williamson, R.W. (1912), *The Mafulu: Mountain People of British New Guinea,* London, Macmillan & Co.

Young, M.W. (1971), *Fighting with Food,* Cambridge University Press.

Young, M.W. (1979), 'Introduction', in M. Young (ed.), *The Ethnography of Malinowski: the Trobriand Islands 1915–18.* London, Routledge & Kegan Paul.

Young, M.W. (1983), 'The Massim: an introduction', *The Journal of Pacific History,* vol. 18, pp. 4–10.

Young, M.W. (1984), 'The intensive study of a restricted area, or, why did Malinowski go to the Trobriand Islands?', *Oceania,* vol. 55, pp. 1–26.

Young, M.W. (1985), '*Abutu* in Kalauna: a retrospect', *Mankind,* vol. 15, p. 184–97.

Young, M.W. (in press), 'Malinowski and the function of culture', in D. Austin (ed.), *Creating Culture,* London, Allen & Unwin.

Manuscript Sources

AA   Australian Archives, Canberra. Malinowski file: CRS A1, item 21/866.

HC   A.C. Haddon Collection, University Library, Cambridge.

MPL   B. Malinowski Papers, British Library of Political and Economic Science, The London School of Economics.

MPY   B. Malinowski Papers, Yale University Library, New Haven.

SML   W. J. V. Saville Letters, Mitchell Library, Sydney.

SP   C. G. Seligman Papers, British Library of Political and Economic Science, The London School of Economics.

Index

Figures in **bold type** refer to plates